The Psychology of Advertising

Advertising is a ubiquitous and powerful force, seducing us into buying wanted and sometimes unwanted products and services, donating to charity (even to causes we have not heard of before), voting for political candidates (even of questionable reputation), and changing our health-related lifestyles for better or worse. The impact of advertising is often subtle and implicit, but sometimes blatant and impossible to overlook.

This book discusses key topics from the fields of social and consumer psychology. Important questions are addressed in the volume, such as:

- What impact does advertising have on consumer behaviour? What causes this impact?
- What are the psychological processes responsible for the effectiveness of advertising?
- How do consumers make sense of advertising messages?
- What messages 'get across' and when and why?

This is the first book to offer a comprehensive and state-of-the-art overview of the psychological findings on the impact of advertising, and to discuss this research in the context of recent developments in the fields of social and consumer psychology. It presents and discusses results of both classic and contemporary studies in an engaging style that avoids highly technical language.

The authors have included a glossary of frequently used concepts which assists student comprehension, making it a unique and invaluable volume for advanced undergraduate and graduate students as well as researchers and lecturers in social psychology, marketing and communications. It is also a useful resource for professionals.

Bob M. Fennis works as a Professor in Consumer Behaviour at the Department of Marketing at Groningen University. His research interests include persuasion, social influence processes and the dynamics of 'automatic' consumer behaviour. His research focuses on such issues as the effectiveness of marketing and selling techniques, advertising effects, and nonconscious influences on consumer goal pursuit and purchase behaviour.

Wolfgang Stroebe is Professor of Social Psychology at Utrecht University. He is a former president of the European Association of Social Psychology, a fellow of numerous psychological societies (e.g. BPS, APS) and co-editor (with Miles Hewstone) of the *European Review of Social Psychology*. One of his major research interests is strategies of attitude and behaviour change, and he has published widely on this topic.

The Psychology of Advertising

Bob M. Fennis and Wolfgang Stroebe

Psychology Press
Taylor & Francis Group

HOVE AND NEW YORK

Published in 2010
by Psychology Press
27 Church Road, Hove, East Sussex BN3 2FA

Simultaneously published in the USA and Canada
by Psychology Press
270 Madison Avenue, New York NY 10016

*Psychology Press is an imprint of the Taylor &
Francis Group, an Informa business*

© 2010 Psychology Press

Typeset in Futura and Century Old Style by
RefineCatch Limited, Bungay, Suffolk
Printed and bound in Great Britain by
TJ International Ltd, Padstow, Cornwall
Cover design by Design Deluxe

This publication has been produced with
paper manufactured to strict environmental
standards and with pulp derived from
sustainable forests.

British Library Cataloguing in Publication Data
A catalogue record for this book is available from
the British Library

*Library of Congress Cataloging in
Publication Data*
Fennis, Bob Michaël, 1968–
    The psychology of advertising / Bob M. Fennis
    and Wolfgang Stroebe.
        p. cm.
    Includes bibliographical references and index.
    1. Advertising—Psychological aspects.
    2. Consumers—Attitudes.   I. Stroebe,
    Wolfgang. II. Title.
    HF5822.F456 2010
    659.101′9—dc22   2009040521

ISBN: 978-0-415-44273-2 (hbk)

Contents

PREFACE   ix

1 Setting the stage   1

THE ORIGINS OF MODERN DAY ADVERTISING   2
THE FUNCTIONS OF ADVERTISING   5
THE EFFECTS OF ADVERTISING: A PSYCHOLOGICAL
PERSPECTIVE   10
CONSUMER RESPONSES   12
SOURCE AND MESSAGE VARIABLES IN ADVERTISING   15
ADVERTISING IN CONTEXT: INTEGRATED
MARKETING COMMUNICATIONS AND THE
PROMOTIONAL MIX   22
CLASSIC AND CONTEMPORARY APPROACHES OF
CONCEPTUALIZING ADVERTISING EFFECTIVENESS   27
PLAN OF THE BOOK   38
SUMMARY AND CONCLUSIONS   39

2 How consumers acquire and process information from advertising   41

CONTENTS

PREATTENTIVE ANALYSIS   43
FOCAL ATTENTION   51
COMPREHENSION   63
ELABORATIVE REASONING   66
SUMMARY AND CONCLUSIONS   70

3 How advertising affects consumer memory — 73

THE STRUCTURE AND FUNCTION OF HUMAN MEMORY   74
IMPLICATIONS FOR ADVERTISING   90
CAN ADVERTISING DISTORT MEMORY?   106
SUMMARY AND CONCLUSIONS   109

4 How consumers form attitudes towards products — 111

WHAT IS AN ATTITUDE? A MATTER OF CONTENTION   112
ARE ATTITUDES STABLE OR CONTEXT-DEPENDENT?   118
HOW DO WE FORM ATTITUDES?   120
HOW ATTITUDES ARE STRUCTURED   133
ATTITUDE FUNCTIONS: WHY PEOPLE HOLD ATTITUDES   136
ATTITUDE STRENGTH   140
SUMMARY AND CONCLUSIONS   149

5 How consumers yield to advertising: Principles of persuasion and attitude change — 153

THE YALE REINFORCEMENT APPROACH   154
THE INFORMATION PROCESSING MODEL OF MCGUIRE   156
THE COGNITIVE RESPONSE MODEL   158
DUAL PROCESS THEORIES OF PERSUASION   160
ASSESSING THE INTENSITY OF PROCESSING   165
PERSUASION BY A SINGLE ROUTE: THE UNIMODEL   182

LOWERING RESISTANCE TO ADVERTISING   184

SUMMARY AND CONCLUSIONS   192

6   How advertising influences buying behaviour   195

THE ATTITUDE–BEHAVIOUR RELATIONSHIP: A BRIEF HISTORY   196

PREDICTING SPECIFIC BEHAVIOUR: THE REASONED ACTION APPROACH   198

NARROWING THE INTENTION–BEHAVIOUR GAP: FORMING IMPLEMENTATION INTENTIONS   202

IMPLICATIONS FOR ADVERTISING   205

BEYOND REASONS AND PLANS: THE AUTOMATIC INSTIGATION OF BEHAVIOUR   207

IMPLICATIONS FOR ADVERTISING: THE RETURN OF THE HIDDEN PERSUADERS   220

SUMMARY AND CONCLUSIONS   225

7   Beyond persuasion: Achieving consumer compliance without changing attitudes   229

SOCIAL INFLUENCE AND COMPLIANCE WITHOUT PRESSURE   231

THE PRINCIPLE OF RECIPROCITY   235

THE PRINCIPLE OF COMMITMENT/CONSISTENCY   238

THE PRINCIPLE OF SOCIAL VALIDATION   244

THE PRINCIPLE OF LIKING   248

THE PRINCIPLE OF AUTHORITY   252

THE PRINCIPLE OF SCARCITY   256

THE PRINCIPLE OF CONFUSION   258

MINDLESSNESS REVISITED: THE LIMITED-RESOURCE ACCOUNT   261

SUMMARY AND CONCLUSIONS   262

NOTES   267

REFERENCES   271

GLOSSARY   303

AUTHOR INDEX   317

SUBJECT INDEX   327

Preface

The idea to write a book which presents a coherent and in-depth analysis of the psychology of advertising was the result of an e-mail exchange between the authors of this book. A few years back, one of us (Wolfgang Stroebe) was writing a textbook chapter on attitude and behaviour change and wanted to add some advertising research to demonstrate the practical use of the social psychological theories discussed in this chapter. Since he could not find any state-of-the-art textbook on the psychology of advertising, he turned to Bob Fennis, whom he knew as an expert in the area of consumer and advertising research. Bob mailed back that, surprisingly, there was no state-of-the-art textbook on the psychology of advertising. Since we both strongly believed that such a book was needed, we decided to write it ourselves. And here it is.

Originally, we had intended to write a book on the *social* psychology of advertising. Since advertisers devise persuasive communications to convince consumers to buy their products, the psychology of advertising can rightfully be considered an application of social psychology. However, when we began planning the content of the book, we realized that we had to include chapters on information acquisition and consumer memory and in writing these chapters to review research and theories that originated in cognitive rather than social psychology. We therefore decided that social psychology of advertising would be too narrow a title and scope; thus we expanded it beyond the original plan and chose to call it 'The psychology of advertising'.

The book differs in a number of important ways from older advertising textbooks. First, we included state-of-the-art research on psychological processes that bear direct relevance for understanding advertising effects, yet have been largely ignored by many of the older books. For example, the burgeoning field of unconscious processes in motivation and goal pursuit has received only scant attention in many textbooks, although such processes are probably responsible for the bulk of typical consumer behaviour in response to advertising. Next, our point of departure in each chapter is always a psychological 'hurdle' that advertisers face when communicating with consumers, rather than some type of advertising practice.

Except for our introductory chapter, in which we describe the wider context of advertising research and practice, and in which we situate our psychological approach, our chapters all address specific psychological processes that determine the influence of advertising on consumers. For example, to answer to the question of 'How consumers acquire information from advertising', the second chapter reviews relevant theories and research from cognitive psychology and applies these to advertising. In this chapter, as in all other chapters, this application is helped by the availability of relevant research conducted in the area of consumer psychology. As a result, our book is intended to be a sophisticated and advanced summary of the host of psychological processes that influence advertising effectiveness. As Europeans, who are familiar with research done in North America, our chapters integrate findings of North American and European researchers. It goes without saying that we have interspersed our discussions of relevant research with numerous examples to illustrate how research findings translate to the real world of advertising and consumers exposed to it.

Probably our most radical deviation from the traditional way of writing advertising books is the total absence of case studies. We do not report case studies, even though we agree that such studies are good for getting students interested. A key reason is that case studies can be misleading. Case studies in advertising books usually describe some particular sales problem encountered by a company and the strategy they developed to address the problem. Usually the strategy 'works' and results in substantial increases in sales. The problem is that one cannot really be sure of this. In the terminology of the classic essay on methodology by Campbell and Stanley (1963), case studies are one-shot studies, which, according to scientific standards, do not allow us to draw conclusions with any degree of certainty. Although it is always possible that the chosen strategy was responsible for the increase in sales, it is equally possible that sales increased for some other reason. Conclusions become even more uncertain, when readers generalize from the case study to a somewhat different case that bears some resemblance with the case study. We believe that a thorough understanding of theoretical principles and of the scientific evidence collected in testing these theories will enable readers to apply knowledge to real life situations better than the case study approach. As Kurt Lewin once said, there is nothing more practical than a good theory.

A further difference between our approach and the traditional approach chosen by other authors in this area is that, in reviewing theories and research, we do not only report the findings as reported by the authors of specific studies, but also describe in some detail the theoretical background of a given study, how authors derived predictions from that theory, how they went about testing these predictions and whether their results supported these predictions. We think that this information is not only essential to allow readers to evaluate themselves whether the conclusions drawn by authors are really valid, but also to help them evaluate whether the conclusions can validly be applied to other contexts.

What kind of readers did we envisage in writing this book? Most obviously, our book is written for advanced undergraduate and graduate students interested in consumer psychology, advertising and promotional strategy, as well as for students in classes in applied psychology, business and communications. We might be flattering ourselves, but we think that researchers interested in these areas will also find the book useful. But this is not all. We think that this book should also be interesting to social psychology students and researchers interested in persuasion and attitude and behaviour change. Moreover, this book might help social psychologists appreciate the rich reservoir of research done in consumer psychology. Consumer researchers often test the same theories and address the same research questions studied by social psychologists, but use advertising and consumer psychology contexts in their studies. Whereas consumer psychologists, who are often social psychologists who moved into consumer psychology, are well aware of relevant social psychological research, social psychologists are often unaware of relevant research done in consumer psychology. The reason for this, as the example given at the beginning of this preface illustrates, is that until now there was no book bringing these literatures together. Now there is: *The Psychology of Advertising*.

As always in writing a book, there are people who helped the authors in improving chapters. We had the privilege to have four outstanding colleagues comment on every single chapter, one of them a social psychologist, the other three consumer psychologists. We are indebted to Curtis Haugvedt, Klaus Jonas, Frank Kardes and Peeter Verlegh for their detailed and extremely helpful comments on all of the chapters of this book. They should not be blamed for any weaknesses of this book, but they surely deserve credit for contributing to any of its strengths.

Bob M. Fennis and Wolfgang Stroebe

Chapter 1

Setting the stage

The origins of modern day advertising   2
The functions of advertising   5
The effects of advertising: a psychological perspective   10
Consumer responses   12
Source and message variables in advertising   15
Advertising in context: integrated marketing communications
        and the promotional mix   22
Classic and contemporary approaches of conceptualizing
        advertising effectiveness   27
Plan of the book   38
Summary and conclusions   39

'As I woke up this morning and stumbled to the bathroom to refresh, I barely noticed the brand of toothbrush and toothpaste I used. I couldn't escape the brand of breakfast cereal though, because it screamed at me in huge typeface to enjoy my "coco-pops". I wanted to check the morning news, so switched on the television, only to find a seemingly endless sequence of commercials on every channel I selected, urging me to buy more cereal, get a consumer loan, choose shampoo X instead of Y, collect a great offer at the nearest car dealership, and phone lawyer Z when I had a conflict at work. I had no interest in any of these products or services. Before setting off for work, I saw a glimpse of yesterday's football match, but the billboards surrounding the playing field were more visible than the ball, so the sponsoring only distracted me from what I wanted to see. On my way to the train station I passed numerous signs, billboards and shop windows, each with their own message and several repeating the same message I had seen a mile back. Of course, I did not want to attend to them, and wasn't even able to do so, since I was using my cell-phone to email a friend. It was only 8.00 am, but by now I had been exposed to over 250 commercial messages ranging from brand names and packaging to billboards, television ads and sponsored events. And of course, none of these messages had in any way affected me, my mood, my thinking or my actions, because I had other things on my mind, and a busy schedule to follow. Or had they?'

After reading this book, the answer to this question will be *yes*, and in more ways than the actor of this anecdote or the reader might have imagined. Although people's lives differ, there is at least one constant, particularly among those living in Western and Asian-Pacific hyper-industrialized societies and that is the ubiquitous presence of advertising. Indeed, the average US consumer is thought to be exposed to more than a 1,000 commercial messages each day. Did you ever wonder whether and how this advertising works? How consumers make sense of advertising messages? What types of messages 'get across', when and why? What impact advertising has on consumer emotions, thoughts and behaviour? That is what this book is about.

Advertising is defined as any form of paid communication by an identified sponsor aimed to inform and/or persuade target audiences about an organization, product, service or idea (Belch & Belch, 2004; Tellis, 2004; Yeshin, 2006). In the present chapter, we set the stage for what is to come in the following chapters by providing the reader with a grasp of the business context, societal context, and academic context in which the material in the other chapters must be situated. As such, the present chapter will touch briefly on several issues that are dealt with in more detail in the coming chapters and will highlight the origins and settings of contemporary thinking and research on the psychology of advertising and its translations in advertising practice. More in particular, we will discuss how advertising practice has evolved through history, how it manifests itself presently, what functions it has in society, and how thinking about its effects has developed to where we are now. We conclude this chapter with an outline of the contents of the other chapters.

The origins of modern day advertising

Advertising was not invented yesterday or the day before, but has a considerable history. As McDonald and Scott (2007) claim, the first type of advertising was what we now term 'outdoor advertising'. Archaeologists have unearthed tradesmen's and tavern signs from ancient civilizations such as Egypt and Mesopotamia, Greece and Rome, indicating that traders and merchants were keen to tell their community what they had to sell and at what price. Similarly, ads for slaves and household products have been found in early written records of the period. Later, town criers and travelling merchants advertised goods and services and in so doing became the forerunners of today's voice-overs in television and radio ads (McDonald & Scott, 2007). The Industrial Revolution between 1730 and 1830 especially boosted advertising practice. This increase can be partly explained by the large-scale diffusion of the division of labour which increasingly necessitated informing consumers of the availability of goods and services, the creation of which they were no longer directly involved in, and partly because the Industrial Revolution greatly accelerated the scale of production, creating an obvious impetus for manufacturers to advertise in order to sell their stock. As a result, markets transformed from being mainly local to regional and finally even global. The Industrial Revolution also illustrates the pivotal role of advertising as a necessary lubricant for economic traffic. Without advertising, we would not be aware that certain products or services exist, and consumption would wane. This in turn would directly slow down production. Thus, whereas advertising cannot be said to *create* consumer needs, it *is* capable of *channelling* those needs by reshaping them into **wants** for specific products and services that manufacturers can supply and that promise to satisfy those needs (cf. Kotler, 1997).

A 'side effect' of these trends was the creation and growing importance of the consumer **brand**: the label with which to designate an individual product and differentiate it from competitors. Since production and consumption became distinct in time and space, consumers needed such an unequivocal label with which they could identify the product of their choice amidst alternatives. Hence, advertising practitioners (who by the mid to end of the Industrial Revolution started to exclusively work as such and thereby created an entirely new profession) were quick to assign unique labels to products and associate them with unique advantages not shared by competitors. The **Unique Selling Proposition** or USP was born, a summary statement used to meaningfully differentiate the brand from the competition. The creation of a compelling USP was to grow to be the key challenge for professional advertisers in 'building' new consumer brands.

The American Civil War and, 50 years later, World War I temporarily slowed down production, only to see an 'afterburner effect' after hostilities ceased and societies had to be rebuilt. After the Depression years and World War II, advertising volumes skyrocketed again, to keep up with the production and consumption pace of the period. The post-war economic boom enabled ever more consumers on an ever widening scale to enjoy new products and services, and the concomitant mass introduction of television increased advertising's reach at an unprecedented rate. This trend is mirrored by the present-day proliferation of the internet as an advertising medium. More generally, a brief history of advertising should include a brief discussion of the evolution of the chief carriers of these ad messages throughout history: the advertising media.

The earliest forms of advertising, as noted, used 'outdoor media': clay tablets, placards, and, from 1400 onward, handbills and poster bills. Martin Luther used this latter medium when advertising his objections to Roman Catholicism by nailing a poster bill on the Wittenberg church door. Outdoor advertising subsequently evolved from poster bills to billboards, which especially in North America grew out to be one of the most eye-catching icons of increased consumerism with brands such as Kellogg's, Heinz, Coca-Cola and Palmolive covering large parts of US public space.

Newspapers and magazines are among the main advertising media, especially since their development in the eighteenth and nineteenth century accelerated. An estimated billion people per day read newspapers, and advertisers have been keen on reaching them, especially with display (regular) ads and classified ads (McDonald & Scott, 2007). Interestingly, despite the introduction of television and, more recently, the internet, newspapers continues to be a popular advertising medium. Although market shares of classified ads are decreasing mainly due to the internet, newspaper advertising is still second in volume after television, with 30 per cent of all main media expenditures (McDonald & Scott, 2007). Similarly, the advent of the internet has not led to the demise of magazine advertising, as audiences are ever more specifically targeted with special interest magazines, which continue to be attractive for advertising aimed at reaching **consumer segments** that share common interests, values, or lifestyles.

Television, radio and the internet complement the array of contemporary mass media. Whereas radio advertising started in the early 1920s in the US, television advertising took off two decades later with a Bulova Watch commercial being shown before a baseball game between the Brooklyn Dodgers and Philadelphia Phillies (McDonald & Scott, 2007). Despite the World Wide Web, television continues to claim the largest share in ad expenditures, accounting for more than $147 billion worldwide in 2005 (McDonald & Scott, 2007). Finally, internet advertising started in 1994 and has ever since seen yearly growth rates of over 25 per cent. At present, the internet appears a complementary rather than a substitute medium. Although it has taken away some of the market share from other media (most notably classified ads in newspapers), the internet will probably coexist next to more traditional mass media, rather than eliminating them as some media gurus have prophesied. In all, despite its humble origins, advertising has grown to be a flourishing business with spending on advertising expected to reach $450 billion worldwide by 2010.

We might look at classic ads with feelings of warm nostalgia or wonder about the sometimes peculiar language use and propositions made, but are the appeals made in those historic ads really fundamentally different from those we find in contemporary advertising? The answer appears to be both yes and no. McDonald and Scott (2007) argue that from the 1800s to the early twentieth century virtually all print ads used what we would nowadays term an **informational** or **argument-based appeal**. They straightforwardly informed consumers what was for sale, at what price and where one could buy it. The approach became known as the 'tell' approach, a more subtle variant of the more pressing 'hard-sell' approach of 'salemanship in print' which aligned a set of persuasive arguments to convince prospective buyers and thus became known as the 'reason-why approach' (Rowsome, 1970, see Fig 1.1).

Partly as a reaction to this aggressive approach, a more subtle 'soft-sell' approach was developed in the early 1900s which sometimes used an **emotional** or **affect-based appeal**, aiming to influence the consumer's feelings and emotions rather than his thoughts. The development of the soft-sell approach was in line with the societal and academic trend of the time increasingly to view human nature as governed by instinct, emotions and non-rational processes (Beard, 2005). Despite the impression that the discussion may have given thus far, Fox (1984) has stated that

Figure 1.1 Vintage advertisement using an informational appeal

argument-based and affect-based appeals have coexisted through the ages, rather than one approach evolving out of the other. Hence, even the beginning of the twentieth century saw illustrations of emotional appeals next to informational ads much like we see today. Indeed, in today's advertising practice, hard-sell and soft-sell appeals still coexist, and sometimes reflect distinct philosophies of the ad agencies about what works in advertising (i.e. use of arguments versus use of emotional appeals to sell products; Kardes, 2002).

The functions of advertising

Imagine a world without advertising. What would it be like? Certainly, there would be no unsolicited harassment by sales representatives, no distraction by neon signs and billboards, no interruptions to movies on TV by commercial breaks. But before sighing with relief, also think of the following. Perhaps, there would also be no newspapers and magazines, no television, no radio. All these media depend on advertising revenues for their existence. There would be fewer great sports competitions such as tennis, football and Formula One, because all depend largely on commercial **sponsorship**. And, on a personal level, your knowledge of 'what is out there', what products are available, with what attributes, at what price and at which outlet, would be seriously impaired. In short, advertising does have its place in society, both at an aggregate and an individual level. In contemporary industrialized societies, advertising serves several functions: facilitating competition, communicating with consumers about products and services, funding public mass media and other public resources, creating jobs, and informing and persuading the individual consumer.

First, advertising facilitates competition among firms. Advertising enables firms to communicate with consumers fast and efficiently, and thereby plays an important role in the competition between firms for consumer **attention**, competition for consumer **preferences**, choice and, of course, consumer financial resources. Second, advertising is the prime, and perhaps only, means companies have to inform consumers about new and existing products. If a firm offers a product that is cheaper than that of competitors, but equally good, they need consumers to learn about this. And the key way to achieve this is by advertising. Relating this to the previous function, as a result, the competitor may go down in price, thus stirring competition between the two. Third, as alluded to before, advertising is a key source of funding for major mass media in the US and many other countries. Newspapers, TV, radio and certainly many free services on the internet (e.g. search engines such as Google or AltaVista) would not exist if it were not for advertising expenditures. On the other hand, to prevent full dependence on advertising revenues, countries such as Great Britain, Germany and the Netherlands still maintain a public service broadcasting system which is publicly rather than commercially financed (e.g. the BBC in Great Britain, or ARD and ZDF in Germany). Fourth, the advertising industry is an important employer. Earlier we referred to the huge estimated volume of expenditures in the industry. Add to this the number of employees in advertising related industries – a total of over 300,000 worldwide in the year 2000, and estimated to grow at a yearly rate of 32 per cent compared to 15 per cent for other industries – and it becomes evident that a world without advertising would produce fewer jobs, less competition, and thus less economic activity.

Related to these societal functions, are two important functions of advertising at the individual level: to inform and persuade the individual consumer. When advertising's function is to inform, the emphasis is on creating or influencing non-evaluative consumer responses, such as knowledge or **beliefs**. When trying to persuade, in contrast, the focus is on generating or changing an evaluative (valenced) response, in which the advertised brand is viewed as more favourable than before or vis-à-vis competitors.

As mentioned earlier, advertising's key objective is often to provide information on what is available, where and at what price. There is one basic motive for an advertiser to use an informational appeal: to communicate something new and potentially relevant about a product, service or idea. At first glance, this would imply that the information function is primarily used for new product or service introductions, but reality appears more complex than that. Use of advertising to inform is made widely and for varying purposes. For instance, Abernethy and Franke (1996) have shown that the information function varies with product category: informational appeals are used more frequently for **durable** goods (e.g. products that can be used repeatedly such as refrigerators, cars, or furniture) than non-durable goods (e.g. food items, cosmetics or holidays). Moreover, ads in developed, industrialized cultures (e.g. the US, Canada) use informational appeals more often than ads in less developed countries (e.g. India, Saudi Arabia, Latin America). What information do informational appeals convey? The study by Abernethy and Franke (1996) revealed that the most frequently communicated types of information are about performance, availability, components and attributes, price, quality and special offers.

There are also moments in the life of a product when specific informational appeals are called for. Typically, products proceed through a **product life cycle**, an inverted U-shaped curve which is related to the diffusion or spreading of a product across the marketplace from its initial introduction to its decline and ultimate demise (see Figure 1.2).

The product life cycle has an introduction stage, a growth stage, a maturity stage and a decline stage. The S-shape depicts the volume of sales and profits at each of these stages. When a product enters the market, advertisers must inform consumers that it is there and thus create brand awareness (i.e. creating the conscious knowledge that the brand exists and that it represents a specific product) and induce product trial. During the growth stage, the focus is on building market share, vis-à-vis the competition, which is frequently achieved by improving the product, or developing brand extensions and communicating them to the consumer. In the maturity stage, consolidating market share becomes paramount, shifting focus to creating consumer brand loyalty and maintaining top-of-mind awareness. Finally, in the decline stage

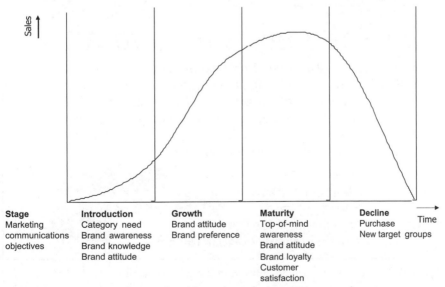

Stage	Introduction	Growth	Maturity	Decline
Marketing communications objectives	Category need Brand awareness Brand knowledge Brand attitude	Brand attitude Brand preference	Top-of-mind awareness Brand attitude Brand loyalty Customer satisfaction	Purchase New target groups

Figure 1.2 Stages in the product life cycle and communication objectives

informational appeals may be used to convey new and additional uses for the product. For instance, advertisers of fast food products may suggest different occasions at which their snacks may be consumed (e.g. not just at a party, but also at the weekend, during lunch, etc.).

For more complex new products or services, advertising may provide a means to 'educate' the consumer about the ways the product or service works. For instance, with the global climate change in mind, a Dutch bank (Rabobank) has recently introduced a new type of mortgage loan, where consumers pay for the loan with a reduced interest rate, while using the money for improving the energy efficiency of their homes, a strategy which not only increases the market value of the property but simultaneously improves the social responsibility image of the bank. The advertising campaign featured a well-known sports celebrity who informed consumers of this new type of loan and its attributes. The information function of advertising is highlighted in the chapters on how advertising affects the processing of information and consumer memory.

For existing products and services, informational appeals are also used when there are problems associated with the product. Advertisers are sometimes forced to use advertising to communicate a **product recall** to inform consumers that they are to return their product to the factory for repair or refunding. Product recalls are frequently issued by law, but may also constitute a voluntary action by the manufacturer, especially when a product's fault may have safety or health implications (see Figure 1.3).

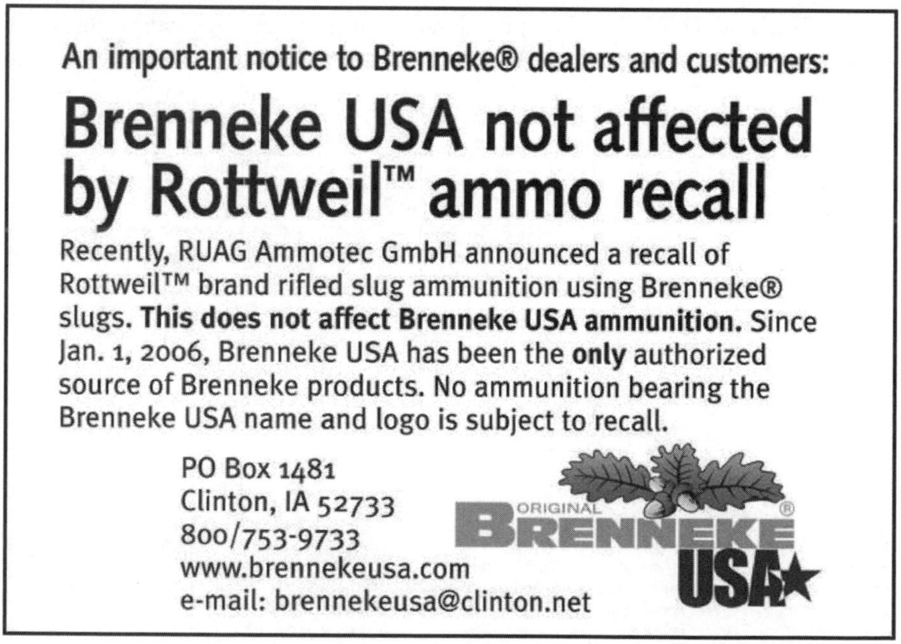

An important notice to Brenneke® dealers and customers:

Brenneke USA not affected by Rottweil™ ammo recall

Recently, RUAG Ammotec GmbH announced a recall of Rottweil™ brand rifled slug ammunition using Brenneke® slugs. **This does not affect Brenneke USA ammunition.** Since Jan. 1, 2006, Brenneke USA has been the **only** authorized source of Brenneke products. No ammunition bearing the Brenneke USA name and logo is subject to recall.

PO Box 1481
Clinton, IA 52733
800/753-9733
www.brennekeusa.com
e-mail: brennekeusa@clinton.net

Figure 1.3 Recall ad informing consumers there is no recall
Reproduced with permission of Brenneke, USA

For example, car manufacturers often use advertising to inform customers that a problem with their model has occurred and they should have it checked at the dealer. Additionally, advertising may have a 'corrective' function when manufacturers or service providers learn that consumers have certain misconceptions or when the product has an overall negative image or reputation.

In an early study examining this issue, Tybout, Calder and Sternthal (1981) addressed a problem that fast-food restaurant McDonald's faced some time ago (see also Kardes, 2002). A rumour spread among consumers that McDonald's used worms to prepare their hamburgers. Of course, the rumour was false, and, surprisingly, although consumers said they did not believe the rumour, sales plummeted anyway by more than 30 per cent (Tybout et al., 1981). Hence, there was a clear need to inform the public that McDonald's hamburgers were safe to eat and as tasty as ever, but how? In a first response, McDonald's simply tried to counter the adverse effects of the rumour by refuting it through advertising, in-store communication and public relations (PR) messages. Print and TV ads emphasizing that McDonald's used '100 per cent pure beef' were intensified, and store managers posted a letter from the Secretary of Agriculture, stating that the 'hamburger produced by these [McDonald's] establishments is wholesome, properly identified, and in compliance with standards identified by Food Safety and Quality Service regulations'. In addition, McDonald's PR advisors stressed that it would hardly make sense to use worm meat since it is even more expensive to process than ground beef.

This concerted appeal to consumer reason, however, failed to have a positive effect. To understand this issue, Tybout et al. (1981) turned to the structure of consumer **memory**, a subject that is dealt with more in depth in chapter 3. They observed that disconfirming beliefs about worms present in consumer memory did not serve as a basis for judgment (see also Grant, Malaviya & Sternthal, 2004). The hypothesized reason was that hearing the rumour made consumers form an associative link in their memory between McDonald's and worms, and every time the brand name was activated, this also activated the associated concept of worms, despite the presence of a belief informing them that the rumour was false.

Of course the activation of the concept of worms is not much of an appetizer, which explains the declining sales (Kardes, 2002). To solve this problem, the researchers reasoned that the brand name McDonald's needed to activate other 'harmless' concepts that could weaken the salience of worms and thus would decrease the tendency for an aversive consumer response. This was accomplished by asking customers to participate in a survey which asked about a wide range of features of McDonald's restaurants, such as the quality of the French fries and milkshakes, the service and quality of the personnel, their friendliness, the cleanliness of the restaurant and the convenience of the location. The idea was that completing the survey would forge the necessary associative links in consumer memory between McDonald's and these attributes, weakening the association between McDonald's and the concept of worms. The results supported this reasoning: those who completed the survey were less likely to think of worms when exposed to the brand name, and showed more favourable evaluations of McDonald's.

The previous study showed that informing consumers may sometimes backfire or be ineffective in changing misconceptions. In that case, the advertiser needs to resort to **persuasion** to reach his objectives, and the Tybout et al. (1981) approach is one clever way of doing so. The persuasion function of advertising becomes espe-cially apparent in Tellis' (2004) definition of advertising as 'any paid message that a firm delivers to consumers in order *to make the offer more attractive to them*' (p. 9, italics added). As is apparent from this definition, the persuasion function mainly differs from the information function in the intention of the sender: information appeals, although they may certainly lead to consumer persuasion, are intended to inform, whereas persuasive appeals are intended to *change* consumer responses. The persuasion function is clearly important as the function of advertising is to aid in the marketing of products and services, and the key function of marketing is to facilitate the 'exchange of value' between manufacturers and consumers (Kotler, 1997). Ultim-ately, it is the persuasion brought about by advertising that should result in buying and using the product or service. Hence, in each of the stages of the product life cycle described above, persuasion strategies will always flank information appeals in order to increase the odds of consumers responding positively to the product or offer.

When the focus is on persuasion, advertising primarily seeks to influence beliefs and evaluative consumer responses, such as feelings, preferences and attitudes (see below). As discussed more extensively in chapter 5, persuasion is aimed at changing such consumer responses via exposure to a communication (Petty & Cacioppo, 1986), sometimes (but definitely not always) through the use of one or more arguments supporting a position advocated by the communicator (Eagly & Chaiken, 1984).

There are two basic strategies advertisers can use to achieve the goal of persua-sion: by directly increasing the attractiveness of the offer or the message, or by reducing consumer reluctance to accept the position. Knowles and Linn (2004) have summarized these approaches as alpha and omega strategies to persuasion. **Alpha strategies** generally serve to increase the tendency to 'move toward the advocated position', and hence influence a consumer's **approach motivation**. In contrast, **omega strategies** can persuade because they reduce or minimize the tendency to move away from the position, and hence influence a consumer's **avoidance motivation**. Alpha strategies in advertising include the use of strong, compelling arguments that justify accepting the message position, the promise of incentives and other inducements for accepting the message position, or communicating scarcity by saying that the product is in short supply, or only available for a limited period. Omega strategies, on the other hand, reduce resistance by directly counterarguing consumer concerns (which might not always be successful as we saw above); distracting consumers to interfere with their concerns regarding the message position; reframing the message so that it does not appear to be a blatant persuasive attack; or using negative emotions such as fear or guilt (Knowles & Linn, 2004). As we will discuss below, alpha and omega strategies translate into various source and message variables in advertising.

The effects of advertising: a psychological perspective

Thinking about the impact of advertising invariably implies choosing a perspective for doing so. In this volume we adopt a psychological perspective where we focus on individual responses to clearly specified advertising stimuli. However, the psycho-logical perspective is by no means the only alternative. Indeed scholars have summar-ized current perspectives on advertising effectiveness (e.g. Poiesz, 1989):

- The *naïve approach* assumes that advertising must be effective, simply because it is so ubiquitous and advertising expenditures are vast and ever increasing.
- The *economic approach* tries to address the effects issue by correlating advertising expenditures with aggregated changes in sales volume.
- The *media approach* conceptualizes advertising effectiveness in terms of the number of individuals in a specific target population who have been exposed to a message. Hence, it conceives of impact as the extent of 'reach' of the message. An effective message in this approach is one where many consumers of the target segment have been exposed, and relatively few consumers outside the target segment. This approach is still a dominant paradigm in advertising practice where commissions and fees for agencies are based largely on effective reach. The problem with this approach is that it cannot inform us on the *impact* of this exposure: it is unclear what happens once a consumer is exposed to the message.
- The *creative approach*, in contrast, claims to provide an answer to this issue, but does so by equating effectiveness with creativity. It assumes that a message is effective to the extent that it is well-made and creative (leaving open what a 'creative ad' is, however). This notion is widespread among advertising agencies where creative directors (in charge of message strategy and production) are frequently the ones who have to convince the advertiser to opt for one or the other type of commercial message.
- Finally the *psychological* approach aims at identifying effects of advertising at the individual level. That is, its objective is to relate specific advertising stimuli to specific and individual consumer responses. Moreover, it seeks to articulate the intrapersonal, interpersonal or group-level psychological processes that are responsible for the relationship between ad stimuli and consumer responses.

The psychological approach is the perspective of choice for the present volume, but it is hardly new. Indeed, more than 100 years ago, in 1904, Walter D. Scott published a paper in the *Atlantic Monthly* entitled 'The Psychology of Advertising'. It is fair to say that this publication marked the beginning of an era in which the subject of advertising's impact on consumers has received overwhelming attention from practitioners, concerned public policy organizations and academics. Similarly, as far back as 1923, Claude C. Hopkins, an advertising professional who worked for one of the predecessors of the well-known advertising agency Foote, Cone and Belding (FCB) had this advice for advertising practitioners: 'the competent advertising man must understand psychology. The more he knows about it, the better. He must learn that certain effects lead to certain reactions, and use that knowledge to increase results and avoid mistakes' (cited in Pieters & van Raaij, 1992, p. 4).

The psychological approach implies not only a focus on the individual, it also requires being as explicit as possible about the types of consumer responses, the types of advertising stimuli affecting these responses, and the types of postulated, causal relations between advertising stimuli and consumer responses.

Consumer responses

Specific outcome measures at the individual level include thoughts, feelings and actions, or, more formally, cognitive, affective, and behavioural consumer responses.

Cognitive consumer responses are beliefs and thoughts about brands, products and services that consumers generate in response to advertising. They include the 'traditional' ad effectiveness indices such as brand awareness and brand (and product) recall and recognition, as well as newly formed associations about products and brands which are sometimes a function of the persuasive information (i.e. persuasive arguments) encountered in advertising. According to our definition of **attitudes**, as categorization of an object (e.g. a product, message or brand) along an evaluative dimension (chapter 4), attitudes should also be considered cognitive responses. Hence, an attitude captures how good or bad we judge an object to be. Similarly, **preferences** of Brand X over Brand Y can also be considered cognitive responses. *Affective responses*, in contrast, entail various more or less transient emotions and moods that can occur as a function of ad exposure and differ in valence (positive versus negative) and intensity (i.e. arousal). Examples include warmth (Vanden Abeele & MacLachlan, 1994), irritation (Fennis & Bakker, 2001), fear, pride, sadness or anger. Finally, *behavioural responses* include the intention and actual behaviour in response to advertising, such as buying the product, choosing a brand, but also product trial, brand switching, and discarding a product.

Assessing advertising effects on consumer responses

Consumer thoughts, feelings and behaviours may be affected by advertising stimuli. But what does 'affected' mean exactly? We need to state the type of relationship that exists between ad stimulus and consumer response. Basically, relationships can be **correlational** or **causal** (cf. Kardes, 2002). When some advertising stimulus (say, the number of arguments in an informational message) and consumer response (say, the attitude towards the product) correlate, then an observed change in one variable is associated with a change in the other: if the number of arguments in the message changes, then the consumer attitude changes. A positive correlation implies that an *increase* in one variable is associated with an *increase* in the other, as when more arguments are associated with a more positive attitude. A negative correlation implies that an increase in one variable is associated with a *decrease* in the other (i.e. more arguments are associated with a more negative attitude). Zero correlation implies that there is no systematic relationship between the two variables. Correlation is informative because it enables the researcher to *predict* the values on one variable when the values of the other are known.

However, in addition to prediction, a psychologist wants to *explain* consumer responses in response to advertising stimuli, and here correlation coefficients fall short. Although correlation is a *necessary* condition for causality, it is not a *sufficient* one. To infer that A *causes* B, three conditions must be met: 1) the antecedent (A) must precede the consequence (B); 2) changes in the antecedent must be associated with changes in the consequence; and 3) no other explanation for the change in consequence must be present than the change in antecedent (i.e. the third variable problem). Correlation only tells us something about condition 2, but not the other two.

The main problem in inferring causality is usually not the temporal sequence, but the third variable problem. For example, if a firm increases its advertising budget for a branded product and subsequently finds that sales have also increased, they can easily check that the increase in advertising preceded the increase in sales (i.e. condition 1). But can they conclude that the increase in sales was really *caused* by the increase in advertising? They might, but they should not, because there could be numerous alternative reasons for the increased sales. There might have been improvements in the product, there might have been environmental changes, which led to an increase in the need for that product (e.g. hot summer weather stimulating soft drink and beer consumption). Even if we were successful in eliminating all obvious third variable explanations for the increase in sales, it would still be possible that some non-obvious cause, which we overlooked, could have been responsible.

As can be seen in this volume, one type of research design is particularly suited to establish causality and that is the experiment. In its most basic form, an experiment involves manipulating one or more antecedent(s), and subsequently assessing its (or their) impact on the consequence. The antecedent is the **independent variable** and the consequence is the **dependent variable. Random assignment** of participants to the different conditions created by manipulating the antecedent(s) ensures that any effects on the dependent variable can be reliably attributed to the independent variable(s). By randomly assigning participants to the various experimental conditions, we can be assured that there were no (statistically significant) differences between participants before the independent variable was manipulated. Thus, any statistically significant difference between conditions that can be observed afterwards is likely to be due to the experimental manipulation.

To return to the earlier example and to demonstrate that the number of arguments in an ad affects consumer attitudes toward the product, we could have opted for a design where we would have experimentally manipulated the number of arguments, for example by creating two ads for the same product, with one ad containing two and the other containing five arguments. Next, we would randomly assign participants to be exposed to either the two-argument or the five-argument version. Potential extraneous variables such as pre-existing differences in the level of consumer **involvement** (the extent of perceived personal relevance of the brand, product or product category), brand familiarity or product knowledge within our sample would not pose a problem, since their influence would be equal in both conditions and thus could not differentially affect the outcome. If we subsequently measured attitudes towards the advertised product and observed that attitudes were more positive in the five-argument as opposed to two-argument condition, we could attribute this difference to our experimental manipulation and conclude that the change in number of arguments (two versus five) *caused* the changes in attitude found (more positive in the five as opposed to two-arguments condition).

Although we could be confident in attributing the difference in attitudes to the difference in the number of arguments presented, we might want to 'dig deeper' and identify the psychological mechanisms that are responsible for the impact of our experimental manipulation on our dependent variable. It seems likely that differences in the amount of thought elicited by the two types of ads were responsible for (i.e. mediated) the greater impact of the ad containing five arguments than the ad with only two arguments. We could test this assumption by measuring the amount of thoughts with the thought-listing technique (Greenwald, 1968; Osterhouse & Brock, 1970) described in chapter 5, and by using this measure in a mediation analysis. A **mediation analysis** attempts to identify the intermediary psychological processes that are responsible for (i.e. mediate) the effect of an independent on the dependent variable. According to a classic article by Baron and Kenny (1986), to demonstrate mediation, we would have to show that (1) the independent variable had an impact on the assumed mediator (i.e. more thoughts after five than two arguments); (2) that variations in the mediator significantly accounted for variation in the dependent variable (i.e. that more thoughts accounted for more positive attitudes); and (3) that controlling for the mediator (i.e. number of thoughts listed) significantly reduced or eliminated the impact of the independent variable on the dependent variable.

It seems plausible that the amount of thinking does not only depend on the number of arguments presented in an advertisement but also on the degree of personal relevance (i.e. consumer involvement) of the advertised product for the target audience. For example, consumers should be more motivated to think about a car advertisement, if they are in the market for a new car (or chronically interested in automobiles) than if they are uninterested in cars and not planning to buy one in the near future. In our hypothetical experiment we ignored differences in involvement by assigning participants randomly to the two experimental conditions. However, since we suspect that differences in the number of ad arguments have a greater effect under high than low involvement conditions, we might conduct a second experiment, in which we manipulate number of arguments (two versus five) *and* level of involvement (low versus high). Such experiments, in which two or more variables are manipulated within the same design, are called **factorial experiments**. We would probably find overall, that five arguments result in more attitude change than two arguments. This would be a **main effect** of number of arguments. However, since the number of arguments should have greater impact on consumers who are highly involved and thus highly motivated to think about the ad, we would also expect a **statistical interaction** between number of arguments and involvement: the main effect of number of arguments on attitudes should be moderated by level of consumer involvement.

In case of *moderation* a given main effect (of A on B) is *conditional* upon a third variable, C, which is labelled the moderator. **Moderators** are individual differences or contextual variables that strengthen or even change the direction of the effect of the independent on the dependent variable. This means that the effect of A on B is different for different levels of C. In the previous example, involvement would be the moderator (C) and the formal hypothesis would be that the effect of arguments (A) on attitudes (B) is moderated by involvement (C), such that the effect is more pronounced when involvement is high rather than low. Moderation would be demonstrated if the *interaction effect* between arguments and involvement (A*C) on attitudes (B) would be significant. Plotting the interaction and probing for the simple main effect of A within both levels of C would then be required to ascertain that the observed pattern was indeed the one we predicted.

The discussion on moderated effects illustrates that we are not assuming that the effects of advertising variables are invariant across consumers. Rather, we need to take the psychological make-up of the consumer and situational constraints into account when making predictions about the effect of some ad factor on some individual outcome measure. That is, the consumer is not a passive recipient, absorbing whatever he is exposed to. He is not a *tabula rasa* but brings his psychological make-up into the influence setting. And this psychological make-up can play an important role in the impact of advertising. Hence, we take the position in the present volume that advertising effects can be best understood as joint or interaction effects between *situational* and *person* variables (cf. Kardes, 2002). That is, an advertising message may have a larger impact on one group of consumers than on another group of consumers, or the direction of the effect may differ for different groups of consumers.

Situational variables are external, environmental variables that act as the independent or moderator variables that affect some consumer outcome (or dependent) variable. Examples of situational variables include source and message variables in advertising stimuli, and other communication tools that make up the marketer's **promotional mix**. Person variables are dimensions that are internal to a specific individual and typically act as moderator variables. These include variables that are specific to a person *and* a situation, such as consumer involvement or pre-existing product knowledge, or they may vary over persons but be constant over situations, such as individual difference characteristics. Individual difference variables include personality traits such as the **need for cognition** or the **need for cognitive closure** which will be discussed in chapter 5.

Source and message variables in advertising

The role of source and message variables will be reviewed extensively in chapter 5. The purpose of the following section is merely to introduce the main concepts. When looking at an advertisement, one might often wonder what the source is of that advertising message. Take the advertisement showing the golf professional Tiger Woods endorsing Tag Heuer watches. Who is the source in this message? Is it Tiger Woods? Tag Heuer? Or a combination (see Figure 1.4)?

In many instances sources are individuals delivering the message. In other instances they are the organization or the brand behind the product or service. One can make a distinction between direct and indirect sources. A direct source is a spokesperson delivering a message or demonstrating a product. An indirect source does not deliver the message but is nevertheless associated with the product or service, for instance the logo of a bank that concludes an ad for a new type of mortgage. In the Tag Heuer ad, Tiger Woods is not speaking directly about the watch to the viewer, but is merely associated with the brand, so must be considered an indirect source in this instance.

Source credibility

Credibility includes the dimensions of source expertise and trustworthiness. We shall see in chapter 5 that while all companies would want their messages to be presented by credible sources, the accumulated research suggests that the impact of source credibility and other **source effects** is sometimes impressive and sometimes negligible.

Figure 1.4 Source variable: Tiger Woods endorsing Tag Heuer watches

Reproduced with permission of Tag Heuer, SA

Source credibility influences message processing and persuasion mainly when recipients are not particularly motivated to process the message. Since this is often the case with advertising messages, it is understandable that companies go to great lengths to foster expertise and trustworthiness (Belch & Belch, 2004). Sales personnel are trained in the product line, and spokespeople are often chosen because of their knowledge and experience with a certain product.

Trustworthiness can be conveyed by stressing that the message source does not have a vested interest in delivering the message. A popular strategy to create the illusion of an uninterested communicator often used in commercials, is to show consumers filmed ostensibly spontaneously using hidden cameras or suggesting that the camera 'accidentally overheard' a conversation about the product by two consumers. This strategy places the viewer in the position of a bystander, rather than a target of the communication. A classic study by Walster and Festinger (1962) suggests that bystanders are more influenced than targets because they tend to let their guard down and be less critical of the message.

Source attractiveness

A source variable that has also received much attention is *source attractiveness*. Many products are sold by appealing to sexual attraction and physical beauty (see Figure 1.5). Sometimes these appeals make sense, for example when selling cosmetics or perfumes where an attractive model directly supports the claim of the product to enhance one's attractiveness, but sometimes they do not as when a car dealer advertises a new model by placing an attractive female model on the bonnet. Nevertheless, there is reason to believe that using a physically attractive source may be a wise thing to do for the advertiser. Eagly, Ashmore, Makhijani and Longo (1991) have summarized research on how people perceive physical attractiveness and conclude that attractiveness frequently functions as a 'halo': observers typically use a **heuristic**, or simple decision rule, of the form: 'what is beautiful is good'. Hence, people who are attractive are also perceived to be more socially competent, well-adjusted and sometimes even more intelligent than their more average-looking counterparts. In the advertiser's reasoning, the attractiveness halo-effect need not stop there: it can easily extend beyond the model itself to positively affect the products with which he or she is associated in the advertisement. Empirical evidence suggests that he is often right in thinking so (see DeBono & Harnish, 1988).

Argument quality and message structure

Advertising message variables that have been studied extensively include *argument quality* and *message structure*. Argument quality refers to *what* is communicated about the product and thus to the strength or persuasiveness of the arguments used to support a position or offer. Areni and Lutz (1988) have suggested that argument quality is based on perceptions of the valence of the argument, as well as the likelihood of occurrence. Hence, a strong argument in advertising is one where a desirable product attribute is highlighted, coupled with the certainty that it will be delivered with the product.

Figure 1.5 Ad appealing to sexual attraction

Message structure refers to *how* product information is communicated and thus to the order of presentation. Presenting the strongest arguments first may be beneficial in terms of increased consumer attention and increased processing intensity (a primacy effect), but arguments at the end may benefit because they are most recently activated in memory (a recency effect, see Haugtvedt & Wegener, 1994; Kruglanski & Freund, 1983). So presenting the best arguments first or last seems preferable to presenting them in the middle of the message. Recent research suggests that distraction might play a role. When consumers are distracted from message processing, an advertiser should save the best for last, but when consumers can devote undivided attention to the message (i.e. when they are not distracted) delivering a punch by presenting the strongest arguments first is preferable (Biswas, Biswas & Chatterjee, 2009).

Two other message variables that are particularly relevant for understanding advertising effectiveness are *message sidedness* and *argument-based vs affect-based appeals*, alluded to above.

Message sidedness

A one-sided message is the classic, biased, lopsided ad that contains only arguments supporting a conclusion favourable to the advertised brand. These messages may be effective, but sometimes they may result in resistance (Knowles & Linn, 2004). Therefore, advertisers may resort to **two-sided advertisements** in which both positive and negative, or supporting and counterarguments are included. For example, a classic two-sided message was the advertising campaign for car-rental company Avis (see Figure 1.6).

In their advertisements, they admitted not being the market leader ('we're number two'), but subsequently turned this potential weakness into a consumer benefit by adding 'so we try harder'. Early research on message sidedness suggests that one-sided message are more persuasive when recipients are favourably disposed to the message issue, but two-sided messages may be more effective when the issue (i.e. the brand) is unfamiliar to consumers, or when their initial attitudes are unfavourable (Hovland, Lumsdaine & Sheffield, 1949; Lumsdaine & Janis, 1953).

Argument-based and affect-based appeals

Advertisements can use different types of appeal. They can appeal to reason and use arguments, or they can use emotions and feelings to get the message across. Hence, they can choose an argument-based or a more affect-based appeal. The efficacy of each of these strategies will depend on the type of product advertised and the involvement level of the audience. Experiential products such as wine, soft drinks, perfumes, paintings or designer clothing are evaluated primarily by personal preference (e.g. taste, flavour, style and design) and thus lend themselves well to affect-based appeals.

In contrast, durable products such as computers or washing machines, but also non-durable products such as washing powders or toothpaste are typically communicated with rational, argument-based appeals. Obviously, some products combine aspects of both types, such as sports cars or watches.

Consumer evaluations of experiential products will be mainly based on affect and will have very little cognitive content. In addition such appeals require little processing motivation to be effective, so they are particularly suitable when consumer involvement is low. It would be difficult to use a rational, argument-based appeal for a

Avis is only No.2 in rent a cars. So why go with us?

We try harder.
(When you're not the biggest, you have to.)
We just can't afford dirty ash-trays. Or half-empty gas tanks. Or worn wipers. Or unwashed cars. Or low tires. Or anything less than seat-adjusters that adjust. Heaters that heat. Defrost-ers that defrost.
Obviously, the thing we try hardest for is just to be nice. To start you out right with a new car, like a lively, super-torque Ford, and a pleasant smile. To know, say, where you get a good pastrami sandwich in Duluth.
Why?
Because we can't afford to take you for granted.
Go with us next time.
The line at our counter is shorter.

Figure 1.6 Two-sided ad, in more ways than one
Reproduced with permission of Avis

particular brand of soft drink, given that the different brands are not all that different and that purchasing decisions are rarely based on an evaluation of objective qualities. Soft drink ads therefore use appeals that play on people's emotions, trying to associate these products with feelings of youth or sexual attractiveness. However, although rarely done, it is not impossible to try reason-based approaches even to the sales of soft drinks. For example, the Pepsi claim that people preferred Pepsi over Coca-Cola in blind tasting or the emphasis of non-cola soft drinks on the absence of caffeine were attempts at more reason-based approaches.

Another type of emotion sometimes played on in advertising is fear. Fear-appeals are also known as **fear-arousing communications**. They try to 'scare the consumer into action' (Kardes, 2002). Fear appeals in advertising frequently refer to *risks* that the consumer can either prevent or reduce by buying the product (e.g. insurance) or by not buying the product (e.g. smoking or alcohol abuse). DePelsmacker, Geuens and van den Bergh (2001) have listed several types of risk that are encountered frequently in advertising:

- *physical:* risk of bodily harm which is used in ads for sportswear (e.g. sports injuries), toothpaste (e.g. cavities) or over-the-counter self-medication (e.g. headache, see Figure 1.7)
- *social:* the risk of being socially rejected, frequently used for personal hygiene products such as deodorants, dandruff shampoo, mouth wash etc
- *product performance:* the risk that competitive brands will not have high quality attributes or will not perform as expected
- *financial:* the risk of losing large sums of money, or spending too much on an inferior competitive product
- *opportunity:* the risk of missing a special opportunity to buy the product because it is in short supply or only available a limited amount of time.

Some advertising agencies claim that affect-based appeals are generally more effective than argument-based appeals (e.g. Leo Burnett). Other agencies claim the opposite (e.g. Ogilvy & Mather). The truth probably lies in the middle as research by Venkatraman, Marlino, Kardes and Sklar (1990) has shown. Their work demonstrated that rational, argument-based appeals and affect-based appeals may be equally effective, albeit for different groups of consumers. More specifically, consumers who enjoyed effortful cognitive activity (i.e. high in the need for cognition) responded differently to rational versus emotional appeals than consumers who disliked such extensive mental activity (i.e. low in the need for cognition). More in particular, consumers low in the

Figure 1.7 An unconventional outdoor ad graphically appealing to pain

Reproduced with permission of Advil

need for cognition were more affected by emotional appeals, whereas their high need for cognition counterparts was more influenced by rational appeals.

Advertising in context: integrated marketing communications and the promotional mix

In addition to source and message variables in advertising, a second class of situational variables that may affect consumer responses consists of the communication tools that make up the marketer's **promotional mix**. The promotional mix includes five types of marketing communications in addition to advertising, namely direct marketing, interactive marketing, sales promotion, public relations (PR) and personal selling. The deployment of these elements of the promotional mix is usually determined through what is commonly referred to as **Integrated Marketing Communications** or IMC (see Smith, Gopalakrishna & Chatterjee, 2006). IMC involves coordinating the elements in the promotional mix to create synergy between them (Belch & Belch, 2004). This implies that advertising (or another promotional element) may under certain circumstances interact with the effect of one or more of the other promotion elements on some consumer response, preferably buying behaviour. When successful, this interaction may result in an enhanced impact on consumer responses. However, as Smith et al. (2006) have noted, empirical demonstrations of the synergetic potential of promotion mix elements remain scarce (see also Naik & Raman, 2003). Nevertheless, DePelsmacker et al. (2001) have documented the successful case of Pioneer, the Japanese brand of consumer electronics. For their twenty-first century strategy, they opted for increasing the strength of the Pioneer brand name. As part of this strategy, an IMC philosophy was adopted in which all promotional mix elements were centralized in and coordinated by one marketing communications department with full control over all communication activities worldwide. Not only were market and consumer research endeavours centralized but also the analysis of competitors' communications, the compatibility and complementarity of all marketing communications, including corporate communications and PR, and even the selection and introduction of new Pioneer personnel. All these activities enabled Pioneer to communicate more successfully than before with one concerted voice with different consumer segments around the world.

Although the promotional mix elements represent distinct types of marketing communications, the development of IMC has also led to a blurring of traditional boundaries between 'classic' advertising and these other tools. For example, regular advertising increasingly offers a direct response opportunity, especially on the internet (e.g. by offering the possibility of leaving an email address, directly forwarding the consumer to the web outlet, or enabling the consumer to get in touch with sales personnel by emailing them). In addition, communication by sales personnel can sometimes 'mimic' advertising, when sales representatives repeat the key message of an ad campaign, or convey the same persuasive arguments as the ad. Therefore, advertising can no longer simply be viewed as invariably non-personal communication, but increasingly manifests itself in hybrid forms, including elements from other tools in the promotion mix.

Direct marketing

In **direct marketing** the firm communicates directly and individually with a potential customer, with the objective of generating a behavioural response from him/her, preferably in the form of a transaction (see Basu, Basu & Batra, 1995). It is claimed to be one of the fastest growing sectors of the US economy (Belch & Belch, 2004). Direct marketing entails such activities as database management (to assess key consumers in the target group), telemarketing, and direct response advertising (advertising with an immediate customer feedback option). Indeed, as Belch and Belch (2004) argue, some companies rely totally on direct marketing efforts at the expense of other, more traditional means of promotion, such as advertising. Examples include household product manufacturer Tupperware and cosmetics manufacturer Avon. Tupperware and Avon products are not sold in regular shops. Instead, both firms use a specific form of direct marketing, in which sales agents visit groups of potential consumers at their house to demonstrate and sell products. In this form of direct marketing, the social function of a home party with its own dynamic of creating a sense of consensus ('all my friends like this product'), and liking for the seller (who is frequently the host or hostess) is as important for the success of this marketing strategy as directly informing or persuading the consumer.

A related form of direct marketing which hinges on actual interpersonal interaction between (sales) agent and consumer is **word-of-mouth marketing**, where the influence agent is not a sales representative of the company, but a commited user of the product. He or she acts as a persuasion agent (sometimes 'seduced' to do so by the promise of a desirable incentive by the company) trying to convince close relatives and friends to try the product as well (see Tuk, Verlegh, Smidts & Wigboldus, 2009). Similar to the in-home selling format described above, word-of-mouth marketing has seen a surge in interest from companies to overcome consumer resistance and scepticism towards convential advertising practices. Similarly, face-to-face interaction is also an essential element of **event marketing**. Here, a sports event or cultural event (such as a soccer match or a rock concert) is used as a 'vehicle' to get in touch with prospective customers, frequently through **sponsorship** of an existing event (chapter 6) or the creation of an entirely new one, closely associated with the sponsoring brand. A key example of event marketing is the Red Bull Air Race, an international stunt flying competition hosted and organized by the energy drink. In line with word of mouth marketing, a key motive driving event marketing is the presumed lowered resistance of consumers toward marketing stimuli in the context of the entertaining event.

In addition, another well-known type of direct marketing is **direct mail** which is a personalized form of advertising, where consumers are typically addressed by their names (for instance by mail catalogues). Consumer databases are increasingly enabling marketers to personalize the offer by relating the demographic data of the addressee to interests, lifestyles and preferences. Direct mail has spurred something of an 'arms race' on the internet between marketers developing increasingly aggressive selling messages and software engineers developing increasingly sophisticated spam-filters trying to prevent these messages from ending up in the consumer's email inbox.

Interactive marketing

Interactive marketing shares the feedback between sender and receiver with direct marketing. Interactive marketing involves using the potential of the internet for marketing products and services, and thus has boomed over the last decade. Four features of the internet make it a suitable medium for interactive marketing. In contrast to traditional media, the internet is synchronous meaning that there is no or only a small time lag between sending and receiving messages. Consumers also have control of *contact*, in that they control the timing and pacing of information. Moreover, they may sometimes also have more control of *content* than they do with traditional media. However, in contrast to face-to-face communication and audio-visual communication, perceived *social presence* defined as the extent of perceived 'personalness', warmth and sensitivity is lower on the internet, although it is increasing through the use of avatars, emoticons and other features simulating human personal interaction (cf. DePelsmacker et al., 2001).

Some authors claim interactive marketing entails more than direct marketing, as the internet allows the consumer to become a 'co-producer' of the products and services offered, and sometimes even create their own personalized products (e.g. Belch & Belch, 2004). A well-known example is the website for Nike sportswear. Consumers can customize their athletic shoes according to their personal preferences and thus create a unique product tailored to their specific wishes and lifestyle.

Sales promotion

Similar to direct marketing efforts, **sales promotion** is focused on generating an immediate behavioural response from the consumer and thus can be considered a form of 'action communication'. Unlike direct marketing, however, it is less concerned with doing so by means of personalizing the message or the offer. In contrast, sales promotions use price-cuts and other forms of temporary incentives to generate sales on an ad hoc basis. Sales promotion tools include monetary incentives (price cuts, coupons or refunds), additional incentives (i.e. chances to win a prize in contests and sweepstakes) and product promotions (i.e. sampling, premiums, or saving cards). In addition to sales, these types of communications can also be used to induce other types of consumer behavioural responses, such as trial purchases, and brand switching.

DePelsmacker et al. (2001) describe five basic functions of sales promotions: to increase market size (by directly stimulating sales); to reward loyal customers (i.e. by providing them with price cuts and other incentives); to make existing customers more loyal; to stimulate trial by new customers; and to support other communications tools. As with the effects of IMC, empirical support for the effects of sales promotion on these types of outcome measures is scarce, but the evidence does suggest a short-term positive effect on consumer purchase intentions and actual buying behaviour (e.g. Dhar & Hoch, 1996). What is less clear, however, is the impact of price cuts and related tools on longer-term consumer behaviour. It may well be that positive effects do not 'stick' and quickly wear off in the longer term and there is even some evidence that sales promotion actions may have negative effects in the long run (e.g. Kahn & Louie, 1990). Negative effects may occur at an aggregated level as sales promotion actions by competing firms may result in ever-increasing promotion costs for similar sales revenues. Moreover, sales promotions may affect the reference price consumers use to form their judgement ('it was on discount before, so why not now?'). This may result in consumers refraining from buying the product when the promotion ends (the 'post-promotion dip') and manufacturers being driven to providing ever more substantial price cuts to induce repeat purchases (DePelsmacker et al., 2001). In addition, sales promotion tools may have the sometimes undesirable effect of making the price the most salient product attribute in the perception of the consumer, thus corroding consumer brand perceptions based on features such as product quality, attributes or performance.

Public relations

Although traditionally not part of the IMC promotion mix, **public relations** can have a substantial effect on the impact of other promotion tools, and thus may be 'aligned' with them in order to maximize effectiveness of an IMC programme (Fitzpatrick, 2005).

Public relations may be viewed as a communication instrument that is used to promote favourable perceptions about the organization as a whole. Hence, its 'theatre of operations' is broader than just the communication between suppliers and consumers, and also includes sponsoring of public events, communication with media gatekeepers, political stakeholders, pressure groups, government bodies and internal employees. Nevertheless, the definition of PR as being aimed at fostering favourable perceptions, is not undisputed. Several scholars argue that PR should not be considered a form of persuasion, but should be viewed as a 'symmetrical' form of communication aimed at the exchange of information between (organizational) senders and their target groups and thus creating a mutual understanding between organizations and their publics (see Grunig & Grunig, 1998). Other authors, however, maintain that this practice still boils down to communication with the aim of fostering favourable evaluations, and hence, is essentially persuasive in nature (Pfau & Wan, 2006). It is this view of PR that yields the most promise of a fruitful integration with other elements of the promotion mix.

Although public relations as an academic discipline has seen a surge in interest in the last few decades, witnessed by increased scholarly attention, and the foundation of journals devoted to the subject, the scientific study of PR-effectiveness has yet to yield unequivocal findings. Nevertheless, in the context of IMC, two types of PR practice may be especially relevant to consider, namely financial public relations and marketing public relations. Financial public relations is aimed at informing and persuading the financial audiences which are essential for the long-term money-raising potential of the company, such as shareholders, potential investors, financial consultants and banks. Marketing PR is directly related to the other elements of the promotion mix with its objective to foster the selling of products and services. Marketing PR entails the promotion of new products and services through free publicity (as when a new car model is tested and reviewed by the press).

Sometimes, instances of marketing PR go wrong as Mercedes-Benz found out when it introduced their new small A-model. To demonstrate the agility of the new car, a 'moose test' was staged in front of the world's press where the little Benz was to slalom around a suddenly appearing moose on the road (actually a set of pylons). However, what should have been a clever PR stunt, turned out to be a car marketer's nightmare as the car flipped over and landed on its side after a few turns. The problem was subsequently solved by Mercedes-Benz, but the damage was done: the A-class has ever since had to live with an inerasable association of instability.

Personal selling

In contrast with the other elements of the promotion mix, **personal selling** is always and by definition a two-way, face-to-face form of communication to inform and per-suade prospective buyers with the aim of yielding a behavioural response from them, either in the sense of an initial purchase of the product or service, or fostering repeat purchases and thus creating customer loyalty. Interestingly, the practice of personal selling has received much attention in (social) psychology as a specific manifestation of dyadic social influence in which an 'agent' tries foster compliance from a 'target', most often through the employment of a specially tailored persuasion strategy (Cialdini, 2009). Compliance entails a more narrow group of consumer responses than persuasion. Whereas persuasion involves changing consumer beliefs and evaluative resonses, compliance is focused solely on overt behaviour and even more specifically on acquiescence following a specific type of communication: a request. We will discuss this research extensively in chapter 6. For now, we will only mention that research findings on the impact of these persuasion strategies has led to the identification of several influence principles that foster the odds of consumer persuasion and compli-ance, such as the principles of commitment and consistency (creating small actions or reframing the consumer's prior responses to appear consistent with the requested response), or reciprocity (creating the tendency to return a favour; Cialdini & Goldstein, 2004; Kardes, 2002). Surprisingly, while social psychology has devoted considerable research attention to understanding the process of personal selling as a special case of social influence, the reverse cannot be said. That is, although social influence principles have been employed widely in the field by sales representatives, fundraisers and telemarketers, they are mainly based on intuition, common sense or 'best prac-tices' sales training. When glancing through sales manuals promising 'effective sales performance in three easy steps', or 'guaranteeing sales success at the first encounter', the lack of scientific corroboration for the assertions is striking. Moreover, even in the academic field of marketing and consumer behaviour, programmatic research on mechanisms and dynamics underlying sales performance tends to lag behind other fields. More specifically, although early research has focused on influence procedures that foster consumer compliance around the late 1970s, early 1980s (e.g. Allen, Schewe and Wijk, 1980; Furse, Stewart & Rados, 1981; Hansen & Robinson, 1980; Reingen, 1978; Reingen & Kernan, 1977; Tybout, Sternthal & Calder, 1983), later studies shifted attention to the related domain of attitude change and information processing research (but see Monroe & Avila, 1986, for a notable exception).

Personal selling has several advantages and disadvantages over other tradi-tional elements in the promotion mix that may facilitate or hinder its effectiveness (DePelsmacker et al., 2001). One key advantage is that personal selling is said to have a higher overall impact on buyer behaviour than many of the other tools, since a sales person can carefully probe symptoms of consumer resistance (see Knowles & Linn, 2004) and try to break through them. Because the customer can provide the sales agent with continuous feedback, he/she can tailor the sales message to the specific needs and wants of the customer thus increasing its effectiveness. Additionally, the impact of face-to-face selling is enhanced through the possibility of demonstrating the product and negotiating on the price, after-sales service, warranties, etc. Furthermore, it is an efficient form of communication since there is no 'waste', in the sense of reaching audience members that are not part of the target group. Potential disadvantages of personal selling include the costs: it is a relatively expensive form of communication. Therefore, although efficient, personal communication has a limited reach and frequency. Moreover, although communication can be tailored to the needs of the customer, this has the disadvantage of the company's lack of control over the content of its messages, and this may increase the risk of inconsistent messages and salesperson behaviour which may engender consumer confusion.

Classic and contemporary approaches of conceptualizing advertising effectiveness

As a starting point for discussing how thinking about the effects of advertising has developed over time, a distinction has to be made between two basic approaches to conceptualize the impact of advertising. Tellis (2004) distinguishes the modelling approach, and the behavioural approach. The modelling approach focuses on the aggregate level. That is, entire markets or market segments are the primary unit of measurement. On the other hand, the behavioural paradigm focuses on individual consumer responses as a function of specific advertising input variables. Hence ad variables function as the independent variables in this paradigm and consumer responses as dependent variables. In contrast to the modelling approach the level of specificity in the behavioural paradigm is typically high, such that the effects of individual ad characteristics (e.g. music in advertising) on specific individual consumer responses are assessed (e.g. consumer favourability of brand-related cognitions). It does so by employing primarily experimental research methods.

Sales-response models

Aggregated models have a long history of research, especially in the fields of management science and business administration (see for example Hanssens, Parsons & Schultz, 1990). These aggregated models are conceptualized as so called **sales-response models** (Arndt & Simon, 1983) or market-response models (see Vakratsas & Ambler, 1999). In short, these models aim to relate advertising inputs such as expenditures to aggregated output measures, such as sales, market share or profits in an effort to gain insight in the aggregated advertising effects as a function of aggregated advertising input. Although the number of variations is potentially infinite, two basic shapes have received the most attention, namely the concave sales response model and the S-shaped model.

According to the concave sales response model (Figure 1.8), sales follow the law

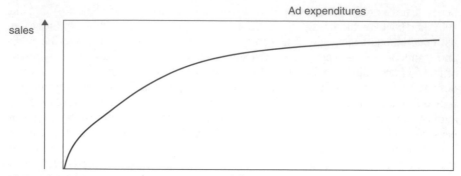

Figure 1.8 Concave sales-response model

of diminishing returns: the incremental impact of advertising on sales diminishes with increasing the communication budget, based on the notion that once the entire population of non-buyers has been reached by an advertising campaign (of which only a sub-sample will convert into buyers), additional ad expenditures will not add much in terms of impact.

Another type of sales-response model is the S-shaped model (Figure 1.9). This model assumes that initial impact of advertising as a function of communication budget is low. In this phase, advertising 'wear-in' takes place (Blair & Rabuck, 1998, see also chapter 4). When this phase is concluded, sales will start to increase exponentially with increasing expenditures, up to a certain saturation point where the impact of advertising will level off, or at least be reduced following a diminishing-returns type of function. After this phase, added investments may even lead to adverse results, such as wear-out brought about by consumers gradually replacing positive evaluations with negative ones as ad repetitions increase (see Nordhielm, 2002).

Although modelling these types of relations constitutes an important step in conceptualizing the aggregate effects of advertising, scholars have been critical of the approach. DePelsmacker et al. (2001), for example, have argued that the aggregate level of analysis may obscure the confounding role of several factors. First, advertising may not be the only causal factor affecting sales. Indeed, any or all of the (other) marketing elements in the promotional mix may have their influence as well. Moreover, these variables may interact in their effects. In addition, factors outside the realm of the advertising company may be (partly) responsible for aggregated effects, such as the communication efforts of the competition, or economic and sociocultural factors. In short, all these factors decrease the possibility of isolating the net effects of advertising on buying behaviour. Even more important is the observation that response modelling is based on input-output representations without regard for the underlying processes that are responsible for the occurrence of a relationship (or lack thereof) between advertising input and sales output. However, sales output evidently is a *behavioural* measure, albeit an aggregated one. Hence, a behavioural approach is needed to complement the modelling approach in understanding advertising effects. The behavioural approach is made up of hierarchy-of-effects models, the cognitive response approach, dual process models and research on unconscious processes in consumer behaviour.

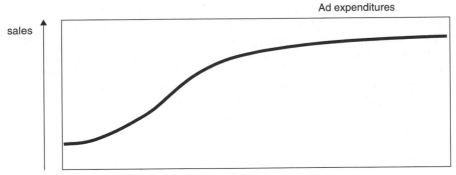

Figure 1.9 S-shaped sales-response model

Early models of individual responses to advertising: hierarchy-of-effects models

Hierarchy-of-effects models do not make the assumption of a direct link between ad message and consumer response, but instead propose several *intermediate* steps. These models are based on the assumption that some form of consumer *learning* takes place following exposure to advertising. More particularly, hierarchy-of-effects models assume that consumer responses to advertising proceed through a fixed set of three learning stages. In the *cognitive* stage consumers engage in directing conscious attention to the target ad and thinking about its content. In the subsequent *affective* stage, thinking gives way to emotional responses and the formation of attitudes or preferences associated with the advertised brand takes place (note that these models assume that attitudes and preferences are affective, rather than cognitive responses). Finally, the third *conative* stage includes behaviour that might arise from exposure to advertising, including (re)purchasing the advertised brand, or (re)using it.

The oldest hierarchy known dating back to 1898 is the AIDA sequence, attributed to E. St. Elmo Lewis (Strong, 1925). The AIDA model was originally developed to understand personal selling, but it was soon thereafter applied to advertising. It proposes a straightforward linear sequence of effects: advertising reaches its impact on consumer behaviour through the sequence of Attention (cognitive stage), Interest, Desire (affective stage), and Action (conative stage). Reflected in the model are the two basic functions of advertising: to inform (reflected in the attention stage, in which advertising is used to create brand awareness) and to persuade (reflected in the interest and desire stage, see Yeshin, 2006). The AIDA model is not only hierarchical in the sense that consumers have to go through each of the stages in a fixed order, it is also hierarchical with regard to the implications for advertising practice (Weilbacher, 2001): if the consumer has never been exposed to the brand before, advertising must induce consumer attention in order to foster brand awareness. If the consumer is aware of the brand but doesn't know any of its attributes, advertising must 'educate' the consumer by first arousing interest, and second, describe the product's attributes in order to induce consumer desire. Once the flame of desire has been sparked, consumers will invariably act upon it, and will buy the brand.

Several variations on this theme have been proposed in which stages have been added or deleted. As summarized by Barry and Howard (1990) these modifications include AIDCA (Attention, Interest, Desire, Conviction, Action), AIETA (Awareness, Interest, Evaluation, Trial, Adoption), and a model suggested by Lavidge and Steiner (1961). This model, which is probably the one cited most frequently in the literature, comprises the following sequence: awareness → knowledge → liking → preference → conviction → purchase. Although these frameworks may have some heuristic value, empirical support for the predictive power to understand advertising effectiveness is largely lacking (Vakratsas & Ambler, 1999). Hence, none of the models provide a valid description of how advertising 'works'.

In addition, hierarchy-of-effects models suffer from several other conceptual weaknesses as well. First, they invariably depart from a cognitive-affective-behaviour sequence, or 'think-feel-do' sequence, and indeed for some types of products, in some situations (e.g. new products and new market expansions), this sequence may provide an apt description of the buying process (Lucas & Prensky, 1997). However, for other products in other situations, the think-feel-do tripartite model will not hold. More specifically, the most pressing problem associated with these hierarchies is that the fixed sequence of processes presupposes a relatively high level of consumer involvement. Once the prototypical consumer is exposed to an ad, it is invariably considered relevant, which spurs his/her interest, induces desire and so on. However, more often than not, high consumer involvement levels are the exception rather than the rule. In the field, these considerations have given rise to alternative taxonomies, such as the Foote, Cone-Belding (FCB) Grid developed by advertising agency Foote, Cone and Belding (Vaughn, 1980, see Figure 1.10) and the Rossiter-Percy-Donovan grid (Rossiter, Percy & Donovan, 1991).

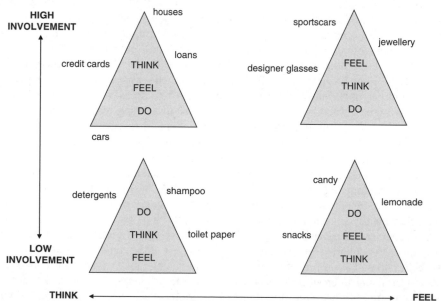

Figure 1.10 Foote, Cone-Belding grid

The FCB grid proposes that advertising could be modelled along two key variables: the extent of thinking versus feeling and the extent of consumer involvement (low versus high). This results in a planning grid with four cells, each representing a combination of the extent of consumer thought and involvement. Brands and products can be placed in one of the four cells based on a consideration of whether the product is selected primarily in terms of its functional benefits or rather in terms of the emotional needs it is assumed to satisfy. In addition, some of these products may be more personally relevant to the consumer than others, and so they will vary in the extent of involvement that is associated with them. Finally, each quadrant has a different sequence including the components 'think', 'feel' and 'do', that is assumed to account for the consumer decision-making process and the processing of advertisements about these products. The quadrant low-involvement/thinking typically includes household products such as detergent, toilet paper, and simple food items. Decision-making proceeds along a do-think-feel hierarchy: consumers buy the brand without any mentionable cognitive or affective process preceding it (for example spurred by the simple observation that their household has ran out of the product). Then, by using the brand, they may learn about its attributes. The evaluation of the usage experience may produce an attitude (which in the grid is equated with the 'feel' component). The quadrant low-involvement/feeling includes products that may be regarded as 'life's little pleasures' (DePelsmacker et al., 2001), such as candy, soft drink, ice cream, etc. They are bought primarily for hedonic reasons, and hence affective considerations weigh more heavily than cognitive considerations (please note the inconsistency in the use of terms, as 'feel' now denotes a 'true' affective, sensory experience). Information processing about these products requires little cognitive effort and decision-making proceeds along a do-feel-think hierarchy: after purchase, the product is consumed eliciting an affective experience, which may (or may not) be followed by learning about the product's attributes. On the high involvement end, the motivation to invest more cognitive effort in information processing is typically larger. The quadrant high involvement/thinking includes products that are associated with considerable (financial) risk such as loans, houses, and cars (although one can dispute the extent to which cars are truly 'think' instead of 'feel' products). Decision-making involves the traditional think-feel-do sequence, in which the consumer first learns about the product's attributes and performance through careful processing of advertising and other sources of information, then develops an attitude (again, the term 'feel' refers to an evaluation here) and subsequently acts in accordance with that attitude. Finally, the high involvement/feeling quadrant is involved with a feel-think-do sequence and includes such products as expensive jewellery, perfume and fashion (where 'feel' refers in part to a true affective, sensory experience – as with perfume – and in part to an evaluation).

Although the FCB grid constitutes a step forward in that it acknowledges that consumers are sometimes less than highly involved and unmotivated to exert the cognitive effort assumed by the classical hierarchies, it suffers from the same shortcoming in that it always assumes some form of sequence involving all three classes of consumer responses. A variant of the FCB-grid, also highlighting the distinction between high and low involvement is the Rossiter, Percy, and Donovan (1991) planning grid. Its aim was to overcome some of the shortcomings of the FCB-grid, most notably the FCB-restriction to two classes of consumer responses: feelings and thoughts. In addition, they stressed the role of brand awareness as a necessary precursor for brand attitudes, both at the point of purchase (where a consumer has to recognize the brand) and prior to purchase (where a consumer needs to recall the brand). In the Rossiter et al. (1991) grid, high and low involvement product types are crossed with two classes of consumer motives. Involvement in their model is defined as the extent of risk perceived by the typical target audience member (although the type of risk remains unspecified). These authors refer to positive and negative purchase motivations, which are reminiscent of goal-approach and avoidance motivations (see Knowles & Linn, 2004). Positive motivations in their grid are labelled 'transformational motivations' and include sensory gratification, intellectual stimulation, and social approval. In contrast, negative purchase motivations are termed 'informational motives' and include problem removal, problem avoidance and normal depletion. Hence, a consumer who notices he has run out of milk and wants to buy a new carton, experiences a negative, informational buying motive. But a consumer who craves milk because he likes the taste so much, experiences a positive, transformational motive. This simple example immediately reveals an inherent weakness in both the FCB grid, and the Rossiter-Percy grid. It invariably links certain levels of involvement and motivation (albeit conceptualized differently) to certain products or product-types, and thus disregards the possibility that the same product may function in a different role for different individuals. Stated more directly, involvement and motivation refer to person variables, not to invariant attributes of a product or advertising stimulus.

To date, hierarchy-of-effects models and planning grids continue to function as a compass for advertising managers guiding them in their decision-making. As recently as 1995, the US Association of National Advertisers released a revised edition of a specific hierarchical framework, termed DAGMAR (Dutka, 1995). It is an acronym for Defining Advertising Goals for Measured Advertising Results and was originally published in 1961 by Russell Colley. According to the model, advertising can yield nine different effects that are hierarchically ordered (see Figure 1.11): starting with category need, via brand awareness, brand knowledge/comprehension, brand attitude, brand purchase intention, purchase facilitation and purchase, all the way up to satisfaction and brand loyalty.

DAGMAR is different from other models, in that it is more explicit with regard to the specific communication objectives that advertising may have in each stage, and hence in the types of advertising research needed to measure the effectiveness of advertising at each successive stage. In addition, the model highlights a basic distinction in evaluative versus non-evaluative consumer responses to advertising, and is thus compatible with the two essential functions of advertising: to inform and to persuade. That is, creating category need, brand awareness, increasing brand knowledge and comprehension all pertain to non-evaluative consumer responses. In contrast, brand attitude, brand purchase intention, purchase facilitation, purchase, satisfaction, and brand loyalty are evaluative in that they are valenced and directional. That is, a successful ad campaign will result in more favourable cognitive and affective responses toward the advertised brand, vis-à-vis competitive brands.

However, what applied to its classic forerunners also applies to DAGMAR: there is no convincing evidence that advertising affects the consumer in the sequence posited by the model, although some of the postulates make intuitive sense. In addition, all models discussed essentially assume a passive consumer whose primary source of

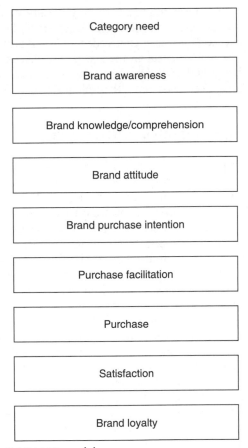

Figure 1.11 The DAGMAR model

influence is advertising. Furthermore, Weilbacher (2001) has summarized a series of problems associated with these models. First, they are only concerned with the effects of advertising as discrete media messages, whereas in reality, effects often come about in interaction with various other marketing factors (including product features, distribution factors and pricing decisions), a point we also stressed in relation to sales-response models. Second, hierarchy-of-effects models represent a simplistic view of human behaviour and response processes, with advertising as the stimulus and overt consumer behaviour as the ultimate response without any regard for underlying processes and moderating conditions. Third, such models are inflexible, since they assume that all ads have the same specific effects. Fourth, especially the models that relate specific effects with ways to measure them (i.e. DAGMAR) suggest that the postulated sequence of effects is valid, since its constituent components can be measured. Indeed, although both advertising recall (a measure of ad awareness) and brand attitude (a measure of the 'persuasive potential' of advertising) can be measured, studies in cognitive and social psychology typically show no or only a weak correlation between recall and attitude change (see also chapter 3), underscoring the lack of construct validity of models in which awareness is a necessary precursor to attitude formation or change (note that the Rossiter et al. (1991) grid is subject to the same concern with its proposition of brand awareness as an antecedent of brand attitudes). Studies have shown that attitude change can occur in the absence of increased recall, especially when such attitude change is the result of thorough and extensive consumer information processing, a subject discussed later in this volume (chapter 5).

Information processing research in advertising

Thinking of advertising in terms of grids or hierarchy-of-effects is reminiscent of a broader trend in marketing and consumer behaviour research in the 1960s and 1970s. As summarized by Simonson, Carmon, Dhar, Drolet and Nowlis (2001), the field in that period focused on 'grand theories': comprehensive models of buyer behaviour that claimed to capture all relevant factors and relationships necessary to provide an exhaustive account of why, when and how consumers buy products and services. A well-known example is Engel, Kollat and Miniard's (1968) consumer behaviour model where buying behaviour was conceptualized as the joint resultant of individual differences (such as personality traits), and environmental influences (e.g. advertising, culture or social class) affecting information processing and decision-making. Although this and other models (e.g. Howard & Sheth, 1969) have proven their value as conceptual frameworks for organizing strands of research findings on advertising and other marketing effects, research generally failed to generate sufficient empirical evidence to support them as generic theories of consumer behaviour. In the early 1980s researchers realized that consumer behaviour, and psychology in general, was too complex to be captured in a single model and instead focused on specific psychological processes that drove consumer judgement and decision-making under specific conditions. Information processing and attitude change became the dominant objects of research in that period.

Cognitive response approach

The **cognitive response model** (Greenwald, 1968; Petty, Ostrom & Brock, 1981) spearheaded the new attention to information processing issues. It shares with the various hierarchy-of-effects models the assumption that some kind of learning takes place in response to exposure to a persuasive message. However, in contrast to a fixed set of consumer responses, the cognitive response approach emphasizes the mediating role of idiosyncratic thoughts or 'cognitive responses' that people generate when being exposed to a persuasive message. The consumer is no longer a passive recipient of an advertising message, but instead actively tries to make sense of it. In essence, the cognitive response approach holds that once a receiver is exposed to a persuasive message, he/she may actively add to and elaborate upon message content. This means that message recipients may come up with counterarguments when they view the message arguments as weak and specious, they may derogate the source of the message, doubt the veracity of the arguments, etc. Conversely, a message containing strong arguments, may provoke more positive thoughts, such as supportive arguments, implementation intentions in line with the advocacy in the message, or favourable thoughts on the credibility of the source of the message. It is the valence of these thoughts (either positive, neutral or negative) that determines the direction of any resulting attitude change. This means that cognitive responding may lead to persuasion, active resistance or a neutral, unchanged position. Cognitive responding is a function of the extent of motivation and ability to engage in elaborative thinking, with higher motivation and ability resulting in more extensive cognitive responding. As Eagly and Chaiken (1993) have noted, it was the first approach at the time to account for the fact that extensive thinking could result in *more* or *less* persuasion, as a function of motivation and ability.

The major shortcoming of the cognitive response approach is its failure to account for the processes that occur when ability and/or motivation are low, other than that the extent and valence of thoughts are less consequential for persuasion. This limits its application to the understanding of many advertising effects, because the prototypical context for advertising exposure is often one of low ability and/or motivation. Starting with the classical observation by Herbert Krugman (1965) that consumer involvement with advertising is typically low, many scholars have stressed the importance of low-involvement consumer judgment and decision-making (e.g. Andrews & Shimp, 1990; Batra & Ray, 1985; Celsi & Olson, 1988; Gardner, Mitchell & Russo, 1985; MacKenzie & Lutz, 1989; Miniard, Bhatla & Rose, 1990; Park & Young, 1986; Smith & Swinyard, 1982). To account for the roles that various source, message, receiver and channel factors can play under conditions of both extensive and less extensive thinking, dual process models have been developed, that build on the heritage provided by the cognitive response approach. The cognitive response approach is discussed more in detail in chapter 5.

Dual process approaches

Like the cognitive response approach in persuasion, most early theories of information processing, social judgement, and decision-making were based on the assumption that individuals are able and willing to engage in careful and time-consuming information processing in order to arrive at a decision. In recognition of the fact that individuals are often neither willing nor able to carefully scrutinize all the information that is available to them but base their decisions on rule-of-thumb heuristics or other effort-saving ways of arriving at inferences, social psychology saw the development of **dual process theories of persuasion**. The dual process approach can be considered one of the cornerstones of present-day social cognition and has helped to reconcile a host of conflicting findings in the field of attitude formation, social judgement, and persuasion.

According to the dual process approach, information processing, judgement and decision-making must be viewed as a continuum. At one end of this continuum, information processing is characterized by controlled, slow, explicit, conscious, deliberate, analytical, effortful, reflective, rule-based, bottom-up processing and judgement. In this 'mode' people typically spend considerable time scrutinizing the advertising message, devote mental resources to the sense-making process, and in so doing carefully construct meaning, beliefs, attitudes, judgement, and – ultimately – behavioural decisions (e.g. purchase decisions in the case of advertising). In this mode, one needs to consciously reflect on and examine the advertising stimulus in a 'mindful' (Langer, 1992) manner. This is the prevalent mode in the extensive processing side of the cognitive response approach. This mode of processing is engaged when the issue in an advertising message is highly involving for the consumer (i.e. is personally relevant), or when the consumer has ample time to scrutinize the message. In these situations, the quality of information pertaining directly to the issue under consideration (i.e. the quality of the persuasive arguments) becomes an important determinant of persuasion. Following cognitive response logic, under these conditions, strong, compelling arguments evoke mostly favourable thoughts which will increase persuasion. Conversely, weak, specious arguments will evoke mostly unfavourable thoughts which will decrease persuasion. Moreover, attitudes that are formed or changed in this mindful manner often show temporal persistence, are predictive of (buying) behaviour and often resist change in response to counter-persuasion (Petty & Wegener, 1999).

However, as stated, consumers often lack the motivation or the ability to engage in this effortful process. Under these conditions, their mode of information processing will be more reflective of the other end of the dual process continuum. It will involve relatively automatic, fast, implicit, impulsive, immediate, experiential, non-conscious, effortless, associative, top-down processing and judgement. In this mode, consumers use prior knowledge, simple decision rules (heuristics), stereotypes, well-learned scripts and other relatively 'quick and dirty' guidelines to effortlessly and rather 'mindlessly' (Langer, 1992) arrive at a decision. In the context of advertising this means that consumers use background music, the attractiveness of the product's endorser, or any other contextual message element as the key basis for judgement. Attitudes formed or changed this way are thought to be less persistent, do not predict behaviour very well, and are vulnerable to counter-persuasion (i.e. are easily changed in the face of countermessages).

Both modes of information processing represent the endpoints on a continuum and so intermediate forms are highly likely (i.e. when motivation and ability are moderate rather than very high or low). Moreover, both modes complement each other and may even interact under specific conditions (Eagly & Chaiken, 1993). Together, they represent a comprehensive spectrum of consumer information processing and judgement in response to various advertising stimuli. Nevertheless, despite the overwhelming evidence supporting the existence of these styles, they still have to find their way to the idiom of the advertising practitioner. Indeed, as Malaviya, Meyers-Levy & Sternthal (1999) contend, many practitioners, especially advertising copywriters, still maintain that in order to be effective, an ad invariably needs to 'break through' an almost vegetative state of consumer media viewing, and then deliver a powerful punchline that consumers need to respond to with a well-articulated and favourable stream of thought, strong emotions and in a resource-active manner (i.e. following an effortful processing style). The most well-known dual process frameworks in the realm of advertising and, more generally, persuasive communication, are the Elaboration Likelihood Model (ELM; Petty & Cacioppo, 1984), and the Heuristic Systematic Processing Model (HSM; Chaiken, 1980) that will be discussed extensively in chapter 5.

Unconscious processes in consumer behaviour

Research on models such as the ELM and HSM has helped tremendously in sorting out what type of advertising variable affects what type of consumer response, driven by what type of underlying process, under what type of conditions, but developments on the psychology of advertising do not end there. From the mid 1990s onward, research increasingly emphasised fully unconscious and automatic processes. As we will discuss in chapters 3 and 6, researchers studying **priming** found that activating a concept in consumer memory could directly affect overt behaviour without the participant being consciously aware that the activation procedure had any influence on the subsequent behavioural response. Moreover, work on *subliminal* priming also showed that people may sometimes not even be consciously aware of the stimulus, let alone its influence, but nevertheless show even complex behaviour as a function of the stimulus that is largely involuntary and automatic. This increased focus on automatic, unconscious processes will hold great promise for advertising research in the future and current developments will be highlighted in the coming chapters of this book. It is a mistake, however, to believe that scholars failed to appreciate the importance and impact of unconscious processes in advertising in more distant times. Indeed, one of the 'founding fathers' of advertising research, Herbert Krugman, pointed out the pivotal role of implicit and automatic processes in learning from advertising more than 40 years ago (Krugman, 1965). Back then, he was among the very few to reflect on these processes, but in the meantime, research on the irrational and unconscious in consumer behaviour has boomed. Indeed, scholars have argued that unconscious effects of advertising probably account for the bulk of consumer behaviour (see Bargh, 2002). For in particular, McGuire (1986) has reviewed econometric evidence that suggests that typical mass media communication effects are rather weak. However, as McGuire points out, these studies do not account for individual level psychological processes that qualify the impact of mass-media messages in important ways. Moreover, econometric studies tend to ignore delayed effects and implicit effects that psychological studies have revealed. When taking such unconscious processes into account, the impact of advertising (and other types of mass-media messages) is far more pronounced than previously thought, as the research findings in this book will show.

Given the largely low-involvement nature of most advertising, it is hardly surprising that implicit processes are the rule rather than the exception when it comes to understanding the psychology of advertising. Ironically, though, in contrast to (social) psychological research, which has made great progress in the last decade in theorizing about and assessing these more subtle, unconscious processes, advertising practice is still rather unconcerned with unconscious and automatic phenomena. For example, models and methods in the profession still stress the importance of brand awareness as a necessary starting point for all other imaginable advertising effects, whereas psychological research increasingly demonstrates that even the most complex forms of consumer behaviour can be brought about without the consumer being aware of the brand or any other advertising-related stimulus.

Plan of the book

The following chapters will discuss key issues in the effectiveness of advertising from a psychological perspective. As the reader will learn, much of the material is directly compatible with the more recent, contemporary approaches of viewing consumer responses to advertising as either the result of reflective, conscious processes, or of more associative, automatic processes. Moreover, in contrast to other books on advertising that depart from a focus on the advertising business, the present volume puts the consumer centre-stage and addresses the key psychological processes and mechanisms that are involved when people and ads 'meet'. In chapters 2, 3 and 4 the focus is on (but not limited to) the information function of advertising. Chapters 5, 6 and 7 highlight the persuasion function. We will see that both functions involve the interplay of cognitive, affective and behavioural consumer responses, and that both involve the complementary roles played by conscious, effortful and more automatic, implicit processes. Moreover, we will show that cognition and affect may sometimes act as precursors of consumer behaviour, and sometimes as a consequence.

Chapter 2 discusses the processes that play a role when consumers attend to advertising, and acquire and process information. Four stages of information processing are highlighted, ranging from pre-attentive analysis (a general, non-goal directed 'surveillance' of the environment), focal attention, comprehension and extended elaborative reasoning. We will discuss what elements of advertising are able to attract and hold consumer attention and which person and situational variables moderate consumer attention, categorization and thinking about products and brands. Hence, this chapter deals with what consumers come to know and think, when intentionally and incidentally exposed to advertising messages.

Chapter 3 continues by focusing on the vast and flexible reservoir consumers need to think: memory and how it is affected by advertising messages. More particularly, chapter 3 will address the issue of how consumers are able to remember advertising messages and the source and message variables that make up these messages over days or weeks and which factors determine whether or not the ad is recalled at the point of purchase. To that end, the chapter discusses the structure and function of human memory and the basic distinction between short and long-term memory. Memory serves an important function in consumer judgement and decision-making in response to advertising, and we will discuss this function at length in this chapter. We conclude the chapter by illuminating two topics that have received less attention but are very important for understanding advertising effectiveness: how consumers forget, instead of remember, ad-related information, and whether advertising can distort consumer memory.

In chapter 4, we shift attention from non-evaluative to evaluative consumer responses when discussing how consumers form attitudes towards products and brands. Attitudes are of central importance in the psychology of advertising, which we underscore by devoting an entire chapter to it. After defining the concept, we present the distinction between implicit and explicit attitudes, and focus on the properties of consumer attitudes. Next, the formation of attitudes and the role of advertising (versus direct experience) in the process is highlighted. The functions of advertising help us understand why some types of advertising are more influential than others in attitude formation.

Chapter 5 extends chapter 4 by discussing principles of persuasion and attitude change. It provides an overview of classic and contemporary approaches to the study of persuasion, starting with the Yale Reinforcement Approach which spearheaded academic research on the issue in the late 1940s. Next, McGuire's stage model of information processing is discussed, followed by the cognitive response approach mentioned previously in the present chapter. Dual process theories and extensions exemplify contemporary approaches to persuasion, which acknowledge that the impact of advertising differs as a function of the consumer's information processing motivation and ability. This chapter not only deals with research on factors that foster attitude change, but also the reverse: consumer resistance to advertising, as well as ways to overcome or lower resistance.

Chapters 4 and 5 contain many references to consumer behavioural intentions and actual purchasing behaviour, without systematically discussing the theoretical relationship between brand attitudes, purchasing intention and purchasing behaviour. This theoretical relationship is featured in chapter 6. We will report research suggesting that an attitude towards a given behaviour is a very important determinant of this behaviour. In addition, we will extend the reasoning underlying implicit and explicit attitudes introduced in chapter 4 by discussing work on the relationship between explicit and implicit attitudes and the extent to which each of these attitudes is predictive of different types of consumer behaviour. However, despite the relevance of attitudes to predicting behaviour, it is not the only determinant. Other factors such as social norms or the perceived or actual control over the behaviour are also influential factors. Finally, automatic and unconscious influences on consumer thoughts, feelings and actions are also highlighted, such as work on the (controversial) notion of subliminal advertising in which concepts such as brand names are activated in consumer memory without the consumer being consciously aware of this activation nor of the stimulus responsible for it.

Finally, in chapter 7 we move beyond persuasion by discussing principles of gaining consumer compliance without changing attitudes. In this chapter, research is reviewed on principles of social influence that are typically employed in-store and at point-of-purchase settings where consumers are seduced to comply with sales requests. The chapter will address the key mechanisms that are responsible for effective social influence, their manifestations in various commercial and non-profit contexts, and the conditions under which the impact of principles of social influence is enhanced or attenuated.

Summary and conclusions

- In this introductory chapter, the stage has been set for the chapters that are to come. The subject of the present book, advertising, is conceptualized as any form of paid communication by an identified sponsor aimed to inform and/or persuade target audiences about an organization, product, service or idea.
- A glance through history revealed that the origins of modern day advertising date back to classical civilizations such as Egypt, Mesopotamia, Greece and Rome. The Industrial Revolution accelerated advertising practice as a result of the massive increase in production scale and the large-scale diffusion of the

division of labour which increasingly necessitated informing consumers of the availability of goods and services. This development also led to the proliferation of brands to identify and label products and services. Print and audio-visual media such as magazines, newspapers, television, radio and the internet are the key carriers of advertising messages and these media appear to be complementary to each other rather than substitutes.

- Advertising serves a variety of societal and individual functions. Societal functions include facilitating competition among firms, funding mass media, serving as a key employer to thousands of professionals worldwide. Individual functions of advertising are twofold: to inform and persuade consumers.
- The next section briefly discussed the psychological approach to advertising's impact, which aims at identifying effects of advertising at the individual level. The objective is to relate specific advertising stimuli to specific and individual consumer responses. Consumer responses include thinking, feeling and doing responses or cognitive responses, affective responses, and conative or behavioural responses. Types of effects of advertising stimuli on these responses include main, mediated and interaction effects. Advertising stimuli include source variables such as credibility and attractiveness, content variables such as argument quality, message structure and sidedness, and types of appeal, such as argument-based or affect-based appeals.
- Advertising is one type of communication that makes up the promotional mix in (integrated) marketing communications. Other promotional elements include direct marketing, sales promotion, public relations and personal selling.
- There are two basic approaches to the conceptualization of the effects of advertising: the modelling approach and the behavioural approach. The modelling approach focuses on the aggregate level and aims to plot advertising inputs (e.g. expenditures) to outputs (e.g. sales). Sales-response models are an example of this approach. The behavioural approach focuses on individual responses to specific advertising stimuli. Classic work on the behavioural approach includes hierarchy-of-effects models. These models assume that consumer responses to advertising proceed through a fixed set of learning stages involving a cognitive, affective and behavioural stage. Additional models such as the FCB grid and Rossiter-Percy-Donovan grid subsequently stressed the role of consumer involvement. These developments are mirrored by research on persuasion, which saw an increased focus on information processing resulting in the cognitive response approach, and ultimately the dual process models and their extensions. Even more recently, these models have been supplemented by work examining unconscious and automatic processes involved in consumer behaviour.
- With the present foundation in place, the next chapter will address the issue of how consumers make sense of advertising. Because there are so many commercial messages around, consumers necessarily have to be selective. This chapter describes what principles guide this selective exposure and how consumers acquire, represent and encode information from advertising.

Chapter 2

How consumers acquire and process information from advertising

Preattentive analysis	43
Focal attention	51
Comprehension	63
Elaborative reasoning	66
Summary and conclusions	70

As we go about our daily business as consumers, we are constantly bombarded with commercial information. Early studies indicate that even before the advent of the internet, and the globalization of the marketplace, the typical American consumer was already exposed to over 300 advertisements a day (Britt, Adams & Miller, 1972), and this number does not include exposure to information provided by sales representatives, package labels, brand logos on products, point-of-purchase displays, and sales promotion material or corporate advertising. As mentioned in chapter 1, the estimate of present-day advertising exposure is in the order of around 1,000 ads per day that compete for attention. With the obvious limits of working memory in mind (Miller, 1956), it is evident that consumers cannot attend to all these messages, so how do they do it?

How do consumers make sense of this abundance of information? How do they select information, attend to it, and process information from advertising? This is the focus of the present chapter. The research in this chapter draws heavily on work in social cognition as conducted in the field of consumer psychology, a field that concerns itself with the psychological antecedents, processes and consequences involved in the acquisition, use and disposal of products and services by consumers (e.g. Haugtvedt, Herr & Kardes, 2008). Social cognition focuses on the way cognitive and affective processes are affected by, and in turn influence, social behaviour (e.g. Bless, Fiedler & Strack, 2004; Moskowitz, 2005).

This chapter is organized around the four stages in the process by which consumers acquire, represent and encode advertising information (see Bargh, 1984; Greenwald & Leavitt, 1984). These stages include 1) **Preattentive analysis**, which involves a general, non-goal directed, 'surveillance' of the environment; 2) Focal attention: after noticing a stimulus, it may be brought into conscious awareness where it is identified and categorized; 3) **Comprehension**, or the process of forming inferences pertaining to the semantic meaning of the stimulus; and 4) **Elaborative reasoning,** or the process by which the semantically represented stimulus is related to previously stored consumer knowledge that allows for simple or more complex inferences.

In terms of the dual process logic that permeates all chapters of this volume, we will see that automatic, non-conscious processes are more influential during preattentive analysis and during focal attention, whereas reflective, conscious processes play an important role during comprehension and elaboration. An important variable that influences how consumers proceed through these stages is **involvement,** or the perceived relevance of an object or issue. Greenwald and Leavitt (1984) have pointed out that involvement determines the allocation of resources needed for nonfocal and focal attention. The type of involvement relevant in this context is **outcome-relevant involvement**, or the extent to which the acquisition and use of a product or brand is deemed to have significant personal consequences for the consumer (cf. Johnson & Eagly, 1989). In the context of consumer decisions, outcome-relevant involvement is determined by such factors as the price of goods but also by consumer goals. Involvement is lower when buying everyday inexpensive consumer goods such as washing powder or toothpaste than when purchasing a washing machine or a new car. However, even though washing machines or cars are expensive, information about them is irrelevant to consumers, unless they are in the market for a new washing machine or a new car (or chronically interested in these goods). Other needs also influence the degree of outcome-relevant involvement. Thus, people pay more attention to information about food, when they are hungry or about beverages when they are thirsty.

When involvement is low, information is processed with very little effort and often outside conscious control. When involvement is moderately low, nonfocal attention turns into focal attention, which is directed at goal-relevant, salient and vivid stimuli (see below for a discussion of factors contributing to stimulus salience and vividness). Moreover, this level of involvement is required when consumers actively relate incoming new information to information already stored in memory to facilitate comprehension. When involvement is relatively high, consumers engage in elaboration, systematic processing, and complex inferential reasoning going beyond the information given to arrive at new beliefs, evaluations and conclusions. (see also chapter 5; Chaiken, 1980; Petty & Cacioppo, 1986).

Preattentive analysis

Very often, consumers learn about products *incidentally*, when they are accidentally and involuntarily exposed to advertising. They read a newspaper and there are ads between the articles of interest, they click on an internet site and there are ads that pop-up at the fringes of the site, and they watch TV and there are commercials interrupting a programme. Consumers may hardly glance at these advertisements, because what they are really interested in is the newspaper article, the information on the internet, or the television programme and not the advertisements. But this does not mean that ad messages fail to have an impact. Information acquisition frequently involves only very little higher-order cognitive activity and is often automatic and nonconscious. This type of preattentive processing is most likely to result in storage of information in **implicit memory**, a nonconscious form of memory distinguished from **explicit memory**. As we will discuss in chapter 3, explicit memory is characterized by a person's conscious recollection of facts or events (Schacter et al., 1993) and by intentional attempts to access that information. In advertising studies, explicit memory is typically assessed through recall or recognition tests (chapter 3). Implicit memory effects occur when previous exposure to a stimulus (e.g. an advertisement) influences our performance on subsequent judgement or choice tasks without the consumer remembering the previous experience or being aware of its influence on performance. In line with chapter 1, this means that implicit memory effects involves information processing that is fast, parallel and effortless (see Chaiken & Trope, 1999). Moreover, as Posner and Snyder (1975) have argued, it also implies that information processing occurs without conscious intention, without necessarily leading to conscious attention, and without interfering with other simultaneously operating mental activities (see also Bargh, 1994; Robinson, 1998; Schneider & Shiffrin, 1977).

Feature analysis and semantic analysis

It has long been assumed that preattentive processing operates 'at the fringe of consciousness' (Reber & Schwarz, 2001) and relies mainly on feature analysis, an efficient and quick analysis of the environment for basic familiarity and significance

(Greenwald & Leavitt, 1984). Feature analysis implies that the memory trace produced through exposure to an advertisement only contains information on the perceptual features such as contours, brightness and contrast of the ad rather than its meaning (Shapiro, 1999). The drawback of feature analysis from the perspective of advertisers is that feature-based memory will only have future consequences (for instance at the point-of-purchase), if the features of the stimulus that are available during judgement or choice are perceptually identical to those that were processed during stimulus exposure. Thus, product choice would only be affected by an ad, if the product on the shelf was perceptually identical to the product as depicted in an ad. Product choice would not be affected by a preattentively processed advertisement, if the product was in a different package from that depicted in the ad or if one was to choose a product from a list of brand names, whereas the advertisement had represented the product pictorially (Shapiro, 1999; chapter 3, this volume).

In the meantime, there is increasing evidence that preattentive processing can include conceptual processing as well, resulting in a *semantic* analysis of the advertised product, capturing the meaning of the product: what the product is, and what it does (e.g. Labroo & Lee, 2006; Shapiro, 1999). Hence, preattentive processing not only includes the basic and physical features of the product, but also more abstract-level attributes: conceptual features such as those pertaining to the nature of the product, the usage situation and the results of use. The advantage of semantic analysis is that an advertisement can influence future choice, even if the consumer is presented at the point of choice with a representation of the product that is perceptually different from how the brand was represented in the ad, for example when the product is sold in a packaged form, but advertised in an unpackaged form, or advertised how it performs during consumption. The only requirement is that both representations activate the same conceptual representation of the product in the consumer's mind. That is, both representations need to activate the same conceptual associations of the brand (i.e. the brand image).

To assess whether incidental ad exposure can induce conceptual processing of an advertisement, Shapiro (1999) instructed participants to read articles that appeared in the right-hand column of a mock magazine, with target ads appearing in the left-hand column. These ads presented pictures of various goods students might want to buy (e.g., computer, briefcase, mobile telephone). The objects were depicted either in isolation, or in a normal usage context. For example, there was a picture either of a briefcase (isolated object) or of a person carrying a briefcase (object in context). The telephone either was presented as isolated object or with a hand holding the telephone (see Figure 2.1).

There were two dependent measures. One involved a catalogue that depicted each advertised object in isolation. The pictures in the catalogue were identical to those presented in the isolated object condition, but differed from those presented in the object in context condition. In addition, the catalogue also contained products that had not been advertised. A second dependent measure involved a catalogue that listed verbal labels referring to the same products as in the picture catalogue. Subjects were given two tasks: First, they had to indicate all the products in the catalogue, which might have been displayed in the advertisements. Second, they could choose from the catalogue eight items they might consider buying once they graduated, but avoid all objects that might have been depicted in the advertisements. Based on the Process

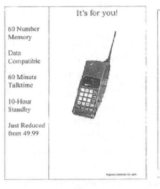

Figure 2.1 Stimulus materials used in Shapiro (1999)

Source: Shapiro (1999). When an ad's influence is beyond our conscious control: Perceptual and conceptual fluency effects caused by incidental ad exposure. *Journal of Consumer Research, 26,* 16–36. Reproduced with permission of University of Chicago Press

Dissociation Procedure of Jacoby (1991),[1] these two measures made it possible to get an unbiased measure of unconscious ad influence processes.

There is evidence that embedding a product in a familiar scene of typical use of that product should facilitate activation of the product concept in memory during exposure (Shapiro, 1999). In contrast, since the *features* of the object are different in the choice situation from the ad presentation, participants should be less likely to remember advertised products in the condition where the ads contained context information, if their memory trace had been based on feature analysis. With feature analysis, participants should perform best under conditions where the products were presented in exactly the same way in the catalogue as they had been presented in the ads.

Supporting the assumption that the ad information was processed semantically, more products were remembered when the products had been depicted in context rather than in isolation and this effect emerged with the picture catalogue as well as the list of verbal labels. Furthermore, based on the Process Dissociation Procedure, Shapiro (1999) concluded that the influence of the advertisements on judgements had operated outside conscious awareness (i.e. preattentive).

Matching activation

A series of studies by Janiszewski (1988, 1990, 1993) sheds additional light on the mechanisms underlying preattentive processing of information and shows that implicit memory effects can be a side effect of conscious attention. Following Friedman and Polson (1981), Janiszewski used the hypothesis of matching activation to account for the impact of incidental exposure to advertising on consumer preattentive responses. Because this hypothesis is based on assumptions from hemispheric lateralization, we have to introduce this concept first before we explain matching activation. **Hemispheric lateralization** implies that our brain hemispheres have evolved specialized processing units for specific types of information. Picture processing involves relatively higher activation levels of the right hemisphere since that hemisphere is tailored towards more holistic, impressionistic processing. In contrast, textual processing involves relatively high levels of activation of the left hemisphere, which specializes in bottom-up, data-driven, feature analysis. The location in the visual field, where information is placed, determines the hemisphere where it is processed (with placement on the right resulting in processing in the left hemisphere and placement on the left activating the right hemisphere). A pictorial advertisement that is not in the foveal field but placed in the *left visual* field encourages use of the holistic processing resources associated with the *right hemisphere*, and consequently, has been shown to be liked better than when placed in the *right visual* field (Janiszewski, 1988). In contrast, because the left hemisphere is geared toward processing text rather than pictures, a textual advertising message benefits from being placed in the right visual field.

The **matching activation hypothesis** assumes that when one hemisphere is activated by the information that accommodates the processing style of that particular hemisphere, the other hemisphere is encouraged to elaborate on secondary material. Thus, greater activation of one hemisphere (e.g. the left hemisphere) will be matched by an increase of processing resources in the opposing hemisphere. What this amounts to is that when resources are mobilized in one hemisphere to process the *focal* information, resources in the other hemisphere are also mobilized and thus ready to process *nonfocal* information. Thus, when brand names or advertising messages are *not* consciously attended to, but happen to be placed in such a position that they can be easily processed by the mobilized but unused hemisphere, such incidental exposure may result in increased unconscious processing (Janiszewski, 1990, 1993). This unconscious processing is thus a by-product or side effect of the processing of focal information and can influence consumer attitudes.

This hypothesis has been tested in an ingenious study by Janiszewski (1990), who exposed participants to an ad for Guerlain's Shalimar perfume. The ad featured the picture of a lady and a slogan ('I am Shalimar') and the brand name (see Figure 2.2). In the four different experimental conditions, the brand name was placed to the left or right of either the picture of the lady (top panel) or to the left or the right of the slogan (bottom panel). One can assume that people who look at the advertisement first look at the picture and then the slogan. The brand name, which is at the periphery of the visual field, is most likely to be processed when it placed so as to be easily processed by the *unused* (but mobilized) hemisphere. When consumers focus on the picture, their right hemisphere will be used and, due to matching activation, this will increase the readiness of the left hemisphere to process *peripheral* information

Figure 2.2 Stimuli used in Janiszewski's (1990) study on matching activation

Source: Janiszewski (1990). The influence of print advertisement organization on affect toward a brand name. *Journal of Consumer Research, 17*, 53–65, Study 1. Reproduced with permission of University of Chicago Press and Guerlain

placed to the right of the picture. Therefore, the brand name is more likely to be (unconsciously) processed when placed to the right rather than the left of the picture. In contrast, reading the slogan will activate the left hemisphere. Since simple words can be processed with equal efficiency by either hemisphere, the brand name has the greatest chance to be processed when placed on the left of the slogan (so as to reach the unused but ready right hemisphere). As we can see from Figure 2.3, the pattern of participants' evaluative responses to the brand name fully supported these hypotheses.

In other words, if Guerlain wants to place the brand name next to the face, they have to put it on the right side, if they want to place it next to the slogan, they have to place it on the left side. Since people, who only glance at the ad, are more likely to look at the face than the slogan, the top right position is probably the best one.

This research indicated that preattentive analysis can manifest itself by the type and extent of consumer information processing as a function of ad placement. But according to Robinson (1998) this is not the only form preattentive mechanisms can take. Robinson (1998) argues that preattentive analysis can also result in instant and nonconscious generation of emotions, particularly negative ones such as fear and anxiety. Robinson argues that in addition to these immediate judgments of valence, urgency assessments can also be made preattentively and act as a precursor to the emotion. When an urgency signal is induced unconsciously, fear and anxiety are the result, presumably prompting the organism to take immediate action to reduce the threat. Hence, this preattentive system serves an important role in situations where immediate action is important for survival.

Although we would not like to claim that advertising and responding to advertising are crucial for survival, the same mechanisms may still play a role in the consumer sphere for instance in consumer responses to fear appeals. Therefore, in a cluttered environment where competing for consumer attention is difficult, using negatively valenced emotions in advertising appeals may pay off when the goal is at least to evoke some sort of consumer response. Of course, once an unconscious sense of urgency is aroused, the advertiser must know what to do with it. Offering a simple

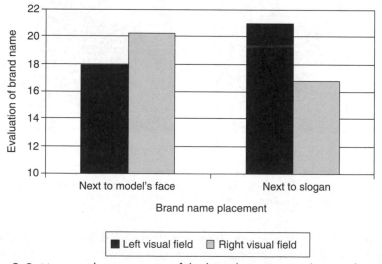

Figure 2.3 Mean evaluative ratings of the brand name according to placement of brand name

and effective remedy to remove the threat, for instance by buying the product, or following up on the advocacy in the message, is then important for advertising effectiveness (De Hoog, Stroebe & De Wit, 2005, 2007, 2008).

An apt illustration of this principle at work is the outdoor ad for Advil pain relievers featured in the previous chapter. The picture of the man graphically suffering from a headache stirs a sense of urgency which is immediately channeled to the Advil brand name and the slogan 'more powerful than pain'. Although fear and anxiety can be aroused unconsciously, Robinson (1998) also points out that the individual's response need not stay unconscious. Valenced information is capable of capturing conscious attention after unconscious preattentive processing, similar to when one hears one's own name mentioned at a cocktail party: the chatter has been processed unconsciously, but hearing one's name leads to focused attention (see Moray, 1959).

The practical implications of findings on preattentive analysis are intriguing. Robinson's (1998) research indicates the importance of content variables in advertising that can act as an unconscious signal of potential relevance to the consumer. In addition, the work on matching activation sheds light on the importance of ad and brand placement in advertising effectiveness. Given the limitations of conscious, focal attention (Miller, 1956), advertisers must rely on other means to get their message across, and the effects obtained as a result of the notion of matching activation may constitute one route to move forward. A clever advertiser may thus profit from the activation triggered by a competitor to enhance evaluations of his own brand. That is, when the competitor's ad is known (which is actually the case, since media planning agencies that buy media time and space also schedule the ads), it makes good sense to place one's own brand name prominently on an even (i.e. left) page of a newspaper or magazine if the ad on the opposite page contains predominantly textual information, and to place a brand name on an uneven (i.e. right) page of that newspaper if the ad on the opposing page features pictorial information (see Janiszewski, 1993). This way, the brand name would benefit from the increased activation of the hemisphere that is not occupied by processing the focal ad. Similarly, for advertisers on the sites of internet versions of newspapers, it would make sense to place the brand name on the left side of the news text to reach the right hemisphere that is not used by the reader.

Preattentive processing and hedonic fluency

To account for the positive effects on brand evaluations by incidental, preattentive processing, **hedonic fluency** is thought to play a mediating role. Hedonic fluency is the subjective ease with which a stimulus can be perceived and processed. This ease is experienced as a mildly positive emotion, which is sometimes used as information to evaluate a stimulus (see Mantonakis, Whittlesea & Yoon, 2008). This fluency can be based on perceptual or conceptual fluency (e.g. Lee & Labroo, 2004; Shapiro, 1999). Perceptual fluency reflects the ease with which the physical features such as modality (e.g. visual versus auditory), shape or brightness can be processed. Conceptual fluency reflects the ease with which the semantic meaning of an object comes to the consumer's minds and thus reflects the processing of meaning.

An important factor contributing to the ease of processing is familiarity: stimuli that have been encountered before have been encoded and represented in memory and are processed more easily once they are encountered again, and this holds also for incidental exposures and nonconscious preattention (see also chapter 4). Therefore, when an ad is encountered incidentally, a subsequent conscious exposure to the ad produces hedonic fluency as a function of the previous exposure. This fluency results in a (mild) positive affect which is subsequently misattributed to the focal ad and brand, producing more favourable consumer responses. In consumer psychology, research on various kinds of fluency (e.g. processing fluency, goal fluency, response fluency) has recently received a great deal of attention (e.g. Lee & Labroo, 2004; Labroo & Lee, 2006) and reflects a surge in interest in unconscious phenomena in the consumer sphere (see Simonson et al., 2001, for an overview).

The hedonic fluency model has also been employed to understand various kinds of memory-induced judgement processes. Focal and nonfocal consumer attention can be directed outward toward ads and brands presented in the consumer's environment, or inward toward product-related information already stored in memory (Kardes, 1994) and hedonic fluency may play a role in both types of processes. In cases of nonfocal attention brought about by hemispheric matching activation that involves processing fluency, attention is clearly directed outward, albeit not consciously.

Another example of the role of hedonic fluency in outward directed attention is work on goal fluency. In a recent series of studies, Labroo and Lee (2006) showed that exposure to sequences of seemingly unrelated ads may affect consumer judgement as a function of the compatibility of the goals that the ads activate. In this research, consumers were exposed to a series of two ads (a prime and a target ad) with either compatible or conflicting consumer goals. If the goal of the target ad and the prime ad were compatible, the target ad produced more favourable product evaluations and higher behavioural intentions toward the advertised products than when the goals mismatched. Labroo and Lee (2006) argued that this effect occurs because the goal activated by the priming ad increases the ease of processing of the target ad, if that ad serves the same self-regulatory goal as the priming ad. In line with the previous findings, this goal fluency results in positive affect that is misattributed to the focal ad and brand resulting in more favourable evaluations and intentions.

When attention is directed inward, rather than outward, fluency effects can also occur. For example, research has shown that simply measuring behavioural intentions increases the likelihood of people actually performing that behaviour, a phenomenon known as the question-behaviour effect (see Fitzsimons & Moore, 2008). Thus, Greenwald, Carnot, Beach and Young (1987) showed that simply asking people whether they intended to vote actually increased voting rates among this group compared to a control group not asked about their behaviour. Similarly, Williams, Block and Fitzsimons (2006), and Fitzsimons, Nunes and Williams (2007) demonstrated that asking adolescents about risky and negative behaviours (such as drug use, drinking behaviour or skipping classes) increased the chances of them engaging in these very behaviours. One explanation for this effect is that asking about some behaviour renders the attitude toward that behaviour (as well as knowledge relevant to that behaviour) more accessible. As a consequence, when that attitude is favourable, the behaviour becomes more likely (see Fitzsimons & Moore, 2008).

Another explanation is put forward by Janiszewski and Chandon (2007), who argue that these findings may be the result of response fluency: asking questions about behaviour increases the hedonic fluency of the response to the questions, making perceptions at the time when the behaviour might be performed more easily, positively affecting the likelihood of that behaviour.

Williams, Fitzsimons and Block (2004) have suggested a clever application of this phenomenon in the market place: conducting market research among consumers should actually increase purchase rates of the products asked about in the survey (unless the initial attitude of consumers towards the product is negative). However, when consumers learn that asking questions may serve a persuasion goal rather than an information goal, the effect should vanish (Williams et al., 2004).

Focal attention

In the processes we have discussed so far conscious awareness played no critical role in consumer judgment and decision-making. However, although conscious information processing is probably of little importance for many consumer decisions and actions (e.g. involving inexpensive goods), advertisers are sometimes successful in bringing their message to conscious awareness of consumers. As a result, marketing stimuli may be identified and categorized. This process invariantly involves some sort of focal attention, and is facilitated when consumer involvement turns from low to moderate. But what factors determine whether information enters **short-term (working) memory** and becomes the focus of conscious attention? Since short-term memory is of very limited capacity (chapter 3), we are highly selective in the kinds of stimuli that we pay attention to. We tend to select a very limited set of stimuli to which we pay focal attention and we tend to neglect stimuli that are nonfocal. Hence, stimuli need special features that make them 'stand out' from the background and capture (and possibly hold) conscious consumer attention. These features can be part and parcel of the stimulus itself or they can reside in the consumer. Examples of the latter include consumer motivation, intentions, preferences and attitudes. When we are in the market for a new automobile, we will notice ads for new models of cars. When we are hungry we will pay attention to cues in the environment that signal food (such as ads for foods, or the 'golden arches' of fast food restaurant McDonald's in the mall). These examples involve voluntary attention to some extent, but as Klinger (1975) and others (e.g. Kahneman, 1973) have suggested, focal attention can also be the product of involuntary processes.

Three classes of stimulus featured have been shown to attract involuntary consumer attention: salience, vividness and novelty (Kardes, 1994; 2002). Advertisers can employ the attention-getting properties of salient, vivid and novel stimuli to increase the chances that consumers will consciously notice their ads.

Salience

Stimulus **salience** refers to the extent to which a stimulus is noticeably different from its environment. Salience is context dependent, and varies over situations. A Harley Davidson motorcycle is salient on a parking lot full of cars, but not amidst other Harley Davidson motorcycles. Salient stimuli draw attention because they are different vis-à-vis their context and therefore possibly interesting. Creating salient ads has become an important objective for advertisers given the increasing **advertising clutter** on TV, print and in other mass media. Because ads are typically grouped together on television in commercial pods, the individual ad must contain at least some stimulus elements that make it stand out in order to be consciously noticed.

Humour is an example of a strategy that advertisers can use to make their ads salient, but only to the extent that neighbouring ads do not use it as well. However, for many product categories 'bandwagon effects' occur in which advertisers copy elements from their competitors if they feel they are effective in attracting consumer attention, thus reducing the likelihood of these ads remaining effective. A short history of insurance ads in the Netherlands nicely illustrates this point. These ads have traditionally used a serious tone of voice, describing the risk of certain mishaps and emphasizing the effectiveness of the insurance product to avert or compensate for the risk. One company, Centraal Beheer, then pioneered a different approach and changed to humour to playfully illustrate the relevance of insurance in risk situations, using a slogan 'even Apeldoorn bellen' ('simply call Apeldoorn': the home town of the company, see Figure 2.4).

The humour proved salient amidst competitors and the company became very successful with it. Consumers started talking about the ads, thus creating what marketers term 'rumour around the brand' although initially brand awareness (i.e. identifying the correct company as the source of the ads) did not profit from the increased attention. It was not long, however, before the majority of competitors in the insurance business followed suit and consequently typical insurance ads turned from serious

Figure 2.4 Still from a commercial for Centraal Beheer insurance using a humour appeal. Reproduced with permission of Centraal Beheer, Achmea

to frivolous. Indeed, humorous advertising messages flooded the market, and ultimately 'killed' the salience effect. As this example suggests, salience is created by contrast, in the present case contrast between the style of a focal advertising message and the majority of messages that make up its environment.

Another technique to enhance advertising salience is to change the camera angle used to focus on the target product. Meyers-Levy and Peracchio (1992) have shown that changing the camera angle from eye level to an upward angle in a print ad increases focal attention and affects the extent to which consumers remember the advertising message. Presumably, the upward angle makes the brand 'bigger than life' and increases the **figure-ground principle**. This principle holds that figural stimuli become focal whereas non-figural stimuli become nonfocal. Hence, the principle captures the process by which stimuli can grab attention and everything else fades into the background. By using an upward the angle the figural properties of the advertised brand increase while simultaneously background stimuli fade into the background (see Kardes, 1994; 2002; Meyers-Levy & Peracchio, 1992). Such salience effects on judgement and decision are likely to be moderated by the extent to which individuals are motivated to process information: they should be at a maximum when processing motivation is low and decrease with increasing processing motivation. Salience effects should exert little influence on judgements and decision-making, when individuals are highly motivated to study an advertisement. In line with this prediction, Meyers-Levy and Peracchio (1992) found the effect of camera angle on product evaluations primarily for low **need for cognition** individuals who have a lower intrinsic motivation to engage in extensive information processing than people high in the need for cognition (chapter 5).

Vividness

Whereas salience emerges as a function of stimulus properties in the context of its background, **vividness** is not assumed to be fully context dependent. Nisbett and Ross (1980) view vivid stimuli as '(a) emotionally interesting, (b) concrete and image-provoking and (c) proximate in a sensory temporal or spatial way' (p. 45). This description suggests that vividness in advertising can be a function of characteristics of the perceiver (i.e. what is emotionally interesting to one consumer may not be interesting to another consumer), or of the advertising stimulus itself (as in the concreteness of product information or the proximity of elements of the ad). Hence, whereas proximity may be an attribute of the stimulus and thus a situational variable, interest and ability for mental imagery are person variables.

Asking creative directors of advertising agencies whether vivid ads are more effective than their pallid counterparts almost invariably produces affirmative answers, but interestingly, despite its intuitive appeal, research on the impact of vividness on persuasion has failed to yield unequivocal results (Taylor & Thompson, 1982). Although some authors reported a positive impact of vividness (e.g. Bone & Ellen, 1992; Fortin & Dholakia, 2005), others have shown that vividness can result in adverse effects (e.g. Frey & Eagly, 1993) and the majority of studies found that that vividness, despite its potential to attract consumer attention, has no traceable impact on persuasion (Taylor & Thompson, 1982).

To account for this prevalence of null findings, a recent series of studies sought to examine the role of individual differences in the effectiveness of vividness in advertising (Fennis, Das & Fransen, 2009). In line with Nisbett and Ross (1980) vividness in these studies was varied by using concrete versus abstract language and the proportion of text versus pictures (with vivid ads showing larger product pictures than pallid ads and using concrete and image provoking language rather than simply stating product attributes). A key hypothesis underlying this research was that concrete and image-provoking information in ads may be perceived and processed differently, depending on the extent to which the perceiver has a high or low intrinsic tendency to engage in visual imagery (measured with Vividness of Visual Imagery Questionnaire, Marks, 1973). High visualizers would be more sensitive than low visualizers to vivid executional elements in advertising and consequently vividness may only prove to be an effective executional element for high as opposed to low visualizers.

In support of this hypothesis, three studies showed that people who scored high on the Vividness of Visual Imagery Questionnaire (Marks, 1973) had more favourable product attitudes after exposure to vivid as opposed to pallid ads (Fennis et al., 2009). This questionnaire asks respondents to rate the vividness of the images formed in thinking about particular scenes and situations. For individuals low in the Vividness of Visual Imagery, vividness in advertising had no impact on brand attitudes. Moreover, this effect was consistently observed for ads for both functional as well as more 'transformational' products (i.e. for products where the experience of product use is more important than the attributes per se, such as champagne, the product featured in one of their studies) and across different experimental manipulations of the vividness construct. In short, the combined results present a compelling case of considering this personality trait and Marks' (1973) instrument of capturing it as a powerful tool in understanding the effectiveness of vividness as an executional style in advertising.

Another way to manipulate vividness is to vary the medium or channel through which information is transferred. This was the approach chosen by Herr, Kardes and Kim (1991). These researchers provided consumers with attribute and anecdotal information about a new personal computer. They kept constant the content of the information, but varied the way it was delivered. In the vivid condition, the attribute and anecdotal information was brought to participants by a trained confederate in a face-to-face setting, whereas a printed format containing the same information was used in the pallid condition. This research showed that in line with McLuhan's classic adage 'the medium is the message' in vivid conditions, anecdotal information proved more effective than attribute information, whereas in pallid conditions a reversed pattern was observed. Hence, when one has to list several points of information, it makes good sense to select a medium that accommodates that requirement, i.e. print. However, when the information is anecdotal and described as a scenario, a more vivid medium is more effective, i.e. a face-to-face, word-of-mouth format.

Apart from individual differences in the tendency to engage in visual imagery, consumer goals also differentiate vividness from salience effects, as implicated by the 'emotional interest' part of the Nisbett and Ross (1980) definition. Using an eye-tracking procedure, Pieters and Wedel (2007) recently showed that the goal of ad memorization resulted in more attention to the body text, pictorial elements and the advertised brand, whereas a brand-learning goal also produced increased attention to the body text, but simultaneously inhibited attention to other, potentially distracting elements in the ad. This research suggests that what is vivid in an ad not only depends on the personality of the perceiver, but also on his/her goals at the time of processing.

Novelty

A third way in which advertising elements may draw (involuntary) attention is through **novelty**. A key factor driving a consumer perception of 'newness' is the extent to which information about the products in advertising is unfamiliar and disconfirms existing consumer expectancies. Product information that disconfirms existing expectations produces a surprise response (see Àlden, Mukherjee & Hoyer, 2000; Teigen & Keren, 2003). An essential feature of surprise is that it mobilizes cognitive resources that are used to resolve the inconsistency between what was expected and what is actually encountered, a process that is frequently at work when humour is employed in an ad (Alden, Mukherjee & Hoyer, 2000). Hence, unexpected information has been shown to result in extended causal reasoning (Hastie, 1984; Weiner, 1985), **counterfactual thinking** (Kahneman & Miller, 1986; Meyers-Levy & Maheswaran, 1992), and cognitive elaboration (Petty, Fleming, Priester & Feinsein, 2001; see also Heckler & Childers, 1992).

At first glance one might think that disconfirming consumer expectancies is always a good thing and indeed after 'free', the word 'new' is believed to be one of the most frequently employed words in product advertising (see Stewart & Furse, 1986), but there are instances where surprise indeed fosters salience, but not in a way the advertiser would like. An important outcome of expectancy violation in the consumer domain is related to product satisfaction. According to Oliver's (1980, 1993; Oliver & DeSarbo, 1988) **expectancy disconfirmation model** consumers form expectancies about product performance before buying a product. These expectancies are in large part shaped by product advertising. After they buy the product, consumers then compare the actual performance with the expected level of performance. If performance exceeds expectation, consumers are surprised and satisfied with the product. However, because of the tendency of advertising to use puffery and exaggerate product performance (Kamins & Marks, 1987) expectations about product performance are often higher than the 'real deal' and consequently expectancy violation brought about by actual product experiences does occur in the market place but unfortunately frequently results in decreased rather than increased consumer satisfaction. This leaves advertisers with an interesting conflict: If they promise too little, they run the risk that consumers will not buy their product, if they promise too much, they run the risk that consumers will be disappointed.

Of course, advertisers can frequently change their advertising execution without necessarily adapting or innovating the target product. What is more, changes in advertising execution need not pertain directly to product attributes but can also include more 'cosmetic' changes. Research on varying ad strategies to increase or maintain novelty is known as the 'repetition-variation hypothesis', which will be discussed in chapter 5 (Schumann, Petty & Clemons, 1991; Haugtvedt, Schumann, Schneier & Warren, 1994).

Categorization

As stated in the introduction of this chapter, an integral part of the focal attention phase in the information processing sequence is categorizing information once it has been brought into conscious awareness and identified. **Categorization** is the process by which incoming information is classified, that is, labelled as belonging to one or more categories based on a comparative assessment of features of the category and the incoming information (see Loken, Barsalou & Joiner, 2008). For example, a Mercedes-Benz may be categorized as a car, as a status symbol, as a German product, as a symbol of capitalism, and so on. Each of these classifications represents an act of categorization. In the advertising and consumer domain, categorization processes are germane to research on product and brand line extensions as a comprehensive review of recent research indicates (Loken, 2006).

Product and brand line extensions. Frequently, advertising is used to communicate new products that are introduced under the umbrella of a parent brand. For example Coca-Cola has introduced Cherry Coke, Porsche has introduced a designer cellphone, Dove has introduced a new shower cream and so on.

The success and survival of these brand extensions depends largely on whether consumers categorize the new product as congruent with the parent brand, or congruent with the key associations the parent brand evokes (at least when associations about the parent brand are positive). Stated more formally, brands may represent categories and consumers frequently use information about the category to make inferences about new category members. Categorizations can be based on comparisons on any salient and meaningful dimension, such as comparisons between product attributes, (i.e. products with different brands that share certain attributes, such as the product category of automobiles), brands (products with different attributes that share the same brand, such as the examples above), or product usage (products with different brands and different attributes that are used in the similar situations, such as breakfast foods). When a new model of an established car brand is introduced, consumers use what they know about the brand to judge the new model (e.g. in terms of its luxury, performance, warranty, etc.) and so categorization often becomes more fine-grained and more elaborate when consumer prior knowledge and involvement increases (see Peracchio & Tybout, 1996).

Categorization processes become easier when the new product shares similarities with existing products that use the same brand name. This is a further example of the effects of perceptual or conceptual fluency in the categorization process. Indeed, many studies suggest that increased similarity-based 'fit' between the parent brand and the extension fosters acceptance of the extension (e.g. Barone, Miniard & Romeo, 2000; Bottomley & Holden, 2001; Klink & Smith, 2001; Loken, 2006). This similarity may prove to be a powerful aid in consumer decision-making, acting as a rule of thumb, or heuristic (see also chapter 5 for an extended discussion on heuristic decision-making), especially when other types of individuating product information (i.e. information on product attributes) are unavailable, or when consumers lack the motivation or ability to critically evaluate such information (Klink & Smith, 2001).

The heuristic value of category membership based on similarity is in line with what Tversky and Kahneman (1974) have termed the **representativeness heuristic,** or the extent to which two stimuli are deemed to belong to the same overall category based on shared similarities. According to Kardes (2002), the representativeness heuristic might be used to predict whether consumers categorize a new product as a true innovation (and hence place it in a category of innovative products) or perceive it as similar to existing products (and place it in a category of established products), in which case it runs the risk of being seen as a copycat or a fad, at best.

Similarity, though, does not guarantee success of brand extensions. A contrasting view purports that moderate dissimilarity of category members rather than extreme similarity or dissimilarity, may actually benefit a brand extension because people sometimes take pleasure in solving moderate incongruities, at least when they have the motivation to do so (Campbell & Goodstein, 2001; Peracchio & Meyers-Levy, 1994). The associated pleasure may be transferred to the focal brand which is consequently evaluated more favourably. Hence a moderately dissimilar extension will be better liked than either an extreme dissimilar or extreme similar brand extension. An example of a moderately dissimilar product is Pringles Potato Chips by Procter and Gamble. Pringles looked new and different, were produced differently from traditional potato chips, and came in an alternative, cylindrical package, rather than a bag. Nevertheless, the shape, feel and taste remained largely similar to the parent product category of potato chips: salty, greasy and 'potato-like'. Hence, the product may have been viewed as moderately dissimilar and, after its introduction, proved successful in gaining its share of the market (but see Kardes, 2002, for an alternative perspective).

Typicality and the pioneering advantage

Apart from research on the processing and evaluation of brand extensions, categorization effects have been found on individual products as well. A well-established finding, for instance, is that the extent to which a specific product is 'prototypical' for a product category, (i.e. the similarity to other category members) influences liking for the product (cf. Loken, 2006). Frequently, more prototypical products are better liked than less prototypical products (Carpenter & Nakamoto, 1996; Folkes & Patrick, 2003; Simonin & Ruth, 1998; Veryzer & Hutchinson, 1998; Zhang & Sood, 2002). For example, a bottle of French Bordeaux may be a more prototypical exemplar of the product category of wine than a bottle of Japanese sake (a wine made from rice), and consequently and *ceteris paribus* may be better liked. However, prototypicality may come at a cost: as we have seen earlier, presenting the product as a prototypical exemplar of a category may not serve the brand in terms of advertising *salience*, where communicating *contrast* between the focal brand and competitors is pivotal. A prototypical product may not easily stand out in comparison to its competitors and thus, the attention-getting potential of ads for prototypical brands may suffer.

On the other hand, there are additional benefits of being considered a prototype. A number of studies have shown that is pays to pioneer a novel product category and thus become (by definition) the most prototypical representative of that category (Carpenter & Nakamoto, 1989; Kardes & Gurumurthy, 1992; Kardes, Gurumurthy, Chandrashekaran & Dornoff, 1993). Research on this **pioneering advantage** has suggested that being first results in a series of strategic advantages in comparison to following brands.

First, there appears to be an inherent advantage: being the first in a product category, means the brand is novel and interesting. Consumers tend to process such information more elaborately, learn more attributes and as a result form more extreme judgements: hence the pioneering brand is liked better (Kardes & Gurumurthy, 1992). Additionally, the pioneering brand is able to 'set the attribute agenda' and thus create a strategic advantage. That is, as the brand defining the category, the pioneer can determine the type of attributes on which category members will be evaluated, which are often categories on which the pioneer scores highest (cf. Carpenter & Nakamoto, 1989). The iPhone is a case in point of a new product category: that of designer cellphones. With the innovativeness and designer image of Apple Macintosh, the iPhone was not only the first, but on the key differentiating attribute (i.e. design) also the best brand, and is still considered the uncontested winner in this category.

Pioneers can make use of a direction-of-comparison effect (Carpenter & Nakamoto, 1989). That is, not only is it the pioneer that gets to decide on what attributes competitors are to be judged, but they are by definition judged on those attributes *after* the pioneer, so competitors are compared to the pioneer, rather than vice versa, and because the pioneer has set the agenda, the pioneer typically 'wins'.

Assimilation and contrast

Categorization is not simply a matter of determining 'what belongs where' based on attributes of the category itself and the potential category member. Research also shows that the process of categorization may directly affect the perception of the attributes themselves. This process is reflected in work on assimilation and contrast phenomena. In **assimilation**, objects are classified as more similar to the parent category than they really are when the object and category are perceived as more congruent and contrast implies a reverse phenomenon (i.e. objects are classified as more disparate from the parent category as a function of incongruence). The perception of attributes of the object can change in the direction of features of the parent category when assimilation occurs. Conversely, in a contrast response, the target is adjusted away from the parent category.

Assimilation occurs when information is made salient, which can be included in the parent category. For example, if you were asked to rate the trustworthiness of (American) politicians just after you have read about Richard Nixon, you would rate politicians less favourably than you would have done, had you not been reminded of the president who had to resign after the Watergate scandal (Schwarz & Bless, 1992). The reason for this assimilation effect is that Nixon is a member of the category 'American politicians' and making Nixon salient pulls the category down. However, if you had to rate the trustworthiness of an exemplar of the category of American politicians, for example the former president Clinton, being reminded of Nixon just before would probably help Clinton. Since you are now rating an exemplar of that category, Nixon will serve as a standard of comparison, and compared to Nixon, Clinton looks as white as snow (despite the Lewinsky affair).

However, Clinton is a special case. He became extremely well-known, not only because he was US president, but also because of his somewhat unorthodox personal affairs. We have a great deal of individuating knowledge about him and therefore do not have to rely on his category membership for information. If we had to evaluate a politician, about whom we knew little except that he was a politician, our evaluation would probably be strongly influenced by his category membership. Thus, being reminded of Nixon, just before you had to evaluate this relatively unknown politician, would probably pull your evaluation down.

Some support for these assumptions comes from a study Wänke, Bless and Igou (2001) conducted in a consumer context. Participants in this study were provided with information about three toasters, the Logan T 5000, the Logan L 500, and the Wellington TA 1 (fictitious brand names). The attributes ascribed to the Logan T 5000 were superior to those of the L 500 and the TA 1. The performance of the latter two toasters was described as similar. Participants were presented with mock advertisements for all three toasters. There were two conditions: one condition emphasized the shared brand identity of the two Logan toasters, with the two advertisements being highly similar in colour, slogans and logo, merely differing in the attributes assigned to the two toasters (the ad for the Wellington looked very different). In the second condition (individual ad), brand membership was downplayed, with the ads for the two Logan toasters looking very different (different colour, different slogans, no logo). In the control condition, only the two inferior toasters (L 500; TA 1) were evaluated. Figure 2.5 displays the ratings of the two target toaster in all three conditions.

If we compare the individual ad condition with the control condition, we can see that informing participants about the superior toaster pulled down the ratings of both inferior machines. Relative to the Logan T 5000, both the Logan L 500 and the Wellington TA 1 looked less good than they did when they were evaluated in the absence of the superior comparison standard (i.e. contrast effect). However, when the common brand membership of the two Logan toasters was made salient, the Logan 500 was not downgraded.

To gain more insight into the psychological processes, which led to these ratings, Wänke et al. (2001) replicated this experiment, but also had the two brand names evaluated. As expected, the evaluation of the Logan brand correlated much more highly with the evaluation of the Logan L 500 toaster in the brand identity than in the individual ad condition. Thus, whereas comparison of the inferior L 500 with the superb performance attributes of the Logan T 5000 decreased the evaluation of the inferior toaster when their common brand membership was not made salient, reminding participants that both toasters were made by the same company dampened the impact of the negative comparison.

One might have expected that information about the common brand membership might even have had a positive effect on the evaluation of the L 500 in the brand identity condition. The information that the L 500 was produced by the same company that also made the superb Logan T 5000 could have increased the evaluation of the L 500 (relative to the control condition). We suspect that the fact that the advertisements provided a great deal of individuating information about both toasters, information which made the L 500 look much worse than the T 5000 might have prevented this effect.

As the perception of the category member can change when it is viewed in context of the parent category, so too can the perception of the parent category when viewed in context of a new member (Loken, 2006). We see this phenomenon at work with brand extensions where new products are introduced under the label of an established brand. The parent brand constitutes the parent category. The extent to

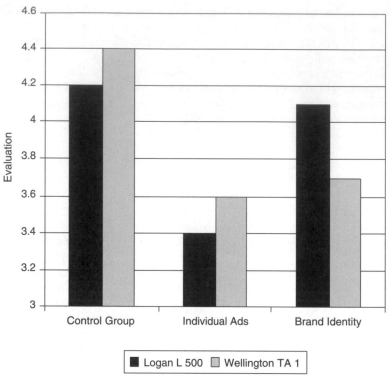

Figure 2.5 Evaluation of the Logan L 500 and the Wellington TA 1

Source: Adapted from Wänke, M., Bless, H. & Igou, E.R. (2001). Next to a star: Paling, shining or both? Turning interexemplar contrast into interexemplar assimilation. *Personality and Social Psychology Bulletin, 27,* 14–29.

which the new product affects the associations and beliefs of the parent category, again depends on the similarity of the new product to the parent category. Similar or moderately dissimilar new products have been shown to affect the perception of the parent brand to a larger degree (either in a positive or a negative direction), than very dissimilar new products, especially when processing motivation is low (Gurhan-Canli & Maheswaran, 1998). Hence, the evaluation of the parent brand category is frequently updated based on consumers' experiences with product and brand line extensions (Erdem, 1998).

A study by Bless and Wänke (2000) suggests the possibility that brand line extensions could even backfire, if the new product line is too dissimilar to the other products of this brand. Bless and Wänke presented participants with the names of 10 well-known TV shows, some of which had been rated as poor and some excellent in a pre-test. Depending on conditions, participants were instructed to select from this list two shows they considered as a (a) typical good show, (b) typical bad show, (c) unusually good show, and (d) unusually bad show. After that, participants had to evaluate the overall quality of TV programmes in general and their own satisfaction with such programmes.

The task of having to select a 'typical' good show motivated participants to focus on the good shows on the list and thinking about all these good shows increased their evaluation of TV programs in general. Similarly, thinking about all the poor shows decreased their evaluation of TV programmes in general. Thus, increasing the cognitive accessibility of positive (negative) category information increased (decreased) the evaluation of the category (assimilation).

Participants, who had been asked to select unusually good (or unusually bad) shows thought about the same shows as participants in the other conditions (after all, they were given the same list of 10 shows). Therefore the same positive or negative memories are likely to have been retrieved. However, instead of considering these shows typical members of the category, they were labelled atypical (and thus outside the category). As a result, these shows were used as standards against which other TV programmes were evaluated. And being evaluated against the best shows, the other TV programmes looked less good than when contrasted against the worst shows.

These findings indicate the dangers involved in too ambitiously extending one's brand upwards. If one attempted a significant upwards extension one should at least make sure that the new product could still be clearly perceived as a member of the brand family (i.e. was not atypical). However, that this strategy can also have drawbacks has been shown in the case of the VW Phaeton, a luxury car built by VW to compete with the most luxurious Mercedes, BMW and even Bentley cars. Car journalists were enthusiastic and some considered the Phaeton one of the best cars ever built. For example, Jeremy Clarkson wrote in the *Sunday Times* of 11 November 2007: 'As a luxury car . . . the Phaeton is better than any of its rivals from Mercedes, BMW, Audi, Jaguar and Maserati'. And yet, the car was a commercial flop. So what went wrong? The main problem is that the car is a Volkswagen and looks like one. This may have been an intentional strategy to have the Phaeton improve the image of the Volkswagen brand. We do not know whether the strategy worked for the Volkswagen brand, but it certainly did not work for the Phaeton.

Impression formation and impression correction

A specific type of categorization occurs when not just products or brands are categorized, but product or brand *users* as a function of associations related to a parent brand category. Fennis and Pruyn (2007) have tested this possibility. In their study, participants were exposed to a picture of a target individual wearing a brand of clothing that differed in 'brand personality'. According to Aaker (1997), brands can have personalities similar to people. In line with the 'big five' factor structure of human personality (e.g. Goldberg, 1992), Aaker (1997) proposed that the concept of brand personality is comprised of five dimensions that can be measured using the brand personality scale. These dimensions are sincerity, excitement, competence, sophistication and ruggedness. Of these, Fennis and Pruyn (2007) choose clothing brands that differed in the extent of competence, the extent to which the brand was associated with personality adjectives such as intelligence, success and confidence (based on a pre-test). Stereotypically, people who are intelligent, successful and confident, frequent different places than people who are not. The former can be seen in multinational businesses, fine restaurants and golf courts, the latter on the factory floor, in cheap restaurants and on camping sites. This match or mismatch between competence and setting was included in the design. In their study, participants were exposed to a picture of an individual wearing a high-competence brand of clothing (i.e. Hugo Boss), or a low competence brand (i.e. Australian), presented either on a golf course, or a campsite. Results showed that participants rated the individual's competence in line with the key association evoked by the brand he was wearing, especially when the setting the individual was placed matched rather than mismatched these associations (i.e. a golf course for the competent brand and a camp site for the incompetent brand) and when participants had ample time for impression formation. When the ability to process the information was limited (i.e. when participants were under time pressure), only the associations evoked by the brand guided the impression formation process. Hence, when participants had ample time to process the information, they used the contextual setting as a cue to the diagnosticity of the brand for inferring the wearer's personality. Hence, the setting functioned as a qualifier for the impact of brand personality on inferred consumer personality. This more individuating impression formation process was not observed when processing ability was limited and only the salient brand personalities were used as a basis for impression formation.

This study is an example of *stimulus-based* impression formation, where salient stimulus information guides the impression formation process. In contrast, Muthukrishnan and Chattopadhyay (2007) conducted a study on *memory-based* consumer impression formation by assessing how firms could overcome the impact of negative (versus) positive initial consumer impressions about a brand. The well-known saying states that you never get a second chance to make a first impression. But perhaps this proverb is not always correct? Muthukrishnan and Chattopadhyay (2007) found out that although it is harder to correct a bad than update a good first impression, there is still hope. They found that overall, impressions based on negative initial information indeed were less amenable to correction than impressions based on positive initial information (due to what is known as the negativity effect, or the higher diagnostic value of negative as opposed to positive information). However, they also reported that presenting new, or updating information in either a non-comparative or a comparative format (i.e. when the new or challenging information about a brand was conveyed in direct comparison with competitors, as we see in comparative product advertising, such as has been the case with Coca-Cola versus Pepsi) influenced the chances of correcting the initial impressions. More specifically, it was found that comparative new (positive) information was more effective than non-comparative information when initial impressions were positive, but that the reverse was true when initial impressions are negative. In that case it pays for an advertiser to try and fix the damage, but without resorting to direct comparisons with competitors. This is attributed to the fact that comparative information motivates recall of previous information and careful processing of the new information. Hence, when the initial impression was negative, a comparative format would motivate increased weighting of this negative information, compared to a non-comparative format resulting in less positive adjusted impressions than when no comparisons were made in the new information.

Comprehension

After preattentive analysis and focal attention, the process of acquiring, representing and encoding information from advertising also entails a phase of comprehension, or the process of forming inferences pertaining to the semantic meaning of the stimulus. This inferential process, where incoming information from advertising messages is related to previously stored knowledge in memory, seems like a self-evident stage, which in the case of advertising should pose no challenge whatsoever to the typical consumer. After all, when thinking about advertising claims, well, it is hardly rocket science . . . or is it . . .? Strikingly enough, an early study on the comprehension of television advertising has found that a stunning 80 per cent of all messages are initially miscomprehended in some way (Jacoby & Hoyer, 1982). Indeed, when focusing on the processes involved in the comprehension process, it becomes clear that comprehending even the simplest of commercial information sometimes posits a formidable challenge with psychological pitfalls, hurdles, biases and faulty inferences lurking along the way.

Message comprehension is considered essential for achieving persuasion according to some theories (e.g. McGuire, 1985) and should therefore be an important factor in advertising effectiveness (but see dual process theories in chapter 5). Indeed, research by Ratneshwar and Chaiken (1991) has demonstrated that at least a moderate level of accurate message comprehension is a prerequisite for certain types persuasion, namely those forms of persuasion where careful, extended and effortful information processing lies at the root of attitude change (see also McGuire, 1985 and chapter 5 for an extended discussion of comprehension's role in the persuasion process). To the extent that comprehension is a prerequisite for persuasion, miscomprehension may pose a problem. However, sometimes miscomprehension (or, more accurately, a lack of full understanding of all the implications of an advertising message), may not be that disadvantageous for an advertiser and oftentimes even serves the goal of persuasion. How can this be so? Part of the answer appears to come from what marketers and advertisers frequently term the **truth effect** of advertising (Sutherland & Sylvester, 2000), or people's tendency to initially uncritically accept information, even when certain elements are not fully comprehended.

Seeing is believing

Believing a message appears to be the default, low effort response and critically reappraising a conclusion is a second step not taken automatically. Gilbert and colleagues have conducted a series of studies on the truth effect that make clear that comprehension and belief are two sides of the same coin (Gilbert, 1991; Gilbert, Krull & Malone, 1990; Gilbert, Tafarodi & Malone, 1993; see also Kardes, 2002). In one of their studies, Gilbert et al. (1990) asked participants to learn words and statements of what they thought was an unknown (Hopi Indian) language. For example, participants were exposed to statements such as 'a monishna is a star', or 'a ghoren is a jug'. Subsequently, participants received feedback that the statements were either true or false, or they received no feedback. In addition, participants were confronted with a distracting task during a number of trials which interrupted the feedback (i.e. they had to perform a tone-detection task after the target word was presented). Later, all statements were presented again and participants were asked to indicate whether the statements were true or false. Although participants made many errors, the results showed that they tended to err on the affirmative rather than on the negating side. As Figure 2.6 shows, the interruption by the distracting tone task did not affect the correct identification of statements that were presented as true, but it did affect the correct identification of statements that were presented as false: when interrupted, participants were less prone to correctly classify these as false and instead perceive them as true. In addition, the distraction task also affected the incorrect classifications, and again in line with the truth effect. That is, when uninterrupted, the number of times true statements were misclassified as false was equivalent to the number of false statements that were misclassified as true. However, when distracted, participants increasingly misclassified false statements as true, but *not* vice versa. Thus, when processing resources are limited (in the present case because working memory is partly consumed with the concurrent task), believing becomes the default option and rejection the – more effortful – correction response.

Subsequent studies (Gilbert et al., 1993) have shown that the effect also holds for more consequential issues. In this research, participants read evidence about two crime reports. Feedback indicated that some reports were true and others were false with the false statement suggesting that the first defendant was guilty and the second was innocent or vice versa. Again participants were sometimes distracted during their reading task. Results indicated that the distraction heavily influenced participants' judgements. They recommended longer prison terms for defendants even when statements were false. In addition, these distracted participants weighted exacerbating or extenuating evidence more heavily than non distracted participants, harshly

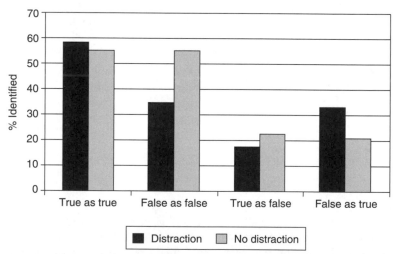

Figure 2.6 Seeing is believing: Identifications and misidentifications of statements used in Gilbert et al. (1990, Study 1)

Source: Adapted from Gilbert et al. (1990). Unbelieving the unbelievable: Some problems in the rejection of false information. *Journal of Personality and Social Psychology, 59,* 601–613

penalizing defendants when false exacerbating information was presented and letting them off the hook more easily when false extenuating information was presented.

What these studies imply for advertising effectiveness is that it is harder to reject than to accept an advertising claim, even when we know or are informed that the claim is false (for instance because we have been warned by a consumer report that the statement is false). In a cluttered media environment where information is constantly competing for our attention, conditions arise that resemble Gilbert et al.'s (1990) interruption condition: consumers tend to make decisions quickly and as effortlessly as possible and when distracted by too many competing messages they are less able (or willing) to 'run the extra mile' and engage in the extra effort needed for disbelieving claims that have initially been accepted even though they were false. For advertisers, this work on the truth effect implies that it pays off simply to keep repeating an advertising claim, since repeating a claim several times (at least to the point of wear-out) will increase acceptance. Within a single advertising message we see this practice reflected in so-called commercial presentations, where sometimes obscure products are advertised in half-hour 'tell-sell' programmes and the claims are repeated over and over again.

Hawkins and Hoch (1992) studied the effects of simple repetition of true and false product claims on validity. Statements included 'Roschips' vitamin C is better for the body than synthetic vitamin C (false)', or 'Prolonged use of Alka-Seltzer can lead to the formation of kidney stones (true)'. Results showed that believability of the claims increased with repetition, especially when participants were asked to rate the comprehensibility of the statements. As argued by Kardes (2002), repetition increases familiarity which increases believability. Ironically, even *repeatedly* highlighting that a claim is false may not undo the truth effect as Skurnik, Yoon, Park and Schwarz (2005) found out. These authors showed that telling consumers that a claim is false may make them misremember it as true. Especially older consumers proved susceptible to the truth effect. Repeatedly stating that a claim was false led to more scepticism in the short run, but surprisingly, also made these consumers more likely to remember it as true after a delayed period. According to Skurnik et al. (2005) a process reminiscent of the well-known **sleeper effect** (see chapter 6) is responsible for the phenomenon: repetition increased familiarity for the claim itself, fostering the perception that it is true (as in the previous studies) whereas it decreased memory for the original context of the claim (i.e. the notification that the claim was false).

Miscomprehension and misleading advertising claims

In these instances, believability proved to be the default mode, regardless of message comprehension. Message comprehension often implies the formation of inferences that go beyond the information given (cf. Kardes, Posavac, Cronley & Herr, 2008). These inferences often lead to miscomprehension when they are formed in response to advertising slogans (Kardes, 1993; Hastie, 1983). Kardes (2002) has summarized advertising tactics and procedures that may potentially lead to miscomprehension, because they lead to faulty inferences. Frequently, these advertising practices actually mislead consumers, and thus have received attention from the US Federal Trade Commission. For instance, *pragmatic inferences* are simple assumptions about statements that are literally true, but figuratively false (see Harris, 1977). An advertising slogan like: 'Brand X may be the best beer in the world' (paraphrasing an actual slogan used by Carlsberg) is literally true, because 'may' means 'perhaps'. But this nuance is typically lost to the information processing consumer that tends to equate 'may' with 'usually' or 'is'. In addition, ad slogans sometimes *omit comparison information*, with consumers frequently providing the missing information, without being fully aware that he/she is doing so often in the direction desired by the marketer. For example, 'Dentists recommend Brand X toothpaste' suggests consensus by its plural form, but becomes less compelling when it refers to two dentists (out of a population of several thousand). Comparison information is also omitted in a slogan such as 'Brand X relieves pain longer!' Longer than what? One minute or two minutes or longer than taking brand Y (the likely inference most consumers will make)? *Juxtaposition* is an alternative means that facilitates certain (sometimes false) inferences. For example: 'be cool, buy Brand X' suggests a causal relationship where buying brand X will make one appear cool, but the causal relationship is inferred, not stated. Similarly, an *affirmation of the consequent* can be misleading because it hinges on reversing cause and effect. For example, a well-known do-it-yourself store advertises with 'If you can see it, you can make it: Brand X' suggests that brand x causes consumers to become handymen/women and build everything they can imagine, whereas this is not stated (see Kardes, 2002 for an extended discussion of these and other potential sources of misleading consumers).

Elaborative reasoning

The previous examples of miscomprehension fall halfway between the stages of comprehension and elaborative reasoning. The 'truth effect' may be the result of processes that are largely outside conscious consumer awareness, and so may some, but not all, of the inferences that consumers make on the basis of sometimes misleading advertising claims. But as Greenwald and Leavitt (1984) have pointed out, inferences made during the final stage of elaborative reasoning typically require full consciousness, because they are usually the product of an effortful and deliberative process. Hence, elaborative consumer reasoning is facilitated when consumer involvement is high rather than low. This stage is characterized as the process by which the semantically represented stimulus is actively related to previously stored consumer knowledge that allows for simple or more complex inferences. These inferences can be based on stimulus information (as in the case of instances of misleading advertising described above) or information that resides in the individual.

Elaborative reasoning is about thinking and thinking can vary along at least three dimensions: the extent of thinking, the valence of thinking and the object of thinking. In chapter 5, the extent and valence of consumer thinking in response to advertising messages will be extensively discussed, so the present overview will focus on the *object* of consumer thinking. Types of thought that have been studied in the consumer domain include item-specific versus relational thoughts (e.g. Malaviya, Kisielius & Sternthal, 1996), thoughts brought about by salient consumer goals (e.g. Escales & Luce, 2004; Nenkov, Inman & Hulland, 2008; Sengupta & Johar, 2002), thoughts about the self (Meyers-Levy & Peracchio, 1992), and meta-cognitive thoughts (e.g. Schwarz, 2004).

Self-schema and elaborative reasoning

A key source for inference making is the self, and in particular the salience of a self-schema. A **self-schema** entails a cognitive generalization about the self that is comprised of a more or less comprehensive set of traits, values and beliefs that exerts a powerful influence on information processing (cf. Markus, 1977). A series of studies by Wheeler, Petty and Bizer (2005) informs us how this influence must be understood. They argued that product information contained in advertising that is congruent with a salient self-schema motivates consumers to process the information in more detail. Hence, issue-relevant information in the ad (i.e. product arguments or claims) is processed more extensively when it is congruent with this self-schema and persuasion is primarily a result of the quality of the argumentation in the ad (see chapter 5 for a more extended discussion of the role of argument quality in persuasion).

In their research, Wheeler et al. (2005) exposed participants to a series of ads. In one study, extroverts and introverts (measured with a personality questionnaire) were shown an ad for a fictitious brand of video cassette recorder that either appealed to extroverts or introverts and that contained either strong or weak arguments. The message frame in the introductory part of the ads was varied to appeal either to introverts or to extroverts. The extroverted version read: 'With the Mannux VCR, you'll be the life of the party, whether the party's in your home or out of it.' An example of a sentence for the introvert frame was, 'With the Mannux VCR, you can have all of the luxuries of a movie theater without having to deal with the crowds.' In addition, argument quality was varied to create ads with strong or weak arguments. An example of a strong argument is, 'The VCR includes a deluxe digital, on-screen timing program that determines how much tape is left, how much time is left in the current program, and how long the current program has been playing.' An example of a weak argument is, 'The VCR includes an eject button on its front face that permits you to remove the video and get a rough idea of how much tape is left.' On the dependent variable of brand attitudes, the authors found that when high extroverts were exposed to the extroverted ad (i.e. when there was a match between ad and self-schema), brand attitudes were a function of the arguments in the ad. Hence, strong arguments resulted in more persuasion and weak arguments resulted in reduced persuasion. When there was a mismatch between self-schema and the frame of the ad, attitudes were less a function of the type of arguments participants were exposed to.

A second experiment replicated these effects with another type of self-schema, namely with individuals rated high and low on the need for cognition (NC): the tendency to enjoy thinking and problem solving. Both high and low NC individuals were exposed to a transcript of a radio commercial for a brand of toothpaste that either matched or mismatched this trait. More specifically, the message framed in high NC terms read: 'I'll bet you're the type of person who likes to look at the details when you make choices. You want to know which choice is best, but you also want to know why.' It concluded with, 'Fluorident: When you think about it, it's the only choice!' The low NC-framed ad began with, 'I'll bet you're the type of person who doesn't like to sit around and think about all of the little details when you make choices. You find what you're looking for and move on with your life.' And concluded with, 'Fluorident: No need to think twice! It's the only choice.' As in their first study, argument quality was varied. Participants who read the strong argument message read, 'Its cool, minty flavour cleans your breath all day, and in a national consumer test, seven out of ten people chose the flavour of Fluorident over the leading brand.' People who read the weak-argument transcripts read, 'Its cool, mint-like flavour cleans your breath for over an hour, and in a national consumer test, three out of ten people chose the packaging of Fluorident over their current toothpastes.' Again, when the message frame matched the salient self-schema of the recipient (in terms of his/her need for cognition in the present case), persuasion was more a function of extended elaboration (i.e. as a function of argument quality), than when a mismatch occurred.

Other studies have confirmed that information processing with regard to the self increases the extent of elaborative reasoning, for instance when processing strong arguments with regard to the self (Burnkrant & Unnava, 1995), although these effects could be offset when processing motivation was reduced or when information processing reached a satiation point and irritation and scepticism set in (Meyers-Levy & Peracchio, 1992; Burnkrant & Unnava, 1995; Loken, 2006). This extensive information processing, however, is not always entirely 'objective' or data-driven. Research also suggests that a salient self-schema can bias information processing in line with the schema, frequently in order to protect or enhance the self (see Johnson & Eagly, 1989, 1990; Petty & Cacioppo, 1986). The bias resulting from an activated self-schema on inference making is also demonstrated by studies showing that attitudes formed or changed as a result of self-schema based processing are largely resistant to correction (Bolton & Reed, 2004).

The research by Wheeler et al. (2005) suggests that elaborative reasoning can result in either increased or decreased persuasion as a function of the quality of the argumentation in the ad the consumer is exposed to. This finding is supportive of the dual process theories of persuasion, which we will discuss in chapter 5. Additional research, however, also suggests that increased elaboration can have adverse effects on persuasion, particularly, when the object of elaboration is negative, irrelevant or nondiagnostic information (e.g. Grewal et al., 1997; Priester, Nayakankuppam, Fleming & Godek, 2004; Schlosser & Shavitt, 2002). That is, in these situations, the 'train of thought' might move the consumer away from the advocated position, especially when the valence of the thoughts is unfavourable, does not pertain to the position advocated in the message, or is not relevant to that position. In addition, thinking too hard sometimes comes at a psychological cost and thus people tend to avoid it (Fiske & Taylor, 1984). Hence, when cognitive effort is not put to good use and appears 'wasted' (i.e. does not lead to a satisfactory conclusion or another benefit), negative affect can be the result (Garbarino & Edell, 1997, see also Loken, 2006 for a review).

Consumer meta-cognition

A specific type of elaborative reasoning occurs when the object of consumer thoughts is not the product, the ad or brand, but the thoughts themselves. When people reflect on their own inner states, and infer something from that process, we speak of consumer **meta-cognition**. Earlier we discussed consumers thinking about the motives of marketers and the misattribution of hedonic fluency. Both types of inferences can be considered meta-cognitive experiences, since they are judgements that are based not on what information consumers perceive (i.e. declarative information), but on how they perceive it and the extent and direction to which they think about their own judgement and evaluation processes and those of others with whom they interact (Loken, 2006; Schwarz, 2004; Lee, 2004). Wright (2002) refers to the concept of 'marketplace meta-cognition' in this regard, which he defines as 'people's beliefs about their own mental states and the mental states, strategies, of others as these pertain directly to the social domain of marketplace interactions' (p. 677). Although meta-cognitive processes can sometimes operate automatically and unconsciously, they can also be the product of more effortful processes (see Lee, 2004), for instance when consumers form meta-cognitive beliefs about marketers' use of persuasion tactics and motives (Friestad & Wright, 1995). Such meta-cognitive beliefs often result in consumer scepticism, distrust and resistance to persuasion, especially when ulterior motives of marketers become obvious to the consumer (see Warlop & Alba, 2004).

However, meta-cognitive inferences do not always decrease the extent of persuasion in response to marketing communications. In discussing consumer meta-cognitive experiences Schwarz (2004) has used the experience of ease of retrieval as an example for a meta-cognitive process, which enhances persuasion. Ease of retrieval is a form of hedonic fluency and refers to the apparent ease with which product and brand related information can be retrieved from memory. People may conclude that the ease of retrieval is diagnostic for the validity of the retrieved information ('what I can easily remember should be correct', a meta-cognitive inference) and may base their judgement in accordance with this ease of retrieval. Information that is easy to retrieve may then positively affect product attitudes.

A striking demonstration that people use ease of retrieval as a diagnostic for the validity of retrieved information comes from studies by Wänke and colleagues (Wänke, Bless & Biller, 1996; Wänke, Bohner & Jurkowitsch, 1997). In their first study (Wänke et al., 1996) participants were asked to list either three or seven self-generated reasons why to use or why not to use public transport. Thus number of reasons was crossed in a factorial design with thinking of positive versus negative reasons. As expected, listing three arguments was considered easier than listing seven arguments. While intuitively one might have expected that somebody who came up with seven arguments in favour of public transport would end up with more favourable ratings than someone who only had to think of three good reasons, the opposite was found. Participants, who had listed seven good reasons felt less positive than those, who had only listed three good reasons. Similarly, participants, who had to come up with seven negative reasons felt less negative than those asked to generate only three negative reasons. The fact that producing seven reasons for (or against) public transport was difficult, persuaded these individuals that things could not really be that good (or bad). When participants (in further experimental conditions) were merely exposed to the arguments rather than having to generate them, the reverse effects (more persuaded by seven than three arguments) was observed.

These findings were replicated in a study in which participants were exposed to an ad that suggested that that they should name one or ten reasons why one should buy a BMW (or why one should not buy such a car). Again, participants were less favourable towards BMW after it was suggested that they should name ten rather than one good reason to buy a BMW (and the reverse was true in the negative condition). Even more striking was the fact that participants were less positive about BMW following an ad that suggested that they think of ten pro reasons than after an ad that suggested that they think of ten contra reasons. These findings demonstrate that meta-cognition is often influential in affecting consumer judgement, because consumers appear to consider these inferences as *diagnostic* and *trustworthy*.

Briñol and colleagues have recently described another form of meta-cognitive judgement where diagnosticity and trust play an important role (e.g. Briñol & Petty, 2009; Briñol, Petty & Tormala, 2004). They have termed this meta-cognitive judgment **self-validation**, reflecting the subjective confidence consumers have in their thoughts and evaluations in response to persuasive messages. Briñol et al. (2004) showed that increasing consumer confidence in positive thoughts enhanced the effectiveness of an advertisement whereas increasing confidence in negative thoughts had the opposite effect. Moreover, one factor that directly contributed to thought confidence was the credibility of the source of the ad, with high credible sources resulting in more thought confidence than low credibility sources. Presumably what high credibility sources have to say is considered more valid than what low credibility sources have to say and the resulting thoughts are perceived as more diagnostic resulting in increased confidence.

Summary and conclusions

- This chapter has reviewed evidence from social cognition and consumer psychology on processes that play a role when consumers acquire and process information from advertising. In line with other chapters in this volume, these processes can be either unconscious, low effort and automatic, or deliberative, conscious and effortful. There are four stages involved in the process of information acquisition and processing.

- Stage 1 is termed *Preattentive analysis*, which involves a general, non-goal directed, 'surveillance' of the environment. In this stage consumers do not intentionally tune in to advertising but get influenced by ad messages nevertheless. Preattentive processing uses both feature analysis and conceptual analysis. The impact of the effects of preattentive processing is mostly based on implicit memory.

  Incidental exposure can direct and capture attention processes in this stage, based on the notion of matching activation, or differential lateral hemispheric activation. The research on matching activation suggests that advertisers need to place great emphasis on the decision where to schedule their message since attention can be directed to or away from the focal ad depending on whether the focal ad can make use of the mobilized attentional resources that are left unused when processing competing ads.

- An important mechanism that can account for many phenomena occurring during the preattentive stage is hedonic fluency, or the misattribution of processing-induced affect to the brand that is featured in an advertisement.

Various types of fluency have been identified in the literature including processing fluency, conceptual fluency and goal fluency

- Stage 2 is coined the stage of *Focal attention:* after noticing a stimulus, it may be brought into conscious awareness where it is identified and categorized. Focal attention can be drawn toward advertising messages involuntarily through stimulus salience, vividness and novelty.
- Salience is the extent to which stimulus features contrast with the environment. Hence, salience is context dependent. The use of humour and an upward camera angle have been examined as instances of salience.
- Vividness is not fully context-dependent but can also be 'person-dependent'. Vivid information in advertising is information that is emotionally interesting, concrete and image provoking and proximate in a sensory temporal or spatial way. Vividness effects have been examined by focusing on personality traits (i.e. the tendency to engage in visual imagery), modality factors and consumer goals.
- A third way in which focal attention can be drawn is through the use of novel information. A key factor driving a consumer perception of novelty is the extent to which information in advertising disconfirms existing consumer expectancies. Sustaining novelty can amount to advertising repetition strategies where cosmetic and substantive changes are incorporated to attract and hold consumer attention

   An integral part of the focal attention phase in the information processing sequence is categorizing information once it has been brought into conscious awareness and identified. In the advertising and consumer domain, categorization processes are reflected in studies on product and brand line extensions. Categorizations are frequently based on comparisons between product attributes, (i.e. products with different brands that share certain attributes, such as the product category of automobiles), brands (products with different attributes that share the same brand, such as the examples above), or product usage (products with different brands and different attributes that are used in similar situations, such as breakfast foods).

- A powerful force driving categorization is the extent of similarity between the parent category (e.g. a parent brand) and the potential category member (e.g. a brand extension), which is reflected in the representativeness heuristic.
- Another categorization phenomenon is the pioneering advantage or the strategic benefit that a newcomer may have in the eyes of the consumer. Pioneering brands may start their own categories and may harvest an inherent advantage, an attribute advantage and a comparison advantage, vis-à-vis competitors.
- Assimilation and contrast are additional manifestations of consumer categorization processes. Assimilation entails the notion that objects are classified as more similar to the parent category to the extent that the object and category are more congruent and contrast implies a reverse phenomenon.
- Impression formation is a specific type of categorization that occurs when not just products or brands are categorized, but product or brand *users* as a function of associations related to a parent brand category.
- Stage 3 is termed *comprehension*, the process of forming inferences pertaining to the semantic meaning of the stimulus. Work on the truth effect shows that

comprehension is an effortful process with people tending to initially believe what they see, and only on second thought correct their initial judgment, if at all. Advertisers can use this bias by simply repeating their claims, since repetition has been shown to increase familiarity which increases believability.

- The fourth and final stage is *elaborative reasoning* or the process by which the semantically represented stimulus is actively related to previously stored consumer knowledge that allows for simple or more complex inferences. Elaboration pertains to consumer thinking and this thinking can vary along at least three dimensions: the extent of thinking, the valence of thinking and the object of thinking. Two examples of the latter include the roles of self-schemata and meta-cognition in elaborative reasoning.

The present chapter dealt with what consumers think, when intentionally and incidentally exposed to advertising messages. In order to think what they think, however, consumers need to draw on a vast and flexible reservoir which we have not described in this chapter, but will turn our attention to next: consumer memory.

Chapter 3

How advertising affects consumer memory

The structure and function of human memory 74

Implications for advertising 90

Can advertising distort memory? 106

Summary and conclusions 109

There is usually a considerable time lag between the time, when we are exposed to mass-media advertisements and the time when we have to make purchase decisions. We might have seen an advertisement on television for a new brand of margarine that claims to lower cholesterol. When a few days later, we see this brand of margarine on the shelves of our local supermarket, we might remember the ad and put one or two packages into our shopping cart. Obviously, without memory, we could not have read or understood the advertisement in the first place, but that is of less interest here. What interests us here is how we can remember the picture and the message contained in an advertisement over days or weeks and which factors determine whether we recall the ad at the point of purchase. These are the questions that we will address in this chapter.

Human **memory** is a system that not only allows us to record, store and retrieve the information that is acquired through our senses, but also influences the way this information is perceived, encoded and stored. **Encoding** refers to the processes involved in getting the information into the system by transforming an external stimulus into an internal representation, which allows us to retain it in the cognitive system. **Storage** involves information retention over time. This storage can be short-term, as when a computer stores information temporarily in the Random Access Memory, or relatively permanent as when our computer stores information on a hard drive. But as everybody knows, who has spent ages trying to find a document in their office that he or she remembers clearly having filed earlier, having stored information does not necessarily mean that we can also find it again. This is where retrieval processes and forgetting come in. *Retrieval* refers to the processes that allow us to find the information stored in our memory and *forgetting* refers to the processes that prevent us from finding it. But in order to understand these different aspects of information processing, we need to understand the functions of the different components assumed to make up human memory.

The structure and function of human memory

During the second half of the last century, thinking about memory has been heavily influenced by the computer metaphor and the metaphor of man as a processor of information. The fact that computers have different kinds of memory proved to be suggestive and during the 1960s a number of models were formulated that conceived of memory as consisting of several separate systems (e.g. Atkinson & Shiffrin, 1968; Broadbent, 1958). The most influential of these was the model developed by Atkinson and Shiffrin (1968), which distinguished three major components of memory, namely *sensory memory, working or short-term memory* and *long-term memory* (Figure 3.1.) According to this model, information is first held very briefly in a modality specific sensory memory. Then, a selection of this information is transferred to the working or short-term memory, before an even smaller amount finds its way into the long-term memory store.

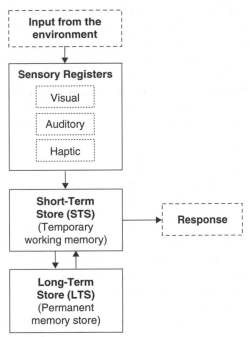

Figure 3.1 The flow of information through the memory system

Source: Adapted from Atkinson & Shiffrin (1968). Human memory: a proposed system and its control processes. In K.W. Spence & J.T. Spence (Eds.). *The psychology of learning and motivation: Advances in research and theory* (pp. 89–195). New York: Academic Press

The model of Atkinson and Shiffrin

Sensory memory

Sensory memory stores are the briefest memory stores. They should probably be considered part of the process of perception, because the information that is stored in these sensory registers is not yet encoded, but stored in the sensory modality in which it has been perceived (Baddeley, 2002). Although all senses have such very short-term registers, research has focused mainly on visual and auditory sensory memory, which Neisser (1967) labeled iconic and echoic memory. These sensory registers store incoming sensory information for less than a second, before the information is either lost or transferred into short-term memory.

Sensory storage was demonstrated for iconic memory in a classic experiment by Sperling (1960), who presented research participants for 50 milliseconds with a matrix of 12 letters, which were ordered into three rows of four letters (Figure 3.2). When asked to recall these letters immediately afterwards, participants could usually only remember four to five letters. There are two explanations for this poor performance: either participants could not scan all the letters due to the short exposure time, or they did scan all of them, but forgot most of them in the time it took them to

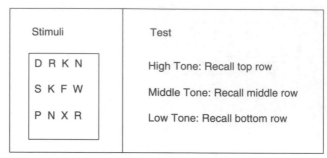

Figure 3.2 The setup of the study by Sperling (1960)

Source: Adpated from Sperling (1960). The information available in brief visual presentations. *Psychological Monographs: General and Applied, 74,* 1–29

report the first five letters. To examine these alternatives, Sperling (1960) told his participants that they needed to report only one row of letters, but that they would only be informed, which row to report, *after* the presentation of the letters had been discontinued. The signal for each row was a tone, with a high tone signalling the top row, a medium-high tone signalling the middle row and a low tone signalling the bottom row. Under these conditions, participants were able to report two thirds of the letters of one row. Since they did not know in advance, which of the rows they would have to report, it has to be assumed that they had the same number of letters available for the other rows as well. Sperling (1960) suggested that participants were reading these letters from a memory trace which was rapidly decaying so that only one row of letters could be read, before the trace had vanished. To assess the duration of the iconic memory trace, Sperling (1960) varied the interval between the offset of the letters and the onset of the cue. He found that the advantage from cuing a single line declined with increasing delay and disappeared when the delay lasted for about 500 milliseconds.

There is evidence for the existence of a similar sensory storage system for sounds (e.g. Efron, 1970a, b; Plomb, 1964). For example, Plomb (1964) exposed participants repeatedly to a 200-millisecond burst of noise that was followed by a second burst. Plomb varied both the interval between the two bursts and the intensity of the second burst. Participants had to detect the onset of the second burst against the background of the decaying trace of the first burst. Consistent with expectations, Plomb found that the second noise needed to be much louder to be detected, if it was presented 2.5 milliseconds rather than 80 milliseconds after the first.

Working or short-term memory

For the information in the sensory registers not to get lost, the raw sensory data that is momentarily held in the sensory registers needs to be turned into some kind of code to be transferred to short-term or working memory. Working memory is a unitary system where input from the different sensory memories is integrated with information from long-term memory to be briefly held in conscious awareness and manipulated. It has very limited storage capacity. Input of new information is only possible if old information is moved out. Since it is the workspace where thinking, problem-solving and decision-making takes place, most information held in short-term memory is information which we are consciously aware of.

The model of Atkinson and Shiffrin (1968) distinguishes memory structures from control processes such as coding or verbal rehearsal. These are strategies used by the individual to memorize or recall material. *Verbal rehearsal* lengthens the period for which information stays in the short-term store and at the same time builds up the trace in the long-term memory.

Long-term memory

Long-term memory is assumed to store nearly unlimited amounts of information for a nearly unlimited period of time. According to the model of Atkinson and Shiffrin (1968) information, which has entered the processing system through modality-specific sensory stores and gone through the limited short-term or working memory, needs to be encoded semantically before entering long-term memory. The more the individual rehearses material the greater the likelihood that it will be stored in long-term memory. Rehearsal requires attention. Thus, in order for information to proceed from short-term to long-term stores, the individual has to pay attention to the information.

Evidence for the multi-systems view of memory

The assumption that short-term and long-term memory should be considered separate systems was quite controversial during the 1960s and this controversy still lingers on today (e.g. Craik, 2002). In his excellent monograph on 'Human Memory', Baddeley (1997) lists the major evidence that had accumulated during the 60s and appeared to support the conception of memory as a multi-storage system.

- *Speed of retrieval*. Retrieval from short-term memory is faster than retrieval from long-term memory,
- *Capacity*. The capacity of short-term memory is much more limited. As George Miller (1956) wrote in his classic article 'The magical number seven, plus or minus two', short-term memory can hold only five to seven pieces of *unrelated* information. (However, these seven items can be seven letters, seven words or seven broad categories, depending on the extent to which information is categorized, or 'chunked' by the individual.)
- *Serial position effects*. Studies of free recall typically indicate that recall is affected by the position of the item within the series. Items presented at the beginning ('primacy') and at the end of the list ('recency') are recalled earlier and more often than items in the middle of the list (Figure 3.3., Glanzer & Cunitz, 1966). Primacy effects are attributed to the fact that individuals have greater opportunity to rehearse the first few items to transfer them to long-term memory. Once short term memory fills up, there is less opportunity to rehearse each item. The last few items are recalled better, because they have not been pushed

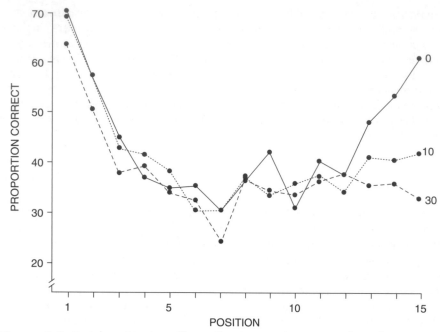

Figure 3.3 Serial positioning effects after 0 second, 10 seconds and 30 seconds delay between presentation and recall test. Recency effects emerge only with immediate recall

Source: Glanzer & Cunitz (1966). Two storage mechanisms in free recall. *Journal of Verbal Learning and Verbal Behavior*, 5, 351–360. Reproduced with permission of Elsevier

out of short-term memory and can therefore be retrieved from there. If recall is delayed by 15 to 30 seconds, this recency effect tends to disappear, whereas the other items of the list are unaffected by this delay (Postman & Phillips, 1965).

- *Memory code.* Short-term and long-term memory appeared to use different forms of coding. Whereas long-term memory seems to rely mainly on semantic codes, short-term memory appears to use acoustic or phonological coding. This evidence comes mainly from studies, which show that when visually presented words or letters have to be learnt, participants are more likely to confuse similar-*sounding* items than items that *look* similar (Conrad & Hull, 1964) or have similar meaning (Baddeley, 1966). For example, a study by Conrad and Hull (1964), in which visually presented letter codes had to be learnt, indicated that the recall errors made by participants were typical for letters that were similar in sound (e.g. P and E) rather than similar-looking (e.g. P and R). This suggested that participants relied on some kind of speech-based code, even though these letters had been presented visually (Baddeley, 1997). Further support for this assumption comes from a study by Baddeley (1966), in which participants had to learn lists of word which either sounded similar (e.g. man, can) or had similar meaning (e.g. big, huge). With immediate recall, similarity of sound resulted in poor performance, whereas similarity of meaning had no significant effect. In contrast, when recall was measured after a filled delay to eliminate short-term memory, similarity of meaning (but not of sound) impaired recall, suggesting that long-term memory relied mainly on meaning in encoding material (Baddeley, 1966).

- *Neuropsychology.* The most impressive evidence against a unitary view of memory comes from neuropsychological studies of patients who suffer from severe amnesia (for a review, see Baddeley, 1997). Patients may have perfectly functioning short-term memories but be seriously impaired in their long-term memory (e.g. Milner, 1966; Baddeley & Warrington, 1970). There are also patients, whose short-term memory is impaired, but whose long-term learning is quite normal (e.g. Shallice & Warrington, 1970).

Problems with the model of Atkinson and Shiffrin

Even though the model of Atkinson and Shiffrin (1968) became the standard model in memory research and dominated thinking about memory for many decades, there was also evidence that was inconsistent with basic assumptions of the model. For example, although the pattern of findings of Shallice and Warrington (1970) discussed earlier supports the conception of short-term and long-term memory as separate systems, it is inconsistent with one of the central assumptions of the model of Atkinson and Shiffrin (1968), namely that information can only reach the long-term memory by passing through short-term memory (Baddeley, 1997). Further problems for the model of Atkinson and Shiffrin come from studies that show that people sometimes do not remember objects clearly even though they are likely to have seen them thousands of times. Such findings seem to be inconsistent with the assumption that information that is frequently rehearsed is likely to be stored in long-term memory. For example, Nickerson and Adams (1979), who asked their US participants to reproduce both sides of an American penny from memory, found that although participants were able to approximate the coin, very few were able to reproduce it exactly. Similarly, a study conducted in Britain during a time when British telephone dials still combined letter and number codes found that of the 50 participants in this research not a single one was able to reproduce the information on the dial totally correctly (Morton, 1967).

There have been several strategies to resolve these inconsistencies. One has been to abandon the idea of different memory systems altogether and concentrate on the way information is processed (Craik & Lockhart, 1972; Craik, 2002) The other has been to reformulate the distinction between short-term and long-term memory in ways that made it consistent with existing evidence (Baddeley & Hitch, 1974). We will briefly discuss both of these approaches.

Levels of processing

Why are the results of the coin study (Nickerson & Adams, 1979) or those on the recall of British telephone dials (Morton, 1967) not all that surprising? If you live in Britain (or in a country of the Euro zone), would you be able to draw a £5 (or €5) note? If, like us, you are unable to reproduce your own currency, even though you have handled it daily, you would probably argue that you never paid much attention to the way the money looked. In a nutshell, this is the basic assumption of the levels of processing approach (Craik & Lockhart, 1972). It assumes that items are remembered better the more we pay attention to them and the more deeply they are processed.

Imagine you are taking part in an experiment, in which you are shown a list of words, with each word followed by a question, which you have to answer:

- RIVER: Is the word in capital letters?
- HOUSE: Does the word rhyme with mouse?
- WINE: Does the word fit in the sentence 'The man drank a glass of _____?'

At this point, you would have no idea that your memory would be tested. Whereas the answer to the first question needs only superficial orthographic encoding, likely to result in relatively short-lived traces, the second question asks for phonological processing producing a somewhat more lasting trace in memory. Finally, the answer to the third question requires semantic or conceptual processing that produces the most durable trace. When Craik and Tulving (1975), who conducted this kind of experiment, later presented their participants with a list of words and asked them to recognize those words that had been presented earlier, the words that had been semantically processed were remembered best, those that had been orthographically processed were remembered least. Findings like this support Craik and Lockhart's (1972) main argument, that there is no need to distinguish between two memory systems to account for differences in the length of time that things are remembered. According to their influential article, longer storage results from deeper processing and not from transfer of information from a short-term to a long-term memory system.

The model of working memory of Baddeley and Hitch

Instead of solving the inconsistency by completely abandoning the concept of short-term or working memory, Baddeley and Hitch (1974; Baddeley, 2002) replaced the model of working memory as a *unitary* system by a *multi-component* working memory model. In this system, a controlling attentional system, the central executive, which has no storage capacity of its own, supervises and coordinates a number of sub-systems. Baddeley and Hitch (1974) focused on two such subsystems, namely the phonological loop, responsible for the short-term storage and manipulation of speech-based information and the visuo-spatial sketchpad, responsible for the short-term storage and manipulation of visual information. In 2000, Baddeley added an 'episodic buffer' to this model, as a place where information from long-term memory and the subsystems of working memory can be temporarily stored, integrated and manipu-lated. It is in this episodic buffer where the so-called consumer consideration set (i.e. the number of brands from a given product category that a consumer is actively choosing from on a given occasion, see Kardes, 2002) manifests itself.

The *phonological loop* consists of two components, a phonological store that briefly holds sounds or speech-based information and an articulatory rehearsal sys-tem that uses subvocal 'inner speech'. Unless speech-based information is subvocally rehearsed, it will fade and become irretrievable within two seconds (Baddeley, 2001).

A second function of the articulatory rehearsal process is to translate written material into phonological code to allow storage in the phonological loop. This process is responsible for the findings reported earlier, that mistakes made in the learning of written letter codes were related to similarity of sound rather than similarity of shape (Conrad & Hull, 1964).

The phonological loop has a finite length. Thus, the memory span for words, that is the number of words we can repeat back immediately after hearing them, is determined by the amount of time it takes to say these words. Our memory span represents the number of items that can be uttered in approximately two seconds (Baddeley, 2001). Thus, the longer the words, the fewer words we will recall without error. This word length effect disappears, when subvocal rehearsal is prevented by articulatory suppression (Baddeley, Thompson & Buchanan, 1975). Articulatory suppression prevents subvocal rehearsal by instructing participants to repeat aloud a simple sound or word (e.g., the, the, the . . .).

The *visuo-spatial* sketchpad is a second subsystem of working memory. It is responsible for the brief storage and manipulation of visual material. It plays an important role in spatial orientation and the solution of visuo-spatial problems (Baddeley, 2001). The visuo-spatial sketchpad and the phonological loop can operate at the same time. There is no interference between the two subsystems. Thus, when asked by somebody to direct them to a nearby street, we can rehearse the street name and at the same time visualize the map of our area to search for the location of the street.

The *central executive* allocates attention and coordinates the two subsystems of working memory. It focuses the available attentional capacity and determines when the phonological loop and the sketchpad are used and how they are used (Baddeley, 2001). It has no storage capacity of its own. The main task of the central executive is to plan sequences of activities. With the central executive having no storage capacity of its own, the problem arises, *how* and *where* the information stored in the phonological loop, the visuo-spatial sketchpad and long-term memory can be integrated. There needs to be a space where all of this information can be temporarily stored and manipulated by the central executive. To address this problem, Baddeley (2000) suggested the addition of an episodic buffer to his model of working memory to serve as an interface between the different systems, each involving a different code.

The *episodic buffer* is a limited-capacity temporary storage system, capable of integrating information from a variety of sources, each involving a different set of codes. To achieve this, the episodic buffer is assumed to use a common multi-dimensional code. It is controlled by the central executive, 'which is capable of retrieving information from the store in the form of conscious awareness, of reflecting on that information and, when necessary, manipulating and modifying it' (Baddeley, 1997, p. 421). For example, it is customary in restaurants in the USA to add a 'voluntary' service charge that constitutes a percentage of the amount to be paid. To calculate this service percentage, one would have to retrieve the information about the customary percentage as well as the rules for calculating percentages from long-term memory. Both will be temporarily stored in our episodic buffer, as will the information about the amount of our bill. The central executive would then be responsible for planning the sequence of actions that need to be performed to come up with an answer. It would allocate attention to the various subsystems and keep track of which parts of the operation have already been performed.

It seems plausible that the phonological loop and the visuo-spatial sketchpad are not the only storage subsystems of working memory. Further temporary storage systems are likely to store information from other senses such as the chemical senses of taste and smell. People are able to remember smells (e.g. the disgusting smell of old cigarette smoke or the lovely smell of fresh flowers). Marketers are well aware of this, and have come up with specific types of ads designed to accommodate the sense of smell (i.e. 'scratch-'n'-sniff' ads). Some people are even able to identify different brands of perfume by their smell. Similarly, connoisseurs of wines are able to identify wines from different regions and often even from different vineyards and years in blind tasting. To succeed in this task, they have to temporarily store taste of the wine they are tasting and compare it to their memories of wines they have tasted in the past. This achievement is the more surprising, because there is no well-developed language to describe these tastes. Experienced wine drinkers are also skilled in selecting wines that complement the food they want to order in a restaurant. Although this can also be achieved with simple rules (e.g. white wine with fish and white meat, and red wine with red meat) such simple rules can be fallible. Experienced wine drinkers will imagine the taste of the dishes they are going to order and then also imagine the tastes of different wines to finally select the wine they think will best complement their food. Thus, various taste experiences have to be retrieved from long-term memory and compared in an episodic buffer. With the few exceptions (e.g. Melcher & Schooler, 1996; Castriott-Scanderbeg et al., 2005), we have been unable to find much research on this issue.

Forms of long-term memory

The long-term memory store is assumed to store nearly unlimited amounts of information for a nearly unlimited period of time. There is evidence that long-term memory is not a single entity but is composed of several different components (Squire, Knowlton & Musen, 1993). Researchers have suggested numerous different and often partly overlapping classifications (e.g. Squire, 1987; Squire, Knowlton & Musen, 1993; Tulving, 1983). The most important distinction is that between forms of conscious and nonconscious memory. These conscious forms of memory have been termed declarative (e.g. Squire, 1987; Squire et al., 1993), explicit (Schacter, Chiu & Ochsner, 1993) or recollective (Baddeley, 1997) memory. The nonconscious forms of memory have typically been referred to as implicit memory. There is some doubt, however, whether implicit memory should really be considered a distinct memory system even by researchers, who regard explicit or recollective memory operating as a single system (e.g. Baddeley, 2002).

Declarative or explicit memory

Declarative or explicit memory is characterized by a person's conscious recollection of facts or events (Schacter et al., 1993). Based on suggestions by Tulving (1983), researchers distinguish two subcategories of explicit memory, namely *episodic* and *semantic* memory. An episodic memory is about a specific event that occurred at a particular place and time, such as your memory of having seen McDonald's new range of hamburgers advertised on TV yesterday evening. In contrast semantic memory refers to the *'mental thesaurus, organized knowledge a person possesses about words and other verbal symbols, their meaning and referents, about relations among them, and about rules, formulas, and algorithms'* used to manipulate them (Tulving, 1983, p. 386). If you were asked to *remember* whether you have ever been in Paris, your episodic memory would be tested. If you were asked you whether you *knew* the name of the capital of France, your semantic memory would be assessed. Most people would not only know the name of the capital of France, but know much more about Paris, even though they would not remember the many episodes during which they acquired that knowledge. The foundations for this knowledge were probably laid during geography lessons in school and later filled up with information personally acquired through reading or visits to that city. Thus, *'semantic memories are the abstracted words, concepts, and rules stored in our long-term memory whose context of acquisition was long ago forgotten'* (Bower, 2000).

Free recall and recognition tests are considered standard tests of explicit memory. In *free recall tests*, respondents, who previously had to learn a list of words, are simply asked to recall as many of the recently presented words as possible. In *recognition tests*, memory of the (previously) learned words is assessed by presenting participants with a list of words consisting of words that had been presented in the earlier list intermixed with words that had not been presented and asking them to identify those words that had been presented earlier. Thus, in asking for intentional retrieval of material from a prior event, both these tests clearly require conscious recollection of a previous experience. In the field, these types of tests dominate the practice of testing advertising effectiveness, whereas tests of implicit memory (discussed next) are far less common.

Implicit memory

Implicit memory effects occur when previous experiences facilitate our performance of subsequent tasks without us remembering the previous experience or being aware of its influence on our performance. Although Herman Ebbinghaus (1885), the founding father of the experimental study of human learning and memory, was already aware of the existence of implicit memory, modern interest in this topic was triggered by research of Warrington and Weiskrantz (1970) with patients, who suffered from organic amnesia. Warrington and Weiskrantz showed that severely amnesic patients, who were unable to remember lists of words when tested with recall or recognition tests, nevertheless performed as well as healthy participants, when assessed with measures of implicit memory, such as word fragment identification or word stem completion tests (Figure 3.4).

In measures of implicit memory instructions refer only to the task at hand and make no reference to prior experiences (Richardson-Klavehn & Bjork, 1988). Thus, in *word stem completions*, participants are presented with the first few letters of each word that had been presented earlier (e.g. com____ for computer) and are asked to present the first word that comes to mind to complete the stem. With a *word fragment identification test*, participants are presented with a few letters of the word

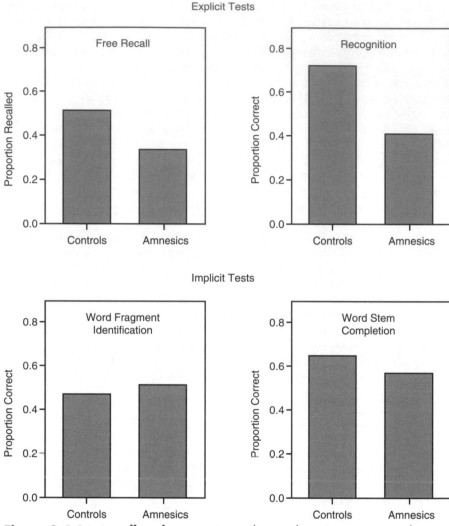

Figure 3.4 Priming effects for amnesics and normal participants on implicit and explicit tests

Source: Warrington & Weiskrantz (1970). Amnesic syndrome: consolidation or retrieval? *Nature, 228*, 629–630, Experiment 2. Reproduced with permission of Nature Publishing Group

(e.g. c_m_u_er) and are asked to name a word that fits (Baddeley, 1997). Other classic tests of implicit memory are *perceptual identification*, where participants who previously had been presented with a list of words are then presented with words from the list as well as other words at very *brief* exposure (e.g. 35 ms) and are asked to identify these words. Implicit memory effects are indicated by the fact that participants identify more of the words that had been previously presented than of the control words that had not been presented. With a *lexical decision task*, participants are either presented with words or non-word letter strings and are asked to decide as quickly as possible whether the presented item was a word or a non-word. Here we expect that lexical decisions about target words are made faster (or more quickly?) than about words that had not previously been presented. *Category instance generation* is a more conceptual measure of implicit memory. Here participants, who had previously learned a list of words, containing among others a set of animals are then asked to name as many animals as they can remember. Implicit memory would be indicated by producing items that had been on the previous list. Whereas these are all verbal tasks, non-verbal measures of implicit memory have also been used. For example, in picture fragment naming, participants are presented with fragments of the pictures they have learned in the first phase and are asked to identify these pictures.

As we have seen from our discussion of preattentive processing and incidental exposure to advertisements in chapter 2, the distinction between explicit and implicit memory effects is of great relevance for advertising research. Since few people expose themselves voluntarily and consciously to advertising messages, probably most advertising effects are due to incidental exposure to advertising. We try to ignore the banner ads that pop up on the internet sites we are studying, or the newspapers ads that interrupt the article we are reading. Even the buses, which pass us by have advertisements painted on their side. In chapter 2, we discussed several effects of this type of incidental exposure to advertisements and most of these effects are mediated by our implicit memory. That incidental ad exposure should result in implicit memory, whereas the content of ads to which we pay attention should be stored in explicit memory is reminiscent of the levels of processing assumption of Craik and Lockhart (1972).

Priming

The most widely used research strategy to demonstrate distinctions between explicit and implicit memory has been priming. Priming refers to the phenomenon that exposure to an object or a word in one context increases the accessibility of the mental representation of that object or word (i.e. the concept or schema) in a person's mind. As a result, the activated concept exerts for some time unintended influence on the individual's responses in subsequent unrelated contexts without the individual being aware of this influence (Bargh & Chartrand, 2000). It is important to note that this conception of priming implies the *existence* of concepts within memory that represent familiar objects or words. When the object or word is presented, this representation will be activated or primed (Baddeley, 1997).

One of the key findings of research on priming, which illustrates the distinction between explicit and implicit memory, is the differential impact of manipulations of processing depth on measures of explicit and implicit memory. In a classic study conducted by Jacoby (1983) depth of processing was manipulated by showing the target words during the first part of the experiment (study phases) either without context (e.g. 'cold'), with the opposite as context (e.g. 'cold–warm') or showing the opposite of the target word, asking participants to generate the target (e.g. 'warm' was shown, and 'cold' had to be generated). Obviously having to generate the target word requires much deeper processing than simply seeing it visually presented. Subsequently memory was either tested with a recognition test (explicit memory) or a perceptual identification test (implicit memory). As one would expect, the performance on the explicit memory test, was worst in the 'no context' and best in 'generate' condition. After all, one is less likely to remember a word, if one has only seen it once than if one had to think of the word oneself. The surprising finding was that the opposite was true for implicit memory, where performance was best when the word had been presented without a context and worst when it had been generated by the participants themselves (Figure 3.5). As further research demonstrated, this type of visual priming is *modality specific*. Priming is considerably reduced or even absent when the target material is in presented auditory form or when participants study

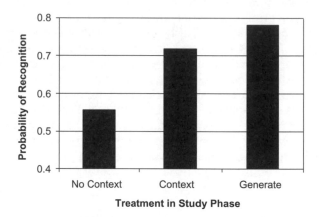

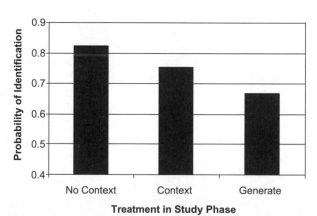

Figure 3.5 Recognition and perceptual identification for words self-generated or shown without context tested with implicit and explicit tests

Source: Adapted from Jacoby (1983). Remembering the data: analyzing interactive processes in reading. *Journal of Verbal Learning and Verbal Behavior. 22*, 485–508, Experiment 2. Reproduced with permission of Elsevier

pictorial equivalents of words. There is also little cross-language priming (Schacter, Chiu & Ochsner, 1993).

Another groundbreaking priming study was conducted by Higgins, Rholes and Jones (1977), who demonstrated that priming could not only increase the accessibility of single concrete lexical memory location corresponding to the stimulus word, but could also activate abstract trait concepts. In the first phase of this study (again presented as an apparently unrelated experiment) participants were either exposed to negative personality terms 'reckless', 'conceited', 'aloof', 'stubborn' or to positive terms such as 'adventurous', 'self-confident', 'independent', 'persistent'. Then in a second and apparently unrelated 'reading comprehension study', they were given a paragraph describing a man called Donald. Although Donald was described as 'always in search of excitement', the description was sufficiently ambiguous to allow positive as well as negative interpretations of his behaviour. Participants, who were asked to form an overall impression of Donald were strongly influenced by the personality traits to which they had been exposed during the earlier 'independent' experiment. They were much more likely to perceive Donald's behaviour in a negative light, if they had been exposed to negative rather than positive personality traits. However, these effects occurred only when the traits were relevant for the interpretation of Donald's behavior (i.e. applicable). Positive (e.g. obedient, neat) or negative (e.g. disrespectful, listless) traits that were not applicable to the behaviour had no effect on overall impression.

In a replication of this study in a consumer context, Herr (1989) used a word puzzle to supraliminally prime the cognitive accessibility of a (price) category of cars. Participants were exposed to a 20-by-20 matrix of letters with words embedded in them which they were to find and circle. Four conditions were thus created. In one group brands of extremely inexpensive automobiles were hidden (such as Chevy Chevette and Ford Pinto), the second type of puzzle included moderately inexpensive cars (e.g. Ford Escort, Chevy Citation), the third included moderately expensive cars (e.g. Pontiac Grand Prix, Mazda RX-7), and the fourth condition included brands of extremely expensive cars (e.g. Mercedez Benz and Porsche). In line with the scrambled sentence task, Herr's (1989) procedure was aimed at priming certain concepts; in the present study the concepts of extremely inexpensive, moderately inexpensive, moderately expensive and extremely expensive automobiles. In an ostensibly unrelated second study, participants were then exposed to an advertisement for another car and were required to rate the price of the target automobile. The ads either featured an unambiguous car (where make and model could be easily identified) or an ambiguous car where make and model information were omitted. Herr (1989) observed an assimilation effect for the ambiguous car: people tended to rate the car in accordance with the prime. Hence, participants exposed to the word puzzle with (extremely) inexpensive car brands embedded in them, rated the ambiguous car as cheaper than participants exposed to the word puzzle with the more expensive car brands. Since participants in the ambiguous condition had little information about the car, they assimilated it into the category that had been made accessible during priming. However, when the car was clearly identifiable (i.e. individuating information was available), the primed category would be used as a standard of comparison and contrast effects were found: Participants rated the car as cheaper when they had previously been exposed to more expensive car brands in the word puzzle or as more expensive, when cheaper brands had been primed.

Like all earlier research, Higgins et al. (1977) and Herr (1989) used supraliminal priming. In *supraliminal priming* the participant is exposed to the priming stimuli as part of a *conscious* task. For example, participants in the study of Higgins and colleagues were shown the priming words (and a number of other words) on variously coloured slides. Although their task was to indicate the colour of the slides rather than to read the words, they were fully aware of these words. Higgins and colleagues assumed, and probably correctly so, that participants were not aware of the underlying pattern or the connection between the priming words and the evaluation of Donald. Hence they are aware of the stimulus, but not its influence.

If researchers want to be certain that participants are unaware of the connection between priming stimuli and subsequent task, they can present priming stimuli subliminally. With *subliminal priming*, the priming stimuli are presented at such a brief exposure that participants remain unaware that any stimulus has been presented. To make sure that the prime stimulus does not linger on in the individual's iconic short-term memory and thus be recognized despite the brief exposure, presentation of the priming stimulus is immediately followed by a letter string, a so-called post mask. (Usually it is also preceded by a letter string. There will also be a fixation point to ascertain that participants focus on the exact space where the priming stimulus will be presented.) With very brief exposure (in presentation in the centre of the visual field usually between 20 to 40 milliseconds) and good masking, participants typically perceive hardly a flash. Nevertheless, the impact of such subliminally presented primes can be similar to that of primes that are presented supraliminally (Bargh & Chartrand, 2000). This has first been demonstrated by Bargh and Pietromonaco (1982) in a conceptual replication of the Donald study. Subliminal presentation of personality traits had a significant effect on the evaluation of Donald.[2] In the meantime a vast number of studies have demonstrated the effectiveness of subliminal primes (for a recent review, see Bargh, 2006).

The finding that subliminal presentation of words or pictures can prime mental representations of words or objects in a person's mind raises the possibility that such procedures could be used effectively in advertising. This is probably a surprising suggestion, because subliminal advertising, after a brief period in the limelight in 1957, was declared as not feasible by more recent authors (e.g. Moore, 1982; Pratkanis & Aronson, 2001). We will discuss the possibility of subliminal advertising later in chapter 6.

Knowledge structures in long-term memory

As we mentioned earlier, to be stored in long-term memory, our perceptions of stimuli and events need to be *interpreted* and *encoded* into some form of cognitive representation. Although the distinction between perception and encoding are fuzzy, encoding usually relies on some kind of prior knowledge. An individual succeeds in the encoding task by relating the stimulus to previous knowledge, by 'recognizing' that the stimulus belongs to a particular category. *Categories* are the most elementary knowledge structure reflecting a class of objects that we believe belongs together (e.g. product categories, such as cars, light beers, breakfast cereals, etc.). By categorizing a stimulus as a chair, a knife or a car, we assign meaning to that stimulus and save ourselves the necessity to have to think about the properties and functions of that object. Thus, once we have assigned an object to a particular category, we go beyond the information given, make inferences about various functions and properties of that object, which go far beyond our perception (Bruner, 1957). For example, if we have categorized a vague shape standing under heap of snow in front of our house as a car, we assume that it has four wheels, an engine, and potentially could be driven away, even though none of these properties are visible.

There is still discussion about how categories are represented in our memory. An early classical view assumed that categories should be represented as a set of *defining features* that apply to all category members. As anybody who ever tried to define a natural category is likely to have realized, the problem is that most natural categories cannot be defined in terms of such features. Furthermore, if category membership were determined by a set of defining features, it would be difficult to explain why some members of a category are more typical than others. For example, chickens or penguins are much less typical for the category of birds than are robins. More recently, therefore, a probabilistic or prototype view of category representation has become accepted that conceives of categories as a list of features, which are typical for the category but not necessarily defining it (Rosch, 1973). Different features may be more or less diagnostic of a category. This view assumes that people abstract category prototypes from their experience with different category members and then classify exemplars on the basis of their similarity to the prototype (Smith, 1999). If concepts are formed around prototypes, then different exemplars will vary in their typicality that is in how closely they match the prototype.

Cognitive psychologists have developed several other terms to refer to more complex units that people use to interpret and encode their perceptions of the world around them. Thus, *scripts* refer to abstract knowledge structures that describe standardized sequences of events and the interrelationship between different (role-) categories (Abelson, 1981). For example, if in a restaurant, we assign a person to the category of waiter, we know that this is the person, with whom to order one's food or to pay the bill. Although some of this information is already contained in the category of 'waiter', we also rely on the restaurant script to derive these predictions. The importance of scripts in guiding our behaviour becomes most apparent when one travels abroad, because cultures or even countries may differ in terms of the scripts that apply to specific situations. For example, in many restaurants in Europe, guests entering a restaurant may directly go to a table that is unoccupied (and without a sign indicating that it is reserved). This would be a norm violation in the USA, often punished by not being served. In the USA a hostess has to be approached, who will lead the guest to a table. Similarly, American restaurants practise a division of labour between waiters that is unfamiliar to Europeans. Thus, the waiters who fill up water glasses in the USA are not taking orders for food or drinks.

Knowledge stored in memory does not consist of isolated bits, but of a network of associations between these items. Although categories represent mini networks of objects that are associated with various features, and scripts are descriptions of the interrelationship between a set of a small number of specific categories, cognitive psychologists have developed more general models that not only describe how categories are represented and interrelated but also the processes through which knowledge may be activated and retrieved (Kunda, 1999). One form of models that has been widely used in memory research are associative network models (e.g. Collins & Loftus, 1975). These models conceive of mental representations of each isolated piece of knowledge as a discrete 'node' connected to other nodes by 'links' of various types. Depending on the specific model, a node may represent a specific category/concept or an attribute. Each concept or attribute is represented by a node. Thus, in the associative network representing our knowledge about drinks, there will be nodes for concepts such as soft drinks, beer, cola, etc., but also for attributes such as 'dry', 'thirst-quenching' and 'tasty'. These concepts and attributes are connected to each other through links. These links are formed (or strengthened, if they already exist) through a process of contiguity. They are formed (or strengthened) whenever items are experienced or thought about together. For example, the link between 'beer' and 'thirst-quenching' may have originally been formed, when an individual drinking his or her first beer experienced this beverage as particularly thirst-quenching. After that, it would have been strengthened every time she/he thinks how thirst-quenching a beer would be or sees an advertisement making this point. Links can vary in strength, but their strength changes only slowly over time (Smith, 1999). In contrast, the level of *activation* of nodes can vary rapidly over time and varies from occasion to occasion (Smith, 1999). When a node is activated because it is actively thought about or perceptually present, this activation spreads to other nodes via the connecting links. Thus, if an individual is *primed* with the word 'thirst-quenching', the activation would spread to all the concepts connected to this feature and their recognition threshold for these concepts would be lowered. Similarly, if one is exceedingly thirsty and thinking about quenching one's thirst, the activation will spread to all the drinks associated with thirst-quenching and the drink, which has the strongest associations with thirst quenching, is most likely to come to mind. Thus the more activated a node is, the more likely it is that it will burst into awareness, be recalled, or be applied to incoming information. In terms of these models, long term memory is assumed to be a single large associative network and short-term memory is considered as the currently activated subset of this network (Smith, 1999).

Implications for advertising

In this second part of the chapter, we will apply the findings of memory research discussed in the first section more specifically to advertising. We will discuss five areas of advertising research, where application of work on memory has been particularly fruitful.

The role of memory in judgements: on the ineffectiveness of traditional measures of advertising effectiveness

One of the standard strategies marketers use to measure the effectiveness of an advertising campaign is to contact consumers, who were exposed to the ad and ask them what they *remember* about the ad or about the advertised product (i.e. recall test), or they might be shown the advertisement and asked whether they *recognize* it (i.e. recognition test). The reasonable assumption underlying this procedure is that people's product judgements (i.e. their attitude towards the advertised product) should be related to their recollection of the evidence on which those judgements are presumably based (i.e. the advertisement). This assumption is incorrect and measures of advertising efficacy based on this assumption are likely to be misleading for at least two reasons. First, as discussed in chapter 2, exposure to advertisements can impact on implicit memory and these effects may not be detectable with measures of explicit memory. Therefore using only recall or recognition measures might result in an underestimation of the impact of a campaign on memory. Second, and more importantly, recollection of arguments made in a campaign may be unrelated to consumers' attitude towards the advertised product, because the targets of advertising campaigns may change their product judgements online, while being exposed to the campaign. As a result, they might be influenced by arguments, even if they cannot remember them, or they might still remember arguments, even though they considered them invalid. We will discuss both of these possibilities in the following two sections.

Implicit memory and the measurement of ad effectiveness

As we discussed in chapter 2, a great deal of advertising exposure is incidental and the advertisements are unlikely to influence explicit memory. Nevertheless, such incidental exposure is likely to leave a trace on implicit memory. This has been demonstrated in a study of the impact of internet banner ads by Yoo (2008). Participants in this study were exposed to three web pages, each page being opened for 45 seconds. Two test banner advertisements and two filler ads (developed by a professional graphics designer) were used. Whereas participants in the control group were exposed to these web pages without the banner ads, ads were included for the two experimental groups on all three web pages, with the test banner ad always appearing on the second web page. There were two attention conditions: Participants in the directed attention condition were told to evaluate the web page in terms of design, content, and usability (directed attention condition). Participants in the non-directed attention condition were led to believe that their understanding of the content of the web page would be tested. This latter condition constituted a realistic simulation of the motivation of the average web user, who surfs the web in search for specific information and not in order to be exposed to advertisements. Implicit memory was assessed with word stem completion tests. Explicit memory was tested with a recognition task, where participants had to select the one banner ad they had been exposed to during the experiment from three ads (one target and three new filler ads).

As expected, participants in both experimental conditions did significantly better than the non-exposure control group on the implicit memory task (word stem completion test). Participants in the two experimental conditions also acquired equally positive attitudes towards the brand, with both groups being significantly more positive than the control group. However, with the ad recognition measure, a big difference emerged between the two experimental groups: The directed attention group did much better than the non-directed attention group and the control group on the measure of ad recognition. In fact, ad recognition of the non-directed attention group did not differ significantly from those of the control group. Even though participants who had concentrated on reading the web text did not remember having seen the banner ads, their attitudes were influenced as much as those of the group that had been instructed to pay attention to the advertisements. Thus, if one had based the evaluation of the impact of the banner ads only on the measure of explicit memory, one would have falsely concluded that these advertisements had been ineffective.

A study by Shapiro and Krishnan (2001) resulted in a similar pattern. Simulating the more conventional TV situation, this study played an audio tape while exposing participants to 12 target and 12 distracter ads, all using fictitious brand names. Attention was manipulated by telling half the participants to focus on the ads and to ignore the audio tape (full attention), whereas the other half were told to focus on the ads, but also listen to the audio tape. They expected to be tested on their knowledge of the programme later (divided attention). In addition to the attention manipulation there was also a delay manipulation: For half the participants the effect of ad exposure was tested immediately (after a brief unrelated filler task), for the other half it was tested one week later (delay condition).

Explicit memory was measured with a recognition task, with participants being asked to choose the correct brand name from two alternatives offered for each 12 target product categories. The implicit memory measure used the same 12 target test product categories and the same two product items for each category as the explicit memory measure. However, twelve distracter categories were added, increasing to 24 the number of product categories offered. Participants were asked to circle for each product category the brand they would like to choose, with no reference being made to the advertisements. Thus, no active search in memory for the previously seen brand name was required.

An analysis of variance conducted on the ad recognition measure of explicit memory resulted in two main effects: recognition was poorer when attention was divided (rather than undivided) and when assessment was delayed (rather than immediate). Tests on the recognition measure against chance revealed that even with divided attention ad exposure significantly influenced ad recognition, but only if there was no delay. After the delay, the effect of ad exposure could no longer be detected. That the divided attention instruction did not eliminate the (immediate) ad exposure effect on ad recognition was probably due to instructions. After all, even with divided attention, participants had been asked to pay attention to the advertisements.

For the measure of *implicit* memory, a markedly different pattern emerged. A comparison of the experimental conditions against the control condition that was not exposed to the advertisements, indicated that exposure to advertisements had a significant effect on the implicit memory measure in all experimental conditions. Furthermore, the analysis of variance revealed that neither the delay nor the attention manipulation had a significant effect on implicit memory. Thus, the effect of ad exposure on implicit memory was as strong under divided as under undivided attention and as strong after a week as it had been when tested immediately

Furthermore, in line with conclusions from the experiment of Yoo (2008) the study of Shapiro and Krishnan shows that sole use of measures of explicit memory to assess the effectiveness of advertising is likely to result in an underestimation of the impact of advertising campaigns on memory. However, as we will argue in the next section, assessing the impact of a campaign on memory, whether implicit or explicit, is not an adequate measure of the effectiveness of an advertisement campaign. After all, the aim of such campaigns is to change consumer attitude towards the product in order to increase the probability that they will buy it. Thus, attitude change achieved by a campaign, rather than memory for arguments contained in the advertisements should be the indicator on which an evaluation of campaign effectiveness should be based. And as we will argue in the next section, the change in attitudes achieved by a communication is often unrelated to the arguments that are remembered.

Memory-based versus online judgments

For many decades, social psychologists assumed that an individual's memory of the arguments contained in a communication would be a good indication of the impact of that communication on their attitudes (Eagly & Chaiken, 1993). There were sound theoretical reasons for this assumption. For example, McGuire's (e.g. 1985) information processing theory of persuasion, one of the early cognitive theories of attitude change, assumed that the change induced by a persuasive communication would be determined by the reception of the arguments contained in that communication (chapter 5). However, empirical tests of this assumption typically demonstrated that message reception, when measured by *recall* of message arguments, was more or less unrelated to attitude change (for a review see Eagly & Chaiken, 1993).

There are a number of reasons why such correlations are typically not obtained. One reason highlighted in a classic article by Hastie and Park (1986) is the distinction between *online* versus *memory-based judgments*. In many situations, we are presented with information, which motivates us to form our judgement at the time we are taking in the information. For example, in most research on impression formation, participants are presented with a series of traits descriptions in order to form an impression of the stimulus person. Participants typically integrate this information immediately into an overall evaluation. Once the impression has been formed, there is little purpose for them to remember all the traits on which their impression had been based.

Similarly, when reading various advertisements about different brands of a product, we are planning to buy, we will probably form an opinion while reading the information. Thus, if we read ads in a computer journal, because we intend to buy a computer, we will probably try to reach a decision, or at least to arrive at a limited consideration set, while we are taking in the information. It is therefore unlikely that we will later remember all the advantages and disadvantages of the different computers we had read about. Furthermore, we are likely to elaborate on some of the information and dismiss other parts and our decision will be based on our reactions to this information rather than the information as it had been presented. Thus, when we make online judgments, integrating the information while we are exposed to it, our evaluations could be relatively unrelated to the product claims, even though we would still be able to recall them at some later time. The situation would be different, if, when reading the various advertisements, we had no intention to buy a computer. If a few days later a friend would ask us advise him on buying a computer, our judgement would be more memory-based. We would probably try to retrieve all the information we had read in the computer magazine and form an evaluation on the basis of the recalled information.

Hastie and Park (1986) tested these assumptions about the different informational bases of online and memory-based decisions in an experiment (Experiment 1) in which participants had to judge the suitability of a man's qualification as computer programmer after hearing a taped conversation between two men. Half of the participants were told beforehand that they had to make this judgement, the other half were only informed of this task after having listened to the tape. After listening to the conversation, all participants had to make the suitability ratings and then recall as much information from the conversation as they could. Results supported predictions. When participants knew beforehand that they had to make this judgement (online task), the correlation between recalled information and evaluation was non significant. In contrast, when participants did not know of this task and had to make the evaluation after having listened to the tape, a considerable correlation emerged between recall and evaluation. Similar findings were reported by Mackie and Ascuncion (1990), who provided participants exposed to a persuasive communication with different processing goals, which either encouraged the online formation of an overall evaluation or discouraged them from making such an evaluation (by asking them to proofread the material or to memorize it). When participants were later asked to indicate their attitude towards the issue argued in the communication, attitudes were only related to recall of arguments for participants, who had been prevented from forming an attitude online (i.e. proofreading or memory goal).

It is important to note that the lack of correlation between recall and judgement in these studies does not imply that after having made their judgements online, participants immediately forgot the information on which they based this evaluation. Since participants, who have been asked to arrive at an online evaluation might often be motivated to process information more deeply, it is even likely that they may have better recall for that information than individuals, who had no particular reason to pay attention to the information they were exposed to. In fact, in the study of Mackie and Asuncion (1990), which we described earlier, the manipulation of processing goals had no impact on recall. So why are the evaluations of individuals who make online judgments unrelated to argument recall? One reason already mentioned earlier (to be discussed in greater detail in our review of dual process theories of attitude change in chapter 5) is that individuals, who are trying to form an evaluation while listening to information, are more likely to elaborate the information they are given. In evaluating the product, they will rely more heavily on their own reactions and elaborations of the original information than on the information itself.

But findings of a study by Kardes (1986) suggest that elaboration of arguments may not be the only reasons for the lack of a relationship between argument recall and product judgement. Kardes presented his participants with information about a stereo set. The set was described either as high in sound quality and low in performance or high in performance and low in sound quality. Cross-cutting this manipulation, respondents subsequently had to rate the set either in terms of sound quality or in terms of dependability. The aim of the manipulation of the judgement task was to motivate participants to either focus on performance- or dependability-related information. In a second session, participants were asked to give a global evaluation of the set, to indicate their purchase intention, and to recall all the product information they had been given during the first session. As expected, participants who had been induced to focus on the negative aspects of the stereo set gave a less positive global evaluation than participants, who had been induced to focus on the positive aspects. More interestingly, however, recall of product information was uncorrelated with the global evaluation and with intention to purchase the set. In contrast, the global evaluation showed a substantial correlation with purchase intention.

But this is not the whole story. In the second session, these participants were also asked to rate the set on eight specific attribute dimensions which were relevant to sound quality or dependability. When these ratings were aggregated into two scales, a dependability scale and a performance scale, these ratings correlated significantly with information recall. Thus, when they were asked to judge the set on the specific performance and dependability dimensions that had been mentioned in the information they had been given, they were quite capable of retrieving this information when making their judgements.

Kardes (1986) draws on Carlston's (1980) dual coding explanation to interpret these findings. According to Carlston individuals store both the original information about the attributes of the products (attribute-based representation) as well as their evaluations based on this elaboration (evaluation-based representation) in separate representations. Each of these representations may be used independently in subsequent judgements. Kardes (1986) concludes that the 'results of the present study suggest that an evaluation-based representation is retrieved for use in making subsequent global memory-based judgments, whereas an attribute-based representation is retrieved for use in making subsequent discrete memory-based judgments' (p. 8). Since it is the global judgements that predict purchase intentions, we have to agree with Kardes' (1986) conclusion that 'measures of memory for descriptive information are poor measures of advertising effectiveness' (p. 9).

Memory factors in brand choice: the role of cognitive accessibility

It is a truism that brand awareness is a necessary precondition for choice: unless consumers are aware of the existence of a brand, they cannot choose that brand (Lavidge & Steiner, 1961). However, consumers rarely consider all the brands they are aware of in making purchasing decisions (and their 'awareness set' is typically smaller than the total number of brands available in the marketplace). They limit themselves to a much smaller *consideration set*, usually consisting of three to seven alternatives (Hauser & Wernerfelt, 1990). The consideration set is defined 'as the set of brands brought to mind in a particular choice situation' (Nedungadi, 1990, p. 264). In this section, we will focus on the role of cognitive accessibility of a brand name as determinant of brand consideration and brand choice.

Purchase situations vary in the extent to which they encourage more *memory-based*[3] or more *stimulus-based* strategies. For example, if we buy a car, we usually have a clear idea about the car we want to buy before we approach a car dealer. Since Mercedes dealers sell only Mercedes and Volkswagen dealers only Volkswagens, it would actually be rather futile to walk into dealerships at random. Most car buyers are therefore likely to have made their decision about the car they want to buy (or formed a consideration set of alternatives) on the basis of information about price, performance, space, etc., long before they enter a car dealership. Thus buying a car is typically a memory-based decision. In shopping in the local supermarket, on the other hand, we often have to follow a different strategy. Our partners may have sent us with shopping lists that merely state product categories rather than brands. Thus, we are supposed to come back with a pack of margarine, a bottle of olive oil and a pound of flour, with the choice between brands for each category left open. Our purchase decisions in this situation would therefore be largely stimulus based.

In the case of memory-based choices the composition of the consideration set will be strongly influenced by the cognitive accessibility of brands on that particular occasion (Nedungadi, 1990). But even in cases of stimulus-based choices, cognitive accessibility of brand names will influence the set of brands considered, because highly accessible brands are likely to attract more attention and to seem more familiar (Lee, 2002; Shapiro, McInnis & Heckler, 1997).

Lee (2002) recently published a series of studies which tested the influence of implicit memory on memory-based and stimulus-based brand choices. In line with the research on implicit and explicit memory discussed earlier (e.g. Jacoby, 1983), she reasoned that differences in conceptual elaboration should have greater impact on memory-based than stimulus-based choices. She manipulated the degree of conceptual elaboration by presenting brands either as single words (e.g. 'Heineken') or as part of a sentence ('He put the case of Heineken in the trunk of his car'). To demonstrate that this type of manipulation has a differential impact on measures of explicit and implicit memory, she conducted a study, in which participants were presented with 12 brand names, either embedded in sentences or as single words. As expected, assessment of explicit and implicit memory in a first experiment, showed that sentences were better remembered in measures of explicit memory (e.g. a cued recall test), whereas words in isolation led to better performance on measures of implicit memory (e.g. word fragments).

More importantly, however, a second experiment demonstrated that these manipulations have a differential impact on memory-based compared to stimulus-based brand choices. For reasons to be discussed below, she did not use product categories such as beers, which are characterized by strong preference hierarchies in her second experiment, but selected product categories for which participants had no strong brand preference (toothbrushes, chewing gum, candy bars and cough drops). In the memory-based brand choice, participants were presented with several product categories and asked to indicate their preferred brand for each category. For example, they were provided with the category 'candy bar' and asked to write down the brand they would most like their convenience store to stock. In the stimulus-based brand choice, participants were provided with two brands for each category (one target brand and one filler) and were asked to circle the brand they would like their convenience store to stock. In line with her predictions, memory-based choices benefited more when the brand name was presented in a context that encouraged elaboration (i.e. as part of a sentence), whereas stimulus based choice benefited more when the brand name was presented in an isolated context.

Priming a brand name increases the cognitive accessibility of that brand name. With totally unfamiliar brand names, priming can increase liking by increasing processing fluency (chapter 2). With more familiar brands, priming is unlikely to result in further increase of fluency. With those brands, unless the prime contains positive persuasive information in addition to the brand logo or brand name, it is unlikely to influence the evaluation of that brand. Since brand choice typically reflects evaluation (i.e. revealed preference), it is surprising that the priming manipulation in Lee's study increased the probability of a brand being chosen. There are two aspects of that study which are likely to have contributed to this effect. First, one could doubt that the decision to want one's local supermarket to stock a certain brand is psychologically the same as purchasing that brand. Since there are likely to be many other places, where participants could buy these items, their recommendation might be more of the nature of a brand consideration than a brand choice. Second, as Lee (2002) cautioned herself, consumers' brand choices will only be influenced by accessibility if they do not have a strong preference for a particular brand or if their preferred brand is not available. In fact, the product categories used in Lee's experiment had been particularly chosen because most participants had indicated that they were quite willing to switch brands if their preferred brand was not available. Lee's (2002) warning points therefore to a serious limitation on the generalizeability of her findings. Thus, increasing the cognitive accessibility of the brand name of Heineken beer (without some additional statements about the positive qualities of that beer) is unlikely to motivate people who prefer a different brand to choose Heineken, unless the bar they find themselves in does not stock their favourite brand of beer.

In addition to increasing the accessibility of the primed brand name, priming can also increase the accessibility of closely associated brands and of the product category to which the brand belongs. This is most likely to happen if the brand is prototypical for the product category and if that particular product category was previously not highly accessible in the individual's mind. This has been demonstrated by Nedungadi (1990) in a study that made use of the fact that his Canadian student participants typically thought of hamburger restaurants when asked to think of fast food restaurants. Restaurants that served only chicken were much less likely to be considered. When specifically asked to list chicken restaurants, a chain called Swiss Chalet (rather than Kentucky Fried Chicken) was the most accessible and preferred brand. Least accessible was a chain called St Hubert. Thus, the memory structure of these participants for fast food restaurants was divided into several categories, with hamburger restaurants being the most accessible and chicken restaurants one of the less accessible categories. And within the category of chicken restaurants, Swiss Chalet was the most and St Hubert the least accessible brand.

Under the guise of having to rate the appropriateness of a set of ads for different types of magazines, participants in the priming condition were exposed to a mock-up trade ad for St Hubert. The ad described the ability of St Hubert's to increase franchise owners' profits and thus *said nothing about the quality of the food served in these restaurants*. In the control condition, participants saw a similar trade ad for a carbonated soft drink. After having completed this task, participants were told that they could have a $1 coupon for a fast food place of their own choice as reward for their participation. They were asked to note down the name for the fast food outlet for which they would like the coupon (choice). Just in case coupons for their preferred restaurant were no longer available, they were also asked to write down the names of other fast food restaurants they might potentially consider (consideration set). After that, brand accessibility was assessed with a word-fragment completion task.

Finally, participants were provided with a list of fast food restaurants and had to indicate their liking for these places.

The priming manipulation did not only increase the accessibility of St Hubert but also of Swiss Chalet. It also increased the probability of both St Hubert (from 0 to 12 per cent) and Swiss Chalet (from 32 to 43 per cent) being included in the consideration set. Thus, memory factors do not only increase the retrieval of a target brand but also that of similar competitors. However, priming only resulted in a significant increase of the probability of Swiss Chalet to be chosen (from 4 to 12 per cent) but not of St Hubert (from 0 to 4 per cent). Finally, priming did not increase participants' liking for either St Hubert or Swiss Chalet. It had no effect on the evaluation of any of these restaurants.

How can we explain these findings? When Canadian students consider fast food restaurants, they tend to think about places which serve hamburgers rather than chicken. Priming them with the brand name of a chicken restaurant therefore did not only increase the accessibility of that particular restaurant, but also of the category of chicken restaurants. Once some participants began to consider chicken restaurants for their fast food dinner, they decided on Swiss Chalet rather than St Hubert, because that was the most positively evaluated restaurant within that particular category. Thus, although the majority of participants still decided to go to a hamburger place, (indirectly) priming the category of chicken restaurants appeared to have induced 8 per cent of participants to choose Swiss Chalet for dinner instead of their usual hamburger joint. Because this effect is likely to have even been stronger if Swiss Chalet had been primed directly, priming of a minor product category can influence product choice. Thus, by reminding individuals that there is an attractive but non-obvious choice alternative, some individuals are likely to choose this alternative, which they would not have thought of unaided.

Under certain conditions even mere exposure to a brand name can increase evaluation by increasing processing fluency (chapters 2, 4). But these effects are limited to stimuli that are unfamiliar. Since the brand name of St Hubert, though not highly familiar, was well-known to participants of this study, mere exposure was unlikely to increase liking for this brand. To improve participants' attitudes towards St Hubert restaurants, the advertisement about St Hubert would therefore have had to contain information relevant for restaurant choice (e.g. about the quality of the food or service). Because the mock-up trade ad about St Hubert did not contain such information, it is not surprising that it did not influence participants' evaluation of this restaurant. Even though the priming manipulation might have induced participants to dine at St Hubert's, if it had been one of a number of equally attractive chicken restaurants. It was the bad luck of St Hubert, or more likely to lack advertising, that participants clearly preferred Swiss Chalet.

To conclude, the set of brands consumers consider when deciding on a purchase is typically not only smaller than the total number of brands available in the market-place but also smaller than the number of brands of which the consumer is aware (Shapiro, MacInnis & Heckler, 1997). The important contribution of the study of Lee (2002) was her demonstration in a consumer context that different types of priming procedures have a differential impact on brand choices that are memory-based as compared to stimulus-based. Thus priming that required a greater degree of conceptual elaboration was more effective for memory-based choices but was less effective when choice was stimulus-based. In the latter case, exposure to the brand name as a single word was most effective. Increasing accessibility of a brand name through priming is likely to influence only the inclusion of a brand in consumers' considerations sets rather than their purchasing decisions (Coates et al., 2004). However, under certain conditions priming can also influence purchasing decisions, namely (1) when individuals have no particular preference for a specific brand (Lee, 2002), (2) when their preferred brand is not available or (3) when an attractive, but less accessible subcategory of a given product category has been primed (Nedungadi, 1990).

Forgetting the message: advertising clutter and competitive interference

That memory fades with the passage of time is nearly a truism: there is a strong positive relationship between forgetting and the passage of time (Baddeley, 1997). However, the passage of time (i.e. the decay of memory traces) is not the only reason why we forget things (Baddeley, 1997). Forgetting is also influenced by our experiences in the period between exposure to information and recall. Forgetting appears to be accelerated if this period is filled with exposure to a great deal of competing information from the same content domain. Explanations of forgetting as due to competing information have become known as interference theories.

That exposure to similar material can interfere with people's memory for material they have already learned has been known to memory researchers for a long time. To describe one classic experiment, McGeoch and McDonald (1931) had research participants, who had learnt a list of adjectives to perfection, subsequently learn new materials that varied in similarity to the original list. They found that the interpolated learning interfered with the recall of the original material and that the degree of interference increased with increasing similarity between the two lists. Learning nonsense syllables after meaningful adjectives resulted in much less interference than learning synonyms. This effect of later learnt material on earlier learning is known as *retroactive interference*.

However, it is not only so that later learnt material interferes with earlier learning; what we have learnt earlier can also interfere with later learning, a phenomenon known as *proactive interference*. A classic study of proactive interference was reported by Underwood (1957), who was puzzled by the extent to which his participants forgot lists of perfectly learnt nonsense syllables during a 24-hour period. Since he did a great number of experiments with nonsense syllables and since the same undergraduate students usually participated in several of his experiments, it occurred to Underwood that the apparent forgetfulness of his participants might be due to interference of material learnt in previous experiments with the material learnt later. When he plotted the amount forgotten by his participants as a function of previous participation in nonsense syllable experiments, he found a clear relationship. The more previous experiments participants had endured, the greater was their forgetting during a 24-hour period.

With hundreds of products advertised daily, proactive and retroactive interference on TV are likely to be rampant. The extent to which multiple messages compete for the consumer's attention has become known as *advertising clutter*. And indeed, according to one report, nearly one in every four minutes of US primetime television now features a commercial or other non-programming message (Downey, 2002). The problem is even worse in daytime television, which has roughly 20 minutes of non-programming every hour. No wonder that viewers exposed to this clutter protect themselves by tuning out, switching channels, replenishing their drinks or going to the bathroom. But even if they pay attention to the advertisements, the sheer volume of information could impair their ability to remember the advertised brand characteristics. We discussed the role of attention in chapter 2. In this chapter, we will discuss the impact of competitive interference on consumer memory for advertising (e.g. Burke & Srull, 1988; Keller, 1987, 1991).

Competitive interference and memory for advertisements

The study of the effect of competitive interference on memory for advertisements has a long history (e.g. Blankenship & Whitely, 1941; McKinney, 1935). However, one of the most systematic studies of these effects was initiated more recently by Burke and Srull (1988). Based on the reasonable assumption that consumers organize information about the attributes of a product by brand name, these authors argued that additional attribute information about a competing brand would impair the consumers' ability to recall old information about the characteristics of this brand. To test this hypothesis, participants were shown (and asked to make judgements about) 12 one-page ads of brands with which participants were unfamiliar. Three of these advertisements were designed as target ads and were later tested for recall. Competitive interference was manipulated by either presenting the target ads in a varied-product context, with other ads promoting different products, or in a same-brand context, with a second ad promoting a product in the same product class. Since the crucial context ads were presented after the target ads, the study tested the impact of retroactive interference.

Burke and Srull (1988) also manipulated processing goals, by asking half their participants to judge each ad in terms of the likelihood that they would buy the particular product. The other half was instructed merely to evaluate the interest value of each ad. Burke and Srull (1988) assumed that their manipulation of processing goals would influence processing depth. Deeper processing was assumed to make the mental representation of the product information less susceptible to retrieval interference. Recall was assessed following an interpolated task. Participants were presented with the brand name and product class designation of each of the target ads and had to report all the information they could recall about the ad (i.e. cued recall). There was evidence of a great deal of competitive interference when target ads were presented with ads of brands from the same product class, but only for participants, who merely had to evaluate interest value. The recall of participants, who had to think about a purchase decision, was not affected by competing information. This finding tends to support the levels of processing interpretation. In a second experiment, Burke and Srull (1988) presented the competing (and non-competing) information before the target ads to assess the impact of *proactive* interference. There was again evidence for interference of competitive ads on recall of product information, but this time the effect was equally strong under both goal orientations. The authors suggest that this could be due to the short time between exposure and testing. Proactive interference effects appear to increase with the passage of time.

In the experiments of Burke and Srull (1988) the similarity between target ad and competitive information was manipulated by exposing participants to information about competing brands in the same product class rather than brands of different product classes. Thus, if we see three different washing machines advertised on TV in one evening, we are less likely to remember the claims made for each of these machines than if only one type of machine had been advertised. However, as Kumar and Krishnan (2004) pointed out, there are other sources of interference, which can also impair recall of advertising claims. One such source is similarity of advertising *execution*. To test this assumption, Kumar and Krishnan (2004) exposed his participants to eight advertisements, of which six were the same in all conditions. The two other ads consisted of the target ad (brand of suntan lotion) and the interfering ad (brand of ice tea). The target ad had a beach scene and the interfering ad had either a beach scene or the scene of a living room. When the task consisted of having to identify brand names and brand claims on the basis of pictures, participants were much less able to match the target ad's picture with the brand name or to remember brand claims when the two ads had similar rather than dissimilar pictures. However, this interference effect disappeared, when product class was used as a cue (Experiment 2). Thus, when participants were asked to recall as much as they could about the ad for suntan lotion or the ad for ice tea, their memory was not affected by the similarity/dissimilarity of the pictures used in the advertisements.

Moderators of the impact of advertising clutter

There are several factors that should moderate the impact of competitive interference on memory. One such factor, which we have already discussed, is the processing goal of the recipient of the ad information. If recipients read or view the ad with the goal of potentially purchasing the advertised product, they are likely to process the information more thoroughly than if they look at the ad without any specific interest in the brand that is being advertised. Although the evidence is not very consistent, one would expect competitive interference to be stronger with more superficial processing.

A second factor likely to moderate the impact of competitive interference is brand familiarity. Brand familiarity reflects the consumer's level of direct or indirect experience with the product (Kent & Allen, 1993). The studies on competitive interference presented so far all used brands that were fictitious. There are cognitive and motivational reasons to assume that the impact of competitive interference would be less strong for brands that are highly familiar. First, recipients will have an established knowledge structure for familiar brands. Since they will integrate the new information within this knowledge structure or schema, the new information will be strongly linked to the brand name. Competitive information will therefore be less likely to affect recall. In contrast, unfamiliar brands are characterized by the absence of an elaborate brand knowledge structure. Recipients are therefore less likely to link the information about the brand claims to the brand name and more likely to link it to the product category. With only weak links between brand name and brand claims, cued recall is less likely to activate brand information.

Consumers might also be more motivated to allocate differential attention to product information in ads for familiar versus ads for unfamiliar products. More extensive processing of an ad might result in better memory for the claims contained in that ad. In a test of the hypothesis that brand familiarity will moderate the impact of competitive interference on recall of brand claims made in advertisements, Kent and Allen (1993) manipulated competitive interference and brand familiarity. For half the participants, familiar brand names were used instead of the unfamiliar brand names. Results showed that competitive interference reduced brand claim recall for unfamiliar but not for familiar brand names. There is some evidence that the protective effect of brand familiarity might not work for all types of interference. In the experiment described earlier, Kumar and Krishnan (2004) also manipulated brand familiarity. They found that if the picture were used as cue, the similarity of pictures resulted in the same interference effects regardless of brand familiarity.

Combating interference due to advertising clutter

Retrieval cues. Marketers have developed numerous strategies to combat interference due to advertising clutter, such as the use of retrieval cues, ad repetition or placing the ad in an advantageous position within the block of advertisements. As the study of Kumar and Krishnan (2004) demonstrated, the use of the picture that was shown in an advertisement as a retrieval cue can be confusing, if similar pictures had been used in several advertisements. However, if the ad pictures used in different ads were quite distinctive, then using ad pictures as cues might help participants to retrieve the brand name advertised and the brand claims that were made in the advertisement. Such a strategy could be particularly helpful in reducing interference from other advertisements for competing brands from the same product category.

This was demonstrated in a study by Keller (1987), who combined the manipulation of competitive interference with the addition of a picture retrieval cue. Competitive interference was manipulated as within-subject factor by the number of competing ads from the same product category that were shown with the target ads. In the low-interference condition, the two target ads were each paired with one other ad from the same product category. In the high-interference condition the two target ads were paired with four other ads from the same product category. Thus, each participant was shown two target ads with low interference and two target ads with high interference. Each ad consisted of a photo, a headline and a number of claims about the qualities of the advertised brand. To test retrieval, participants were given a booklet that contained a picture of a mock package for each of the four target products. In the 'no retrieval cue condition', this was all the information that was given. In the 'retrieval cue condition', a corner of the mock package displayed a small reproduction of the original ad photo and the photo headline. Participants were asked to note down all they could remember about a particular ad. These manipulations resulted in two main effects, with interference impairing the recall for ad claims, and retrieval cues facilitating recall. Thus, as we have seen before, if people were exposed to several ads about different brands of the same product category, their memory for the information about a specific brand was impaired. However, the damaging effects of interference could be partly remedied by placing retrieval cues at the point of purchase. These cues appeared to serve as a strong reminder of the advertisement.

Repetition of advertisements and spacing. Although Burke and Srull (1988) reported some evidence to suggest that message repetition becomes less effective with competitive interference, showing advertisements repeatedly is still considered one of the main strategies to combat advertising clutter (e.g. Appleton-Knapp, Bjork, & Wickens, 2005). After all, the positive relationship between number of trials and recall is one of the basic findings of memory research (Bower, 2000). It is therefore not surprising that effects of advertising repetition have been studied extensively. However, much of this research has focused on the impact of repetition on product attitudes rather than message recall. Whereas the relationship between ad repetition and recall is monotonic and positive, the impact of ad repetitions on product attitudes is curvilinear and likely to decrease after few repetitions (for a review, see Sawyer, 1981). We will discuss this research in chapter 5, which deals with processes of persuasion, and focus here on its effects on message recall.

The impact of ad repetitions on recall is strongly influenced by the way these ads are being spaced. Spacing the repetitions of an advertisement rather than massing them can substantially increase the probability of message recall. The benefits of spacing study trials had already been discovered by Ebbinghaus (1985/1964), who found that spreading his study sessions over three days nearly halved the time he had to spend on actively studying his lists. There are a number of theoretical explanations that can explain this effect. The most plausible ones are the attention hypothesis, the encoding variability hypothesis and the retrieval hypothesis. According to the *attention hypothesis*, people pay less attention to a second or third presentation of the same advertisement, if they realize that it is the same and that they miss nothing if they ignore it (Hintzman, 1976). The *encoding variability hypothesis* predicts that spaced presentations enhance recall, because spacing can increase encoding variability (Appleton-Knapp, Bjork & Wickens, 2005). Variation in how information is encoded is assumed to facilitate subsequent recall because it allows for the formation of more cue-target associations. If the repetition is presented immediately after the first presentation of the advertisement, there will be little change in the individual's mental state or the context and the stimulus will be encoded the same way as the first time. However, if time lapses and intervening events occur between the two presentations of the ad, then the change in context and in the individual's mental state should result in a second encoding that is different from the first one, increasing the probability of later recall (Appleton-Knapp et al., 2005). The *retrieval explanation* is based on the conception that retrieval itself is a learning event. Each time information is retrieved from memory increases the probability that it can be recalled the following time. A second assumption is that the more difficult the act of retrieval, the more potent it will be as a learning event. Thus, according to the retrieval hypothesis, the spacing effect is due to the fact that with increasing time between the first and second presentation of an advertisement, the retrieval of the advertisement should become more and more difficult. At some point, however, the time interval becomes too long and retrieval becomes too difficult.

Appleton-Knapp and her colleagues conducted four experiments to test these interpretations, at least for novel material and short intervals. In one of the experiments, they exposed participants to an advertisement either once or twice (together with many ads for other products). The number of other ads shown between the first and the second presentation of the target ad ranged from 0 to 4. Furthermore, the ad repetition consisted either of exactly the same ad or an ad with a changed layout. After a distractor task, participants had to complete a cued recall test of brand names of the products that had been presented to them. There was a significant main effect of spacing. Spaced ads were remembered better than ads that had been repeated back to back. Most interestingly, however, there was also an interaction between spacing and variation of layout. Compared to exact repetitions, the variation of layout improved recall at short spacing intervals, but impaired recall at longer intervals.

How should one interpret this finding? Superficially, it appears to support the encoding variability hypothesis, except that one would have expected a main effect of variation rather than an interaction. Similarly, the attention hypothesis would also have led one to expect a main effect of variation. The authors argued that their findings are most consistent with the retrieval hypothesis. The repeated advertisement acts as a retrieval cue for the cognitive representation of the first advertisement. Since an exact replication of the first ad would be a better retrieval cue than a replication with a different layout, the variation in layout makes retrieval more difficult. For this reason, it facilitates recall. However, with a longer time interval between the two presentations, when retrieval becomes more difficult, the varied layout may no longer act as a successful retrieval cue and retrieval fails. In contrast, retrieval with the identical advertisement as retrieval cue is still successful. The findings of Appleton-Knapp and colleagues (2005) are also broadly consistent with the conclusions based on an extensive meta-analysis of spacing effects in verbal learning (Janiszewski, Hayden & Sawyer, 2003). However, all of these studies are short-term studies done under artificial laboratory conditions and mostly with novel materials. One would like these conclusions tested in field studies.

Serial position. Serial position effects are some of the most reliable findings of memory research. When participants are asked to learn a list of words or nonsense syllables, they will recall the items presented first and last better than items that were presented in the middle, although the recency effect disappears if there is a delay between presentation of the words and recall (Figure 3.3). Since television advertisements are typically presented in blocks (the well-known commercial breaks), it is an interesting question whether memory of commercials shows the same serial position effects.

This question has been studied in large field studies in the Netherlands (Pieters & Bijmolt, 1997) and the USA (Zhao, 1997) as well as a series of experiments (Terry, 2005). The study in the Netherlands was based on surveys conducted between 1975 and 1992 among over 39,000 television viewers, involving brand name recall for 2,677 television commercials (Pieters & Bijmolt, 1997). These television viewers were interviewed between 10 and 30 minutes after a commercial block. After it had been established that they had been watching TV, they were asked to recall the television commercials they could remember. Results showed a primacy effect, albeit a weak one. Recall was better for commercials shown early rather than late in a block. Other factors influencing recall were the duration of a commercial (longer commercials were remembered better) and competition, defined as the number of commercials that appeared in the same block. As in previous research, competition had a negative effect on recall.

The US study assessed brand recall of commercials that had been shown during Super Bowl football broadcasts, one of the most popular programmes in the United States (Zhao, 1997). A telephone survey was conducted with 1,134 television viewers, who were phoned during the 4 days after the 1992–1994 games. Those who said they had watched the game were asked to list all the advertisements they remembered seeing during the games. The findings of this study mostly replicated those of Pieters and Bijmolt (1997). Again there was evidence for a primacy effect, with the first commercials being better remembered than the last ones. There was also evidence for competition effects. Advertisements were more likely to be recalled, if fewer commercials had been shown within a commercial break. Surprisingly, there was no effect on duration, with short commercials resulting in as much recall as longer ones.

The experimental studies conducted by Terry (2005) also revealed primacy effects. Student participants were exposed to series of commercials, which in some of the studies were embedded in a TV programme. In Experiment 1 participants were asked to view and subsequently recall four sets, each showing 15 commercials. For some of the sets recall was tested immediately, for others there was a brief delay during which participants had to work on a filler task (for some participants research was tested both immediately *and* with a delay; Figure 3.6). Results replicated the

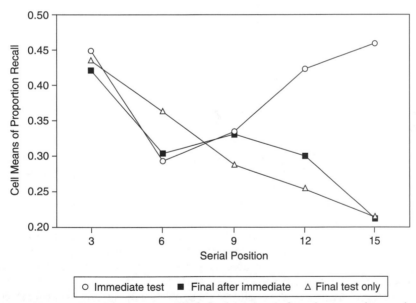

Figure 3.6 Mean proportion recall of product names from lists tested immediately following presentation (immediate test); recall from those lists during the end-of-session test (final after immediate); and recall during the end-of-session test of previously untested list (final test only)

Source: Terry (2005). Serial position effects in recall of television commercials. *Journal of General Psychology, 132,* 152–163

pattern we are familiar with from studies of word lists (Figure 3.3). When recall was immediate, both primacy and recency effects emerged. With delayed recall, the recency effect disappeared. Since field studies only assess delayed recall, the latter findings for delayed recall replicate those of the two field studies in showing primacy but not recency effects.

The primacy effect is probably due to the commercials shown early in a block being processed more deeply (i.e. receiving more rehearsals) than commercials that were shown later. The fact that there was a recency effect with immediate recall rules out the explanation that viewers switched off their attention during later commercials. However, unlike the TV viewers in the field studies, the experimental participants knew that their recall would be assessed. They might therefore have paid more attention to the total set of advertisements than could be expected from the average TV viewer.

Can advertising distort memory?

Marketers have known for some time that exposure to advertising about a product before experiencing it can influence the consumer's experience. In fact, the evidence to be discussed in chapter 4 that information about the brand or the country of origin of a particular product can affect consumers' judgement of that product is at least partly an effect of advertising. More recently, evidence has also been accumulating that advertising presented after experiencing a product can distort consumers' memory of their experience. For example, Levin and Gaeth (1988) had student participants rate the taste of ground beef on several qualitative dimensions (good tasting, greasy, high quality and fat) after having sampled the taste of that meat. Participants also received a verbal description of a key characteristic of meat, namely its fat content. They were either informed that the meat was 75 per cent lean (positive framing) or that it was 25 per cent fat (negative framing). Half of the participants were given this information before tasting the meat, the other half immediately afterwards. Framing did significantly affect ratings, with the effect being most marked for the fat/lean scale and least for the bad/tasting versus good/tasting scale. Thus, the frame had the greatest impact on the dimension most related to the frame, and least impact on the dimension closest to the tasting experience. There was a weak tendency for effects to be smaller when the framing was given after rather than before the tasting, but this effect did not even approach statistical significance.

The time order effect was further explored in a study by Hoch and Ha (1986), who exposed their participants to advertisements praising the high quality of JC Penny Polo shirts either before or after they were given the opportunity to inspect the quality of six different brands of polo shirts (including a shirt from JC Penny). The control group assessed the quality of these shirts without being shown any ads. Exposure to ads praising the JC Penny product resulted in a significant increase in quality ratings of JC Penny shirts (not of competing brands), and this effect was considerably stronger for participants, who saw the ad before rather than after the quality test.

Hoch and Ha (1986) attributed the impact of advertisements shown before people evaluated the quality of a product to selective information search. People experience what they expect to experience, at least with products that are not easily evaluated. The authors further concluded that the effect of advertisements shown afterwards reflects a distortion of individuals' memories of their evaluation, involving 'some form of selective retrieval, with possibly a reinterpretation of the retrieved evidence in the light of the ad claims' (Hoch & Ha, 1986, p. 230). Hoch and Ha (1986) suggested that the effects of advertising on selective information search and on selective retrieval are most likely to occur for products or product dimensions that the average consumer finds difficult to judge. They tested this assumption in a study (Experiment 1) in which they compared the impact of advertisements shown *before* a quality assessment of polo shirts (as a product category that is difficult to judge) and of paper towels (identified in a pilot study as a product category for which quality judgments can be made with greater ease). Consistent with their hypothesis, advertisements only affected the quality assessment of polo shirts but not of paper towels. Since there is no reason to assume that ambiguity would have a stronger effect when advertisements are shown after rather than before the quality assessments, we can probably conclude that post-experience memory distortions are also more likely to occur for quality dimensions which the average consumer finds difficult to assess. When linking these findings with a well-known distinction in types of product attributes on the basis of their 'objective' verifiablity before or after purchase, post-experience memory distortions may be more likely to occur for so-called 'experience' and 'credence' product attributes than for 'search' attributes (see Wright & Lynch, 1995).

A series of studies conducted by Braun (Braun, 1999; Braun-LaTour & LaTour, 2005) suggests that matters may be somewhat more complicated. We would like start out our discussion of this research with Braun's (1999) first study, even though this study did not manipulate time order but presented the ad information always afterwards. Braun's experiment had several features, which distinguishes it from earlier studies. First, in contrast to previous studies, where participants were exposed to ads either immediately before or immediately after the product assessment, participants in Braun's study had to spend 15 minutes on a distraction task between the two phases of the experiment. Second, she manipulated the quality of the stimulus that had to be evaluated. Participants, who were asked to judge the taste of a brand of orange juice, were either presented with good, moderately good or bad tasting juice. Her main dependent measure was an identification task, where participants had to identify the tested orange juice from among 5 different samples of orange juice ranging from extremely bad tasting (sample 1) to extremely good tasting juice (sample 5).

Approximately 15 minutes after the taste test, half of the participants were shown ads with instructions that assured deep processing. The text of one of the ads asked readers to 'imagine the taste of fresh squeezed orange juice . . . it's sweet, pulpy and pure'. The control participants in the control group were not shown any advertisements. As expected, participants' accuracy in identifying the tasted orange juice was somewhat higher for individuals who had not been exposed to the advertisements than for participants who had read the ads (46 per cent correct versus 26 per cent correct choices). Furthermore, participants, who had been exposed to the ads, were more likely to err in the positive direction (Figure 3.7).

In an extended replication of this study, Braun-LaTour and LaTour (2005) added 'time order' and 'time between ad exposure and product test' as additional factors to the design. (In order to keep the design from becoming too complex, they

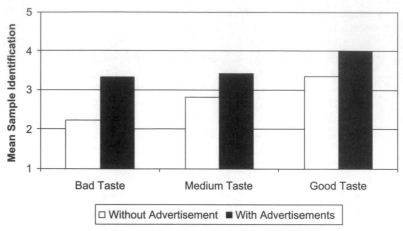

Figure 3.7 Taste identification of the three kinds of orange juice

Source: Adapted from Braun, K.A. (1999). Postexperience advertising effects on consumer memory. *Journal of Consumer Research, 25,* 319–334.

used only one taste of orange juice, namely the juice with the poor taste.) There was a main effect of delay on identification, with advertisements having greater impact with delay than without delay. More interestingly, however, there was also a delay by time order interaction. When there was no delay between ad exposure and taste test, results replicated those of Hoch and Ha (1986), finding greater ad effects when the ad was presented before rather than after the taste test. However, when there was a delay, this effect was reversed. Under these conditions, the advertisement had greater impact when it was presented after rather than before the taste test.

The authors interpret their findings in terms of reconstructive memory (e.g. Loftus, 1980). According to this conception of memory, every act of remembering involves a reconstruction of information and this process is susceptible to inaccuracies. When a memory test is given, the event is reconstructed on the basis of all the relevant information and this includes the information from the advertisement as well as from one's own experience. In terms of this conception of memory, it is plausible that inclusion of the ad information in the reconstruction is most likely when there is a time lag between the two events. With no delay between their own tasting experience and the advertisement, participants will still have a clear memory of their own experience and will rely most heavily on this information in making their judgment.

The findings of Braun-LaTour and LaTour (2005) paint a somewhat depressing picture of our future as consumers. According to these studies, we should be unable to trust our own experience, because we could never be sure that it is really our own rather than having been distorted by persuasive advertisements. However, the findings of Hoch and Ha (1986) suggest limiting conditions to this kind of distortion, namely that the effect of advertising on selective retrieval is most likely to occur for experiences, which are ambiguous rather than clear-cut. Although Braun-LaTour and LaTour (2005) argued that their bad tasting orange juice was so bad as to be unambiguous, taste perceptions may be particularly susceptible to external influences, because we lack good descriptive verbal labels for taste experiences (Melcher & Schooler, 1996). But even within the taste domain, Cowley and Janus (2004) failed in their attempt to convince their participants that they had drunk grapefruit juice when in fact they had experienced orange juice. Furthermore, Cowley and Janus (2004) found a tendency for this effect to be moderated by familiarity. Participants who reported to be unfamiliar with the taste of orange juice were slightly more susceptible to the distorting influence of the advertisement than were individuals who had expressed familiarity with the taste of orange juice. Taken together these findings suggest that advertisements are most likely to distort our memory for experiences that have been rather ambiguous. According to our interpretation of the evidence, people who are familiar with a product and confident in their ability to judge the quality of that product, are unlikely to be susceptible to the distorting influence of advertising messages.

Summary and conclusions

- This chapter reviewed different theories of memory and also applications of these theories to research on advertising.
- The memory model of Atkinson and Shiffrin 1968), which served as the standard model for three decades, distinguished three major components of memory, namely sensory memory, working or short-term memory and long-term memory. According to this model, information is first held briefly in sensory memory, which is sensory specific (e.g. visual, auditory). A selection of information is then transferred to short-term or working memory. In this limited-storage, short-term store, the input from the different sensory memories is integrated with information from long-term memory to be briefly held in conscious awareness and manipulated. The more attention the individuals pay to the information and the more they rehearse the information, the greater the likelihood that it will be transferred to permanent storage in long-term memory.
- In response to critique of the model of Atkinson and Shiffrin some researchers abandoned the idea of different memory systems. Thus, Craik and Lockhart (1972) argued that there is no need to distinguish between two memory systems to account for differences in the length of time that information is remembered. According to their 'levels of processing' hypothesis, longer storage is the result of deeper processing and not of transfer of information from a short-term to a long-term memory system.
- A different solution was suggested by Baddeley and Hitch (1974; Baddeley, 2002), who replaced the model of working memory as a unitary system by a multi-component working memory system. In this system, a controlling central executive, which has no storage capacity, supervises and coordinates two subsystems, the phonological loop (a store that briefly holds sound) and the visuospatial sketchpad for the brief storage of visual material. Both subsystems can operate at the same time.
- There is evidence that long-term memory is not a single entity. One distinction is between explicit and implicit memory. Whereas explicit memory is characterized by a person's conscious recollection of facts and events, implicit memory is unconscious. It is inferred from the fact that previous experience influences

performance on subsequent tasks. Implicit memory is important for the understanding of the effects of much of advertising exposure, because people are often exposed to advertisements, while paying attention to other information. This type of incidental exposure results in implicit rather than explicit memories.

- Traditional measures of advertising effectiveness based on recall or recognition of advertisements assess explicit memory. Since advertising is more likely to influence implicit rather than explicit memory, measures of implicit memory need to be used to assess the impact of advertising.

- But even implicit memory measures may not be a very valid measure of advertising effectiveness, because recollection of the content of advertisements may be unrelated to product evaluations (i.e., attitudes) formed on the basis of these advertisement,

- Increasing the cognitive accessibility of brand names through advertising is likely to influence the inclusion of a brand in a consumer's consideration set (i.e., the set of brand brought to mind in a particular choice situation). This is most likely to influence choice when consumers have no particular preference for a specific brand or when the preferred brand is not available.

- Consumers are exposed to a multitude of competing advertisements, which compete for their attention (advertising clutter). To combat interference due to advertising clutter, advertisers have developed several strategies, such as the use of retrieval cues, ad repetition and placing the ad in an advantaged position within a block of advertisements.

- As a final point, we discuss evidence that advertising can distort consumer memory of products. Since brand images are at least partly the product of advertising and since brand images are assumed to influence product evaluation (brand equity), these findings should not be unexpected.

Chapter 4

How consumers form attitudes towards products

What is an attitude? A matter of contention   112
Are attitudes stable or context-dependent?   118
How do we form attitudes?   120
How attitudes are structured   133
Attitude functions: why people hold attitudes   136
Attitude strength   140
Summary and conclusions   149

As we discussed in the previous chapter, one of the standard strategies marketers use to measure the effectiveness of an advertising campaign is to contact consumers who saw the ad and ask them what they *remember* about it or to show them the ad and to ask whether they *recognize* it. We already questioned the assumption underlying this procedure, namely that people's evaluation of a product (i.e. their attitude towards the advertised product) should be closely related to their memories for the evidence on which those judgements are presumably based. In this chapter, we will formally introduce and define the concept of attitude, discuss how attitudes are formed, structured and what function they serve.

What is an attitude? A matter of contention

Attitudes are considered major determinants of behaviour by practically all social psychological models of behaviour (Eagly & Chaiken, 1993). Even though consumers' purchase decisions are influenced by a variety of factors (to be discussed in chapters 6 and 7), their attitudes towards the product and the brand are powerful predictors of buying decisions. People tend to buy products they consider attractive or useful and avoid buying products they think of as unattractive or useless. To illustrate the importance of the concept of attitude, social psychologists often cite the statement of Gordon Allport (1935) that attitude was the single most important concept in social psychology. The fact that the journal *Social Cognition* (2007) has devoted a special issue solely to the definition of the attitude concept does not only provide a more recent indication that the attitude concept has remained important, it also suggests that researchers have still not agreed on a definition. This lack of agreement poses a problem for social psychologists as well as advertisers. As we will see in the following section, the way we conceptualize attitudes is important for understanding advertising. It helps to pinpoint at what level advertising affects consumer responses and what drives the impact of advertising on purchasing behaviour.

Defining the concept

Why have social psychologists not been able to reach closure in their attempts to define one of their most central concepts? Before we discuss areas of disagreement, let us focus on three aspects of the definition on which most social psychologists agree, namely (1) that attitudes are *evaluative* responses (2) that they are *directed* towards some *attitude object* and (3) that they derive from, or are based on, three classes of information (cognitive, affective/emotional and behavioural; Eagly & Chaiken, 1993, 2007; Zanna & Rempel, 1988).

People's attitudes reflect the way they evaluate the world around them, their likes and dislikes. Consumers' attitudes towards brands such as Coca-Cola or McDonald's are based on their brand image; that is, on their thoughts, feelings and expectations about the brand. Some people like Coca-Cola or McDonald's; others loathe soft drinks and fast food and like good wines and fine restaurants. Any discriminable aspect of our physical or social environment can become an attitude object. Attitude objects may be abstract (e.g. materialism; conspicuous consumption) or concrete (e.g. Nescafé;

Volkswagen). They may be (real or fictitious) individuals (e.g. Cindy Crawford; Michelin's 'Bibendum') or categories (e.g. computer games; soft drinks). The assumption that attitudes are always directed towards an attitude object distinguishes them from other concepts such as mood, which involve more diffuse evaluative reactions.

Since we will discuss the bases of attitudes in greater detail later in our section on the formation of attitudes, we can be brief here. Most attitude theorists agree that attitudes can derive from three general classes of information or experiences and that the basis for any given attitude can vary (e.g. Eagly & Chaiken, 1993; Zanna & Rempel, 1988). A person's attitude towards an object can be based on cognitive information about the attributes that characterize the object. This knowledge can derive from the individual's own appraisal of the attitude object (i.e. direct experience) or from communications about the object (e.g. advertising). Attitudes can also be based on affective or emotional reactions evoked by the attitude object. For example, Coca-Cola uses music and pleasant scenes in its advertisements in the hope that the positive emotions aroused by these stimuli will become associated with the brand through classical or evaluative conditioning. Some attitude objects (e.g. spiders) may even elicit strong emotional or affective reaction on first exposure. Finally, attitudes can be based on behavioural information. For example, people sometimes infer their attitudes from their past behaviour towards the attitude object. This assumption was central to Bem's (1965, 1972) self-perception theory. He argued that people rarely have direct, privileged information about their attitudes and therefore often have to infer them from their own behaviour. Thus, if one were asked whether one liked Coca-Cola, one might infer one's brand attitude from the frequency with which one has recently drunk it ('I drink it a lot, therefore I must like it').

What then are the areas of disagreement regarding the definition of attitude? Since this is not the place to enter into a discussion of the finer points of this controversy, we will highlight only the major point of contention, which also touches on the role of advertising in shaping or changing attitudes, namely whether attitudes should be defined as a *predisposition* to evaluate an attitude object in a particular way or as the evaluative response itself. Let us illustrate this point by presenting what is still the most influential definition of attitudes, namely that, 'Attitude is a psychological tendency that is expressed by evaluating a particular entity with some degree of favour or disfavour' (Eagly & Chaiken, 1993, p. 1).

Eagly and Chaiken (1993, 2007) postulate that this predisposition to evaluate is expressed by three types of evaluative responses, namely cognitive, affective or behavioural evaluative responses. Cognitive evaluative responses consist of the beliefs people hold about the attitude object. These beliefs reflect the connection people see between the attitude object and various attributes. Cognitive evaluative responses can range from extremely positive to extremely negative. Some people believe that soft drinks are thirst-quenching or hamburgers tasty, whereas others think that they contain loads of calories and are terribly bad for weight-control.

Evaluative responses of the affective type consist of the feelings, moods and emotions people experience when confronted with the attitude object. The fact that reading about terrorist acts or the torture of people suspected of terrorist activities makes one feel sad and depressed reflects a negative affective reaction towards these attitude objects, whereas the elation most Americans appear to feel when seeing their flag reflects a positive emotional response.

Evaluative responses of the behavioural type consist of the intention to act or the overt actions people perform in relation to an attitude object. For example, the fact that somebody displays a 'Vote Smith for Mayor' sticker on his or her car suggests a positive evaluation of this candidate, whereas the 'No more atomic power stations' sticker would indicate a negative evaluation of atomic power stations. Since behaviours are often influenced by a variety of motives, their evaluative implications are more ambiguous than is the case for cognitive or affective evaluative responses. Buying three cases of Heineken beer in a supermarket may be the indication of extreme liking for that particular brand of beer, but it might also have been motivated by the fact that there was a special offer at an attractively reduced price.

Implicit and explicit attitudes: challenging the unity of the attitude concept

The definition of attitude as an evaluative tendency that underlies the expression of attitudes in terms of cognitive, affective and behavioural responses implies a certain consistency between different types of evaluative responses: we should feel good about brands about which we hold positive beliefs and we should also tend to buy these brands. Apart from a host of scholars, most professional communicators, such as marketers and fundraisers also entertain this view of consumer attitudes (perhaps because it is the only way these professionals can assess the effectiveness of their endeavours and hence depend on this notion in establishing the success of their work), but evidence is accumulating that challenges this view. This conception, which had already come under pressure due to the discrepancy often observed between verbal expressions of attitudes and overt actions (e.g. LaPiere, 1934; Wicker, 1969) was further challenged by the research conducted on implicit attitudes[4].

Implicit attitudes are evaluations, of which the individual is typically not aware and which influence reactions or actions over which the individual has little or no control. In contrast, **explicit attitudes** are evaluations of which the individual is consciously aware and can be expressed using self-report measures. The types of measure most frequently used are semantic differential scales (bipolar adjective scales) and Likert scales. Semantic differential scales have scale endpoints or anchors, labelled by adjectives with opposite meanings (e.g. good–bad; positive–negative; favourable–unfavourable). To measure an explicit attitude toward some object (say, Nike athletic shoes), a researcher presents the individual with the object (either through a picture of Nike shoes, the brand name or the actual product) and asks the person to rate the object using the pairs of adjectives. An overall attitude towards Nike athletic shoes can then be computed by summing or averaging the scores on the individual items. When using Likert scales, participants are presented with a series of statements (e.g. 'I like Nike athletic shoes' and 'I think Nike athletic shoes are good') and are asked to indicate the extent to which they agree with each of the statements, using response categories that vary from 'strongly agree' to 'strongly disagree'. Again, an overall attitude index is computed by summing or averaging the scores on the items. In contrast, implicit attitudes require a new technology to unobtrusively assess them. Research on implicit attitudes reopened the old controversy about the discrepancy between attitudes inferred from explicit self-reports and those derived from the way respondents behave.

Since there is some disagreement among attitude researchers whether it is the attitude or the procedure used to measure it, which is implicit, we will start our discussion on implicit attitudes with the description of the first workable procedure developed to assess implicit attitudes, namely the **affective priming method** of Fazio and his colleagues (Fazio, Sanbonmatsu, Powell & Kardes, 1986; Fazio, Jackson, Dunton & Williams, 1995). With this procedure, individuals are presented on each trial with a prime (the name or picture of an attitude object). Immediately afterwards they are presented with positive or negative adjectives (e.g. words such as 'useful', 'valuable' or 'disgusting') and are asked to decide as fast as possible whether the adjective was positive or negative. The time it takes people to make this judgement (i.e. response latency) constitutes the dependent measure.

The basic assumption is that the attitude prime automatically activates an evaluative response and that this response will either facilitate or inhibit the evaluative response to the next stimulus (i.e. the adjective). Whether the evaluative response activated by the prime will facilitate or inhibit the subsequent response will depend on whether prime and target are evaluatively similar or dissimilar. Suppose that the attitude prime is a picture of a spider and that respondents evaluate spiders negatively. Presentation of the spider prime should automatically activate a negative evaluation. If the target adjective that is presented immediately afterwards is also negative (e.g. the word 'disgusting'), respondents will be able to indicate the evaluative connotation of the target adjective relatively quickly. In contrast, if the target adjective is positive (e.g. attractive), then the fact that the attitude prime has just activated a negative evaluative response might slow down the respondent's reaction.

Fazio, Jackson, Dunton and Williams (1995) used this procedure as an unobtrusive measure of prejudice. The attitude primes in their study were pictures of white or black faces. For each student participant and each picture, a facilitation score was computed by subtracting the reaction time when the target adjective was preceded by a face, from the reaction time of a control condition, where the adjective had been presented without priming. If we assume that the white participants were prejudiced against black people then presenting them with a black face should facilitate their responses to negative target attributes but inhibit responses to positive target attributes. This effect should not occur with white faces. The pattern of results supported this prediction. By the same token, the procedure may be used to assess implicit attitudes toward consumer products, at least to the extent that the researcher suspects that there may be a discrepancy between explicit and implicit consumer attitudes. A case in point are 'controversial products', such as clothing brands with strong negative connotations. For example, right-wing extremists in Europe have shown a tendency to select specific clothing brands to underline their group membership. Brands they use include Lonsdale and New Balance (shoes). Although the manufacturer of these brands is in no way related to or supporting these groups, consumers may nevertheless have developed an explicitly negative attitude toward these brands, which may differ from any implicitly held attitude, something that the affective priming method could reveal.

A problem with the affective priming method is that although the pattern of data may be consistent with the researchers' a priori assumptions about the prejudice or negative attitudes of their participants, such consistency does not constitute scientific evidence. In the case of prejudice, what we need is the validation of the priming measure with an independent measure of prejudice of proven validity. There is no shortage of such measures, but the problem is that the best validated ones are all self-report scales. Since there are strong norms against racial prejudice particularly in academic environments and since individuals have control over their answers to such self-report questionnaires, their scores on such measures are unlikely to correlate with a measure based on their automatic reactions. And indeed, the facilitation scores on the priming measure were uncorrelated with scores on the modern racism scale (McConahay, 1986).

Since they anticipated this outcome, Fazio and colleagues included a number of unobtrusive measures in their study. For example, the black experimenter had been asked to rate how friendly participants had been in their interactions with him. This rating correlated significantly with facilitation scores. Respondents for whom negativity had been activated in the priming task behaved in a less friendly manner when they later interacted with the black experimenter. In contrast, these friendliness ratings did not correlate with the modern racism scale. This finding was the first support for the hypothesis that on socially sensitive topics such as prejudice, measures of intrinsic attitudes are likely to correlate with attitudinally relevant behaviours over which individuals have little control, but are less likely to be predictive to evaluative responses that are controllable (e.g. responses to a verbal measure of prejudice)

If the lack of correlation between the facilitation score and the modern racism scale were indeed due to the fact that most of the prejudiced participants tried to hide that they are prejudiced, then such a correlation should emerge for any participant who did not care whether he or she was perceived as being prejudiced. Fazio and colleagues (1995) tested this assumption in a further experiment (Study 3), in which they replicated their first study, but included a newly constructed scale that assessed people's motivation to control racial prejudice. In line with predictions, they found that the less their participants were motivated to control their prejudice, the stronger became the relationship between the modern racism scale and the facilitation score.

An alternative measure that is frequently used to assess implicit attitudes is the **Implicit Association Test** (IAT) devised by Anthony Greenwald and colleagues (e.g. Brunel, Tietje & Greenwald, 2004; Dasgupta, Greenwald & Banaji, 2003; Nosek, Greenwald & Banaji, 2007). Like the affective priming method, the IAT uses response latencies to infer implicit attitudes. In essence, the procedure assesses the strength of an association between two concepts with positive and negative evaluations. The response latencies are derived from the participants' use of two response keys which have been assigned a dual meaning. This procedure is often used for assessing stereotypical or otherwise biased attitudes. For instance, when used to assess prejudice toward ethnic minorities, participants in the IAT are presented with words on a computer screen that fall into four categories: minority-related words, majority-related words, positive words and negative words. The participants assign each of the words presented to one of these four categories by pressing one of two keys. For example, in a first trial, participants are required to press the 'Z' key on the computer keyboard when a word is a majority word *or* a positive word and to press the 'M' key when a word is a minority word *or* a negative word. In a second trial, the task is reversed and the participant is required to press the 'Z' key when a word is a majority word or a *negative* word and to press the 'M' key when a word is a minority word or a *positive* word. The computer records the response latencies for each of the categorizations.

The logic underlying the technique is that if the participant's attitude toward minorities is negative, response times will be shorter when minority words share the same key with negative words than with positive words.

Support for this notion was found in the classic Greenwald et al. (1998) study on racial attitudes. In this experiment, participants were first asked to categorize names which are either believed to be prototypical African-American (e.g. 'Latonya') or not (e.g. Betsy) as black or white on two corresponding keys. Next, participants categorized a sample of clearly valenced words such as 'poison' or 'vacation' as either pleasant or unpleasant using the same two keys. In the critical phase, and in line with the previous example, participants were presented with the combination of black/ unpleasant versus white/pleasant words using the assigned keys, and subsequently the combinations where reversed, i.e. black/pleasant and white/unpleasant. The pairing of the words was counterbalanced between sessions to prevent any order effects and response times were recorded. In this experiment, participants were faster (i.e. showed shorter response latencies) when black was paired with unpleasant than pleasant words, an indication of racial bias.

The IAT could be useful for the indirect assessment of consumer attitudes and other responses toward controversial products (e.g. weapons, drugs), brands (e.g. brands associated with soccer hooliganism, such as Lonsdale or Fred Perry) or advertising executions (e.g. fear appeals or sexual appeals). Although the IAT is a rather new measure of attitudes (Fabrigar, Krosnick & MacDougall, 2005), it is also still fairly controversial (Blanton & Jaccard, 2006; Blanton, Jaccard & Christie, 2007; Rothermund & Wentura, 2004). Most importantly, the processes driving the IAT results are as yet not well understood (Fazio & Olson, 2003).

There is now a great deal of evidence that for socially sensitive issues such as prejudice, the association between explicit and implicit measures is very low (for reviews, see Dovidio, Kawakami & Beach, 2001; Fazio & Olson, 2003; Friese, Hofmann & Schmitt, 2008). Similarly, numerous studies have replicated the finding of Fazio and colleagues (1995) that implicit racial attitudes are reliable predictors of subtle interracial behaviour (for reviews, see Dovidio et al., 2001; Fazio & Olson, 2003). For example, Dovidio et al. (1997) reported a correspondence between attitude estimates based on a priming measure and nonverbal behaviours displayed while interacting with a black or white interviewer. Thus, the implicit measure of prejudice predicted lower levels of visual contact with the black interviewer and higher rates of blinking, both not predicted by the measure of modern racism. Wilson et al. (2000) found their priming measure of prejudice significantly related to the number of times white participants touched a black confederate's hand in a task where they had to share a pen. Finally, in a study of prejudice towards fat people, Bessenoff and Sherman (2000) found that a priming measure involving photos of fat and thin women correlated with the distance at which participants would later place their chair away from that of a fat woman. In a sense, modern advertising faces the same discrepancy between explicit and implicit consumer responses. Not many consumers are willing to admit that they are often heavily influenced by advertising in their shopping behaviour and thus, scales designed to tap the persuasive influence of advertising often reveal a sceptic and resistant consumer. Nevertheless, more implicit measures do reveal advertising's impact on consumer perceptions and behaviour.

The discordance between implicit and explicit measures of attitude challenges our conception of attitude as a unitary concept. In fact, one of the more intriguing explanations for this discordance is the theory of dual attitudes suggested by Wilson et al. (2000). These authors explained the discrepancy between implicit and explicit attitudes by suggesting that persuasive advocacies (such as advertising) or novel experiences might often result in the creation of a novel, second, attitude without replacing the old one. Wilson and colleagues define dual attitudes as different evaluations of the same attitude object, one on an automatic, implicit level, and one on a controlled, explicit level. For example, people who were brought up on McDonald's and Kentucky Fried Chicken, may have later learnt that, from a nutritional perspective, fast food ought to be avoided. In contrast to the traditional view, which holds that these individuals have now abandoned their love of fast food, Wilson et al. (2000) would suggest that they now hold dual attitudes towards fast food: an implicit positive attitude and a more recently constructed explicit negative attitude. This model would yield the prediction that the attitude individuals are likely to endorse at any given point in time will depend on whether they have the cognitive capacity to retrieve the explicit attitude, while suppressing the old, implicit attitude. Extending the Wilson et al. (2000) notion, advertising (as well as health education) could be considered a powerful force creating secondary attitudes that may exist alongside, rather than in lieu of, earlier formed, implicit attitudes toward consumer products.

Are attitudes stable or context-dependent?

A further challenge to the dispositional definition of attitude comes from evidence that indicates that attitudes are often context dependent. The way we define the concept has implications for the stability we expect of people's attitudes. Eagly and Chaiken's (1993) proposal that evaluative responses reflect an inner tendency implies that people's attitudes should be relatively stable over time. With this assumption, Eagly and Chaiken are consistent with a tradition in attitude research which conceives of attitudes as learned structures that reside in long-term memory and are activated upon encountering the attitude object (e.g. Fazio & Williams, 1986). This perspective has been termed the 'file-drawer model', because it conceives of attitudes as mental files which can be consulted for the evaluation of a given attitude object (Schwarz & Bohner, 2001).

In recent decades, this view has been challenged by evidence that suggests that attitudes may be much less enduring and stable than has traditionally been assumed (for reviews, see Erber, Hodges & Wilson, 1995; Schwarz, 2007; Schwarz & Bohner, 2001; Schwarz & Strack, 1991; Tourangeau & Rasinski, 1988). According to this perspective, attitudes fluctuate over time and appear to 'depend on what people happen to be thinking about at any given moment' (Erber et al., 1995, p. 433). Proponents of this 'attitudes-as-constructions perspective' reject the view that people retrieve previously stored attitudes in making evaluative judgements. Instead, they assume that individuals make their judgments online, based on the information that is either presented or comes to mind in any given situation. This conception of attitudes as online judgements is inconsistent with the view that evaluative judgements are the expression of an underlying tendency (e.g. Schwarz, 2007).

There is empirical support for both stability and malleability of attitudes. There is evidence that political attitudes can persist for many years or even a lifetime (e.g. Alwin, Cohen & Newcomb, 1991; Marwell, Aiken & Demerath, 1987), but there is also evidence that attitudes change with changing context. For example, Wilson and his colleagues demonstrated that attitudes can change when people analyze their reasons for holding them and that this change can occur for a wide range of attitude objects, including political candidates (Wilson, Kraft & Dunn, 1989) and dating partners (Wilson & Kraft, 1993).

How can these inconsistencies be reconciled? One potential solution suggested by theorists who subscribe to the attitude-as-construction perspective is to deny that their position implies that attitudes should be unstable and therefore not predictive of behaviour. They argue that even if attitudinal judgments are made online each time we encounter the attitude object, attitudes should remain stable to the extent that at each point in time respondents draw on similar sources of information (Erber et al., 1995; Schwarz & Bohner, 2001). For example, since neither the taste of Coca-Cola nor their advertising campaigns are likely to change dramatically over the years, our brand attitude towards Coca-Cola is likely to remain stable, even if it were formed on a day-to-day basis.

Because it seems implausible and impractical that people construct their attitude anew each time they encounter an attitude object, we tend to subscribe to an alternative solution, namely that attitudes can be placed on a continuum of attitude strength. This continuum ranges from issues which are either so novel or irrelevant for individuals that they have not (yet) formed an attitude, to issues which are both familiar and important to individuals and towards which they have strong, well-developed attitudes. By increasing the strength of attitudes, advertising serves an important function here. Through heavy advertising initially unfamiliar brands can become household names which are highly accessible in people's mind (e.g. Heineken beer; Absolut Vodka). We would further argue that attitude strength does not only influence the stability of people's attitude but also whether attitudinal judgments are formed on-line or based on memory. When people are asked to evaluate novel and unfamiliar stimuli they have no alternative but to form their evaluation online based on the information at hand. In contrast, when they are asked to evaluate an attitude object with which they have been familiar for many years and about which they have a great deal of information, they are likely to have made up their minds a long time ago and are therefore able to rely on this evaluative knowledge structure in making their judgement. We will discuss this question further in the context of our discussion of attitude structure.

Implications for the definition of the attitude concept

The evidence discussed in this section presents problems for dispositional definitions of the attitude concept. Both the discrepancy often observed between implicit and explicit attitudes and the context dependence of attitudes are difficult to reconcile with the assumption that these different evaluative responses are the expression of an underlying tendency. Although such a reconciliation is not impossible and plausible explanations have been suggested (e.g. see Eagly & Chaiken, 2007; Fazio, 1990), we tend to favour the definition suggested by Zanna and Rempel (1988) of **attitudes** as 'the categorization of a stimulus object along an evaluative dimension' (p. 319). This definition does not imply that attitudinal judgments reflect some underlying disposition and affective and behavioural responses are considered correlates of evaluative judgments. If one does not limit categorization to a cognitive process but includes positive and negative affective responses occurring below the level of awareness, the Zanna and Rempel definition would be more consistent with the evidence reviewed above than a definition of attitudes as a reflection of a tendency to evaluate.

How do we form attitudes?

As we have seen, there is consensus among attitude theorists that attitudes derive from cognitive, evaluative/affective and behavioural information. In this section, we will discuss how this information is used to form attitudes. This discussion is complicated by the fact that it is difficult to distinguish clearly between processes of attitude formation and attitude change. We will use two criteria to make this distinction. Attitude formation rather than change is involved when the issue or object is novel and unfamiliar to the target individuals. A second characteristic, although less diagnostic, is that attitude formation is typically based on low effort cognitive processes that require little cognitive elaboration such as evaluative conditioning or heuristic processing. It is these processes, which we will discuss in this section.

The formation of cognitively based evaluative responses

Beliefs about an attitude object such as a brand of soft drink, car or air conditioner, are based on information individuals have gathered about this object. This information can either derive from personal experience with that brand or indirectly through reading or being told about it. For example, we can learn about the attributes of a new car directly by going on a test drive, or indirectly through the information conveyed by advertisements, test reports or recommendations from friends or acquaintances. Finally, we may also use heuristics in predicting quality, such as the brand-quality heuristic (e.g. Rolls Royce builds excellent cars), the country of origin heuristic (the best cheeses come from France) or the price–quality heuristic (you get what you pay for).

Attitudes based on direct experience versus memory

In an early review of a research programme on the differences between attitudes that are based on direct or indirect experience, Fazio and Zanna (1981) reported that direct experience resulted in more information about the attitude object than indirect experience. Furthermore, attitudes based on direct experience were held with greater confidence, were more stable over time, and were more accessible in memory than attitudes that derived from indirect experience. But most importantly, Fazio and colleagues (e.g. Fazio & Zanna, 1981; Regan & Fazio, 1977) demonstrated that attitudes based on direct experience were more predictive of future behaviour. As we will discuss later, these are all properties that distinguish strong from weak attitudes.

In many of their studies, Fazio and colleagues (e.g. Regan & Fazio, 1977; Fazio, Chen, McDonel & Sherman, 1982) used an experimental paradigm in which participants either read verbal descriptions about some activities (e.g. a set of puzzles) or were given the opportunity to experience these activities themselves. Subsequently, they would indicate their attitude towards these activities to assess how well their attitude predicted the time they spent with each of the activities, when given the opportunity to freely engage in them. For example, in a study by Regan and Fazio (1977), participants either received a description of five intellectual puzzles or were given the opportunity to try out each of those five puzzles. After having rated the interest value of each of the puzzles, they were given a free-play period, in which they were allowed to play with any of the puzzles. When the correlation was computed between interest value and the order in which the puzzles were attempted, this correlation was much higher for individuals in the condition with direct rather than indirect experience.

In later publications, Fazio and colleagues (e.g. Fazio, 1990; Fazio, Chen, McDonel & Sherman, 1982; Fazio & Williams, 1986) proposed that the fact that attitudes derived from direct experience were more accessible in memory than attitudes based in indirect experience was responsible for their greater impact on behaviour. This view has been challenged by Doll and Ajzen (1992), who argued that it was the greater temporal stability of experience-based attitudes rather than their accessibility that was responsible. A person's attitude towards an activity reflects his or her expectations about how enjoyable this activity is likely to be. The more these expectations prove to be consistent with the actual experience, the better the attitude will predict actual behaviour. It seems likely that an attitude based on previous experience with an activity will be a better predictor of the actual interest value of an activity than an attitude based on a verbal description.

Doll and Ajzen tested this hypothesis in a study in which participants' attitudes towards several computer games were measured after they had either been given the opportunity to try each game or been shown a video recording of somebody else playing these games. Participants then had 45 minutes to play with the different games. The time spent on each game was the dependent variable. Afterwards their attitude towards the games was measured again to assess attitude stability. Consistent with the findings of Fazio and his colleagues, experience-based attitudes were better predictors of the time participants spent with each game than attitudes based on indirect experience. However, supportive of the explanation offered by Doll and Ajzen rather than that of Fazio and colleagues, a test of mediation indicated that attitude stability rather than accessibility was responsible for this difference. In the meantime, evidence has accumulated that indicates that both groups of researchers have been correct. A recent meta-analysis of mediating processes in the attitude behaviour relationship found both greater attitude accessibility and greater stability to be independently responsible for the fact that experience-based attitudes were better predictors of behaviour than attitudes that were based on indirect experience (Glasman & Albarracin, 2006).

The impact of direct experience on the attitude-behaviour link emphasizes the importance of marketing tools to promote direct experience in addition to classic advertising: tools such as 'scratch-'n'-sniff' cards[5], test drives or free samples. However, in our ever-changing world past experience is not always a reliable guide for future behaviour. A wine which may have been delicious on a lake terrace in sunny Italy might taste much less good when drunk on a cold winter's night in the Netherlands. The predictive validity of experience-based attitudes will depend on the similarity between the context in which the experience is gained and that in which the actual behaviour is performed. Thus, if there is a dramatic change in context between the trial and the performance sessions, the advantage of experience-based attitudes over attitudes based on indirect experience may be lost.

This was demonstrated by Millar and Millar (1996), who manipulated the hedonic orientation of their participants in a study in which they had to solve puzzles. Again, participants first formed their impression of these puzzles either based on direct experience or written descriptions. It was known from an earlier study (1996, Study 1) that without specific instructions, student participants find solving such puzzles fun. Experience-based attitudes were therefore likely to reflect the enjoyment participants had with these puzzles. However, in the second phase, Millar and Millar (1996) spoilt the enjoyment of half of their participants by leading them to expect that their analytical ability would be assessed after the free play period with the puzzles and that playing these puzzles would increase their analytical ability. No such instrumental orientation was induced in the other participants. Consistent with predictions, attitudes based on direct experience were better predictors of behaviour than attitudes based on indirect experience in the normal (hedonic) condition, but not in the condition in which an instrumental orientation had been induced. In the instrumental condition experience-based attitudes were no better than attitudes based on indirect experience in predicting behaviour. That attitudes based on direct experience are better predictors of behaviour only when the motivational orientation (instrumental versus hedonic) during the experience is consistent with the motivational orientation during the later activity has been confirmed in the meta-analysis of Glasman and Albarracin (2006). Marketers appear to have intuitively grasped this principle and usually focus on hedonic descriptors in advertising for products that customers buy for enjoyment rather than instrumental purposes (e.g. food and drink).

Another factor which determines the impact of direct as compared to indirect experience is expertise and trustworthiness of the source of the information. Here marketers work under a serious disadvantage, because people tend to distrust the information they receive through mass media advertising. Marketers often try to overcome this handicap by attributing their communications to apparently trustworthy sources, such as the actor in toothpaste advertisements dressed up as a dentist or an apparently unsuspecting customer caught on film just when he or she was praising a product. Although it is doubtful whether many consumers can be duped by such procedures, there is no a priori reason why consumers should *always* trust their own experience more than evaluations presented in mass media communications. Thus, even if a test drive with a car was satisfactory, the average driver may be dissuaded from buying that car by a negative report in a respected car journal. Similarly the opinions of wine writers like Robert Parker exert a tremendous influence on wine purchasing behaviour. The impact of these sources is due to the fact that they are perceived both as trustworthy (i.e. they are not paid for expressing a certain opinion) and highly expert. The effect of such source characteristics on the impact of socially-mediated information on people's attitude is an important research area of persuasion research and will be discussed in chapter 5 of this volume.

Using heuristics to form attitudes towards products

Individuals often rely on simple heuristics to form attitudes towards people or objects. Such heuristics are learnt 'if-then' relationships or expectancies, which can be based on own experience, based on shared cultural beliefs (e.g. stereotypes), or acquired through advertisements. The influence of **stereotypes** (i.e. beliefs about the attributes of members of an outgroup) on attitudes towards members of that group has been extensively studied in research on prejudices (for a recent review, see Dovidio, Gaertner & Saguy, 2007). In the area of consumer behaviour, consumers are particularly likely to use heuristics to form an attitude towards a product, when product quality is difficult or ambiguous to ascertain (Hoch & Deighton, 1989). The most frequently used heuristic cues (i.e. the if-part of the if-then relationship) in the area of consumer behaviour are brand names, country of origin and even its price.

That a strong *brand name* triggers important associations stored in the memory of consumers has been widely demonstrated (Aaker, 1997). The beliefs, feelings, and evaluations triggered by a brand name are referred to as **brand image**. Although people can (and sometimes do) learn these associations through their own experience or through communications from friends and acquaintances, brand images are typically strongly influenced by advertising. Thus, people have learnt to associate Rolls-Royce cars or Rolex watches with high-quality engineering and workmanship, even though they may never have driven a Rolls-Royce or owned a Rolex watch. Brand images are the consumer equivalent to stereotypes in intergroup relations. We tend to judge members of different national or ethnic groups not just on the basis of their individual characteristics but also on the basis of our stereotype about this group and these stereotypes are only partly based on personal experience. Thus, we may think of Italians as emotional, of the British as conservative and the Germans as efficiently boring and these expectations tend to colour our perception of the Italian, British or German we may happen to meet (Dovidio et al., 2007). The impact of such stereotypes on people's judgements of, and behaviour towards, members of an outgroup is referred to as prejudice and considered bad. The impact of a brand image on people's judgement of, and behaviour towards a branded product is referred to as **brand equity** (the value added to a product by a brand name) and considered good, at least by advertisers. To be fair to advertisers, though, since there is less variability among the exemplars of branded products as man-made categories than among the natural categories of Italians, British and Germans, brand images are likely to be more accurate descriptions of branded products than stereotypes are of members of an ethnic group or nationality.

One of the early studies on the impact brand names and the brand name heuristic have on the evaluation of products is a study by Allison and Uhl (1964), who assessed the influence of beer brand names on perception of the taste of different beers. Participants in this US study were beer drinkers who were given five different beers to taste at home. One week they had to taste the beers from unlabelled bottles, the second week the bottles were labelled. The design was a mixed within and between subjects design, with each participant having to rate three of the five brands of beer. When quality was evaluated in blind tasting, there were no significant differences in ratings. Thus, even though (according to the authors), trained tasters were able to distinguish between those beers, the untrained participants were not. However, significant differences in taste ratings did emerge, when participants tasted the beers with their proper labels attached. Since the labelled beers were the same those participants had earlier rated without labels, these findings suggest that the taste differences were induced by the brand image of these different beers. It is interesting to note that all beers tasted significantly better when drunk out of labelled rather than unlabelled bottles. This difference might reflect a prejudice against no-name products.

Another study conducted in the USA, in which three beers were tasted either with or without labels found that beer drinkers were able to distinguish between the three beers (described as a nationally distributed ultra-premium beer, a nationally distributed popular-priced beer and a regionally distributed inexpensive beer). The ultra-popular premium beer was rated most positively in blind tasting and this difference increased when tasters were informed about the brand name. Thus, although the blind tasting showed that the popular beer deserved its popularity, the brand information still enhanced the good taste even further.

That a brand name associated with high quality can improve product ratings was also demonstrated in a study conducted in Switzerland by Fichter and Jonas (2008). These authors attributed the same fictitious newspaper article either to a high quality national paper (*Neue Zürcher Zeitung*) or to a sensationalist national newspaper (*Blick*). In line with previous findings, the quality of the article was rated much higher when it was attributed to the high-quality rather than the sensational newspaper.

Information about **country of origin** of a product is another heuristic people use in judging products. There is much evidence that consumers make use of the information about the country of origin in judging the quality of a product (e.g. Hong & Wyer, 1989; Verlegh & Steenkamp, 1999). In fact, laws about the display of the country of origin have originally been introduced to provide the consumer with cues about quality. For example, country of origin indications such as 'Made in Germany' were introduced in Britain by the Merchandise Marks Act 1897, to mark foreign products more obviously, as British society considered foreign products to be inferior to domestic. However, this move backfired as the term 'Made in Germany' was soon associated with product reliability, quality and even perfection (Wikipedia, 2008a).

Food is one of the product categories for which the country of origin information is considered particularly important. First, consumers tend to believe that ethnic food products are likely to be better if they come from the country from which the food originated. For example, since pasta is a national dish of Italy, pasta sauces with Italian names have an edge in the market. Thus, in advertising their pasta sauce, Bertolli uses Italian mamas, who prepare the sauce in big pots in country-Italian surroundings.[6] That country of origin information can affect the tasting experience has been demonstrated by DeBono and Rubin (1995) in a study described in more detail later. These authors demonstrated that the same cheese tasted better to American consumers (at least those who were image conscious), when it allegedly came from France rather than Kansas.

In a meta-analysis of 41 studies of the country of origin effect published between 1980 and 1996 (reporting 278 individual effect sizes), Verlegh and Steenkamp (1999) estimated the overall effect of this variable as moderate to strong ($r = .39$), The effect size was strongest for perceived quality of a product and smallest for purchase intention, with attitude judgements falling in between.

Another important heuristic consumers use in evaluating product quality is the *price–quality* heuristic, namely the expectancy that 'if expensive then good', and conversely, 'if inexpensive then bad' (see also Rao & Monroe, 1989 for a review). The power of the price–quality heuristic has been systematically assessed in a series of studies by Cronley et al. (2005). These researchers also tested the moderating role of three important factors on the price–quality inference effect: information load, presentation format and the need for cognitive closure, or the desire to arrive at an opinion and avoid confusion, ambiguity and indecision (see Kruglanski & Webster, 1996). In one of their studies, Cronley et al. (2005) requested participants to rate different brands of wines. Different types of information were presented per brand, namely the brand name, the geographical region from which the wine originated, the type of grape used to make the wine, a quality rating ranging from 1–100 and the price. The types of information presented in that study are similar to information given in typical product comparison sites you can find on the internet (e.g. www.kelkoo.com or www.pricegrabber.com). They manipulated information load by varying the number of brands listed (50 versus 25). They also varied the format: half of the participants were presented with a rank ordered list of brands, based on the quality ratings, and the other half of the participants received the list in random order. Need for cognitive closure was manipulated by asking participants either to make a quick judgment, which was to be pooled with the judgments of the other participants (high need for cognitive closure) or to be careful and precise in judging the wines, because their responses would be weighed heavily (low need for cognitive closure). The list of wines was composed such that there was a modest correlation between price and quality ($r = .27$).

Participants were asked to predict the quality of the brands and as expected they showed a strong reliance on price–quality heuristic: the average *subjective* price–quality correlation was much higher than the *actual* correlation in the list ($r = .83$), suggesting that price had a far greater influence on quality judgments than other types of information. In line with the heuristic value of price information, Cronley et al. (2005) also reported that the expected correlation between price and quality was especially high when information load was high and need for cognitive closure was high. Under these conditions there were both ability, and motivational forces at work to prompt the use of the price–quality heuristic. A large amount of information triggers the use of simplifying procedures, because that is the most sensible way to deal with the overload. In addition, when time limits the possibility for careful responding, and a careful response is not desired anyway (as in the high cognitive closure condition) this also motivates the use of a shortcut. Finally, the use of the price–quality heuristic was also more pronounced when product information was presented through a rank-ordering, rather than randomly presented. The authors explained this by arguing that random information promotes bottom-up, data-driven processing, a process in which participants will naturally come across heuristic disconfirming evidence, i.e. instances of high quality wines at low prices and vice versa. Encountering this disconfirming evidence diminishes the diagnosticity of the price–quality heuristic. In a follow-up study Cronley et al. (2005) also showed that the price–quality heuristic affected overt choice behaviour. Participants who used the decision rule were prepared to pay more for a bottle of wine of their choice, than participants who were less prone to use it.

Recent work by Plassmann, O'Doherty, Shiv and Rangel (2008) showed that the influence of the price–quality heuristic extends beyond consumer ratings and can colour the actual consumption experience when using a product. Tasting the same wine, participants in this study enjoyed the wine significantly more when the price tag read $45 than when the price was a mere $5. And this was not a simple case of consumer snobbery. Plassmann and her colleagues had the neurological data to corroborate the 'authenticity' of the consumption experience: when tasting the expensively labelled wine, participants' brain centres associated with pleasure (i.e. the medial orbitofrontal cortex) became more activated than when tasting the 'cheap' wine. Hence, the price heuristic can turn into a self-fulfilling prophecy: the quality of the product actually improves with increasing price!

Unfortunately for the money-saving consumer, the process works both ways. This was demonstrated by Shiv, Carmon and Ariely (2005) who labelled the phenomenon a placebo effect. They found that consumers who got a product at a discount (e.g. an energy drink thought to increase mental acuity) derived less actual benefit from the product (i.e. solved fewer puzzles) than consumers who had paid the regular price. Consumer expectations were found to mediate the effect: expecting a poor product resulted in the actual experience of the product as less than satisfactory. Thus, using the price–quality heuristic in evaluating a product can alter the actual efficacy of the product. For these effects to occur though, price information must be considered diagnostic by consumers and there must be no other easy way of inferring product quality than price information.

A heuristic which appears to serve a similar function when it comes to services, rather than tangible products, is duration. Yeung and Soman (2007) found that service customers tended to infer higher quality of services when duration increased, especially in relation to price (that is, when the duration:price ratio increased). Interestingly, although ambiguity or uncertainty frequently drives the employment of the price quality or duration heuristic, consumers are sometimes blinded by its impact. Research by Oxoby and Finnigan (2007) suggests that overreliance on these decision rules can lead to a blocking effect, where consumers tend to actively ignore other, sometimes more diagnostic, types of evidence indicative of product quality.

The formation of evaluative responses based on affective or emotional experience

There are essentially three pathways to the acquisition of evaluative responses based on affective or emotional experience. Initially neutral stimuli can acquire positive valence through repeated exposure (*mere exposure*) or through association with events that already have positive or negative valence (*classical or evaluative conditioning*). As a third possibility, individuals' may use the affect evoked by the stimulus or the stimulus context as information about this object (*affect-as-information*).

Mere exposure

Zajonc (1968) was the first to demonstrate the effect of mere exposure on attitudes towards novel and unfamiliar stimuli in a classic series of experiments in which

'Turkish words' (actually nonsense syllables) or Chinese-like characters were presented to subjects at varying frequencies (ranging from 0 to 25 times) at short durations. Afterwards, participants were asked to indicate how positive they believed the meaning of these words or characters to be. Zajonc (1968) found that attitudes towards these stimuli became more positive with increasing frequency of exposure, an effect that was more pronounced at lower rather than higher frequencies. The mere exposure phenomenon has been used to explain advertising 'wear-in': the observation that an advertisement's impact only increases after an 'incubation period' of one or several initial exposures where effects are absent or minimal.

Zajonc's study aroused a great deal of interest. In the 20 years following its publication more than 200 experiments were conducted to study mere exposure effects. A meta-analysis of these experiments did not only demonstrate that the exposure–attitude relationship is a robust and reliable phenomenon, but also that the effect is stronger with a longer period of delay between exposure and attitude measure and, most interestingly, that stimulus recognition is not necessary for the exposure effect to occur (Bornstein, 1989). In fact, the exposure effect was stronger when stimuli were presented subliminally rather than supraliminally. Finally, Bornstein also found that the effect levels off after 10 to 20 exposures.

That exposure effects could be used for the advertising of new brands has been demonstrated in several studies (e.g. Blüher & Pahl, 2007; Fang, Singh & Ahluwalia, 2007). Participants in the study of Fang and colleagues (Experiment 1) were asked to read a five-page article on online education, with banner ads rotating for five seconds each on top of the article on the computer screen. There were five filler ads and one target ad. The target ad featured the fictitious brand name 'Pretec' for a digital camera. The target ad was presented either 0, 5 or 20 times. When liking for the different banner ads was assessed at the end of the study, frequency of exposure had a significant and positive effect on attitudes towards the target ad.

A study by Blüher and Pahl (2007) is particularly interesting, because they demonstrated a mere exposure effect on behaviour. In their study citizens of a small German town were approached in a park and asked to participate in a study about town monuments. Those who agreed were shown a folder with 11 photos of landmark buildings, which they were asked to name. In the two experimental conditions, advertising boards were placed in the corner of five of the photos. These boards either showed the brand logo of 'Zitro', a lemon bonbon or of 'Pfeffi' a peppermint sweet (Pfefferminz in German). In the control group, participants were shown photos without advertisements. After participants had named the buildings, they were offered the choice between two bags of sweets as small thanks for their participation. The sweet bags either displayed the brand logo of the Pfeffi or the Zitro. In both experimental condition, participants showed a clear preference for the sweets that had been advertised on five of the 11 photos in their folder.

Why does frequency of exposure increase liking? The currently most widely accepted explanation for the exposure effect assume that frequency of exposure increases perceptual fluency, the ease with which information is processed (e.g. Bornstein & D'Agostino, 1994; Winkielman, Schwarz, Fazandeiro & Reber, 2003; see chapter 2). According to this theory, repeated exposure to a stimulus results in a representation of that stimulus in memory. When the stimulus is encountered again, this representation will make it easier to encode and process the stimulus. The 'hedonic fluency model' assumes that the increased ease of processing is experienced as pleasant and that this positive affect will be used as information in the evaluation of the stimulus (Winkielman, Schwarz, Fazandeiro & Reber, 2003). In support of this latter theory, studies using physiological measures indicated that photographs of faces that had been seen repeatedly evoked more zygomatic (cheek) muscle activity (an indication of positive affect) than unfamiliar pictures (Harmon-Jones & Allen, 2001). The familiar photographs were also more liked and liking ratings correlated with the measure of muscle activity. Finally, the positive effects of high fluency on attitudes are eliminated when participants are offered an alternative explanation (pleasant music) for their pleasant feelings (Winkielman, Schwarz, Fazandeiro & Reber, 2003).

Classical and evaluative conditioning

Through **classical conditioning** a neutral stimulus that is initially incapable of eliciting a particular response (the conditioned stimulus, or CS) gradually acquires the ability to do so through repeated association with a stimulus that already evokes this response (unconditioned stimulus, or US). The well-known example of such an initially neutral stimulus is the tone which Pavlov's dogs heard before receiving food. After these two stimuli had been paired repeatedly, the dogs began to salivate when hearing the tone (the conditioned response, or CR). When Staats and Staats (1958) adapted this paradigm to the study of attitudes, they used words that elicited positive (e.g. attractive, vacation) or negative (e.g. failure, ugly) evaluation as unconditioned stimuli and European nationalities as conditioned stimuli. (It seems that in the late 1950s American students held relatively neutral attitudes towards most European countries, except perhaps towards the main opponent in World War II.) The unconditioned stimuli were presented auditorily immediately after the visual presentation of the name of a nationality (CS) in an experiment that was ostensibly testing whether subjects could separately learn verbal stimuli that had to be processed through different channels. For half the student participants Dutch was consistently paired with negative and Swedish with positive adjectives, while the order was reversed for the other half. Several other nationality names were paired with neutral words and used as controls. When the target nationalities were later evaluated on semantic differential rating scales, the nationality that had been paired with positive words elicited a more positive rating than the nationality that had been paired with negative words.

Strategies based on this type of conditioning are widely used in advertising, even though pictures of supermodels, beautiful scenes or engaging music are typically used as unconditioned stimuli. Products are displayed in pleasing contexts that often have little relationship to the function of the product that is being advertised. The use of this strategy is based on the assumption that the positive affect or mood elicited by beautiful scenery, lovely music, or beautiful people will somehow be transferred ('rub off') on the advertised product. And there is ample evidence that it works (e.g. Bierley, McSweeney & Vannieuwkerk, 1985; Gorn, 1982; Grossman & Till, 1998; Stuart, Shimp & Engle, 1987; Shimp, Stuart & Engle, 1991; Till & Priluck, 2000). For example, Grossman and Till (1998) paired the picture of a fictitious brand of mouthwash (Garra) with either very pleasant or neutral scenes. The pleasant scenes were a tropical beach with a boat, a picture of a railway track leading to a snow-covered mountain, and a nature scene with a panda. In order to avoid the manipulation becoming too obvious they also used a number of filler products that were associated with neutral pictures. There was also a control condition in which the same pictures were used but presented in random order. Evaluation of the target product was measured immediately and with delays of one and three weeks. In support of predictions, the consistent association of the fictitious Garra mouthwash with pleasant pictures in the experimental condition resulted in a significant increase in the positive evaluation of this product (relative to the control condition) and this effect was maintained over the three week period (Figure 4.1), although there appears to be a slight but non-significant decrease over time. Since Grossman and Till (1998) assessed persistence by asking their participants to respond to the attitude measure three times (i.e. repeated measure design), it is important to note that these persistence effects have also been replicated with between subjects designs (e.g. Grossman & Till, 1998, Study 2; Till & Priluck, 2000, Study 2).

How does this type of evaluative conditioning work? In Pavlovian or classical conditioning, the CS (e.g. tone) serves as a signal for the occurrence of a biologically significant environmental stimulus (e.g. food). When the dog hears the tone it 'expects' the food and salivates in anticipation. If the tone is repeatedly presented without the food, the conditioned response is extinguished. This explanation of conditioning as signal learning does not fit the evaluative conditioning that occurs in attitude learning studies. It seems unlikely that at the end of the experiment the participants in the

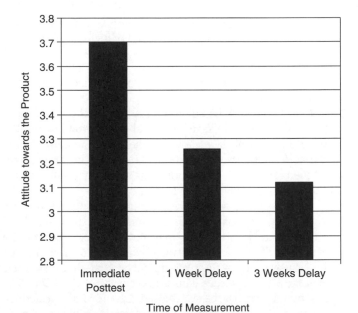

Figure 4.1 Persistence of an evaluatively conditioned brand attitude

Source: Adapted from Grossman & Till (1998). The persistence of classically conditioned brand attitudes. *Journal of Advertising, 27*, 23–31, p.27

study of Staats and Staats expected the Dutch to be attractive and the Swedes to be ugly. Furthermore, if the CS in evaluative conditioning served as a signal, these effects should not occur when participants are unaware of the contingency between CS and US. Although the question of whether conditioning effects occur without awareness of the CS–US contingency is still hotly debated (e.g. Pleyers, Corneille, Luminet & Yzerbyt, 2007), the fact that effects have been demonstrated with subliminal conditioning (Krosnick, Betz, Jussim & Lynn, 1992; for a review, see DeHouwer, Hendrickx & Baeyens, 1997) or under other conditions that made awareness rather unlikely (e.g. Olson & Fazio, 2001) suggests that such changes in evaluation *can* occur without awareness of the association between CS and US. Finally, evaluative conditioning is relatively resistant to extinction (e.g. Baeyens et al., 1988).

Although there is agreement that evaluative conditioning differs from of Pavlovian conditioning (De Houwer, Thomas & Baeyens, 2001), there is no consensus about the processes underlying evaluative conditioning. It seems increasingly likely that evaluative conditioning effects can result from several different processes. One of these processes is misattribution, by which the evaluation triggered by the US is mistakenly attributed to the CS. As a consequence, the CS acquires the valence that was originally associated with the unconditioned stimulus (Jones, Fazio & Olson, 2009). This process does not require awareness of the association between CS and US.

Another path through which evaluative conditioning can occur, requires (or at least benefits from) awareness of the association between CS and US. As Fishbein and Middlestadt suggested, CS–US pairings might produce evaluative conditioning effects by causing individuals to form specific beliefs about the CS. For example, Kim, Allen and Kardes (1996) demonstrated that after repeatedly pairing Brand L Pizza boxes with images of a race car, participants were more likely to believe that Brand L Pizza would be delivered hot and fast. Furthermore, these beliefs partially mediated participants' attitude towards this brand of pizza. And finally, these effects were stronger for participants who had been aware of the contingency in the pairing of Brand L Pizza with a race car.

Whereas the first process is based on the transfer of affect from the US to the CS, the second process appears to involve inferential belief-formation resulting from a misattribution of some aspect of the meaning of the US to the CS. Even though it is nowhere implied that Brand L Pizza House delivers their calorific products by race car, the association of the Pizza brand with the race car somehow creates in participants' minds the belief that Brand L deliveries are fast.

Neither of the two processes involves signal learning. Thus, even though consumers may not expect pleasant music to sound when they see the Coca-Cola brand logo and experimental participants may not assume to be transported into the tropics when seeing the Garra mouthwash, exposure to these products makes them feel good, because it elicits the pleasant mood that they felt when hearing the music or seeing the pleasant scenes. This is good news for Coca-Cola. The positive evaluation of this brand that has been achieved through its repeated association with pleasant music and happy people in commercials is likely to remain, even if people consume the drink in their homes without music and in the absence of happy people.

Affect-as-information

The **affect-as-information hypothesis** suggests a completely different way in which the association of pleasant scenes or lovely music with a product could increase liking for that product: Feelings may sometimes influence evaluations through feeling-based inferences rather than through repeated association with the stimulus. According to the 'how do I feel about it' heuristic, individuals infer their attitude from their present mood state. Rather than basing their attitude on their evaluations of the attributes of an attitude, people might rely on the feelings they experience as they hold the representation of the object in their minds and these feelings may be influenced by context factors as well as the attitude object (Pham, 1998). The affect-as-information hypothesis further suggests that this misattribution should disappear, when people are given reason to discount their mood state as information about the attitude object.

These hypotheses were first tested by Schwarz and Clore (1983) in a study on the impact of weather on life satisfaction. People interviewed about their life satisfaction on a sunny day reported greater satisfaction than people interviewed on a rainy day. Schwarz and Clore further demonstrated that the impact of weather conditions on life satisfaction disappeared when the interviewers (during the phone interview) casually asked about the local weather condition. Presumably, this made people attribute their mood to the weather.

Although shop owners have no control over the weather, they use other strategies to improve the mood of their customers, such as in-store music or even a complimentary glass of champagne. It is interesting to note that such strategies are more likely to be used in shops that sell clothes or luxury goods than in hardware stores. Owners of hardware stores probably suspect that pleasant music does not affect sales of kitchen knives or electrical sockets. And they are right, because such context effects occur mainly when feelings towards the target are regarded as relevant for its evaluation (Clore, Schwarz & Conway, 1994). One factor determining this type of relevance is whether the motive underlying the consumer behaviour is consummatory or instrumental (Pham, 1998). Consummatory motives underlie consumer behaviour that is in themselves rewarding (e.g. going to a restaurant; reading a novel) and attitudes towards these behaviours are most likely to be influenced by contextual affect. Actions that are not in itself rewarding, but means to a goal (e.g. attending a lecture for course credit) are driven by instrumental motives and are less likely to be influenced by contextual affect. Thus, one's mood state is more likely to influence the decision whether to buy a nice, but not essential, addition to one's wardrobe than to buy a set of kitchen knives or a replacement for a garden hose. In line with these assumptions, Pham (1998) demonstrated that a mood manipulation affected participants' intention to go to a movie, when movie-going was introduced as a relaxing episode, but not when it was perceived as a means to writing a better essay.

The formation of evaluations based on behavioural information

We have already discussed the pivotal role of behaviour (as direct experience) on attitude formation. In this section we review two additional pathways through which evaluations can be influenced by past behaviour, namely self-perception (Bem, 1972) and reinforcement (e.g. Hildum & Brown, 1965; Insko, 1965). The idea that people sometimes derive their attitudes from their past behaviour was central to Bem's (1972) self-perception theory. Bem argued that when people had to report their own attitude, but had little information about what their attitude might be, they tended to assume that their attitude was consistent with their own recent behaviour towards the attitude object. Thus, somebody, who, prompted by a person rattling a collection box, had just donated some money to a charity, might henceforth assume that he or she had a positive attitude towards this charity. However, Bem (1972) specified that self-perceived behaviour would influence attitudes only to the extent that internal cues were 'weak, ambiguous or uninterpretable'.

The assumption that self-perceived behaviour can influence attitudes towards that behaviour was first demonstrated by Salancik and Conway (1975). These authors found that their participants expressed more positive or more negative attitudes towards being religious after completing questionnaires that were designed to either increase the salience of their pro-religious or of their anti-religious past behaviour.[7] Using this manipulation in a study of attitudes towards being an environmentalist, Chaiken and Baldwin (1981) later demonstrated that this effect occurs only for people with weak attitudes (attitudes of low evaluative-cognitive consistency) towards being an environmentalist. Individuals who held strong attitudes towards being environmentalists were not affected by the salience manipulation. We will present further evidence on this point in our section on attitude strength. However, to mention one implication here, novel and unfamiliar brands (for which consumers may not have strong attitudes) may particularly benefit from self-perception processes brought about by the direct experience marketing tools mentioned earlier.

Studies of the impact of reinforcement on attitudes typically assessed the effects of verbal reinforcement of stated attitudes. For example, Hildum and Brown (1965) had Harvard student participants respond with agreement or disagreement to attitude statements about the Harvard philosophy of offering a broad and general course of study. For half of the participants the interviewers responded with 'good' every time participants agreed with a positive attitude statements or disagreed with a negative statement, for the other half, the opposite response pattern was reinforced. Participants who had been reinforced in the positive direction ended up showing a more positive attitude towards the issue than those reinforced in the negative direction. That this apparent attitude change did not merely reflect a social desirability response was demonstrated by Insko (1965), who had students of his psychology class interviewed by telephone about some local issue. Again, half the participants were reinforced for favourable attitudinal responses, the other half for unfavourable responses. When these students were one week later given an attitude questionnaire that included questions about the relevant issue among a range of other issues, it could be shown that the groups who had been differentially reinforced differed in their attitude even one week later. Although these were studies of attitude change rather than formation, this procedure could as well be used in studies of attitude formation.

How attitudes are structured

As we have seen, attitudes are evaluations of an attitude object which are based on cognitive, affective and behavioural information. Attitude structure or the way the different types of information are integrated into an overall evaluation has therefore been an important area of attitude research. This part of the chapter will focus on the relationship between beliefs about an attitude object and the evaluation of this object. As we will discuss later in a section on attitude strength, attitude structure affects the durability of attitudes, their stability, their resistance to influence and their impact on behaviour.

Expectancy–value models

Expectancy–value models are the most widely accepted models to express the relationship between beliefs and attitudes. These models conceptualize beliefs as the sum of the *expected values* attributed to the attitude object. Thus, beliefs have two components, namely an expectancy component and a value component. The expectancy component reflects the individual's confidence (i.e. subjective probability) that the attitude object possesses the attributes they associate with it. Thus, we may be quite certain that the new Mini has great road holding, trendy looks and little baggage space, but we may be much less certain whether it also has great acceleration. If we were asked to indicate our subjective probability for each of these attributes, we would probably rate the probability lower for the last characteristic than of the first three. Our level of confidence in attributing these attributes to this car would depend on our level of information. If we had just done a test drive or read a test report in a car journal, we would be more certain than if our information were based on a discussion we overheard in a pub. However, our attitude does not only depend on our confidence that the object possesses certain characteristics, but also on the value we attach to these characteristics. If we were asked to rate these characteristics on evaluative rating scales, most people would rate trendy looks, great road-holding, and good acceleration more positively than a small baggage space, with the extremity of ratings depending on our needs with regard to the car (e.g. a bachelor would probably rate the lack of baggage space less negatively than a family man). According to expectancy–value models attitudes can be predicted by multiplying the valuation of each attribute with the subjective probability with which it is perceived as linked to the object. Thus, the expectancy–value model of attitudes can be summarized as follows:

$$A_o = \sum_{i=1}^{n} \text{Expectancy} \times \text{Value}$$

with A_o being the attitude towards the object, conceived of as the summed total of the valuation x probability product for each attribute associated with the attitude object.

The first expectancy–value model of attitudes was proposed by Rosenberg (1960). According to this model, people's attitude towards some attitude object is a function of the extent to which they perceived the attitude object as a means to the attainment of important values or goals. The more instrumental an attitude object was perceived to be in helping the attainment of positive values or goals and blocking the attainment of negative values or goals, the more positively they would evaluate the object. People's attitudes were predicted to be a function of the perceived instrumentality of the attitude objects in reaching a goal and the value which they attach to that goal. Thus, perceived instrumentality reflects the subjective probability (i.e. expectancy) that the attitude object would help to attain positively valued goals and block negatively valued goals. While Rosenberg's (1960) model was successful in predicting people's attitudes towards having members of the Communist Party address the public or having black people move into one's neighbourhood, it would be less useful in predicting attitudes towards brands of cars or soft drinks. Our attitudes towards the brands are likely to be determined by their *intrinsic* qualities (e.g. road holding, taste) as well their instrumentality in helping us to attain important goals (increased mobility, quenching thirst).

It was Fishbein, who developed the approach into a general theory of attitude (1963; Fishbein & Ajzen, 1975). Fishbein's model can be expressed as follows:

$$A_o = \sum_{i=1}^{n} b_i e_i$$

where A_o is the attitude towards the object, action or event o; b_i is the belief i about o (expressed as the subjective probability that o is associated with the attribute i); e_i is the evaluation of the attribute i; and n is the number of salient attributes.[8] In testing this model, Fishbein and Ajzen (1975) demonstrated repeatedly that attitudes correlated highly with their summed expectancy-value products. They also found that each attitude object was associated with a very limited number of salient beliefs. By demonstrating that individuals' attitudes were determined by a small number of beliefs that were accessible at the time of the measurement, Fishbein and Ajzen (1975) anticipated the attitude-as-construction view of attitudes.

Are beliefs the cause of attitudes?

Another aspect in which the models of Fishbein and Rosenberg differ, is in their assumptions about the causal relationship between beliefs and attitudes. Fishbein's model is essentially an *information integration* theory. The model assumes that people's attitudes towards a brand are completely determined by the information they possess about the product attributes, or more specifically, the beliefs which are salient at the time they express their attitude. In contrast, Rosenberg's (1960) model is a *consistency* theory. Consistency theories make the assumption that individuals try to achieve consistency between their evaluations and their beliefs.[9] Thus, whereas both models would predict that changing people's beliefs would result in attitude change, only Rosenberg would make the additional prediction that changing people's evaluation of the attitude object should result in changes in their beliefs about the object.

There is some empirical support for this second prediction. In a series of classic experiments, Rosenberg (1960) demonstrated that by changing people's evaluation towards 'the idea of Negroes moving into White neighbourhoods' through post-hypnotic suggestion, he not only changed their attitudes but also achieved significant changes in their beliefs about this issue. Further support for the notion of an evaluative-cognitive consistency comes from studies, which demonstrated that more consistent attitudes were better predictors of behaviour (Norman, 1975) and more resistant to social influence (Chaiken & Baldwin, 1981; Norman, 1975, Experiment 3) than attitudes of low consistency.

It is interesting to speculate about the relationship between the antecedents of attitudes and the types of responses which constitute a particular attitude. It is important to note that, although attitudes can be based on three classes of information, not every attitude is likely to have strong cognitive, affective and behavioural components. In fact, some attitudes might even have only one of the three components. For example, an attitude that is based on evaluative conditioning might only consist of an evaluation without any cognitive content. The individual might feel good (or bad) when exposed to the attitude object, without really being aware of any reason for this feeling. Similarly, an individual might read about a new attitude object, without developing any strong feelings towards this object. This fact is important for strategies of persuasion, because it would seem plausible that such strategies should focus on those components of an individual's attitude toward an object which are the predominant determinant of that attitude.

Attitudes towards the advertisement and the dual mediation hypothesis

With his demonstration of the impact of changes in the evaluation of an attitude object on beliefs about that object, Rosenberg (1960) anticipated a controversy that emerged in research on consumer behaviour several decades later, when Mitchell and Olson (1981) questioned Fishbein's position that beliefs about product attributes were the only mediator of advertising effects on brand attitudes. Participants in their study were exposed to mock advertisements about a fictive brand of facial tissues. In different conditions, advertisements either contained explicit verbal claims about the softness of a particular brand of tissue or simply the brand name and a half-page colour photograph that connoted softness (e.g. a fluffy kitten) but no product claim. Since pictures of fluffy kittens also convey the idea of softness, it is not surprising that even the pictorial ads affected (softness-)beliefs about the brand. More importantly, however, participants' attitude towards the advertisements influenced brand attitudes, even when beliefs about brand attributes and the evaluation of these attributes (i.e. evaluative beliefs) were statistically controlled. In fact the evaluative belief and the rated evaluation of the advertisement (A_{ad}) together mediated fully the impact of the advertisements on attitudes towards the various brands of facial tissue.

Based on these findings, MacKenzie, Lutz and Belch (1986) later developed the **Dual Mediation Hypothesis** of advertisements. According to this hypothesis, the attitude towards the advertisements influences brand attitudes through two pathways, namely indirectly, via brand cognitions and directly, via evaluative conditioning (Figure 4.2). First, exposure to the advertisement elicits the expectations that use of the brand will have a number of positive consequences. One reason for this to happen

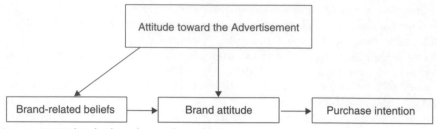

Figure 4.2 The dual mediation hypothesis

Source: Adapted from MacKenzie et al. (1986). The role of attitude toward the ad as a mediator of advertising effectiveness: A test of competing explanations. *Journal of Consumer Research,* 23, 130–143, p.131

could be that the positive affect created by a liked advertisements increases the target's willingness to accept the claims about the product made in the advertisement. Second, exposure to the advertisement elicits positive affect which will be transferred to the brand through processes of evaluative conditioning. Thus, the liking for the advertisement will 'rub off' on the product resulting in greater liking for the product. These effects are stronger in studies that use novel brands suggesting that the existence of prior brand, attitudes reduces the impact of ad attitudes (Brown & Stayman, 1992).

Attitude functions: why people hold attitudes

Attitudes serve an important function in helping us to adapt to our physical and social environment. Every day, we are confronted with a multitude of stimuli and forced to make innumerable decisions about whether to approach or avoid them (Fazio, 2000). Categorization and attitude formation are the two basic processes, which enable us to bring order into this chaos. By using similarity in attributes or function to classify widely differing stimuli as belonging to categories such as furniture, dogs or vegetables, we substantially reduce the complexity of our environment. Attitudes as stored evaluations help us to separate the good from the bad, to approach those stimuli which contribute to our survival and increase our well-being and to avoid stimuli which threaten our survival and lessen our well-being.

Theories about functions of attitudes were first proposed half a century ago, but until recently had little impact on attitude research (Katz, 1960; Smith, Bruner & White, 1956). So why should today's students of attitude and advertising research be interested in attitude functions? Katz answered this question already in 1960, when he argued that in order to be successful in changing a person's attitude we must know why the person holds that particular attitude and tailor our arguments accordingly. Both attitude formation and attitude change must be understood in terms of the needs they serve and as these motivational processes differ, so too will the techniques for attitude change (Katz, 1960).

Katz (1960) distinguished four functions of attitudes: First, attitudes help us to organize and structure our environment to interpret and make sense of otherwise chaotic perceptions (*knowledge function*). Second, attitudes help us to maximize our rewards and minimize penalties in interactions with our physical and social environment. They help us to approach those stimuli, which in the past have been associated with positive reinforcements and avoid stimuli that have resulted in punishments (*instrumental or utilitarian function*). Bruner and colleagues (1956) combined both of these functions in their *object-appraisal* function. Because attitudes were defined as categorization of stimuli along an evaluative dimension, every attitude, regardless of other functions it might serve, can be assumed to serve the object appraisal function (Fazio, 2000).

Individuals might also hold and express attitudes because they reflect values that are central to their self-concept or because they hope that expressing these attitudes might help them to maintain relationships with important groups (*value-expressive function*). For example, people might express liberal attitudes either because such expression confirms their self-understanding as liberals or because such expression conforms to the norms of important reference groups and helps them to gain or maintain status within these groups. Since this function serves private as well as public social identity goals, we will refer to it as *social identity function* of attitudes (Shavitt, 1990). Finally, attitudes may sometimes help us protect our self-esteem by avoiding having to acknowledge harsh truths about oneself or about threats from our environment. For example, since it is unpleasant to accept that one's health is threatened, people might distort or deny information about health threats in their environment (*ego-defensive function*).

Most applications of functional theory to advertising focused on differences in the functions of different attitude objects rather than the functional value of holding different attitudes (e.g. Shavitt, 1990). Thus, this research combined the theory of attitude functions with the approach of Rosenberg (1960) on functions of attitude objects. Most of this research compared brand attitudes based on a utilitarian perspective compared to attitudes based on an image-oriented perspective. The relevance of this type of functional approach to research on advertising derives from the fact that some products are associated with different functions for different people, whereas other products are typically associated with the same function for everybody. For example, everybody buys salt or washing powder for instrumental reasons. There is little image gain to be achieved by buying salt or washing powder of brand A rather than brand B.

For other products, there can be greater image gains associated with certain choices than others. For these products, people's choices might differ, depending on the importance they attach to image gains rather than instrumental value. For example, watches can vary in price from less than a hundred euros to more than a hundred thousand euros. One reason, why some watches are expensive (but only one reason), is that they have mechanical movements handcrafted by watchmakers, whereas the less expensive watches have electronic movements. Since even the cheapest electronic (quartz) movement will be an order of magnitude more accurate than purely mechanical movements (Wikipedia, 2008b), it seems likely that individuals who spend thousands to buy a Rolex or Cartier watch with mechanical movements are motivated by needs other than that of keeping the exact time.

Research on the functional approach to advertising has either used an individual difference approach (e.g. DeBono, 2006; Snyder & DeBono, 1985) or an object-based approach (e.g. Shavitt, 1990). The individual difference approach has focused exclusively on one individual difference variable, namely self-monitoring. It is assumed that differences between individuals' scores on the **self-monitoring scale** (Snyder, 1974) distinguish people for whom image aspects of a product are particularly important from those for whom these aspects are less important. High self-monitors tend to be concerned about the image they project to others and they are highly skilled in adjusting their self-presentations to match differing social and inter-personal expectations. As a result, high self-monitors often display substantial changes across situations in the way they present themselves. In contrast, low self-monitors try to behave in line with their own feelings and attitudes and thus maintain a high degree of consistency in their behaviour across situations. Because they value their social impression more than low self-monitors, high self-monitors are more affected by image-appeals. Self-monitoring studies can therefore also be considered as illustrations of the value expressive function of attitudes.

In an early test of this hypothesis, Snyder and DeBono (1985) demonstrated that high self-monitors preferred image-oriented advertisement to quality-oriented ads. One of the advertisement they used showed a picture of a bottle of Canadian Club whisky on the blueprints of a house. The image-oriented text stated, 'You're not just moving in, you're moving up'. In contrast, the product-quality oriented text claimed, 'When it comes to great taste, everyone draws the same conclusion' (p. 589). High self-monitors did not only think that the image-oriented advertisement was more effective than the quality-oriented ad, they were also willing to pay more for a product that was advertised with image- rather than quality-oriented arguments. Snyder and DeBono (1985) even found differences in participants' willingness to use a product, depending on how it was advertised: high self-monitors were more willing to use a product that was advertised with an image- rather than a quality-oriented advertisement and the reverse was true for low self-monitors. Although replications of these studies have generally indicated that high self-monitors are more responsive to image-oriented advertisements and low self-monitors to quality-based appeals, results have not been robust and inconsistent findings have been reported (for a review, see DeBono, 2006). We will return to this issue below.

The differential impact of image factors on attitudes and judgements of individuals, who differ in degree of self-monitoring has also been demonstrated in studies of judgements of the quality of products (DeBono, Leavitt & Backus, 2003; DeBono & Rubin, 1995). In an early experiment, DeBono and Rubin (1995) used the country of origin of a product as their image cue. As mentioned earlier, there is much evidence that consumers make use of the information about the country of origin in judging the quality of a product (e.g. Allison & Uhl, 1964; Jacoby et al., 1971; Fichter & Jonas, 2008). Food is one of the product categories for which the country of origin information is considered particularly important. For example, even though outstanding cheeses are produced in the United States or Germany, France still has the image of producing superior cheeses. De Bono and Rubin (1995) made use of this stereotype by having their participants rate the taste of two cheeses, one of them very pleasant tasting, the other of unpleasant taste. Half the participants was told that the cheese they were tasting came from Strasbourg in France, the other half that it came from Mulburry in Kansas. The dependent measure was the sum of responses to questions about taste, buying intention and the intention to recommend the cheese to others. Two analyses of variance conducted separately for high and low self-monitors resulted in a main effect for country of origin for high self-monitors and a main effect of taste for low self-monitors. None of the other effects reached acceptable levels of significance.

DeBono, Leavitt and Backus (2003) reported a conceptual replication of the findings of DeBono and Rubin (1995), using the attractiveness of the packaging of a product rather than country of origin as image cue. DeBono et al. (2003) demonstrated that the attractiveness of the packaging had differential effects on high and low self-monitors. When high and low self-monitoring men and women evaluated a perfume/cologne that varied in pleasantness of scent as well as the attractiveness of its packaging, evaluations of low self-monitors were mainly influenced by the actual scent of the product, whereas high self-monitors were mainly influenced by the attractiveness of the bottle from which it came (Figure 4.3).

As we mentioned earlier, the functional approach makes the basic assumption that persuasive messages are most effective, if the arguments match the function which the attitude object serves for this particular individual. The findings of Snyder and DeBono (1985) reported earlier that high self-monitors found image-oriented arguments more persuasive than quality-oriented arguments is consistent with this assumption. However, even if marketers would be able to know the self-monitoring scores of target audiences, the fact that these audiences are unlikely to be homogeneous with regard to these scores would make tailoring of arguments difficult, at least for mass media campaigns.

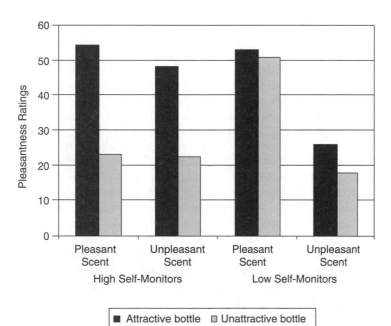

Figure 4.3 Mean evaluations of pleasant and unpleasant smelling perfume/cologne by attractiveness of bottle

Source: Adapted from DeBono et al. (2003). Product packaging and product evaluation: An individual difference approach. *Journal of Applied Social Psychology, 33*, 513–521, p.519

In this respect, the object-based approach is more promising. The object-based approach assumes that (1) some objects are reliably associated with one particular attitude function; and that (2) persuasive appeals about these objects are likely to have the greatest impact, if they match the function served by these objects. Shavitt (1990) tested these assumptions in two studies. In the first study she had participants categorize various objects either as serving an instrumental function (e.g. air conditioners; coffee) or a social identity function (e.g. perfume). She then constructed two advertisements for each of these objects, one containing instrumental the other social identity arguments. When participants were asked to list the thoughts and feelings that went through their minds when reading each of these advertisements, they produced more favourable thoughts for advertisements that contained arguments, which matched the function of the particular object.

It is plausible that if a product category mainly serves an instrumental function, arguments that assure us that a particular product serves this function particularly well are likely to be more effective than image-oriented arguments. Conversely, if one desires a product on account of the image benefits it is likely to convey, then image-oriented arguments would be more effective than quality-oriented arguments. However, Petty and Wegener (1998a) suggested another reason, why functionally matched messages are more effective than mismatched messages. They argued that matched messages are more likely to motivate individuals to scrutinize the arguments contained in a message than do mismatched messages.

This suggestion is interesting, because it would offer a potential explanation (in terms of variations in argument strength) for some of the inconsistencies in this research mentioned earlier (DeBono, 2006). According to dual process theories of persuasion (e.g. Chaiken et al., 1989; Petty & Cacioppo, 1986; chapter 5), an increase in processing motivation should increase the persuasive impact of a message only if that message contains strong arguments. If a message contains mainly weak arguments, increasing processing motivation should reduce the persuasive impact of a message. Thus, matched messages should only be more effective than mismatched messages if they contained strong arguments. Petty and Wegener (1998a) supported this hypothesis in two studies, in which high and low self-monitors were presented with messages that either matched or mismatched the functional basis of their attitude and that contained either strong or weak arguments.

Thus, Katz (1960) was right when he suggested that in order to be successful in changing a person's attitude we must know why the person holds that particular attitude and tailor our message accordingly. But the argument that one has to promise consumers image-gain for products which serve image functions and high quality for products that serve instrumental functions in order to persuade them to buy a product is only part of the story. Because functionally matched arguments appear to increase processing motivation, arguments have to be strong as well as matched to be optimally persuasive.

Attitude strength

Some attitudes exert powerful impact on thinking and on behaviour whereas others have little or no effect. This distinction has been referred to as attitude strength (Krosnick

& Petty, 1995; Visser, Bizer & Krosnik, 2006). The concept of **attitude strength** links aspects of attitude structure and attitude function. Krosnick and Petty (1995) suggest that stronger attitudes are characterized by four attributes: (1) higher stability over time; (2) greater impact on behaviour; (3) greater influence on information processing; and (4) greater resistance to persuasion. In this last section of the chapter we will discuss some of the properties of attitudes or attitude structure, which are assumed to be determinants of attitude strength. The role of advertising and other persuasive communications in influencing attitude strength will be discussed in chapter 5.

Accessibility

It seems plausible that more highly accessible attitudes are more likely to exert a strong influence on information processing and behaviour than attitudes, which first have to be constructed on the basis of new information. Cognitive *accessibility* of an attitude refers to how easily or quickly the attitude can be retrieved from memory. The speed with which an attitude can be retrieved from memory is presumed to indicate the strength of the association between the representation of the attitude object and the evaluation (Fazio, 1995). With regard to brand attitudes, the accessibility of a brand (i.e. the ease with which consumers can recall or recognize the brand and thus also retrieve the beliefs associated with that brand) has been referred to as **brand awareness** (Keller, 2009). Accessibility has typically been measured by measuring response time, that is the time it takes the individuals to report their attitude when asked to indicate it as quickly as possible. Attitude accessibility is negatively related to ambivalence, when people have mixed feeling about the attitude object (Bargh et al., 1992), but unrelated to evaluative–cognitive consistency (Chaiken et al., 1995).

Highly accessible attitudes have been found to be *more predictive of behaviour* than attitudes of low accessibility. In a study conducted by Fazio, Powell and Williams (1989) participants were presented with 100 consumer products on a computer monitor and had to indicate whether they liked or disliked each of products by pressing one of two keys. Afterwards they were given a choice of 5 out of 10 of these products (e.g. Snicker's candy bar, Star-Kist Tuna, Planters peanuts) as a token of appreciation for having participated. Highly accessible attitudes were better predictors of product choice than were attitudes of low accessibility. Other studies have also supported the assumption that accessibility moderates the attitude-behaviour relationship (Fazio & Williams, 1986). Consumer attitudes towards products, of course, can be more or less predictive of a pivotal form of consumer behaviour: purchasing the product. Since attitude strength also moderates this relation, it pays for advertisers to invest in increasing attitude strength among consumers, for instance by increasing advertising frequency.

There is also evidence that highly accessible attitudes are *more resistant to social influence*. For example, Fazio and Williams (1986) measured attitudes towards the then president Reagan in the 1984 presidential campaign and found that highly accessible attitudes were better predictors of whom one voted for four months later than attitudes that were of low accessibility. Although there was no measure of attitude change, the fact that accessible attitudes were a better predictor of voting behaviour after a four month election campaign suggests that these attitudes were less influenced by the arguments that were aired during this campaign. A more direct test was reported by Bassili and Fletcher (1991), who measured attitude accessibility during a telephone interview. Respondents were presented with a counterargument, after they had responded to a question concerning job quotas for women. Some of the respondents changed their minds after having been exposed to the counterargument and this change was related to attitude accessibility.

Attitude importance

It would also seem plausible that attitudes towards issues, which are important to the individuals, are more strongly held than attitudes towards unimportant issues. *Attitude importance* is usually measured by asking people how important an attitude object is to them personally, how deeply they care about it, and how concerned they are about it (Boninger, Krosnick, Berent & Fabrigar, 1995). One important determinant of attitude importance is the relevance of the attitude to cherished values of the individual. A second important determinant is the relevance to self-interest. Using a procedure frequently employed in tests of dual process theories of attitude change (Petty & Cacioppo, 1986), Bizer & Krosnick (2001), who manipulated self-interest by telling some of their participants that a proposed new university policy will affect them, whereas others were led to believe that the policy had already been rejected, found their manipulation to affect perceived importance. A third determinant of importance is the perceived relevance of an issue for the interests of important reference groups. There is evidence that important attitudes are more stable than unimportant attitudes, are more predictive of behaviour and also more resistant to social influence (for reviews, see Boninger et al., 1995; Visser et al., 2006).

Attitude knowledge

Because the importance of an attitude object reflects the degree of caring and concern about an attitude issue, one would expect that people would also be more motivated to acquire knowledge about important rather than unimportant issues. However, knowledge often accumulates simply as the result of exposure to information about an object. Since exposure to an attitude object either through direct contact or indirectly (e.g. media) is not necessarily related to the importance of that object, it is not surprising that knowledge about an attitude object is only moderately positively related to its importance (Visser et al., 2006). Consistent with this interpretation, Visser and colleagues (2006) found attitude-relevant knowledge associated with both attitude importance and media use (Visser et al., 2006).

Individuals with a high level of knowledge about an issue should be better able to evaluate the validity of arguments about that issue than individuals with little knowledge (e.g. Chaiken et al., 1989; Petty & Cacioppo, 1986). Thus, people who are well-informed about a particular product category should be more influenced by strong arguments about a particular product belonging to that category, whereas uninformed people might be more influenced by heuristic cues such as price or country of origin information. In support of these assumptions, Wood and colleagues

(1985) found that the quality of arguments that were presented in a communication had greater impact on attitudes of knowledgeable participants than on individuals with little knowledge about the issue. In contrast, the attitudes of low knowledge individuals were more influenced by heuristic cues. Unfortunately, Wood and colleagues (1985) did not control for attitude importance, even though amount of knowledge was significantly and positively correlated with a measure of importance. It is thus unclear to what extent the pattern of findings was due to differences in knowledge or differences in processing motivation.

Attitude certainty

Attitude certainty refers to confidence individuals have in the validity or correctness of their own attitude. Although attitude certainty is correlated with extremity, with people being typically more certain of their extreme rather than their neutral attitudes, the two dimensions are conceptually distinct. It is possible to hold even a neutral attitude with a high degree of certainty. Attitude certainty has also been found to be moderately positively correlated with importance (Visser et al., 2006). Individuals are more certain of attitudes on important rather than unimportant issues. People also tend to be more certain of attitudes which derive from their personal experience (Fazio & Zanna, 1981), that come to mind easily (Haddock et al., 1999) and for which they perceive a high degree of consensus (Visser & Mirabile, 2004). Attitude certainty has also been found to be associated with a number of important consequences (Petty, Briñol, Tormala & Wegener, 2007). Attitudes held with greater certainty are more resistant to change (Tormala & Petty, 2002) and more predictive of behaviour (Fazio & Zanna, 1981).

Ambivalence

Attitudinal ambivalence has been considered one of the most important strength-related dimensions of attitudes. **Ambivalence** can be defined as a state in which an individual gives an attitude object equivalently strong positive or negative evaluation (Thompson, Zanna & Griffin, 1995). That we sometimes appear to both like and dislike an attitude object is difficult to reconcile with a bipolar conceptualization of attitudes discussed earlier, which assumes that the evaluative processes underlying attitudes are reciprocally activated and interchangeable. As potential solution of this problem a two-dimensional perspective of attitudes has been suggested (e.g. Cacioppo, Gardner & Berntson, 1997). This perspective assumes that for many attitudes, positive and negative evaluations, rather than being the endpoints of a continuum that ranges from positive to negative, are stored in memory on two separate dimensions, one ranging from neutral to positive and another from neutral to negative.

There are two strategies to assess ambivalence. It can either be measured as an *experienced* state, or calculated from evaluations as *structural* ambivalence (Jonas et al., 2000). With measures of experienced ambivalence individuals are asked to express their feelings of ambivalence (e.g. 'I find myself torn between two sides of the issue of . . .'). The structural approach is based on the definition of ambivalence as the coexistence of positive and negative evaluations. Individuals are first asked to rate the positive qualities of the attitude object, disregarding all the negative qualities (Kaplan, 1972). After that they are asked to rate only the negative qualities, ignoring all the positive aspects. These two ratings are then combined into an index, with ambivalence being highest when the two ratings are both *similar* and *extreme*.

Indices of structural and experienced ambivalence show only moderately positive correlations that range from .35 to .45 (Jonas, Broemer & Diehl, 2000). These moderate correlations suggest that the two measures overlap but also reflect different aspects of ambivalence. One possibility is that structural ambivalence is only one of several types of ambivalence that contribute to experienced ambivalence. Support for this assumption comes from a study of Priester and Petty (2001), who demonstrated that experienced ambivalence, but not structural ambivalence, is influenced by the individual's perception of the existence of discrepant attitudes within their social network. Another reason for the moderate relationship could be that individuals are not fully aware of the degree of ambivalence that exists within their attitude structure. Consistent with this assumption, a recent study by Newby-Clark, McGregor and Zanna (2002) found that the association between the two types of measures increased when the cognitive accessibility of the conflicting evaluations was increased.

If one assumes that individuals have a need to be consistent in their evaluation of an attitude object (e.g. Heider, 1946), the two types of ambivalence should have different consequences for information search and processing. As Jonas and colleagues (2000) argued, unless individuals are aware that their attitudes are ambivalent, they should feel no need to resolve this ambivalence through additional information or deeper thinking about the attitude object. Although we agree that the experience of ambivalence is a necessary condition for motivating information search, we would question whether it is also sufficient. Unless there is some need to integrate the information into an overall evaluation (e.g. because some action regarding the attitude object is required), experienced ambivalence may not motivate information search. It seems further plausible that the realization that one's attitude is ambivalent should only motivate individuals to search for further information about the attitude object, if they *expect* that additional information would help them to resolve this inconsistency.

Attitudinal ambivalence has been found to be related to several attributes characteristic of attitude strength. Attitude objects associated with greater structural ambivalence are less cognitively accessible (evidenced by greater evaluation latency) than attitude objects associated with less ambivalence (e.g. Bargh, Chaiken, Govender & Pratto, 1992; Harreveld van der Pligt, de Vries, Wenneker & Verhue, 2004). In some (e.g. Bargh et al., 1992; Jonas, Broemer & Diehl, 2000), but not other studies (e.g. Armitage & Conner, 2000; Bassili, 1996) ambivalent attitudes have also been found to be less stable than non ambivalent attitudes. That findings with regard to stability are inconsistent is not surprising. Since an ambivalent attitude consists of two evaluatively different components, the stability of ambivalent attitudes will depend on situational factors, or more specifically, on the extent to which the same aspects of the attitude are salient at both time of measurement.

Ambivalent attitudes have also been found to be less predictive of behavioural intentions and behaviour than non ambivalent attitudes (Armitage & Conner, 2000; Jonas et al., 2000). Since attitudes can only predict behaviour to the extent that they are stable, one would expect that it is their instability, which makes ambivalent attitudes such poor predictors of behaviour. However, whereas Jonas and colleagues found evidence for this type of mediation, Armitage and Conner (2000) did not. This suggests that attitude stability is not the only factor that can affect the predictive qualities of ambivalent attitudes.

There is considerable evidence that ambivalent attitudes are less resistant to social influence than are non-ambivalent attitudes. For example, Armitage and Conner (2000) found that an attitude change intervention had greater persuasive impact on individuals with more rather than less structurally ambivalent attitudes. Similarly, Hodson, Maio and Esses (2001) showed that consensus information about how many of their fellow students were swayed by a videotaped debate about social welfare had greater impact on participants who held structurally ambivalent attitudes towards social welfare than on participants, whose attitudes were not ambivalent. Tourangeau, Rasinski, Bradburn and D'Andrade (1989) found stronger interview question order effects for attitudes that were ambivalent rather than non-ambivalent.

Finally, ambivalence has been found to be positively related to processing motivation (Maio, Bell & Esses, 1996). In a study, which assessed the impact of processing motivation on message-induced attitude change with regard to ambivalent and non-ambivalent attitudes, Maio and colleagues (1996) exposed Canadian students to a message about Chinese immigrants to Canada. By manipulating the strength of the arguments contained in the message, these researchers were able to assess depth of message processing. [Argument quality affects mainly those individuals who think about the message (Petty & Cacioppo, 1986; chapter 5)]. Maio and colleagues found that individuals, who were ambivalent[10] about Chinese immigrants, were more strongly affected by the strong than the weak message, whereas message strength had little effect on non-ambivalent individuals. Furthermore, attitude change was mediated by thought favourability for ambivalent but not for non-ambivalent individuals. That it is the experience of ambivalence which motivates processing depth has been demonstrated by Nordgren, Harreveld and van der Pligt (2006). These authors showed that the message processing of ambivalent individuals was biased in the direction of their more polarized evaluation. As a result of this biased processing, participants could reduce their ambivalence.

Our discussion of ambivalence has so far been limited to ambivalence in *established* attitudes. Such ambivalence is likely to differ from the ambivalence aroused by exposure to evaluatively inconsistent information during the *formation* of a new attitude. This issue is particularly relevant for the consumer domain, because the information consumers receive about products is often evaluatively inconsistent. From what we know about ambivalence so far, one would expect that attitudes formed on the basis of such ambivalent information, would be less predictive of behaviour than attitudes that are formed on the basis of consistent information. However, the opposite prediction could be derived from dual process theories of attitude change (Chaiken et al., 1989; Petty & Cacioppo, 1986; chapter 5 this volume). According to these theories, attitudes that are formed on the basis of elaborate processing are more predictive of behaviour than are attitudes based on superficial processing. Since it is more difficult to integrate inconsistent than consistent information, one would expect that participants who were presented with evaluatively inconsistent information would have to engage in deeper processing to form an overall evaluation. From this perspective, one would expect that attitudes formed from evaluatively inconsistent information should be more predictive of behaviour than attitudes that were based on consistent information. This is precisely what Jonas, Diehl and Broemer (1997) found in a pioneering study in which they manipulated ambivalence by exposing their participants either to evaluatively consistent or inconsistent information about a (fictitious) brand of shampoo.

We would argue that the findings of Jonas and colleagues (1997) are limited to situations, where individuals both feel a need to form an overall evaluation *and* succeed in integrating the evaluatively inconsistent product attributes of information into an overall evaluation, because they have all the details cognitively accessible. Support for this assumption comes from a study of Sengupta and Johar (2002), who provided their participants with information about a fictitious product (video recorder) at two points in time, separated by an intermittent task. Whereas at Time 1 participants learned that this video recorder outperformed competitive products on a number of important technical features, half the participants learned at a later time that this video recorder was inferior to the competition on two other important technical dimensions. Cross-cutting this manipulation, half the participants were instructed to memorize the product information given at Time 1 (memory instruction), whereas the other half were given no memory instruction. Without instructions to memorize, participants were therefore likely to form evaluation online and forget the product details given at Time 1. They would only remember that they thought the particular video recorder was a good product without remembering anymore why they thought so. When presented with the negative information at Time 2, these participants would find it difficult to reconcile the inconsistent information with their earlier attitude. In contrast, participants who still remembered all the product details given at Time 1 would have little difficulty to integrate the different information into an overall attitude.

As predicted, Sengupta and Johar (2002) replicated the findings of Jonas et al. (1997) only under memory instruction conditions, when participants had all the information available and were able to integrate it into an overall attitude. When participants were unable to integrate the inconsistent information, the pattern reversed. Product attitudes formed on the basis of inconsistent information became weaker predictors of behaviour than attitudes that had been formed on the basis of consistent information. It is important to note here that these students were unlikely to possess much expert knowledge about video recorders. If they had had such knowledge they might have remembered the product information give earlier, even without instruction to memorize.

Evaluative–cognitive consistency

As we discussed earlier, **evaluative–cognitive consistency** refers to the consistency between people's attitudes towards an attitude object and the evaluative implications of their beliefs about the object. It is operationalized as the absolute difference in the z-scores of the attitude and the z-scores of summed instrumentality x value products[11], with higher differences implying greater inconsistency (Chaiken et al., 1995; Maio et al., 1996). Some researchers consider evaluative–cognitive consistency a subtype of ambivalence, namely ambivalence between different dimensions as distinguished from ambivalence within the same dimension (i.e. simultaneous positive and negative evaluation) discussed so far. However, the fact that evaluative cognitive consistency has been found to be uncorrelated to both experienced (Jonas et al., 2000) and structural ambivalence (Maio, Bell & Esses, 1996) suggests that evaluative–cognitive consistency and attitudinal ambivalence should be considered distinct constructs.

And yet, as we mentioned earlier, there is considerable evidence to suggest that evaluative–cognitive consistency is an aspect of attitude strength. For example, evaluatively–cognitively consistent attitudes have been found to be more stable than inconsistent attitudes. Thus, Norman (1975) obtained higher test-retest correlations for consistent rather than inconsistent attitudes towards volunteering for psychological research. Chaiken and Pomerantz (1992; reported in Chaiken et al., 1995) observed a similar difference in temporal stability attitudes towards corporal punishment. Norman (1975) also found consistent attitudes towards volunteering to be better predictors of subsequent behaviour than inconsistent attitudes. Finally, studies have demonstrated that more consistent attitudes are more resistant to social influence (Chaiken & Baldwin, 1981; Norman, 1975, Experiment 3) than attitudes of low consistency.

Attitude strength and the context dependence of attitudinal judgments

In our discussion of the file-drawer model of attitudes versus the attitude-as-construction model, we already suggested attitude strength as the moderating variable responsible for the conflicting evidence on the context stability of attitudes. There is a great deal of evidence from studies manipulating a wide range of context factors, to support this assumption with regard to a variety of different determinants of attitude strength. Thus, as mentioned earlier, Hodson et al. (2001) demonstrated that consensus information had greater impact on individuals with ambivalent rather than non-ambivalent attitudes. Similarly, Tourangeau et al. (1989) found ambivalence to moderate the impact of the order interview questions on reported attitudes. Although Bishop (1990) and Krosnick and Schuman (1988) failed to replicate this pattern, Lavine, Huff, Wagner and Sweeney (1998) demonstrated that this failure to find evidence for the moderating role of attitude strength was due to the fact that strength was assessed with a single, dichotomous item.

Finally, several studies supported the prediction from self-perception theory (Bem, 1972) that when internal cues about attitudes are 'weak, ambiguous or uninterpretable' people infer their attitude from their own behaviour (Chaiken & Baldwin, 1981; Haddock, 2002; Holland, Verplanken & Van Knippenberg, 2002). We already mentioned the study of Chaiken and Baldwin (1981), who experimentally increased the salience of either the pro- or the anti-environmentalist past behaviour of their participants and found that this manipulation affected only the attitudes of individuals whose pre-experimental attitudes had been of low evaluative–cognitive consistency and thus weak. Individuals whose attitudes had been highly consistent were not affected by this manipulation.

Further evidence of the moderating role of attitude strength on the impact of self-perception comes from a study that used accessibility experiences for their manipulation of context effects (Haddock, 2002). In this study, British participants were asked to think either of two or five negative attributes of the then British prime minister Tony Blair. In a second step, their attitude towards Tony Blair was measured. One would expect that if somebody had retrieved five negative attributes of Tony Blair, such a person would have a more negative attitude towards Blair than a person who only had to come up with two. However, as Schwarz et al. (1991) had shown in an earlier study on a different issue, the opposite result can be expected. In making their judgements, participants use their perception of the ease with which they can access the information about the attitude object as the cue on which they base their evaluation. Since it is more difficult to come up with five than two negative attributes, participants in the five-attribute condition will infer from the difficulty they had in coming up with the required number of negative attributes that they must not hold a very negative attitude. Consistent with these predictions, Haddock (2002) found that individuals asked to think of five negative attributes liked Blair more than participants, who only had to think of two negative attributes (Figure 4.4). But consistent with the assumed moderating role of attitude strength, this effect emerged only for participants, who were uninterested in British politics (i.e. had weak attitudes). The manipulation had no effect for people with strong interest in British politics.

Finally Holland and colleagues (2002) did not only demonstrate that weak attitudes are influenced by people's perception of their own attitude-relevant behaviour, they also showed that the causal direction between attitude and behaviour reversed for strong attitudes. Holland and colleagues (2002) measured their participants' attitude towards Greenpeace during two sessions one week apart. In Session 2, participants were also given an opportunity to donate money to Greenpeace, and this donation took place either before or after the attitude measurement. This clever design made it possible to assess not only the impact of behaviour on attitudes (when Session

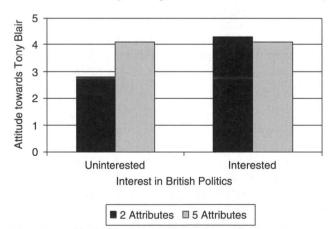

Figure 4.4 The impact of accessibility experiences on attitudes towards Tony Blair of individuals who are interested or uninterested in politics [higher scores indicate more positive attitudes (range 1–7)]

Source: Adapted from Haddock (2002). It's easy to like or dislike Tony Blair: Accessibility experiences and the favourability of attitude judgments. *British Journal of Psychology, 93,* 257–267, p.262

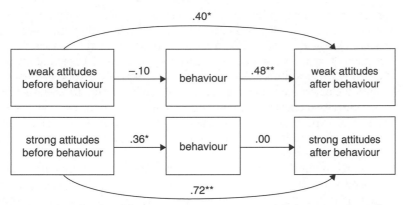

Figure 4.5 Standardized betas in a regression model depicting the influence of attitude strength on attitude-behaviour and behaviour-attitude relations. *p<.05, **p<.01

Source: Holland et al. (2002). On the nature of attitude-behavior relations: The strong guide, the weak follow. *European Journal of Social Psychology, 32,* 869–876, p. 874. Reproduced with permission of Wiley-Blackwell

2 attitude was measured after the donation), but also to assess the impact of attitudes on behaviour (when Session 2 attitude was measured before the donation). They found that attitude strength assessed in Session 1 moderated the impact of behaviour on attitudes (Figure 4.5). Behaviour had a significant impact on Session 2 attitudes of individuals with weak attitudes but did not affect attitudes of participants, who originally had held strong attitudes. In contrast, donation behaviour (i.e. amount of money donated) was predicted by strong but not weak attitudes. Thus, this last study did not only replicate earlier findings that attitude strength moderates the impact of self-perceived behaviour on attitudinal judgments (Chaiken & Baldwin, 1981; Haddock, 2002), it also replicated the findings of studies that demonstrated that attitude strength moderates the attitude-behaviour relationship (e.g. Armitage & Conner, 2000; Fazio et al., 1989; Jonas et al., 2000; Norman, 1975).

Summary and conclusions

- The first section of the chapter reviewed the controversy surrounding the definition of the attitude concept. Researchers agree that attitudes are evaluative responses and directed towards some attitude object. But there is disagreement as to whether to define it as a predisposition to evaluate or as the evaluative response itself. Although the dispositional definition seems very plausible, the fact that some attitudes are constructed on the spot and that people's explicit attitudes sometimes differ from their implicit attitudes speaks against this definition. In this volume, we therefore opted for the definition of attitudes as 'the categorization of a stimulus object along an evaluative dimension' (Zanna & Rempel, 1988).
- The second section of the chapter discussed processes of attitude forma-

tion. Attitudes derive from cognitive, evaluative/emotional and behavioural information and we discussed the various processes through which these different classes of information influence attitude formation. Research on the formation of cognitively based evaluative responses has focused mainly on the question whether attitudes that are based on a person's direct experience with the attitude object are better predictors of behaviour than attitudes that derive from indirect experience (e.g. verbal descriptions, pictorial material). We concluded that experience-based attitudes are better predictors of behaviour, but only if the situation in which the attitude is formed is similar to that in which behaviour is assessed.

- Our discussion of the formation of attitudes based on affective or emotional experiences focused on three processes, mere exposure, classical or evaluative conditioning and the affect-as-information hypothesis. With mere exposure effects, liking for initially neutral stimuli increases with frequency of exposure. The more often individuals are exposed to a stimulus, the more they like it. The mere exposure effect is strongest at first exposure and levels off after 10 to 20 exposures. Furthermore, it is not necessary that individuals are consciously aware of the fact that a stimulus has been presented. In fact, the mere exposure effect was stronger when stimuli were presented subliminally rather than supraliminally.

- In classical or evaluative conditioning, initially neutral stimuli are presented together with stimuli, which are positively or negatively evaluated. After repeated association some of the valence of the evaluatively polarized stimulus transfers to the neutral stimulus. Studies have shown that both the mere exposure effect and evaluative conditioning can be used in the advertising of new brands.

- Finally, the affect-as-information hypothesis suggests a more cognitive route through which an evaluatively polarized stimulus context can affect attitudes towards a neutral stimulus. Thus, rather than being automatically linked to the neutral stimulus through association, pleasant store music or other pleasant contextual factors might influence the evaluation of a product through the 'how do I feel about it' heuristic. Individuals might misattribute the pleasant mood caused by the context to the product and as a result, evaluate the product more positively.

- In our discussion of attitude formation based on behavioural information we considered two mechanisms, namely that people infer their attitudes towards an object from their past behaviour (self-perception theory) and that their attitude is influenced by the consequences of their past behaviour (instrumental conditioning). In support of Bem's self-perception theory, perceived past behaviour affected attitudinal judgements only when attitudes were weak, but not when they were strong.

- The third section of this chapter focused on attitude structure. Attitude structure reflects the way in which the different types of information are integrated into an overall evaluation. We discussed two issues, namely the relationship between attitudes and beliefs, and the dual mediation hypothesis of advertisements. It is important to understand how beliefs about an attitude object are integrated into an overall evaluation, because persuasive communications, which are the most important strategy of attitude change, typically aim at changing the individual's beliefs about an attitude object. According to the dual mediation hypothesis, advertisements can influence attitudes towards brands not only through changing the individual's beliefs about the attributes of a particular brand but also by eliciting positive affects that 'rub off' on the product through evaluative conditioning.

- In the fourth section of this chapter, we discussed the functions of attitudes. We argued that attitudes help us to adapt to our physical and social environment, by indicating, which stimuli one should approach and which one should avoid. Understanding attitude functions is important for strategies of attitude change, because one must know, why somebody holds an attitude in order to be able to change it.

- Advertising research on attitude functions has mainly been concerned with the distinction between products, which serve an instrumental function (e.g. aspirin, salt, air conditioners) and those that serve an image function. The relevance of functional theory for research on advertising derives from the fact that some products are associated with the same function for everybody, whereas others can serve different functions for different people. For example, watches can serve merely as timepieces, but they can also be used as display of wealth to gain status with one's social environment. It appears that the personality dimension of self-monitoring is an important individual difference variable which differentiates individuals who attach great value to image from those who focus more on the quality aspects of a product.

- Since some attitudes exert a powerful impact on our thinking and behaviour, whereas others have little or no effect, the fifth and final section of this chapter focused on determinants of attitude strength. Some of the determinants of attitude strength (e.g. attitude importance) are related to attitude function, others (e.g. ambivalence, evaluative–cognitive consistency) are related to attitude structure. The concept of attitude strength therefore links aspects of attitude structure and function. Attitude strength determines whether an attitude is relatively stable or highly context dependent. Understanding the determinants of attitude strength therefore helps us to understand why attitudes vary in the extent to which they are resistant to change and predictive of behaviour.

- This chapter focused on attitude formation and the various mechanisms by which people develop attitudes about attitude objects with which they are not familiar. As we have seen, most of the processes which mediate attitude formation require little cognitive processing capacity. There was therefore little need to discuss determinants of processing capacity or processing ability in this chapter. The following chapter on persuasion will focus on attitude change in response to arguments or other information about the attitude object. Since the impact of arguments on people's beliefs will not only depend on the strength those arguments and the credibility of the people making them, but also on the motivation and ability of the target to think about the arguments, processing motivation and ability will become a major theme of chapter 5.

How consumers yield to advertising: principles of persuasion and attitude change

The Yale reinforcement approach — 154
The information processing model of McGuire — 156
The cognitive response model — 158
Dual process theories of persuasion — 160
Assessing the intensity of processing — 165
Persuasion by a single route: the unimodel — 182
Lowering resistance to advertising — 184
Summary and conclusions — 192

In the previous chapter, we discussed how attitudes are formed, structured and what function they serve. This chapter will present theories of persuasion. Theorists of persuasion differ in how narrowly they define the concept. For example Eagly and Chaiken (1984) define persuasion narrowly as aimed at changing beliefs and attitudes through the use of 'relatively complex messages that consist of a position advocated by a communicator and (usually) one or more arguments designed to support that position' (p. 268). Since advertisers rarely resort to complex messages in their attempts to persuade consumers to buy their products, much of advertising would not be considered persuasion according to this definition. We will therefore use here the more liberal definition of the concept given by Petty and Cacioppo (1986) in their classic monograph *Communication and Persuasion* They define **persuasion** as any change in beliefs and attitudes 'that results from exposure to a communication' (p. 5).

Although, like Packard in his influential book *Hidden Persuaders*, we view much of advertising as a form of persuasion, the social psychological theories of persuasion and social psychological research into the impact of persuasive communications on attitudes and behaviour discussed in this chapter have little affinity with the sinister techniques of manipulating the subconscious of consumers discussed by Packard. However, persuasion is not the only strategy, which advertisers have at their disposal and attitude change is not the only path through which marketers can influence buying behaviour. Thus, in chapters 6 and 7 we will describe some techniques, which might have made good reading in Packard's book.

The Yale Reinforcement Approach

The beginnings of social psychological research on persuasion can be traced to World War II, when the information and education branch of the US army initiated surveys and experiments to assess the impact of army propaganda films on the morale of their soldiers (Stroebe, Hewstone & Jonas, 2008). One of the social psychologists who became heavily involved in this work was Carl Hovland. Originally a learning theorist and a PhD of Clark Hull, one of the most famous learning theorists, Hovland became fascinated by the experimental study of the determinants of attitude change. After the war, Hovland returned to his academic career and founded the Yale Communication and Attitude Change Program. This programme attracted brilliant young researchers from a variety of universities and generated a stream of collaborative research that defined attitude change research for decades to come.

Hovland, Janis and Kelley (1953) stated at the outset that they did not attempt to present a systematic theory of persuasive communication (p. 6). The guiding assumption of the **Yale Reinforcement Approach** was that 'exposure to a persuasive communication which successfully induces the individual to accept a new opinion constitutes a learning experience in which a new verbal habit is acquired' (p. 10). Hovland and colleagues suggested that recipients of a persuasive message will silently rehearse the arguments together with the recommended response and their own initial attitude. They will only accept the recommended attitudinal response if the incentives associated with this response are greater than those associated with their own original position. Incentives were conceptualized very broadly. First and foremost, they referred to the rewards or punishments (i.e. costs) recipients anticipated as a consequence of accepting or rejecting the position advocated. For example, the minor inconvenience of putting on seat belts is far outweighed by the major reward of not having your face ruined or even worse, getting yourself killed. However, more generally, rewards also included self-approval stemming from the feeling that one's beliefs and attitudes were rational and consistent with important values (Eagly & Chaiken, 1993; Hovland et al., 1953).

Communication and Persuasion (Hovland et al., 1953), the first of a series of four influential volumes, was organized around the issues raised by Lasswell's famous statement that in order to understand persuasion one must know '*Who* says *what* to *whom* with *what effect*' (Lasswell, 1948, p. 37). The volume presented innovative experimental research on the impact of communicator credibility, on features of the communication such as fear-arousing appeals or the organization of persuasive arguments, on individual differences in susceptibility to persuasion, and on the extent to which attitude change was maintained over time. Although they never developed this into a systematic theory, Hovland et al. (1953) also hypothesized that the impact of any of these factors on attitudes could be mediated by three different processes, namely attention to the content of the communication, comprehension of the message or acceptance of the conclusions advocated by the communication. For some factors, their effect on all three processes would be in the same direction, for others it would be in opposite directions. Thus, attributing a communication to an expert rather than an inexpert source might increase both attention and acceptance of a communication and facilitate attitude change through both of these processes. In contrast, supporting arguments in a fear appeals (e.g. in favour of use of seat belts) with gory colour pictures (e.g. of a face mutilated through close contact with a windscreen) might put more force to the argumentation, but at the risk of people averting their gaze to avoid these pictures.

Hovland and colleagues (1953) reported a series of innovative studies conducted to test their theoretical approach. In studies on **source effects** (i.e. the impact of the source of a communication on persuasion), they demonstrated that attribution of a communication to either a prestigious or a non-prestigious source influenced the target's evaluation of the communication. Thus, the same communication about whether antihistamine should be sold without prescription was judged as less fair and resulted in less attitude change if it was attributed to a prestigious source (the *New England Journal of Biology and Medicine*) than to a mass circulation monthly magazine.

They also studied the impact of **fear-arousing communication** on the acceptance of a recommendation that would reduce the threat. Thus, in their classic dental hygiene experiment (see also Janis & Feshbach, 1953), they used three levels of fear appeal strength, with the highest level threatening cancer and inflamed gums and also using vivid pictures of tooth decay and mouth infections. They found that the weakest appeal was most effective in changing attitudes and behaviour. Since there was no evidence for differences in comprehension across the three conditions, it seemed unlikely that this inverse effect was caused by pictures interfering with the processing of the message. Hovland et al. (1953) therefore introduced the concept of 'defensive avoidance' to explain their findings, arguing that the strong fear appeal was so threatening that it was more effective for recipients to reduce fear by rejecting the appeal as alarmist rather than accepting the recommendation. As plausible as this interpretation appears to be, the findings of a negative association between level of threat and attitude or behaviour change has rarely been replicated in later research

(De Hoog, Stroebe & de Wit, 2007). As we will discuss later, most studies show that recipients' willingness to accept a recommendation increases with increasing strength of the fear appeal.

The information processing model of McGuire

Although the learning theory approach of the Yale group did not fit well with the predominantly cognitive perspective of post-war social psychology, the ideas developed by Hovland and colleagues (1953) had a lasting impact on attitude change research. This was mainly due to William McGuire (1968, 1969, 1985), a former member of the Yale Communication Research Program, who dominated persuasion research from the 1960s to the 1980s. In his **information processing model** McGuire elaborated two ideas that were suggested but never systematically worked out by Hovland and colleagues (1953), namely (1) that there are different stages involved in the processing of persuasive communications; and (2) that determinants of persuasion could have different impact at different stages.

McGuire (1968, 1969, 1985) distinguished five stages of persuasion and proposed that the probability that a persuasive message will result in behaviour change is the joint product of the probability that the message is successful in passing each of these stages: (1) attention, (2) comprehension, (3) acceptance, (4) retention and (5) behaviour: 'The receiver must go through each of these steps if the communication is to have an ultimate persuasive impact, and each depends on the occurrence of the preceding step' (1969, p. 173). Thus, if the ultimate objective of advertising a consumer product (e.g. a shampoo) on television is to persuade viewers to buy it, viewers have to proceed through all five steps for the advertisement to be effective. If viewers use the opportunity of the commercial break in the programme to go to the toilet or to get a drink (attention), the advertisement will fail to have the desired effect. But even if a viewer does not leave the room, he or she may not be sufficiently interested in hair care to listen to the arguments contained in a shampoo ad. (For this reason such ads usually contain pictures of silky hair rather than arguments.) With such advertisements lack of comprehension is less likely to be a problem, because the message is typically kept simple. But even if the message is attended to and comprehended, it has to pass another major hurdle namely that viewers believe the claims made in the advertisement (acceptance). If the advertisement is sufficiently convincing to overcome this hurdle, viewers will still have to remember the brand name *and* maintain their attitude towards this particular brand of shampoo until their present supply runs out and they go to their supermarket to replenish (retention). Since they are likely to be exposed to advertisements for competing brands in the meantime, there is a considerable chance that they change their minds again. But even if they do not, their supermarket may not sell the brand and they may thus simply buy the brand they always use (behaviour).

Since the model implies that message receivers must go through each of these steps for the ad to have persuasive impact, McGuire's framework offers an explanation why it is often so difficult to induce behaviour change through advertising or other information campaigns. However, like similar stage models suggested in the area of advertising and consumer psychology (e.g. Lavidge & Steiner, 1961), one has to question whether recipients really have to go through these steps for the advertisement to be effective. McGuire's theory assumes that persuasive messages need to be *systematically* processed (i.e. that recipients need to read, understand and think about the arguments) in order to have impact. As we discussed in chapter 4, there are a variety of ways by which messages can influence, even without having been carefully processed. Recipients may develop a positive attitude towards a product without understanding the message, because the product is endorsed by their favourite film star (identification), because it is accompanied by beautiful music or presented in a beautiful context (evaluative conditioning) or simply because of the frequency with which recipients are exposed to the logo or name of a brand. While consumers are unlikely to be motivated to carefully and systematically process a message describing a shampoo or a soft drink (even if they were thirsty or in need of a shampoo), processing motivation is likely to be higher for more complex and expensive products such as cars, cameras or washing machines, at least for those of us who are considering buying a new car, camera or washing machine in the near future. Thus, a stage model may be more applicable in such situations.

The second idea of the Yale group systematically developed by McGuire (1968) was the suggestion that determinants of persuasion can have different effects at different stages of the persuasion process. He used a simplification of his stage model to discuss this idea. This simplified model focused on the two stages most important in social psychological studies of persuasion, namely reception of the message (combining attention and comprehension) and acceptance. According to this two stage model of persuasion, the probability of a communication influencing attitudes [P(I)] is the joint product of the probability of reception [P(R)] and acceptance [P(A)].

$$P(I) = P(R) \times P(A)$$

McGuire (1968) applied this model to a research issue that had resulted in numerous conflicting findings, namely personality differences in influenceability. McGuire (1968) attributed these contradictory findings to the fact that most personality characteristics have opposing effects on reception and acceptance and illustrated this using intelligence as an example. People are more likely to understand a message the more intelligent they are. However, more intelligent people are also likely to be more critical and therefore less likely to accept everything they hear or read. If we assume that personality factors have opposing influence on reception and acceptance, we predict a curvilinear relationship, with the maximum level of influenceability found at some intermediate level of the personality characteristic. The variability in the complexity of messages across different persuasive contexts provides a further possibility to test this model. With very simple persuasive messages as they are typically used in conformity studies, persuasion should mainly be moderated by the impact of the personality variable on acceptance. With very complex messages, however, persuasion should mainly be moderated by individual differences in reception.

An early meta-analysis of studies of individual differences in influenceability by Rhodes and Wood (1992) provided limited support for the McGuire model. The predicted curvilinear relationship could be found for self-esteem, with individuals of moderate self-esteem being most easily influenced. Insufficient data were available to test the presence of a curvilinear relationship for intelligence. More problematic for

McGuire's model is the fact that Rhodes and Wood (1992) failed to find the expected variation across influence contexts in the relationship between self-esteem and influenceability. Thus, the same patterns emerged from both persuasion and conformity studies. This raises doubt about the assumption that reception is an important mediator of message-based persuasion (but see Mackie & Asuncion, 1990). Thus, although the two step reception–acceptance model is highly plausible, it did not fare well in empirical tests. In particular, the assumption that learning of the message content is essential for persuasion received little empirical support (Eagly & Chaiken, 1993). The reason for this, as we will argue in our discussion of the cognitive response model in the next section, is that this assumption is wrong.

The cognitive response model

The development of the **cognitive response model** in the 1980s substantially advanced our understanding of the processes that mediate the impact of persuasion on attitudes. The cognitive response model was developed by Greenwald, Petty and their colleagues at Ohio State University partly to explain the frequent failure to find a correlation between argument recall and attitude change, despite evidence that recipients had systematically processed the message arguments (Greenwald, 1968; Petty, Ostrom & Brock, 1981). The model stresses the importance of the thoughts individuals generate – and thus rehearse and learn – in response to a persuasive communication (i.e. 'cognitive responses'; Greenwald, 1968; Petty, Ostrom & Brock, 1981). The passive listener of the McGuire model is replaced by an active thinker, who engages in a silent discussion with the communicator and argues for or against the arguments contained in a communication. Listeners are active participants, who relate the communication to their own knowledge. In doing so, they often *elaborate* the message arguments and consider information that is not contained in the communication to generate thoughts for or against the arguments presented by the communicator. It is these cognitive responses to the message arguments produced by the recipient rather than the message arguments themselves which determine the impact of the persuasive communication on attitudes. And it is these cognitive responses rather than the arguments themselves, which are remembered later. This assumption would explain the low correlations typically observed between measures of message learning and persuasion.

Although the idea that cognitive responses might be an important mediator of the impact of persuasive communication on attitudes had already been considered earlier (e.g. Festinger & Maccoby, 1964; Hovland, 1951), the Ohio State Group made two major contributions, which turned the cognitive response approach into a testable theory. The first contribution was methodological, namely the development of the **thought-listing technique** (Greenwald, 1968; Osterhouse & Brock, 1970), which enabled them to assess the processes assumed to mediate attitude change. With this technique, subjects are asked to list all the thoughts or ideas they had while listening to the communication. After elimination of thoughts that are irrelevant to the communication, the relevant thoughts are then categorized by participants or external raters into those which are favourable to the position advocated by the message and thoughts which are generally unfavourable. An index based on these thoughts can then be used to assess the extent to which cognitive responses mediated the impact of a communication on attitudes. The second major contribution of the researchers at Ohio State was theoretical. Earlier research had invoked cognitive responses mainly to explain the production of *counterarguments* which *reduce* persuasion (e.g. Festinger & Maccoby, 1964). Common sense would suggest that if we think about a persuasive communication and scrutinize the arguments contained in the message, we will discover weaknesses and inconsistencies and will therefore be reluctant to accept the recommendation.

This is often true, but only if there are weaknesses and inconsistencies in the communication. With strong and well-reasoned arguments, thinking about them might in fact reduce our reluctance to change our minds. Petty, Wells and Brock (1976) therefore extended the concept of cognitive responses to include *positive* cognitive responses. They argued that, although cognitive responses to weak arguments would reduce persuasion, thinking about strong and well-reasoned arguments would produce favourable thoughts which would *enhance* persuasion. Thus, the favourability (positive or negative) of the cognitive response triggered by message arguments will depend on the quality of these arguments (Figure 5.1). However, as we discussed earlier, some messages are thought about much more than others. Thus, since recipients process messages more or less intensively, persuasion should depend on both (1) the extent to which recipients engage in message relevant thoughts and (2) the favourability of these thoughts. Increasing message-relevant thinking should increase persuasion for strongly argued messages that mainly elicit favourable thoughts. For weakly argued messages that elicit mainly unfavourable thoughts, increasing message relevant thinking should decrease persuasion.

In addition to explaining the frequent failure to find argument recall correlated with attitude change, this extended version of the cognitive response model can also explain inconsistencies in research on distraction and attitude change. **Distraction** is an interesting variable for marketers, because even if individuals keep watching TV during commercials, they are likely to start conversations or glance at their newspapers. On the basis of the McGuire two step model, one would expect that until it begins to interfere with reception, distraction should enhance persuasion by impairing a recipient's ability to counterargue. And indeed, persuasion-enhancing (e.g. Festinger & Maccoby, 1964) as well as persuasion-reducing (e.g. Haaland & Vankatesan, 1968) effects of distraction have been reported. However, Petty and colleagues (1976) argued that the persuasion-reducing effect of distraction was not necessarily due to

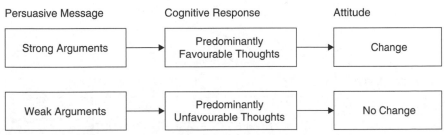

Figure 5.1 Cognitive response model

Source: From Stroebe (2008). *Strategies of attitude and behaviour change.* In M. Hewstone et al. (eds.). *Introduction to social psychology: A European perspective.* Oxford, UK: Blackwell.

impairment of comprehension but to impairment of the ability of recipients of a well-argued communication to produce positive thoughts, which might have persuaded them to change their attitude. According to this explanation, distracting individuals would reduce the persuasive impact of a (well-argued) communication, even if *comprehension* was not impaired.

To test these assumptions, Petty and colleagues (1976, Experiment 1) had student participants listen to either a well-argued or poorly argued counterattitudinal message in favour of a substantial increase in study fees. Distraction was manipulated by having participants monitor the appearance of a visual stimulus while listening to the communication. Intensity of distraction was varied by having the stimulus appear either every 15 seconds (low distraction), every five seconds (medium distraction) or every three seconds. There was also a 'no distraction' control condition. Attitude change was assessed with two questions asking agreement with the position advocated by the communicator. Consistent with predictions, increased distraction increased attitude change for weakly argued messages but decreased change for strongly argued messages (Figure 5.2). Furthermore, the thought-listing data indicated that both the increase and the decrease in persuasion were mediated by thought disruption. Disruption impaired participants' ability to produce counterargument for the weak message, but reduced the number of favourable arguments for the strong message.

Dual process theories of persuasion

Dual process theories of persuasion are an extension of the cognitive response model. Their major theoretical contribution is twofold: (1) In contrast to the cognitive response model, which assumes that attitude change is always mediated by argument

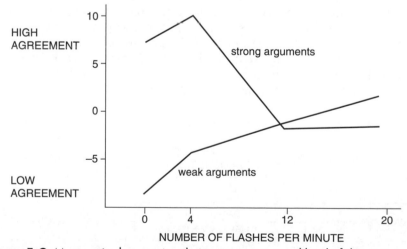

Figure 5.2 Mean attitude score in relation to message and level of distraction

Source: Petty et al. (1976). Distraction can enhance or reduce yielding to propaganda: thought disruption versus effort justification. *Journal of Personality and Social Psychology, 34, 874–884*

relevant thinking, even if the extent to which recipients think about arguments may be minimal, dual process models acknowledge that recipients may sometimes take short cuts and accept or reject the position recommended by the communicator *without* thinking about message arguments. (2) Dual process theories specify the factors which determine the intensity of message processing and thus the conditions under which attitude change will be mediated by message-relevant thinking. There are two dual process theories of persuasion, namely the **Elaboration Likelihood Model (ELM)** of Petty and colleagues (e.g. Petty & Cacioppo, 1986; Petty & Wegener, 1998b) and the **Heuristic-Systematic Model (HSM)** of Chaiken and colleagues (e.g. Chaiken, 1980; Chaiken, Liberman & Eagly, 1989; Chen & Chaiken, 1999). Since there is a great deal of overlap between these theories, we will integrate them into one theoretical framework.

Dual process theories distinguish two routes to persuasion, which form the endpoints of a continuum of *processing intensity*. The '*central route to persuasion*' is taken when recipients carefully and thoughtfully consider the arguments presented in support of a position. We will refer to this type of processing, which is identical to the processes assumed by the cognitive response model, as **systematic processing**. The second route reflects the fact that people often change their attitudes without thinking about the arguments contained in a communication, for example, because an expert or a trusted friend has made a recommendation or because the issue is unimportant. Petty and Cacioppo (1986) called this mode of attitude change the '*peripheral route to persuasion*'. Whereas the ELM subsumes the whole range of mechanisms which cause persuasion in the absence of argument scrutiny (e.g. evaluative conditioning, mere exposure) under this peripheral route, the HSM considers only *one* low effort process, namely *heuristic* processing. We will adopt the HSM position and consider heuristic processing as the low effort endpoint of the continuum of processing intensity.

Heuristic processing refers to the use of simple decision rules (rules of thumb or heuristics) in deciding on whether to accept or reject a persuasive communication (Chaiken, 1980). For example, people may have learnt from experience that statements by experts tend to be more accurate than statements by non experts. They may therefore use the decision rule 'experts can be trusted' in response to indications that a communicator is an expert (Eagly & Chaiken, 1993). Or they may have learnt that people whom they like can be trusted. They will therefore apply a 'liking-agreement heuristic', such as 'People I like usually have correct opinions' (Eagly & Chaiken, 1993).

Dual process theories distinguish between two types of qualitatively different information, which message recipients use when trying to decide whether to accept or reject the position advocated by a communicator, namely the arguments contained in the communication, and heuristic cues such as the expertise or attractiveness of the communicator. According to dual process theories of persuasion, message arguments offer better and more reliable evidence for the validity of a position advocated by a communicator than heuristic cues, but heuristic cues are easier to process. Therefore, when recipients are *unmotivated* or *unable* to engage in more effortful systematic processing, they tend to rely on heuristic cues and use heuristic processing to evaluate the validity of an advocated position. In contrast, when the recipients of a message are motivated and able to process a message, they will invest the effort to engage in argument scrutiny (Figure 5.3).

Processing motivation is important because unless an issue is relevant to recipi-

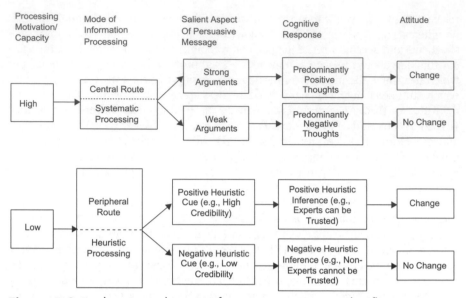

Figure 5.3 Dual process theories of persuasion: Top panel reflects systematic processing (central route). Bottom panel reflects heuristic processing

Source: From Stroebe (2008). Strategies of attitude and behaviour change. In M. Hewstone et al. (eds.). *Introduction to social psychology: A European perspective.* Oxford, UK: Blackwell.

ents, they will not expend much effort in thinking about arguments for or against the issue. Processing ability is important because in order to judge the validity of the arguments contained in a communication a person needs knowledge, time and peace of mind (i.e. absence of distraction). Processing motivation determines the standard of evidence we set ourselves (mostly unconsciously) for accepting an advocated position as valid. Although we all know from courtroom dramas about 'beyond reasonable doubt' as the gold standard for such decisions, we are typically willing to accept lesser criteria in real life, especially when we do not really care whether a statement made in an advertisement is really justified. However, even if we aspire to a high degree of certainty in our decisions, a low level of processing ability may prevent us from reaching the standard of evidence we strive for. Thus, even if we want to be certain that the new video recorder we are planning to buy will be state of the art, we may have neither time nor technical understanding to make sense of the wealth of the information about the permanently changing systems in this area.

It was originally assumed that the two heuristic (peripheral) and systematic (central) processing modes are compensatory: the more individuals relied on systematic processing, the less they would use heuristic processing (Petty & Cacioppo, 1986). If individuals were motivated and able to process the arguments contained in a communication systematically, they should have no need for short-cuts and use of heuristic processing. More recently, it has been suggested that the two modes of processing can *co-occur*, if systematic processing of arguments does not allow one to arrive at a clear-cut conclusion, for example, because the arguments contained in a communication are ambiguous (Bohner, Moskowitz & Chaiken, 1995; Chaiken & Maheswaran, 1994).

To complicate matters further variables can affect persuasion in multiple ways, depending on the extent to which a message is processed systematically (Petty & Cacioppo, 1986). For example, according to the 'affect-as-information' hypothesis (Pham, 1998; Schwarz & Clore, 1983) discussed in chapter 4, mood can influence attitudes as a heuristic cue ('how do I feel about it' heuristic). However mood can also influence a recipient's motivation to scrutinize arguments and to think about the content of a message, with people in a good mood being more likely to engage in heuristic processing. Thus, in a study that manipulated the mood of recipients of a message, Bless, Bohner, Schwarz and Strack (1990) found that argument quality affected attitude change only for participants in a bad mood. When put into a good mood, participants apparently felt no need to scrutinize arguments. Bless and colleagues (1990) reasoned that a happy mood informs people that all is well and that their environment is safe, thereby reducing their motivation to scrutinize the arguments contained in a communication.

To give another example for the **multiple-role assumption**, depending on the level of processing motivation, the attributes of an endorser of a product can be used as a heuristic cue to influence attitudes towards a product, but they can also serve as an argument. To illustrate, Figure 5.4 shows an advertisement in which the triple Olympic gold medallist Ben Ainslie endorses a brand of watches. If one just glances at the ad, Ainslie acts as a heuristic cue (at least for those who are British, like sailing and have heard of him). However, on closer scrutiny, the text below the picture informs us that Ben has worn this watch during the races. This is a content cue. Sailing is a wet sport and if the watch still works after several races, it must be quite sturdy and certainly waterproof.

So far we have discussed processing motivation only in terms of intensity of motivation, varying from being totally unmotivated to being highly motivated to think about a message and to reach a high degree of certainty about its validity. We have assumed that listeners want to form an *accurate* view on the issue being communicated. The assumption that processing is guided by an 'accuracy motivation' probably holds for the majority of communication contexts. However, acknowledging that people are not always unbiased listeners to a communication, Chaiken and colleagues (1989; Bohner et al., 1995) have extended the dual process framework to incorporate two further processing motives or goals, namely *defence motivation* and *impression motivation*. One reason why we are not always unbiased listeners is that we may have a strong preference for a particular position (i.e. *defence motivation*). One condition likely to induce defence motivation is the need for positive self-regard. Understandably, most people prefer to believe that they are intelligent rather than stupid or healthy rather than sick. Other conditions likely to induce defence motivation are vested interests, attitudinal commitment or a need for consistency. A second class of motives likely to bias information processing has been termed *impression motivation*. This motive refers to the desire to express attitudes that are socially acceptable. The processing goal of impression-motivated recipients is to assess the social acceptability of alternative positions in order to accept attitudinal positions which will please or appease potential evaluators.

Defence-motivated as well as impression-motivated processing can be heuristic as well as systematic. Under defence motivation, people will use heuristics selectively to support their preferred position or, when processing systematically, attend more to

Figure 5.4 Ben Ainslie with his Corum watch

Reproduced with permission of Corum, Suisse International Herald Tribune, August 30–31, 2008, p.3

arguments supporting their position than to opposing ones. Impression-motivated heuristic processing involves the use of simple rules to guide one's selection of socially acceptable attitude positions. In impression-motivated systematic processing the same goal is reached through evaluating the available evidence in terms of their social acceptability.

In the following, we summarize the basic assumptions of dual process theories:

- The extent to which recipients of a persuasive communication engage in message relevant thinking and elaborate message arguments can be represented as a continuum of processing intensity that ranges from heuristic processing to intensive systematic processing.
- The intensity of processing is determined by recipients' processing ability and processing motivation.
- There are two types of qualitatively different information, which people use in evaluating the validity of a position advocated by a communicator, namely message arguments and heuristic cues (e.g. communicator expertise). Heuristic cues are typically easier to process than message arguments, but message arguments frequently provide more reliable information about the validity of the position advocated by the communicator.
- Whereas communicators rely mainly on easy to process heuristic cues when processing motivation and/or ability is low (i.e. low processing intensity), increasing processing ability and/or processing motivation increases processing intensity and thus reliance on arguments rather than heuristic cues. However, individuals might draw on heuristic cues even under high elaboration, if arguments are ambiguous and argument relevant thoughts do not result in a clear-cut conclusion.
- Variables can affect persuasion in multiple ways and act as heuristic cue under low elaboration, while influencing processing under moderate or high levels of elaboration.
- Communicators are mostly motivated by the wish to form a valid picture of reality (accuracy motivation). However sometimes their processing can be influenced by the need to defend a preferred position (defence motivation) or their wish to hold attitudes, which are socially acceptable (impression management).

Assessing the intensity of processing

Petty, Cacioppo and their colleagues developed two strategies to evaluate the extent to which recipients of a message engage in message processing (Greenwald, 1968; Petty, Wells & Brock, 1976). As we mentioned earlier, one major theoretical contribution of the Ohio State researchers to the study of persuasion was the development of a measure of cognitive responses, namely the thought-listing technique. This technique can be used to assess the extent to which attitude change is based on systematic processing. If attitude change is due to systematic processing, then (1) recipients should have generated some thoughts favourable to the position advocated by the communicator; and (2) the relative favourability or unfavourability of these thoughts should be correlated with the amount of attitude change. (3) A favourability index (e.g. the ratio of favourable thoughts to total number of relevant thoughts) should act as a mediator of the impact of the manipulated variables on attitude change with systematic but not under heuristic processing.

The manipulation of argument quality provides an even more powerful tool for assessing the extent of systematic (central route) processing. Persuasive appeals containing strong arguments should stimulate mainly favourable thoughts in recipients who engage in systematic processing, and result in substantial attitude change. In contrast, weak arguments should trigger mainly negative thoughts and fail to result in attitude change. The more recipients are motivated and able to engage in systematic processing, the stronger should be the impact of the manipulation of argument quality. The combined use of an argument quality manipulation (as one of the independent measures) and thought-listing (as one of the dependent measure) should therefore provide a valid tool for diagnosing the extent to which individuals engage in systematic processing of the arguments contained in a communication.

Processing ability, processing intensity and attitude change

Anybody who has tried to buy a computer, a television set or a sound system knows how important processing ability is for the comprehension of the arguments presented by salespersons. These people seem to love to impress their customers with techno-babble, the exact meaning of which remains hidden to large sections of the (older) population and, one might suspect, also to the sales personnel themselves. Intelligence and education are of limited use in such situations. Although highly intelligent and/or highly educated individuals are likely to have developed general strategies that allow them to acquire and process complex information more efficiently than less intelligent or less educated individuals, intelligence and education are unlikely to be highly correlated with knowledge in those content areas which are not part of the school curriculum. Unless one has an understanding of the workings of computers, sound systems or washing machines, being intelligent or having a classic education will be of little use in buying such appliances.

The impact of working knowledge on processing ability

We would argue that the amount of working knowledge the individual possesses in a given area is the most important personal factor influencing processing ability. Suppose some politician has been accused of using subliminal messages against the opposing candidate in his campaign, triggering a lengthy discussion of the feasibility of subliminal advertising in the mass media, including the radio station you are listening to on your car radio. As a student of psychology or marketing you are knowledgeable about the potential of these techniques (particularly after having read this book). Thus, you will more easily be able to comprehend the arguments but, drawing on your fund of knowledge, you will also be better able to critically evaluate them. Your knowledge about this area, at least if it is cognitively accessible, provides a standard that allows you to detect the strengths and weaknesses of the information provided in the broadcast. People without such knowledge will be much less able to critically evaluate the incoming information

Wood, Kallgren and Preisler (1985) tested these assumptions in a study, in which they exposed student participants to a counterattitudinal message arguing against the preservation of the environment. Participants were divided into three groups on the basis of their knowledge assessed in a pretest. Two factors manipulated were argument quality and message length. Long messages contained the same information as short messages but were simply more wordy. Message length was manipulated as heuristic cue. There is evidence that at low processing intensity message length acts as heuristic cue with longer messages considered more valid than shorter ones (Chaiken, 1980). The findings of this study were consistent with theoretical assumptions: overall, more knowledgeable participants were less influenced by the communications than participants with little knowledge. However, this main effect was moderated by two interactions. Argument strength influenced only the most knowledgeable individuals, whereas message length affected only the least knowledgeable. Thus, the most knowledgeable participants were influenced by the arguments contained in the message, whereas the least knowledgeable were influenced by the heuristic cue of message length. Further evidence for the assumption that knowledgeable individuals engaged in more intense processing was provided by the results of the thought-listing task: The more knowledgeable participants listed significantly more content-oriented thoughts than the least knowledgeable individuals.

Further support for the assumption that knowledge about the issue under discussion moderates the impact of heuristic cues comes from a set of studies by Maheswaran (1994), who used a product's country of origin as heuristic cue likely to affect product evaluations (**country-of-origin effect**; e.g. Hong & Wyer, 1989; DeBono & Rubin, 1995). In the positive country of origin condition, a fictitious new stereo-system was alleged to have been produced in Germany, whereas production was attributed to Thailand in the negative condition. Pilot testing had indicated that American students associate high quality with stereo-systems produced in Germany but held low quality expectations for systems manufactured in Thailand. Cross-cutting this manipulation, argument strength was manipulated by attributing either superior technical characteristics to these systems (strong arguments) or giving them an average performance and describing them as equal to the competition (weak arguments). Participants were divided into highly knowledgeable experts or not very knowledgeable novices on the basis of a knowledge pretest (Figure 5.5).

The pattern of attitude change that emerged was consistent with hypotheses. Overall, attitudes towards the stereo-systems were influenced by both country of origin and argument strength. However, these main effects were moderated by two interactions. Whereas experts were only influenced by argument strength, novices were only influenced by country of origin. Results of a thought-listing task indicated that experts generated more thoughts about the attributes of these systems and these thoughts were more positive in the strong rather than the weak argument condition. In contrast, novices generated more thoughts about country of origin and these thoughts were more positive in the favourable rather than the unfavourable country of origin condition. Finally, for each group the predominant thoughts predicted their evaluations.

Maheswaran (1994) conducted an interesting conceptual replication of this study, in which he demonstrated that, if arguments do not allow one to draw clear-cut

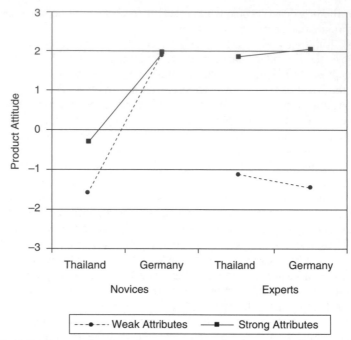

Figure 5.5 Product evaluation of stereo systems by experts and novices by country of origin and argument strength

Source: Maheswaran (1994). Country of origin as a stereotype: Effects of consumer expertise and attribute strength on product evaluations. *Journal of Consumer Research, 21,* 354–365, Table 2, p.359

conclusions, individuals will rely on heuristic cues even under high processing intensity. He again manipulated the favourability of the country of origin of the product (a personal computer) but presented participants with ambiguous attribute information. Under these conditions both experts and novices relied on the country of origin information in evaluating the product.

The impact of distraction on processing ability

Of the environmental factors that can influence an individual's ability to process information, distraction has probably the most powerful effect. Suppose you are driving leisurely on a motorway listening on your car radio to an interview with a politician who is sceptical about climate change. Although you have no strong feelings about the issue, you find his argumentation weak and you are able to counter most of his arguments. But then you exit the motorway. You have to find your way in a maze of busy roads and are no longer able to concentrate on the arguments. Since your ability to produce counterarguments is now impaired, you might be at risk of being influenced by the communication. As we discussed earlier, the impact of distraction on the extent to which people are influenced by a persuasive communication will depend on the quality of the arguments presented. Distraction will reduce attitude change when arguments are strong, but increase it with weak arguments (Petty et al., 1976).

The impact of message repetition on processing ability

Whereas issue-relevant knowledge and distraction would come to mind easily when thinking about factors which facilitate or impair message processing, message repetition is much less obvious. Most of us have probably been annoyed about the repetitiveness with which the same advertisements appear night after night on our television screens. We will therefore wonder why message repetition should facilitate message processing. However, while we are probably thinking about the one liners employed in many TV advertisements, the experiments testing this hypothesis used messages that contained relative complex arguments. Thus, Cacioppo and Petty (1979) exposed student participants over earphones to a message arguing for an increase in the university budget to improve standards of teaching. Whereas the counterattitudinal version suggested that this increase would be financed by an increase in tuition fees, the pro-attitudinal version suggested that it would be financed externally. The need for this budget increase was then justified by a series of strong and highly persuasive arguments. Depending on condition, students were exposed zero (control group), one, three or five times to this message. At the end of the session they had to fill in a post-experimental questionnaire, which assessed their own attitude towards increasing the university budget.

The pattern of findings for attitude change was the same for the pro- and the counterattitudinal message. Whereas argument recall increased monotonically with frequency of exposure, attitude change showed a curvilinear relationship with frequency of exposure. Change increased between 0 to three exposures, but decreased afterwards (i.e. at five exposures). When thoughts were assessed in a replication of this experiment (Experiment 2) an interesting pattern emerged. Up to three exposures, message repetition increased the number of favourable thoughts and decreased the number of counterarguments. However, further repetition reversed this effect. It resulted in an increase of counterarguments and a decrease of favourable thoughts. Cacioppo and Petty (1979) explained these findings with a two-stage model. Initially, repetition of arguments provided recipients with opportunity to think about and elaborate the message. Since these arguments were strong, greater elaboration resulted in an increase of favourable thoughts and a decrease of counterarguments, leading to increased acceptance of the message. However, when message repetition was further increased, tedium set in. Boredom motivated people to attack the now tedious argumentation.

It is important to note that the findings reported by Cacioppo and Petty (1979) are likely to be caused by two specific aspects of the experimental situation, namely the use of strong and persuasive arguments and choice of a topic that was personally relevant to the student participants. Let us look at the effect of both of these factors in turn. If the positive impact of a *small* number of repetitions is due to the fact that repetitions provide increased opportunity to favourably elaborate the strong arguments, then repetition should result in an immediate decrease of attitude with weak arguments. Cacioppo and Petty (1989) supported this hypothesis in a study in which they manipulated argument quality. Whereas exposure to strong arguments resulted in an increase in change from one to three repetitions, repeated exposure to weak arguments led to immediate decrease in change. A lowering of processing motivation should result in a decrease in recipients' willingness to elaborate message arguments. As a consequence, tedium will set in earlier at a smaller number of repetitions (Claypool, Mackie, Garcia-Marques, McIntosh & Udall, 2004).

Marketers try to avoid or at least delay tedium by varying their advertisements. This variation can either be cosmetic or substantial. With *cosmetic variation*, non-substantive features of an advertisement that are not essential in evaluating the product are altered. In contrast, *substantive variation* is defined as a change in message content, for example in the type of arguments made about the qualities of the product. Schumann, Petty and Clemons (1991) hypothesized that cosmetic variation will delay tedium only at very low processing intensity. Once processing intensity increases cosmetic variation will be ineffective and only substantive variation will reduce tedium.

Schumann and colleagues (1991) tested these hypotheses in two studies, which manipulated frequency of repetition (one, four and eight exposures) and product relevance. The advertisements were for a new pen (Omega 3). There was a drawing of the pen with a slogan and several statements describing attributes of the pen. The first study tested the effects of cosmetic variation against ads that remained unchanged. Cosmetic variation altered the layout, font and the colour of the pen, but kept the arguments the same. Consistent with predictions, cosmetic variation reduced the impact of tedium slightly under low but not high product relevance. However, as we can see (Figure 5.6; top panel), the effects were not impressive and centred mainly around four exposures. If ad repetition had increased liking for the product at all, the effect had already disappeared at four exposures. With further repetition, tedium set in and liking for the product decreased significantly. With high product relevance cosmetic variation made no difference either at moderate or high exposure frequency. In contrast, substantive variations of features of the advertisement in Study 2 had its impact under high rather than low product relevance. Whereas none of the differences reached significance under low product relevance, under high relevance substantive variation of the advertisement resulted in greater liking of the product with 4 than with only 1 exposure. (Figure 5.6; bottom panel).

So far our predictions were always based on the assumption that some semantic processing of message arguments occurred, even under low product relevance. However people often look at ads, without really processing any of the text message. For example, readers of news magazines might glance at advertisements, but then go to the next page without reading any of the ad's text. It is interesting to consider what happens under these conditions. An experiment by Nordhielm (2002) provides an answer to this question. The stimuli in her experiment were ads about 16 fictitious products. The ads contained a picture, a slogan and one line of text describing a specific benefit of the product. These ads were presented either three, 10 or 25 times under one of two processing conditions. With deep processing instructions, participants were told that the various products would soon be introduced nationally and that they should try to assess how likely it would be that each brand would be successful nationally. These instructions are likely to produce moderately intense

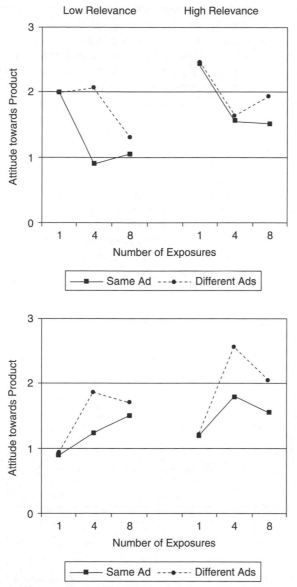

Figure 5.6 The impact of cosmetic and substantive variation strategies on product attitude with different levels of repetition. (Top panel: Cosmetic variation. Bottom panel: substantive variation

Source: Adapted from Schumann et al. (1991). Predicting the effectiveness of different strategies if advertising variation: A test of the repetition-variation hypothesis. *Journal of Consumer Research*, *17*, 192–202. Table 1, p.197

processing of the advertising layout and text. The purpose of the shallow processing instructions was to induce superficial scanning of the advertising layout, while at the same time preventing that any of the text was read. Participants were told that in some of the ads a logo had been embedded subliminally and that they should try to identify the ads with such a logo. The ad presentation session was followed by a 10-minute filler task. Then participants were presented with the 16 target ads and a number of filler ads and had to indicate their attitude towards each of these products.

With deep processing, attitude change followed the familiar curvilinear pattern (Figure 5.7), even though the downturn only occurred at 10 exposures, instead at 3, as in the study of Cacioppo and Petty (1979). Even more interestingly, however, there was no downturn with shallow processing. Furthermore, whereas the attitude change pattern is correlated with the net number of favourable thoughts produced by participants under deep processing, no systematic relationship between thoughts and attitudes emerged under shallow processing. This pattern is consistent with the assumption that under deep (but not shallow) processing, attitude change was mediated by favourable and unfavourable thoughts. So how can we explain the findings for participants in the shallow processing condition? Nordhielm (2002) interprets her results in terms of increased perceptual fluency. Thus, as with the mere exposure

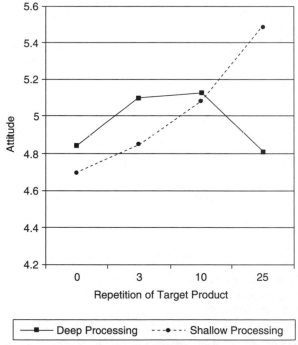

Figure 5.7 The effect of frequency of target product exposure and level of processing on attitude

Source: Nordhielm (2002). The influence of level of processing on advertising repetition effects. *Journal of Consumer Research, 29*, 371–382, Figure 2, p.378

studies reviewed in chapter 4, frequency of exposure to these advertisements is likely to have increased perceptual fluency which, in turn, resulted in greater liking for these advertisements.

Processing motivation, processing intensity and attitude change

Personal relevance as motivator

Personal relevance (i.e. the importance of an outcome for the individual) is the major variable affecting processing motivation. Most people are probably uninterested in the performance of different washing machines and will not even glance at washing machine advertisements or read comparative test reports published in consumer report journals. However, this attitude is likely to change on the day their own washing machine breaks down and needs to be replaced. Due to technical incompetence or lack of time (i.e. ability factors), some individuals will refuse to get involved in systematic information search and simply walk into a shop and buy the brand recommended by the salesperson. For others, the need to have to choose one particular brand of washing machines from the multitude of appliances on offer will act as a powerful *motivator* to critically read advertisements and test reports. If the information about one of these machines is perceived as cogent and persuasive, favourable attitudes will develop. However, if the information about a particular brand is perceived as weak and specious, no favourable attitudes will result. Thus, only if an issue is important to them will recipients of a communication be motivated to scrutinize information about this issue and only then should argument quality influence the amount of attitude change. For unimportant decisions people are unlikely to expend much cognitive effort on scrutinizing arguments and will instead rely on heuristic cues, such as a recommendation from a neighbour, friend or salesperson.

The best known experimental test of these hypotheses is a study by Petty, Cacioppo and Goldman (1981). Student participants in this study were told that their university was undergoing a process of academic re-evaluation and that they should evaluate the quality of a set of policy statements about the exam system at their university that had been made by a variety of groups. They were then given an attitude discrepant communication that argued for a substantial change in the exam system. The message was either attributed to an expert source (Carnegie Commission on Higher Education) or an inexpert source (a class at a local high school). Personal relevance was manipulated by leading students either to expect that these changes would be instituted before they graduated (high involvement) or long after they had left the university (low involvement). Under the guise that their own attitude could have influenced their evaluation of the quality of these statements, participants were then asked to indicate their own attitude towards this issue. The pattern of findings was consistent with predictions: argument quality affected attitudes only under high involvement, with more attitude change when arguments were strong rather than weak. In contrast, source expertise influenced attitudes only under low involvement conditions, with more attitude change when arguments were attributed to a high rather than low status source.

This is also one of the few studies which included a no-message control group. In order to avoid arousing suspicion, experimental attitude change studies often do not assess the attitudes of participants before exposure to the message. Unless one includes a control group of individuals who are not exposed to message arguments (and thus presumably display the attitude experimental participants had before they were exposed to the message), it is impossible to check, whether the use of weak arguments or of an incompetent source has a negative influence on attitudes (i.e. boomerang effect). Petty and colleagues (1981) found no significant evidence for such a deterioration in attitudes. Although this may be surprising at first, it makes a great deal of sense. As long as weak arguments are merely specious, they are uninformative rather than negative.

Two years later, Petty, Cacioppo and Schumann (1983) published a replication of this experiment, using a simulated advertising context. Participants in their study were exposed to an advertisement about a fictitious brand of disposable razors (Edge Disposable Razors). The critical advertisement was embedded in a booklet which contained ads about other products. Four versions of the ad were used which varied in terms of two factors: quality of arguments supporting the brand (strong, weak) and the celebrity status of the featured endorser of Edge (celebrity, average citizen). The strong arguments mentioned the 'unsurpassed sharpness' due to 'new advanced honing method' or the reduction of risk of cuts 'due to a specially chemically formulated coating'. Weak arguments stated that the razor was designed 'with the bathroom in mind' or 'floats on water with a minimum of rust'. The endorser were either a famous athlete or the citizens of a small town in California. Personal relevance was manipulated by leading participants in the high relevance condition to believe that they would be allowed to choose a brand of disposable razor at the end of the study *and* that the Edge razor would be marketed in their area. Under low personal relevance, participants were not promised a choice of disposable razors and were informed that the Edge razor would not be marketed in their area. The main dependent measure was their attitude towards the razor brand.

In line with predictions, personal relevance interacted with both celebrity status of the endorser and argument quality, with celebrity status influencing attitudes mainly under low involvement condition and argument quality being mainly effective under high involvement conditions (Figure 5.8). Thus, whereas involved participants formed their attitude on the basis of argument scrutiny, participants in the low involvement condition were not influenced by argument quality. They used the status of the endorser as heuristic cue and formed a more positive attitude towards the Edge brand when it was endorsed by famous athletes rather than the citizens of a town in California.

It is interesting to note that this study was actually a conceptual replication of an earlier advertising experiment that had not quite worked out as expected. In this earlier study Petty and Cacioppo (1980) used a fictitious brand of shampoo as product. They manipulated personal relevance and argument quality using the same methods as in their later study. However, instead of employing endorser status as their source characteristic, they manipulated the physical attractiveness of a female endorser of the shampoo. In line with prediction, argument quality had a greater impact on attitudes under high than low involvement. However, contrary to predictions, physical attractiveness had the same high impact under high and low relevance. As a reason

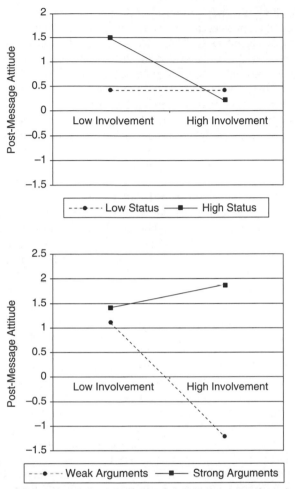

Figure 5.8 Top panel: Interactive effect of involvement and endorser status on attitudes towards Edge razors. Bottom panel: Interactive effects of involvement and argument quality on attitudes towards Edge razors. (Scores cold range from −4 to +4)

Source: Adapted from Petty et al. (1983). Central and peripheral routes to advertising effectiveness: The moderating role of involvement. *Journal of Consumer Research, 10*, 135–146, Table 1, p.141

for this inconsistency, Petty and colleagues (1981) suggested that physical attractiveness (particularly the attractive hair of the endorser), while serving as a heuristic cue under low involvement, might have functioned as visual evidence for the effectiveness of the product under high involvement (i.e. an argument).

This assumption was theoretically elaborated by Kirmani and Shiv (1998), who introduced the concept of 'source congruity' reflecting the match between cognitively accessible endorser associations and attributes associated with the brand. They suggested that source congruity, while irrelevant under low processing intensity, becomes important under high processing intensity. Thus, in the study of Petty and Cacioppo (1980) described above, physical attractiveness was used as heuristic cue under conditions of low processing intensity. This effect will probably have been based on the 'liking-agreement heuristic', because it is likely that physically attractive sources are liked more than less attractive sources. Whether the good looks of the endorser have any relevance for the product they endorse (i.e. existence of source congruity) is unimportant under these conditions. In contrast, when processing intensity is high, source congruity becomes important and the physical attractiveness of the endorser will affect brand attitudes only for products for which physical attractiveness is relevant.

Support for this assumption comes from a study by Kang and Herr (2006) which, in addition to processing intensity, systematically manipulated the relevance of the characteristics of the endorser to the attributes of the product they endorsed. They had either a physically attractive couple or a couple of average physical attractiveness endorse either a (fictitious) brand of razors (called again 'Edge razors') or a brand of computer processors. They reasoned that the attractiveness of the endorsers could serve as a source of information for the razor, but not the computer processor. Argument quality was not manipulated and was low for both products. The authors used cognitive load to impair processing ability in the low processing ability/motivation condition and increased processing motivation in the high ability/motivation condition by telling participants 'that they would be asked to fill out a questionnaire regarding the ad' (2006, p. 126). Consistent with predictions, when processing ability had been lowered source attractiveness had a positive influence on attitudes towards both products, regardless of product category. In contrast, when participants' processing ability had not been impaired (and their motivation had been increased by the expectation to have to answer questions about the advertisements) source attractiveness affected attitudes only towards the relevant product (razor) but not towards the irrelevant product. Thus, when participants were neither able nor motivated to pay much attention to the content of the advertisements, they used the physical attractiveness of the product endorsers as a (positive) heuristic cue, regardless of whether it was relevant or irrelevant to the product advertised. In contrast, when they were motivated to process the message, physical attractiveness appeared to have acted as a content cue and influenced attitudes only for the product for which it was relevant.[12]

In an innovative study, Shavitt, Swan, Lowrey and Wänke (1994) manipulated source congruity through inducing different processing goals. They reasoned that the physical attractiveness of endorsers should be irrelevant if they endorsed a restaurant, at least for people, who were only interested in the quality of the food. In contrast, individuals who are impression-motivated and like to go to places where the 'in-people' hang out, would find physical attractiveness a relevant cue. Shavitt and colleagues (1994) primed either a sensory orientation or an impression motivation in participants, who had to evaluate a fictitious restaurant under either high or low processing motivation. In line with predictions, for participants for whom a *sensory orientation* had been induced, endorser attractiveness influenced restaurant evaluation only under low but not under high processing motivation. The reverse was true when *impression motivation* had been induced: physical attractiveness influenced participants only under high but not under low processing motivation.[13]

The notion of source congruity does not only apply to physical attractiveness but also to other attributes of a source. For example, Clint Eastwood, who is strongly associated in people's mind with the attribute 'ruggedness' should be a congruent source for endorsing products associated with ruggedness (e.g. mountain boots; chronometer watches) but not for products, which are not considered rugged. Thus, he should be a more effective endorser of a brand of mountain boots rather than Gucci loafers or of a TAG Heuer chronometer rather than a Jaeger Le Coultre gold watch, at least under conditions where recipients are motivated to think about an advertisement and are accuracy motivated. In contrast, Tom Hanks or Gary Grand would do better for the gold watch than the chronometer. Kirmani and Shiv (1998) reported several studies, which tended to support this hypothesis.

Fear as a motivator

Fear-arousing communications are widely used in health education campaigns, but are less common in the advertising of consumer products. The products they are most often used for in advertising are hygiene products and over-the-counter medication. Adverts for these kind of products usually point out that the use of a given product would protect individuals against some unpleasant health impairment (e.g. cavities, flatulence, incontinence). Fear-arousing communications mostly consist of two parts, a fear-appeal warning individuals of some health threat and an action recommendation that advises individuals about how to protect themselves against this threat. Their use is based on the reasonable assumption that the more one scares people about the consequences of their health-impairing behaviour, the more willing they should be to accept the recommended action.

One of the most successful advertising campaigns based on fear appeals was the campaign which introduced Listerine mouthwash in the 1930s. Listerine was originally developed in the nineteenth century as a surgical antiseptic, but as such was not a best-seller. The success story of Listerine began when the Warner-Lambert Company promoted it in the 1920s as a mouthwash that would cure bad breath. The problem at that time was bad breath was not really considered a social catastrophe and the concept of mouthwash was unknown. Furthermore, accusing people of having bad breath would not have been a popular message. Thus, the early ads for Listerine invented the medical term 'halitosis' instead. The slogans of this famous campaign played on people's fear of being rejected by their social environment. And in a brilliant move to broaden the consumer basis, it emphasized that people themselves would never know whether they had the problem: 'Even your best friend won't tell you. Listerine is good for halitosis.' Or 'Often a bridesmaid . . . never a bride'. Our favourite Listerine advertisement of that series has the title 'The one true friend she has'. It shows a beautiful young woman standing in front of a bird cage. According to the sad story beneath the picture, she used to have hundreds of friends and looked forward to a brilliant marriage, only a few years earlier, and yet today, she is 'a rather pathetic figure despite her wealth and her charm'. She suffers from halitosis 'a damning, unforgiveable social fault'. And halitosis, the ad continues, is 'a definite daily threat to us all', which people themselves are often unable to recognize. Therefore, 'intelligent people recognize the risk and minimize it by regular use of full strength Listerine'.

Thus, these Listerine ads first created fear of an impending threat and then offered a remedy that would protect individuals against this threat. By persuading people it could cure a problem they never knew they had, the Listerine advertising campaign was increadibly successful, even though, according to the American Medical Association, mouthwashes do not correct bad breath for any length of time (Leipkin & Lipsky, 2003).[14]

As we mentioned in our discussion of the Yale program, research on fear-arousing communication has initially been guided by the drive-reduction model of fear appeals (Janis & Feshbach, 1953). This model assumes that individuals, who are informed of an impending health threat, will be motivated to search for responses that reduce the threat. When a recommended action promises to protect them, and thus reduces fear, it will be reinforced and become part of the individual's permanent response repertory. The model predicts that higher fear should result in more persuasion, but only if the recommended action is perceived as effective in averting danger.

Because part of the empirical evidence was inconsistent with the drive model, Leventhal (1970) introduced a more cognitive theory, the 'parallel response model' which no longer assumed that emotional arousal was a necessary antecedent of the adaptation to danger. According to this model, a threat is cognitively evaluated and this appraisal can give rise to two parallel or independent responses, namely danger control and fear control. Danger control involves the decision to act as well as actions taken to reduce the danger. Fear control involves actions taken to control emotional responses (e.g. use of tranquillizers or alcohol) as well strategies to reduce fear (e.g. defensive avoidance). These responses typically have no effect on the actual danger. Witte (1992) later extended the parallel response model by adding the plausible assumption that the perceived efficacy of the recommended response determines whether individuals engage mainly in danger or in fear control. If a recommendation seems effective in averting a threat, individuals will engage in danger control, if it appears ineffective, they will mainly focus on fear control.

There are two problems with all of these models: First, there is no empirical evidence for the predicted interaction between threat and response efficacy (De Hoog, Stroebe & de Wit, 2007; Witte & Allen, 2000). Second, even though the two parallel response models assume that cognitive appraisal mediates the impact of persuasion on attitude and behaviour change, they make no predictions about these processes of information processing. The stage model of processing of fear-arousing communications was developed to address these deficiencies (Das, de Wit & Stroebe, 2003; De Hoog, Stroebe & de Wit, 2005, 2007, 2008; Stroebe, 2000). According to this model, the important determinants of the intensity of processing are the perceived severity of a health threat and personal vulnerability (i.e. personal relevance of the threat). If both severity and vulnerability are low, individuals are unlikely to invest much effort into processing information about this threat and will rely on heuristic processing. But even at low severity, individuals who feel vulnerable will begin to pay some attention and process information about the risk systematically, though at low intensity. If a health threat is severe, individuals are likely to systematically process information about this threat, even if they do not feel vulnerable. The reason for this deviation from dual process predictions is that severe health threats can always become personally relevant, even if one does not feel vulnerable at the moment. Thus, an epidemic that is only prevalent in some distant continent might suddenly spread to Europe and a virus, which mainly endangers gay men, might suddenly enter the heterosexual population.

Most interesting, according to the stage model, is the situation where individuals feel vulnerable to a health threat that is also severe. Since the threat is severe, individuals will be motivated to engage in systematic processing. However, since feeling at grave risk is also very unpleasant, individuals will be motivated to engage in systematic processing that is defensive (i.e. biased systematic processing). In appraising the fear appeals, they will be highly motivated to minimize the risk. They will engage in a biased search for inconsistencies and assess the evidence with a bias in the direction of their preferred conclusion (e.g. Ditto & Lopez, 1992; Liberman & Chaiken, 1992; Sherman, Nelson & Steele, 2000). However, if the arguments in the appeal are strong and persuasive, individuals may not succeed in minimizing the threat. Their main hope now is that the recommended action will really protect them against the impending risk to their health. They will engage in biased processing of the recommended action. This will involve attempts to make the recommendation appear highly effective, because only then will individuals feel safe. Thus, defence motivation will lead to a *positive* bias in the processing of the action recommendation and will heighten the motivation to engage in the protective action regardless of the quality of the arguments supporting this action.

A recent meta-analysis based on 95 published studies of the efficacy of fear appeals supported most of the predictions of the stage model (De Hoog et al., 2007). As predicted, the attitudes towards the health recommendation were only affected by severity of the health threat and argument quality but not by personal vulnerability. A person's attitude towards an action recommended as protection against a serious health threat should depend only on the strength of the arguments in favour of that action and not on whether the individual him or herself is at risk. In contrast, both vulnerability and severity influenced intention to perform a protective action and even actual behavior and these effects were not moderated by the efficacy of the recommended protective action. Finally, it made no difference whether the health risk information was accompanied by pictorial material. Thus, adding pictures of diseased lungs to the health warning on cigarette packs is unlikely to increase the efficacy of these messages.

An analysis of the cognitive and affective responses triggered by these communications was also consistent with predictions of the stage model. Both vulnerability and severity induced fear and negative affect in respondents. More importantly, however, analyses of cognitive responses supported the hypotheses of the model about differences in biased processing of fear appeals as compared to action recommendations. Feeling vulnerable to a severe health threat triggered thoughts attempting to minimize the threat (i.e. denying, downgrading or criticizing the fear appeal) and at the same time stimulating positive thoughts about the value of the action recommendation. This last finding does not only explain the consistent failure to find an interaction between the efficacy of the recommended action and the seriousness and personal relevance of the health threat, it also explains why anxious or desperate individuals often take recourse to all kinds of treatments of totally unproven efficacy.

Individual differences in processing motivation

So far we have investigated the impact of external or situational variables on process-ing motivation. These variables are most interesting to marketers, because situational contexts can be influenced. However, the extent to which individuals think about message arguments is not only influenced by situational factors but also by individual differences. There is evidence that individuals vary in the extent to which they engage and enjoy effortful cognitive activity that is in their **Need for Cognition**. Cacioppo & Petty (1982) constructed a scale that measures need for cognition and makes it possible to place individuals on a continuum from a very low to a very high need for cognition. Consistent with dual process predictions, persuasion studies demonstrate that argument quality has a greater impact on attitudes of individuals, who are high rather than low in need for cognition (for a review, see Cacioppo, Petty, Feinstein & Jarvis, 1996).

Need for cognitive closure is another individual difference variable that has been shown to influence the intensity with which individuals process information (Klein & Webster, 2000). The need for cognitive closure has been defined as 'the desire for a definite answer on some topic, any answer as opposed to confusion and ambigu-ity' (Kruglanski, 1989, p. 14). This need is assumed to reflect a stable individual difference (measured with the Need for Closure Scale; Webster & Kruglanski, 1994) as well as a state that can be induced by the situational context. One of the situational factors known to induce need for closure is time pressure. Suppose you are going on vacation to some tropical island and you decided to buy a camera at the airport. If you have ample time before your plane leaves, you will look at a range of different cameras, have all their advantages and disadvantages explained and then select one, which promises to be most suitable for your needs. In contrast, if you have only a few minutes before boarding starts but you really want to buy a camera, you have to rely on heuristic cues to reach your decision. You might choose the camera recommended by the salesperson (experts know what is good), you might buy their most expensive camera (expensive must be good) or the camera of a brand that is familiar to you (if even I have heard of it, it must be good).

The assumption behind the need for closure scale is that people with a chronic-ally high need for closure behave as if they were always in a rush. Klein and Webster (2000) tested the hypothesis that dispositional (i.e. personality trait) need for closure influences the depth of information processing. They argued that if heuristic cues are made available, individuals with a chronic high need for closure will rely more on these cues, whereas individuals with low need for closure will scrutinize arguments to form an opinion. In support of this hypothesis they found that individuals, who were relatively high on dispositional need for closure used heuristic cues to form an attitude about a position argued in a message, if such heuristic cues were made available. If such cues were not available, they formed their attitude on the basis of message arguments. In contrast, individuals low on need for closure always relied on arguments, regardless of whether or not heuristic cues were made available. Although Klein and Webster (2000) did not manipulate processing motivation, this pattern suggests that participants must have been at least moderately motivated to process the information.

Processing intensity and stability of change

According to dual process theories of persuasion, attitude change induced by systematic processing is more persistent than change induced by heuristic (peripheral) processing. High levels of issue-relevant cognitive activity are likely to require frequent accessing of one's attitude towards the issue targeted by the persuasive attempt. This activity should have two effects: it should result in better recall of one's cognitive responses to the message and it should increase the number of linkages between an attitude and the structure of beliefs in which it is embedded, making this structure internally more consistent and thus also more resistant to counterarguments.

Haugtvedt and Petty (1992) tested these hypotheses with two studies, in which need for cognition was used to vary processing motivation, In the first study, individuals high or low in need for cognition were exposed to a TV commercial about an answering machine. The commercial, which was embedded with other advertisements in a television programme, contained both strong arguments about the answering machine as well as variables that could serve as strong heuristic cues, so that both the high and the low need for cognition participants would develop equally positive attitudes towards the product. And indeed, there were no significant differences in attitudes immediately after the communication. However, when attitudes were reassessed two days later, the product attitudes of the high need for cognition participants had decayed significantly less than those of low need for cognition individuals. Thus, consistent with predictions, the attitudes of high need for cognition individuals (based on greater elaboration of message arguments) were more persistent than those of low need for cognition participants (based on heuristic cues). In a second study, these authors further demonstrated that the more elaborated attitudes of high need for cognition individuals were also more resistant to a message attacking the attitude. Haugvedt and Petty (1992) found that attitudes of individuals with low need for cognition changed more after exposure to an opposing message than did attitudes of individuals with high need for cognition.

In another study Haugtvedt, Schumann, Schneier and Warren (1994) demonstrated that attitude persistence and resistance to persuasion may be determined by different factors (see also Haugtvedt & Kasmer, 2008). Haugtvedt and colleagues made use of the manipulations developed by Schumann and colleagues (1990) described earlier in our discussion of advertisement repetition (Omega 3 pen). Haugvedt et al. employed three conditions with ad repetition, one with substantive variation of the advertisement, one with cosmetic variation and one in which the same ad was repeated three times. Attitude towards the product was measured immediately, one week after the communication, and a third time after participants had been exposed to a negative communication about the product. This communication employed relatively weak arguments (with no overlap with the arguments used in the substantive variation condition).

When measured immediately after the communication (Figure 5.9), attitudes in the two variation condition did not differ from each other, but were significantly more positive than those in the other two conditions (same ad three times; single exposure). This finding is consistent with the assumption that ad repetition is mainly effective when it employs ad variation.

Since arguments contained in an advertisement would be remembered better, if they had been repeated three times rather than only once, one would expect most decay in the single exposure condition. In the other three conditions, there should be relatively little decay in attitudes. And as we can see from Figure 5.9, the findings of this study were consistent with this prediction.

Most interesting, however, was the impact of the weak attack on participants' attitudes towards the pen. Here one would expect that those participants who had been exposed to the substantive variation and had thus heard a variety of different positive arguments about the pen, should be most able to resist the unfavourable information about the product. Consistent with this expectation, findings showed that attitudes of participants in the condition with substantive variation remained significantly more positive than those of participants in the other three conditions (Figure 5.9). Thus substantive variation in ad repetition does not only help to avoid tedium, it also increases the resistance of individuals against the negative impact of counterarguments.

Persuasion by a single route: the unimodel

Dual process models have provided such powerful conceptual instruments to account for complex relationships between variables such as processing motivation, processing

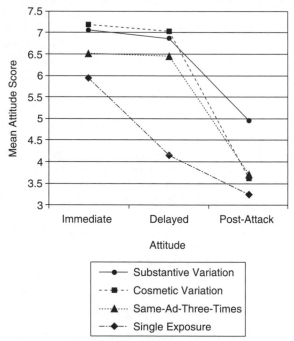

Figure 5.9 Variation and attitude persistence

Source: Adapted from Haugtvedt et al. (1994). Advertising repetition and variation strategies: Implications for understanding attitude strength. *Journal of Consumer Research*, 21, 176–189, Table 2, p. 185

ability and type of information that it seems ungracious to be critical. However, by more and more obliterating the distinction between heuristic cues and message arguments, dual process theorists have brought this criticism on themselves. Originally, these theorists assumed (or were at least widely understood to assume) that recipients of a persuasive communication based their conclusion about the validity of a communication *either* on heuristic cues *or* on message arguments and that they used the one under low processing motivation/ability and the other under high processing motivation/ability. This was very clear. But then matters got slightly confused with the 'multiple mode' assumption that a cue could also serve as an argument. One really had to be very careful in choosing one's examples of cues and arguments. When the champion skier Bode Miller held up his skis after having won a race to display their brand name, this could be a heuristic cue (Bode Miller uses this brand of skis) or an argument (if he won on them, they really must be fast). But worse was to come, when Chaiken and colleagues accepted that the two types of information could co-occur and that even highly motivated individuals would go back to using heuristic cues when message arguments would not allow them to draw clear conclusions (Chaiken & Maheswaran, 1994).

It was thus not an act of murder but more of euthanasia, when Kruglanski and colleagues with their **unimodel** (e.g. Kruglanski & Thompson, 1999; Kruglanski, Thompson & Spiegel, 1999) suggested that the two (arguments and heuristic cues) were *functionally equivalent* in constituting two separate content categories of evidence for drawing conclusions from persuasive communications. More specifically, the unimodel considers both message arguments and heuristic cues as evidence that can be used in an 'if X then Y' assertion. For example, the persuasive impact of the expertise heuristic derives from the recipient's prior belief in the premise 'if someone is an expert, his or her statements can be trusted'. Thus, the fact that Bode Miller uses a particular brand of ski can only serve as an indication of ski quality, if one holds the prior belief that 'top athletes use top equipment' (and that the skis Bode Miller uses are on sale to the public). Similarly the fact that Bode Miller won a race on a Brand X ski could only serve as persuasive argument if one believed that 'Skis, on which one can win races, must be good'. Thus, according to the unimodel, persuasion can be characterized as a singular process of drawing conclusions from available evidence (Kruglanski & Stroebe, 2005). It does not matter whether this evidence is contained in an argument or comes from a heuristic cue.

So how does the unimodel explain the interactions observed in many studies between type of information and processing intensity. The unimodel shares with dual processing theory the assumption that depth of processing will depend on processing motivation. And because heuristic cues are typically more easily processed than message arguments, they will be the preferred information of individuals, who are not terribly motivated to think about a communication. The unimodel rejects the notion that heuristic cues are typically less valid than message arguments. There are strong and weak heuristic cues as there are strong and weak arguments. For example, the information that a particular brand of TV was the only one in its class that came out highly recommended in a test conducted by a highly regarded consumer report journal is a strong heuristic cue, and probably stronger than most statements about some technical attribute of such a TV. In contrast, the information that a racing driver endorses a particular brand of watches is a weak heuristic cue, because it probably says more about the amount of money paid to that racing driver for the endorsement than about the quality of this particular brand of watches.

That lazy information processors base their judgements mainly on heuristic cues is further aided by the order in which information is presented: the information about heuristic cues is typically presented before the message arguments in practically all studies. Thus, the heuristic cues were not only briefer and less complex than message arguments, they were also presented first. And as Kruglanski and colleagues (e.g. 2005) demonstrated, if one establishes the level of expertise of a message source with a lengthy account of the presumed expert's qualities instead of implying expertness by a professorial title, source expertise influenced attitudes only under high rather than low processing motivation.

This analysis of the process of drawing conclusions from message arguments or heuristic cues also explains why it is impossible to develop a priori criteria for strong and a weak arguments. The relevance of the information contained in a message argument or a heuristic cue for the evaluation of the position advocated in a communication will always depend on the belief systems of the members of the target audience.

Lowering resistance to advertising

In their attempts to persuade consumers of the value of their products marketers face major disadvantages. Consumers often try to avoid exposure to advertising. They turn over print ads and switch channels (or leave the room) during commercial breaks on television. With digital recorders they now even have the possibility to eliminate commercial breaks altogether before viewing a recorded programme. But even if consumers are exposed to an advertisement, their awareness of persuasive intent might increase their resistance to persuasion and decrease the impact of the message.

When reading an advertisement or listening to a commercial on TV, consumers are typically aware of the intention behind the message, namely to persuade them to buy the advertised product. Even the most gullible consumer is unlikely to take any of the claims made in an advertisement at face value and will tend to derogate the source as well as the arguments. Consumers are probably more willing to believe product information given by sales personnel in shops, even though their belief in the trustworthiness of these individuals will depend on factors such as the range of products being sold and their client-status within this particular store. On entering a BMW dealership, one will be more willing to believe statements about the relative merits of different types of BMW than claims about the superiority of BMW cars over comparable models produced by Mercedes or Audi. In contrast, when shopping for a computer in an electronic store that sells a range of different brands, one might trust a salesperson to give a relative unbiased description of the attributes of different brands, even though one might be wary of any strategy that nudges one towards buying a more expensive brand. If one were a regular customer in that store, one would hope that the sales personnel would value customer satisfaction higher than a quick sale and thus refrain from giving too biased a description of the products on offer.

The different types of attributions customers make in different sales situations have been analyzed by theories of persuasion knowledge. Persuasion knowledge refers to the theories consumers have developed about the motives, strategies and tactics of marketers as well their beliefs in their ability to resist these tactics (Friestad & Wright, 1994; Campbell & Kirmani, 2000). In the context of this chapter, we will focus only on one aspect of persuasion knowledge, namely the impact of the attribution of intention to persuade. There is evidence that the perception of a communicator's intention to persuade increases resistance in recipients of a message (for a review, see Wood & Quinn, 2003).

Social psychological research has used two strategies to study the impact of perceived intention to persuade on resistance to persuasion: recipients of a message were either given information about the (counterattitudinal) arguments contained in a communication or they were informed of a communicator's intent to persuade without being told about the content of the message they would be exposed to. Both types of manipulation increase recipients' resistance to persuasion but for different reasons. The expectation of being exposed to counterattitudinal arguments will motivate recipients to access the reasons that support their own position. They will use these reasons to generate arguments to refute the persuasive communication. However, to generate counterarguments recipients have to be motivated to do so (i.e. personal relevance). They need further time to generate arguments. Thus, warning of the content of a communication reduced impact only (1) if the topic of the communication was personally relevant; and (2) if there was a short delay between exposure to the communication and the measure of change (e.g. Chen, Reardon, Rea & Moore, 1992). Content warnings proved ineffective, if participants were distracted during the period of delay (Chen et al., 1992).

In contrast, merely warning recipients about persuasive intent without providing information about the direction of the arguments contained in a communication induces resistance even without a delay period, suggesting that the impact of these warnings is not mediated by counterargumentation. This is plausible, because individuals who merely know that they will be the target of a persuasive attempt without having any knowledge of the kind of persuasive arguments to expect, will be unable to prepare themselves against this attack by producing counterarguments (Hass & Grady, 1975). Hass and Grady (1975) offered a motivation explanation for this increase in resistance. They suggested that warning individuals that they will be exposed to a communication aimed at changing their attitudes produced psychological reactance (Brehm, 1966). Psychological reactance is a motivational state that can be triggered by the perceived threat to one's attitudinal freedom implied by a social influence attempt and motivates individuals to re-establish their freedom, for example by resisting the influence attempt. Perceived intention to persuade might motivate recipients to engage in biased processing of the communication or to simply disregard the message as invalid.

Is there any hope that once this reactance subsides, the targets of an advertisement might still remember the arguments and find them persuasive after all? Thus, if advertisements for Brand X computers contained a number of extremely persuasive arguments, would it not be possible that recipients would remember these arguments much longer than the fact that they originated from the people who produced this particular product and thus might not have been unbiased?

This is not as improbable as it sounds as research on the so-called sleeper effect has demonstrated. In an advertisement, the source of the arguments acts as a *discounting cue*, which decreases the impact of the arguments contained in an advertisement. The term sleeper effect refers to the phenomenon that the impact of a message increases over time, because after some delay, recipients of an otherwise influential message might recall the message but no longer remember the source (e.g. Hovland & Weiss, 1951; for a review, see Kumkale & Albarracin, 2004).

Unfortunately, at least for advertisers, the conditions under which sleeper effects occur are rarely realized in advertising contexts. According to a meta-analysis of research on the sleeper effect conducted by Kumkale and Albarracin (2004), one of the preconditions for the sleeper effect to occur is that message arguments had strong initial impact. Thus recipients first have to accept the arguments as plausible and convincing, before discounting them on account of the source. This was most likely when recipients of the message were highly motivated to think about the message *and* received the discounting cue (e.g. source information) only *after* they had processed the arguments. This makes a great deal of sense, because if the discounting cue comes before the message, recipients might not pay attention to the message or not be motivated to think about the message arguments. Unfortunately, this is precisely the situation, which characterizes most advertising contexts.

Two-sided advertisements

Two-sided advertising is one of the strategies which marketers employ in their attempt to reduce the resistance to persuasion (see chapter 1). Two-sided advertisements differ from the usual one-sided ads in that they mention some negative features of a product in addition to emphasizing its positive attributes. Such ads not only have the advantage that they stand out from the advertisement clutter, they also appear as more honest and might therefore have more impact. There is substantial evidence that two-sided ads reduce counterarguing (e.g. Kamins & Assael, 1987; Swinyard, 1981), are viewed as more credible than one-sided advertisements (e.g. Kamins & Assael, 1987; Pechmann, 1992; Smith & Hunt, 1978; Swinyard, 1981) and that they are more effective in enhancing perception of the advertised brand on those characteristics which are described as positive (e.g. Etgar & Goodwin, 1982; Pechmann, 1992; Swinyard, 1981).

Unfortunately, this positive effect of two-sided advertisements does not always translate into a superiority in influencing *overall* brand evaluation or purchasing intention. While some studies find two-sided appeals superior to one-sided appeals on brand attitudes or purchase intention (e.g. Etgar & Goodwin, 1982; Pechmann, 1992) others fail to find any difference (e.g. Kamins & Assael, 1987; Swinyard, 1981). Even refuting the negative attribute in the two-sided advertisement does not seem to make a difference (Kamins & Assael, 1987). However, there is some evidence that attitudes formed on the basis of two-sided advertisements which included a refutation of the negative information may be more resistant to counter-attack (e.g. Szybillo & Heslin, 1973) or disconfirming information (e.g. Kamins & Assael, 1987). Furthermore, including a refutation in an advertisement may be essential if consumers are already aware of the fact that the advertised product is deficient in an important attribute and if it is likely that the competition may 'attack' on the basis of this attribute (Crowley & Hoyer, 1994).

In their integrative framework for the understanding of two-sided advertisements Crowley and Hoyer (1994) discuss some of the conditions under which two-sided advertisements might result in more positive overall brand evaluations. One of their recommendations for achieving a positive overall brand attitude is the use of an 'optimal proportion of negative information'. They argue that this proportion is optimal when credibility gains are at their optimal level (i.e. when adding further negative information does not increase credibility). Based on previous research they suggest that the negative information should not exceed two-fifths of the information contained in an advertisement. Furthermore including negative information on important product attributes should be avoided.

These conclusions are consistent with an analysis in terms of the Fishbein model of attitudes (1963; Fishbein & Ajzen, 1975), which we discussed in chapter 4. According to this model, a person's attitude towards a brand is determined by the strength (i.e. subjective probability) of the person's beliefs that a brand possesses a number of attributes and the evaluation of these attributes. The overall attitude is reflected by the sum of the products of each (attribute-)evaluation times the subjective probability that the brand possesses that particular attribute. If we consider only the evaluation, adding negative to positive information in a two-sided advertisement should lower the overall evaluation compared to a one-sided advertisement that focuses only on the positive product features. This decrease should be stronger, the greater the number of negative attributes and the more negative their evaluation. However, since mention of negative attributes increases the credibility of an advertisement and thus the strength (i.e. subjective probability) of a recipient's belief that the brand also possesses the positive features reported in the advertisement, the impact of the negative information should be compensated to some extent. There is likely to be an optimal point beyond which further addition of negative attributes no longer increases credibility and thus results in a deterioration of the overall attitude.

The optimal procedure would be to mention only negative attributes which are trivial or of which the consumer is already aware. However, this strategy has to be used with care. While one should certainly avoid admitting serious product deficiencies, the strategy of admitting utterly trivial deficiencies may be too obvious and thus fail to increase the credibility. Pechmann (1992) even argued that disclosure of negative attributes that consumer could find out prior to purchase (e.g. price, limited range of package sizes) is less effective in increasing credibility than disclosure of features that can only be evaluated after purchase or consumption of a product.

It is interesting that one of the few studies in which a two-sided communication resulted in a more positive brand attitude than the one-sided communication used negative attributes which were implied by the positive brand attribute emphasized in the advertisement (Pechmann, 1992). The two-sided advertisement that described the creamy good taste of an ice cream mentioned also that it was high in calories. A pretest had shown that creamy taste and calorie content were perceived as negatively correlated. Thus, mentioning the higher calorie content was not only unsurprising to participants, it increased the credibility of the claim that the ice cream had a creamy taste. (At the time of this study, calorie content was considered much less important than creamy taste, an evaluation which might have changed in the meantime).

Product placement

If you ever wondered why James Bond, for years a keen Aston Martin driver, switched to BMW, product placement is your answer. BMW probably offered more than Aston Martin for the privilege of having their cars sensationally crashed (or in this case sawed in two) in a movie seen by millions of people. **Product placement** (sometimes also called brand placement) refers to the 'paid inclusion of branded products or brand identifiers through audio and/or visual means, within mass media programming' (Karrh, 1998, p. 33). It is one of the more unobtrusive ways in which advertisers seek to persuade consumers without having to resort to more blatant influence attempts which are frequently met by consumer resistance (another one is sponsoring, see next). Since the producers of the placed product pay for the privilege, they must expect benefits from product placement such as an increase in brand recognition or an improvement in brand attitudes. As an integral part of a programme, this form of advertising avoids the problem of channel switching. As a disguised form of advertising the intention to persuade is also less likely to be perceived. Product placement can be categorized according to two dimensions, namely modality and centrality to the plot (e.g. Russell, 2002; Yang & Roskos-Ewoldsen, 2007). Modality refers to whether the brand name is only seen (e.g. a logo) or also mentioned. Centrality refers to the relevance of the product use to the plot. Three levels of centrality have been distinguished. *Background* is when the product is shown or mentioned in a scene but not used by any of the main characters (e.g. if we see a package of Lipton tea on a shelf in a kitchen scene). More central is the situation where the product is used by one of the main characters but in a way that has no particular relevance to the story (e.g. if the main character uses Lipton tea bags to prepare a cup of tea). Most central is the situation when the product plays a role in the story, such as saving the main character or helping to solve a problem in a movie (Yang & Roskos-Ewoldsen, 2007).

Studies of the effect of product placement have either made use of existing movies (e.g. Yang & Roskos-Ewoldsen, 2007) or TV shows (e.g. Cowley & Barron, 2008; Law & Braun, 2000) or they have written and filmed their own screenplay (Russell, 2002). Participants are given some unrelated reason (i.e. a cover story) to view these films and are often presented with the dependent measures in an apparently unrelated experiment. The most frequently used measures of the efficacy of product placement have been measures of explicit memory such as recall and recognition measures (e.g. Gupta & Lord, 1998). More recently, measures of implicit memory have also been employed (e.g. Law & Braun, 2000; Yang & Roskos-Ewoldsen, 2007).

There is a great deal of evidence that plot centrality influences explicit memory. For example, Gupta and Lord (1998) have shown that products prominently placed in a movie have greater impact on recall and recognition measures than products placed subtly. Similar findings were reported by Law and Braun (2000) and Yang and Roskos-Ewoldsen (2007). In contrast, implicit measures were not affected by level of placement, even though placement per se (i.e. whether a product was placed or not placed in a film) had a significant effect on implicit measures in the studies of Law and Braun (2000) and Yang and Roskos-Ewoldsen (2007). This pattern is consistent with the research on implicit memory discussed in chapter 3 that indicated that depth of processing was important for explicit but not implicit measures of memory. Finally, attitudes towards the brand assessed with an explicit measure were more positive when the brand was used by the main character rather than when the product was only presented in the background (Yang & Roskos-Ewoldsen, 2007).

To assess whether product placement can also influence behavior, Yang and Roskos-Ewoldsen (2007) included a behavioural choice task in their study. They measured choice by asking participants after the apparent end of the experiment to choose a product as a token of appreciation for participating in the research. Participants who saw the target brand in the movie were more likely to choose that brand compared to participants who were not exposed to that brand. Choice was not affected by level of placement and the effect of placement on choice remained even after participants' explicit attitudes had been statistically controlled for. It is important to note, however, that this choice involved low-involvement products and that individuals were likely to decide without investing much thought.

But the news about product placement is not all positive. There is also evidence that product placement can backfire. The fact that Yang and Roskos-Ewoldsen found attitudes towards the placed brand to be more positive when the brand was used by the main characters suggests that the main characters in their movie clips were all likeable. An experimental study using rap videos showed that brand use by disliked actors results in a negative brand attitude (Schemer, Matthes, Wirth & Textor, 2008). Schemer and colleagues manipulated participants' attitude towards the artist in a rap video with (fictitious) articles attributed to a regional newspaper that described the artist either positively or negatively. Participants then viewed one of two professionally produced rap videos. In the experimental condition, the artist wore a branded T-shirt, in the control condition a neutral T-shirt. The impact of this product placement on brand attitude was significantly influenced by viewers' attitude towards the artist. Compared to the control condition, being worn by a liked artist increased attitude towards the T-shirt brand, whereas being worn by a disliked artist resulted in a more negative brand attitude.[15] Since actors sometimes misbehave, product placement could have unforeseen negative effects. Just imagine that at the time when OJ Simpson was still a popular sports personality and (small time) actor, some firm had paid for him to use one of their products in a movie that might still be screened on late-night TV today.

Disliked actors are not the only reason for product placements to backfire. Viewers who like a program and regularly view it might also be irritated by blatant product placement. This has recently been demonstrated by Cowley and Barron (2007), who presented participants who were (or were not) fans of *Seinfeld* with one of three episodes of that popular US sitcom. One version contained no product placement, whereas the other two versions did. The version with product placement differed in the centrality of the placement. Whereas in the central version the products was connected to the plot and mentioned more than once, placement was background and subtle in the other version. Compared to the 'no placement' control condition, blatant placement resulted in a decrease in attitudes towards the placed products in fans of *Seinfeld*, but improved attitudes of people, who did not particularly like this sitcom. Mere background placement had no effect on attitudes.

Although recent studies (e.g. Cowley & Barron, 2008; Gupta & Lord, 1998; Law & Braun, 2000; Russell, 2002; Yang & Roskos-Ewoldsen, 2007) have greatly improved our understanding of product placement, a great deal is still unknown. For example, we do not really know how the impact of product placement compares to that of regular advertising, except that product placement can reach individuals who habitually avoid watching advertisements. Furthermore, studies of product placement have typically been conducted with low involvement products and we can only guess how it works with expensive high involvement products. Finally, we do not know how unpleasant experiences that befall main characters in a film soon after he or she has used a branded product moderate the impact of product placement on brand attitudes.

Sponsorship

Commercial sponsorship has become a multi-billion-dollar business. Investment in sponsoring has grown from $850 million in 1985 to nearly $9 billion in 2000, and worldwide from $2 billion in 1984 to more than $23 billion in 1999 (Meenaghan, 2001). Sponsorship is of particular importance for the tobacco industry, because it allows them to continue to promote their brands even after being banned from using mass media advertising in many countries. Given the enormous commercial investment in sponsorship, it is surprising how little is known about its effects on brand attitude and purchase intentions.

Sponsorship can be defined as a technique by which a commercial organization financially supports an entity (i.e. event, programme, team, person, cause) in order to associate the organization's name with this entity in the media and to use the entity for advertising purposes. There are different types of sponsorship, with the most important being *programme sponsorship* and *event sponsorship* With programme sponsorship the advertiser assumes the total financial responsibility for the production of the programme. The advertiser also provides the commercials that are shown during the programme. This type of sponsorship is extremely expensive but it can also be effective because the advertiser can also influence the content of the programme and the placement of the advertisements (Wells, Moriarty & Burnett, 2006). With event sponsorship, a company contributes to the costs of an event in order to be allowed to link its brand name to the event. In addition to this communication objective, commercial sponsors often also have trading objectives, mainly to secure the monopoly to sell its goods at the event. For example, Heineken sponsors several golf tournaments which allow them not only to link their name to these tournaments but also gives them the exclusive merchandizing rights so that only Heineken beer is available at these tournaments (Jalleh, Donovan, Giles-Corti & Holman, 2002). This may force individuals who prefer other brands to try Heineken, an experience which might (or might not) persuade them to stay with Heineken in the future. Since more is known about event than programme sponsorship, we will focus on event sponsorship in the remainder of this section.

There are various ways in which event sponsorship could influence brand awareness and brand attitude. The mere fact that the brand logo or brand name of the sponsor will be clearly associated with, and prominently displayed at, the event should increase brand awareness. With relatively unknown brands frequent exposure should lead to increased feelings of familiarity with the brand name or logo (i.e. increased fluency). According to the 'hedonic fluency model' discussed in chapter 4, an increase in the ease of processing a stimulus is experienced as pleasant and this feeling should result in greater liking of the brand. Furthermore, sponsorship of an event links the name of the sponsor to the event. Provided that the event is liked, both evaluative conditioning and balance theory would lead one to expect that this association should result in a transfer of positive affect from the event to the sponsor and increase brand attitudes.

Much of the research on sponsorship has used recall measures to test whether viewers correctly recalled the name of a sponsor who supported a particular event. There is evidence that viewers of sports event pay very little attention to sponsor billboards (e.g. d'Ydewalle, van den Abele, van Rensberger & Coucke, 1988). They may therefore not even realize that an event is sponsored by a particular organization or if they do realize, they might forget it again. Consumers use various heuristics in trying to recall event sponsorship, particularly a 'relatedness or congruity' heuristic and a 'market prominence' heuristic. They will remember better if a track and field event is sponsored by a company that produces athletic shoes than if it is sponsored by a brewery. However, even this memory may be biased in favour of prominent brands, particularly in cluttered media environments where learning the event–sponsor association is difficult (Pham & Johar, 2001). Thus, viewers might mistakenly remember that a particular track event had been sponsored by Adidas, even if in fact it had been sponsored by a less known brand of sports shoes (Pham & Johar, 2001).

The fact that congruent sponsorships are better remembered than incongruent sponsorships could seriously limit the attractiveness of sponsorship deals because many product categories lack self-evident links to sports, arts or good causes. However, even if obvious links do not exist, they can be created and recall can be improved if the event sponsorship is flanked by advertising measures that forge a relationship between sponsor and event (Cornwell, Humphreys, Maguire, Weeks & Tellegen, 2006). In an experiment in which participants were given the fictitious information that either the Sony entertainment conglomerate (congruent sponsorship) or the Heinz food company (incongruent sponsorship) had sponsored the new Moonlight Music Festival, the memory disadvantage for the food company could be largely alleviated by informing participants that according to Heinz officials 'the sponsorship is ideal, as the young people attracted to the festival are those likely to opt for easy-to-prepare foods' (Cornwell et al., 2006, p. 314).

Cornwell and her colleagues (2006) did not assess the impact of the sponsorship information on attitudes towards Sony or Heinz. In fact, little is known about the impact of sponsorship information on brand attitudes. This is unfortunate, because message recall and attitudes are rarely related in studies of the impact of persuasive communications (Eagly & Chaiken, 2003) and the same could be true for sponsorship recall and attitudes towards the sponsor. After all, whether a sponsor brand will profit from linking itself to some event will not only depend on people's attitude towards the event but also on their thoughts (i.e. cognitive responses) about the sponsor's motive in supporting the event. For example, when Cornwell and colleagues (2006) added to their explanation of the link between Heinz and a music festival that Heinz was 'excited about this move to target young adults and views this sponsorship as the perfect starting point' (p. 314) they turned off some young adults, who may have been less happy than officials of the food company about being targeted by Heinz.

Support for the importance of respondents' thoughts about a sponsorship deal comes from a survey conducted in central Ohio to assess the impact of corporate sponsorship of sports teams at Ohio State University (Madrigal, 2001). This is one of the few studies, which focused on attitudes towards sponsors and even assessed purchasing intentions. Attitudes towards purchasing products made by sponsors of Ohio State University athletic teams were more positive, the more individuals identified with these teams and the more they believed that sponsorship resulted in reduced admission costs to sporting events. In turn, purchasing attitudes were a major predictor of purchasing intentions. The fact that respondents' identification with a sports team was a major predictor of purchasing attitudes and intentions suggests that the impact of sponsorship deals on attitudes and intentions is largely limited to those who identify with a particular team or activity. Furthermore, the fact that, next to respondents' identification with the sports teams, their belief that corporate sponsorship lowered ticket prices influenced their purchasing attitudes and intentions indicates that people's interpretation of the sponsorship are important determinants of the impact of such sponsorships on brand attitudes and brand purchasing intention. Since Madrigal (2001) did not include recall measures in his study, the results of this study provide no information about the relationship between brand recall and brand attitudes.

There are numerous interesting questions which have not yet been addressed by research on the impact of sponsorship deals on brand attitudes and purchasing intentions. For example, since we know of no study that used implicit as well as explicit measures, we do not know whether sponsorship may have effects on implicit attitudes and the choice of low involvement products, even if individuals cannot recall the link between an event and its commercial sponsor. We can also only guess about the impact of sponsorship deals which link companies to events that trigger negative publicity. For example, what happens if a commercial sponsor supports a team which sinks to the bottom of its league or fails to win any races? And what happens if the sponsor then abandons this team by stopping sponsorship? Or what happens if a sponsor supports a sports team that becomes involved in a major doping scandal (as seems to happen regularly with bicycle racing teams). Or what effect on attitudes towards sponsor companies had the sponsorship of the recent Olympic torch relay which triggered intense anti-China protests? We cannot answer any of these questions with confidence but we would speculate that none of these sponsorship deals would have had the positive impact on brand attitudes and purchasing intentions probably hoped for (and paid for) by commercial sponsors.

Summary and conclusions

- Based on the conceptualization of advertising as one form of persuasion, this chapter reviewed social psychological theories of persuasion as well as research which applied these theories to advertising. The theoretical development in the area of persuasion can be categorized into four stages:
- Stage 1 is represented by theories which assume that persuasion involved the learning of persuasive arguments contained in a communication (e.g. Yale Reinforcement theory; McGuire's information processing model). Despite some valuable insights, these approaches were finally disproved by the consistent failure to find recall of message arguments related to extent of persuasion.

- Stage 2 is represented by the cognitive response model which replaced the passive learner of arguments with an active respondent, who engages in a silent discussion with the communicator and responds to arguments contained in the communication either with supportive arguments or with counter-claims. This model also contained the motivational assumption that the extent to which recipients are willing to think about a message and to engage in this silent dialogue will depend on their involvement with, or personal relevance of, the issue presented in the communication. This theory was finally integrated into dual process theories of persuasion.

- Stage 3 is represented by dual process theories of persuasion which abandon the assumption that the acceptance of message arguments will *always* have to be based on a systematic processing of these arguments. These theories acknowledge that recipients may sometimes take short cuts and accept or reject the position recommended by the communicator *without* thinking about message arguments. Dual process theories further specify the factors which determine the intensity of message processing and thus the conditions under which attitude change will be mediated by message-relevant thinking. There is a great deal of empirical evidence that supports the assumption that recipients, who are able and motivated to process a communication base their decision to accept or reject the position advocated by a communication on careful scrutiny of message arguments, whereas communicators, who are unable or unmotivated to systematically process a message tend to rely on heuristic cues (e.g. communicator credibility, country of origin information).

- Stage 4 is represented by the unimodel, which abandons the dual process assumption of a *necessary* link between extent of processing motivation/ability and type of cue used. Whereas the so-called heuristic cues are typically easier to process *and* often less valid than message arguments, this is not necessarily the case. There are weak message arguments and strong heuristic cues. Furthermore, as already recognized by dual process theorists (e.g. Bohner et al., 1995; Chaiken et al., 1989; Chaiken & Maheswaran, 1994), even highly motivated recipients rely on heuristic cues, if the arguments contained in a communication do not allow them to arrive at a clear-cut decision about the validity of the position advocated by a communicator. The strength of the unimodel is that it can account for all the findings accumulated in research guided by dual process theories. The weakness of the unimodel is that it produced only few empirical predictions, which cannot be explained in terms of the dual process logic. Thus, the importance of the unimodel lies more in the theoretical clarity it provided than in its power to open (and integrate) whole new realms of empirical research.

- The last part of this chapter discussed strategies marketers use to deal with one of the major weaknesses of advertising, namely that the perceived intention to persuade triggers resistance to persuasion in recipients of advertising messages. Marketers have developed three strategies to address this problem, namely the use of two-sided communications, product placement and sponsoring. Two-sided communications try to appear unbiased by admitting some minor deficiencies of the advertised products. Although this strategy increases recipients' trust in the positive product claims made in an advertisement, there is little evidence that this strategy results in more positive brand attitudes. Product placement is disguised advertising, in which movie or TV characters use a particular product (or appear to have the product in their household or at their workplace). If used wisely, product placement can improve viewers' brand attitude and purchasing intention. Finally, sponsoring tries to improve brand attitudes by linking the brand (or more precisely the producer of the brand) to some positively valued event or TV programme.

- The last two chapters contained many references to purchasing intention and purchasing behaviour, without systematically discussing the theoretical relationship between brand attitudes, purchasing intention and purchasing behaviour. This theoretical relationship will be the topic of chapter 6. We will not only demonstrate that attitudes towards a given behavior are the most important determinant of this behavior, we will also discuss the relationship between explicit and implicit attitudes and suggest that each of these attitudes is predictive of different types of behaviour.

How advertising influences buying behaviour

The attitude–behaviour relationship: a brief history	196
Predicting specific behaviour: the reasoned action approach	198
Narrowing the intention–behaviour gap: forming implementation intentions	202
Implications for advertising	205
Beyond reasons and plans: the automatic instigation of behaviour	207
Implications for advertising: the return of the hidden persuaders	220
Summary and conclusions	225

The last two chapters focused on attitude research. Chapter 4 discussed how consumers form attitudes towards products and chapter 5 reviewed principles of persuasion and attitude change to explain how advertising influences consumer attitudes. The reason for our interest in consumer attitudes and the impact of advertising on these attitudes is that attitudes are believed to be one of the major determinants of consumer choice and buying decisions. It is nearly a truism that if we can persuade consumers to develop a positive attitude towards a given product, they will also be likely to buy it. However, as we will argue in this chapter, matters are more complicated. Although attitudes are an important determinant of consumer behaviour, other factors such as social norms or the perceived or actual control over the behaviour are also influential factors.

The first part of the chapter will review theorizing and research on the influence of attitudes, social norms and perceived behavioural control on behaviour performed consciously and deliberately. However, by focusing nearly exclusively on processes of deliberate, conscious information-processing and decision-making, consumer research has neglected automatic and unconscious processes, which are also likely to exert a powerful impact on consumer behaviour. Fortunately, as of the mid 1990s, consumer research appears to have become aware of this omission in its theorizing, and by now is devoting substantial attention to unconscious influences on consumer thoughts, feelings and actions (see Simonson et al., 2001, for an overview). This research will be reviewed in the second part of this chapter.

The attitude–behaviour relationship: a brief history

There was general agreement among early social psychologists that human behaviour is guided by social attitudes. Some early writers even defined the field of social psychology as the scientific study of attitudes (Bogardus, 1931; Thomas & Znaniecki, 1918). Gordon Allport (1935) expressed this enthusiasm in his famous opening statement to his classic handbook chapter on attitudes when he stated that the 'concept of attitude is probably the most distinctive and indispensable concept in contemporary social psychology' (p. 798).

At the time of writing his chapter, Allport was probably unaware of a study by the sociologist LaPiere (1934), which might have dampened his enthusiasm. Between 1930 and 1933 LaPiere had travelled with a Chinese couple across the USA and had stayed in 66 hotels and camping places and eaten in 184 restaurants and cafés. Even though there was extreme prejudice against Chinese in the US at that time, only one auto camp refused accommodation. When LaPiere later wrote to all of these establishments whether they would accept members of the Chinese race as guests, he received 128 answers of which 92 per cent were refusals and only one was a clear acceptance.

LaPiere's study would not meet the more stringent methodological criteria of today: first, LaPiere did not measure attitudes but behavioural intentions. Second, it is unclear whether the persons answering his letters were really the same individuals who had admitted the Chinese couple as guests. But most importantly, the individuals answering questions about whether they would admit or serve a 'member of the Chinese race' as guests are likely to have had an image of a Chinese that had little resemblance to the well-dressed Chinese couple (accompanied by a Caucasian) facing those who had agreed to provide service or accommodation. However, the LaPiere (1934) study triggered a number of further studies, which had similarly dismal results. By the late 1960s, at least 45 studies had been reported, many of them laboratory experiments, in which researchers had found virtually no relationship between measures of verbal attitudes and observations of actual behaviour deemed to be relevant to these attitudes (Ajzen & Fishbein, 1977, 2005). Many of these studies tried to relate attitudes of white Americans towards African-Americans to some specific behaviour towards an African-American individual, who was usually a confederate of the experimenter. For example, Himelstein and Moore (1963) used attitudes towards African-Americans to predict whether white participants would be influenced in their decision to sign a petition by whether a black participant (confederate) agreed or refused to sign. They found that the decisions of their white participants were unrelated to petition signing of the black. Others unsuccessfully used attitudes towards racial or ethnic groups to predict conformity with members of these groups making use of classic experimental conformity situations (e.g. Berg, 1966; Bray, 1950; Malof & Lott, 1962). But such failures were not restricted to measures of prejudice. Researchers also failed to predict job performance, absenteeism, and turnover from job satisfaction attitudes (e.g. Bernberg, 1952; Vroom, 1964) or to predict cheating in the classroom from attitudes towards cheating (Corey, 1937). Summarizing this research in an influential review, the sociologist Wicker (1969) reached the following conclusion: 'Taken as a whole, these studies suggest that it is considerably more likely that attitudes will be unrelated or only slightly related to overt behaviours than that attitudes will be closely related to actions. Product-moment correlation coefficients relating the two kinds of responses are rarely above .30, and often are near zero' (p. 65).

Wicker's pessimism regarding the attitude–behavior relationship had dramatic impact on the social psychology of that period. After all, Allport's (1935) assessment that attitudes were the most indispensable construct in social psychology was even more true in the 1960s than it had been in the 1930s. And all this research had been conducted in the conviction that attitudes would be related to behaviour. To discover suddenly that they might have studied marks on evaluative rating scales, which were totally unrelated to behaviour, came as a shock to attitude researchers and aggravated the crisis of confidence which had taken hold of social psychology at that time (see Stroebe, Hewstone & Jonas, 2008).

The issue was resolved when less than a decade later, Ajzen and Fishbein (1977) published their classic analysis of research on the attitude–behaviour relation. They argued that Wicker had asked the wrong question. The important question was not *whether* attitudes were related to behaviour, but *when* were they related. With their **principle of compatibility** Ajzen and Fishbein (1977) specified the conditions that had to be met to find such a relationship. They argued that the problem in much of the earlier research had been to relate a global attitude (e.g. attitude towards African-Americans) to a very specific behaviour (e.g. conformity). According to the principle of compatibility, measures of attitudes will only be related to measures of behaviour, if both constructs are assessed at the same level of generality. As Ajzen and Fishbein (1977) pointed out, a specific *action* is always performed with respect to a given *target*, in a given *context*, and at a given *point in time*. Since attitudes towards a racial group only specify the target, one cannot expect any single behaviour to be related to this attitude. After all, prejudice towards some racial group can be expressed in a multitude of different ways: Prejudiced individuals might decide not to sit next to members of that group, might not want to work with them, might not want them as neighbours, might not want them as friends or might not greet them. Each of those behaviours will be influenced by situational factors as well as prejudice. For example, sometimes one might have no choice where to sit or with whom to work. And people might overcome their prejudice against Asians, if the Asian grocery shop is open longer hours and offers fresher fruit and vegetables at lower prices. Therefore, to assess whether there is a relationship between prejudice and behaviour, one needs to construct a behavioural index that aggregates across a *representative* variety of prejudicial actions, performed in a *representative* range of contexts, across a *representative* range of times.

There is evidence that such aggregate behaviour indices correlate highly with global measures of attitudes. For example, Fishbein and Ajzen (1974) related participants' attitude towards religiosity to a set of 100 behaviours that were relevant to religiosity. Whereas the attitude was practically unrelated to most individual behaviours it was highly related to an aggregate measure across all 100 behaviours. Similarly, Ajzen and Timko (1986) reported that a measure of global attitude towards health maintenance, which did not correlate significantly with the specific self-reported frequency with which respondents performed *specific* health protective actions, showed a substantial correlation with a behavioural index that aggregated the performance of a wide variety of health protective behaviours. These behaviours related to different aspects of health and had been performed in a variety of contexts and times.

Since marketers are usually interested in influencing or predicting specific consumer behaviour, these findings appear to be bad news. However, the principle of compatibility cuts both ways: if we are interested in predicting specific behaviour, attitude measures would be compatible if they assessed the attitude towards performing the specific behaviour. Thus, Ajzen and Timko (1986) were able to predict specific health behaviour from equally specific attitudes towards these behaviours. For example, the reported frequency with which respondents had 'regular dental check-ups' correlated .46 with respondents' attitudes towards 'having regular dental check-ups'. Further support for the importance of compatibility was provided by a meta-analysis of eight studies that manipulated levels of compatibility between attitude and behaviour measures while holding other factors constant (Kraus, 1995). The behaviours studied ranged from participation in a particular psychology experiment to blood donations and self-reported use of birth control pills. Kraus (1995) reported a mean correlation of $r = .13$ at the lowest level of compatibility as compared to $r = .54$ when compatibility was high.

Predicting specific behaviour: the reasoned action approach

As we discussed earlier (chapter 4, this volume) attitudes towards a specific behaviour result from the likelihood with which one expects that behaviour to lead to a number of specific outcomes, with each outcome weighted by the value the individual attaches to that outcome. For example, a prospective car buyer's attitude towards buying a big sports utility vehicle (SUV) will be determined by the likelihood that buying this car will lead to a number of consequences (e.g. the pleasure, greater safety, high running costs, environmental pollution), each of these consequences multiplied by the valence the individual attaches to these consequences. However, even though attitudes towards a specific behaviour (and thus also the behavioural beliefs on which the attitude is based) are good predictors of that specific behaviour, they are not the only determinant. Behaviour is also influenced by social norms and by environmental factors that constrain the individual's ability to engage in this behaviour. For example, if the prospective car buyer's wife is a member of an environmentally progressive (i.e., green) party, he might not want to sacrifice his marital happiness for the sake of increasing his driving enjoyment. Furthermore, the dramatic increase in petrol price might have increased the costs of running the car beyond his means.

Several theories have been developed to improve the prediction of specific behaviours by taking account of such additional factors (for a review, see Conner & Norman, 2005; Stroebe, 2000). The most influential ones have undoubtedly been the **theory of reasoned action** (Fishbein & Ajzen, 1975) and the extension of that theory, the **theory of planned behaviour** (Ajzen, 2005). Both theories predict behavioural intentions (i.e. the motivation to perform a specific behaviour) and assume that the impact of attitudes and other components on behaviour is mediated by the intention to perform that behaviour.

According to the theory of reasoned action, the intention to perform a specific behaviour is determined by a person's attitude towards that behaviour and by **subjective norms**. A person's attitude towards a specific behaviour will be determined by the individual's belief (i.e. perceived likelihood) that performing that behaviour will result in certain positive or negative consequences and the evaluation of these consequences. Usually a given attitude is determined by a very limited number of salient (i.e. highly accessible) beliefs (Ajzen, 2005; Fishbein & Ajzen, 1975). **Subjective norms** combine two components, namely normative beliefs and motivation to comply. Normative beliefs are our beliefs about how people who are important to us (i.e. reference groups) expect us to behave. For example, a businessman, who would very much like to by a big luxury SUV, might also know (i.e. normative belief) that many of his customers are extremely environmentally conscious and would frown on such a purchase. However, whether he will actually decide against the purchase will depend on his motivation to yield to this normative pressure. That Governor Schwarzenegger (California) is no longer driving a huge, petrol-slurping and environment-polluting Hummer SUV may be due to becoming environmentally more conscious, but it is also likely to have been influenced by the environmental attitudes of his electorate. The more positive a person's attitude towards a specific behaviour and the more this behaviour is also expected by others important to that person, the more likely it will be that that a person will form the intention to perform the behaviour.

Sheppard, Hartwick and Warshaw (1988) argued that the theory of reasoned action primarily applies to behaviours (e.g. stopping eating cakes; applying for a consumer loan) and not to goals (losing weight; obtaining a consumer loan) that result from that behaviour, because the achievement of goals usually depends on other factors in addition to the individual's behaviour. Thus, people might not lose weight, even though they stopped eating cakes and they might not get the consumer loan, even if they applied for it. Although this is a valid point, the intention to stop eating cake is also a goal, simply a more specific goal than the goal of losing weight. Furthermore, even individual behaviours are rarely under complete individual control but depend on the availability of resources or on the willingness of other people to cooperate. Thus a wealthy consumer might have planned to buy a Mercedes SL Sports Convertible, but due to a fall in the value of her stock portfolio might decide to go for a less expensive option. On a more everyday level, people often plan to buy a product of a particular brand at their supermarket, but end up buying a different brand, because stocks of their preferred brand have run out.

To acknowledge the fact that people often fail to act on their intentions because they lack the ability, resources, or willpower to do so, the theory of planned behaviour added **perceived behavioural control** as a third component to the theory of reasoned action. Perceived behavioural control can be assessed directly by asking respondents to indicate the extent to which performing a given behaviour was under their control. Alternatively, one can measure perceived behavioural control indirectly, by asking people to list the factors, which might prevent them from engaging in a specific behaviour as well as how likely this was going to happen. Although ultimately no behaviour is totally under an individual's volitional control (e.g. I cannot blow my nose, if I lost my handkerchief), some behaviours are more controllable than others are. For example, going for a walk is more controllable than playing tennis, because I can walk on my own, but depend on a tennis partner for playing tennis.

The theory of planned behaviour assumes that perceived behavioural control affects behaviour *indirectly* through intentions, but can also have a *direct* link to behaviour that is not mediated by intentions (Figure 6.1). The assumption that perceived behavioural control influences intentions is consistent with expectancy-value theories of motivation. In forming intentions to perform an action or to reach some goal, people take their own resources and capabilities into account. People who lack the ability or opportunity to achieve some goal will adjust their intentions accordingly, because intentions are partly determined by the perception of the probability that a goal can be reached. For example, unless they have authored best-selling textbooks or inherited from rich relatives, professors of psychology will not form the intention to buy a Bentley or Ferrari. Similarly, beginners on the ski slopes will not form the intention to go down black runs (colour marking for the most difficult slopes).

The direct relationship between perceived behavioural control and behaviour, which is not mediated by intention, is intuitively less plausible. It also has a somewhat different theoretical status from the link that is mediated by intention. Whereas perceived behavioural control has a *causal* influence on intention (i.e. people usually do not intend to purchase goods, if they have no conceivable way of affording them), the *direct* link from perceived behavioural control to behaviour is *predictive* rather than causal: it depends on the accuracy of the individual's perception of behavioural control. For example, a businesswoman, who decided before the recent economic crisis to buy a bigger apartment, intended to make regular down payments on her mortgage. However, when her firm made her redundant soon afterwards, she was unable to do so. Since her failure to keep up with her down payments was due to factors beyond her control, her intention would have been a poor predictor of her behaviour. If her loss of employment had also been totally unexpected, taking perceived control over meeting her financial obligations into account would not have improved predictions. However, if the woman worked for a firm that had already been loss-making before the economic downturn (e.g. Ford or GM) and was therefore expecting to be laid off in the near future (preventing her from meeting her financial obligations), taking account of her perceived behavioural control over making down payments in addition to her

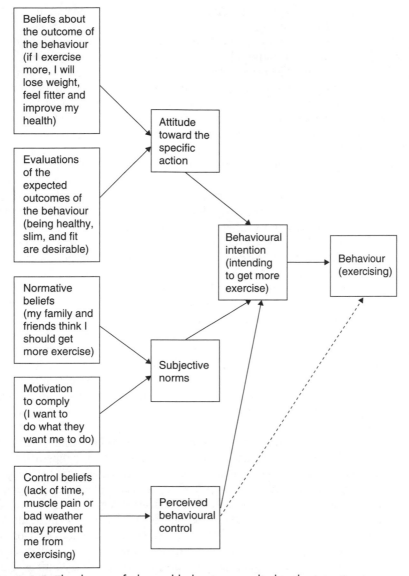

Figure 6.1 The theory of planned behaviour applied to the intention to engage in physical exercise

Source: Stroebe (2000). *Social psychology and health* (2nd ed.). Buckingham: Open University Press

intention to do so would have improved predictions of her behaviour (i.e. a direct link, not mediated by intention). However, since it would have been the fact that she was laid off (i.e. actual control) and not the fact that she correctly anticipated it (perceived behavioural control), which prevented her from continuing to make down payments, the relationship between perceived behavioural control and behaviour would have been predictive rather than causal.

A great number of studies have tested the theories of reasoned action and planned behaviour and their findings have been summarized in several meta-analyses (e.g. Albarracin, Johnson, Fishbein & Muellerleile, 2001; Armitage & Conner, 2001; Sheppard et al., 1988). These meta-analyses support the basic assumption of these models that intentions can be predicted by the components of these model and that measures of intention, in turn, allow a good prediction of behaviour. Based on a meta-analysis of 142 independent studies of a wide range of behaviours, Armitage and Conner (2001) reported an average multiple correlation of attitude, subjective norm and perceived behavioural control with intention of $R = .63$, suggesting that these three components accounted for 40 per cent in the variance of behavioural intentions. Similar correlations were reported by Albarracin et al. (2001) in their meta-analysis of 96 data sets on condom use. However, it is important to note that these tests assessed the accuracy of the predictions of the theories of reasoned action and planned behaviour rather than the processes assumed to lead to the formation of intentions. Thus, the empirical support for these models does not necessarily imply that their process assumptions are valid.

The weighted mean correlation between intention and behaviour range from .45 (Albarracin et al., 2001; Randall & Wolff, 1994) to .53 (Sheppard et al., 1988). Thus, the intention to perform a specific behaviour accounts for 20 per cent to 28 per cent of the variance in measures of that behaviour. Adding perceived behavioural control to intention in the prediction of behaviour increases the explained variance in behaviour on average by another 2% (Armitage & Conner, 2001). The contribution of perceived behavioural control to the prediction of behaviour depends on the extent to which a specific behaviour is under individual control. Thus, it will be lower with behaviour such as attending classes or reading one's book than with stopping smoking or keeping to one's diet.

With the amount of error variance due to less than perfect reliability and validity of measures used, even a perfect theory would never account for 100 per cent of the variance in behaviour. Thus, these estimates of variance accounted for in behaviour are likely to seriously underestimate the strength of the association between intention and behaviour. However, even if we accept that numerous measurement artefacts attenuate the association observed between intention and behaviour, the gap between intention and behaviour remains large enough to have motivated researchers to develop techniques that would reduce it. The most successful technique, which we will discuss in the next section, has been to persuade people to form more specific intentions.

Narrowing the intention–behaviour gap: forming implementation intentions

How can we increase the likelihood that individuals act according to their intentions? One of the most successful strategies is the formation of an **implementation intention**. Whereas behavioural intentions have the form 'I intend to do X' (e.g. I intend to stop smoking), implementation intentions involve the form 'I intend to do X in situation Y' (i.e. if situation Y, then behaviour X; e.g. I intend to stop smoking at 12 o'clock on New Year's Eve). Thus, implementation intentions are more specific goals than behavioural intentions. The efficacy of implementation intentions is typically assessed in studies in which implementation intentions are induced after intentions have been measured, by asking half of the participants to name time and place in which they intended to perform a given behaviour.

For example, Sheeran and Orbell (2000) asked all the women in a medical practice in England, who were due for a cervical smear test, to indicate the strength of their intention to go for a cervical smear test within the next three months. Half of these participants were then instructed to form implementation intentions by asking them to indicate when, where, and how they would make an appointment to have the smear test. Asking individuals to form implementation intentions significantly increased attendance rate from 69 per cent of individuals without to 92 per cent with an implementation intention. The two groups did not differ in the strength of their behavioural intention. Similar results have been reported in numerous studies and over a wide range of behaviours. In a recent meta-analysis of 94 independent studies, Gollwitzer and Sheeran (2006) reported an effect size of medium-to-large magnitude ($d = .65$) for the effect the induction of implementation intentions had in reducing the intention-behavior gap.

How do implementation intentions work? One reason why people fail to act on their intentions is because they simply 'forget' to act when the opportunity arises. By specifying the time and situational context in which behaviour should be performed, the mental representation of the specified situational context cues becomes activated and highly accessible, making sure that people remember their intention when they encounter the situation, in which they planned to act. Furthermore the formation of an implementation intention will also create (or strengthen) the association between the situational cues and the response that is instrumental for obtaining the goal. As a result, the formation of an implementation intention increases the probability that people will remember the action intention when the specified situation arises (Webb & Sheeran, 2007).

In support of these assumptions Sheeran (2002) found in a reanalysis of the data of the Sheeran and Orbell (2000) study that 74 per cent of participants made their appointment for the smear test on the date that they had specified in their implementation intention. More direct evidence for the memory effect of implementation intentions comes from a study by Aarts, Dijksterhuis and Midden (1998). In this study, student participants were asked to go to the cafeteria (apparently to list the price of various food items), but to collect beforehand, on their way to the cafeteria, a consumption coupon at a departmental office. The location of the office was described as being 'down the corridor', 'directly after the first swing door' and 'near the red fire hose'. To induce implementation intentions, half of the participants were requested to plan the steps that are required to collect the coupon. Participants in the control condition were required to plan the steps necessary to spend the coupon (unrelated planning condition).

After some intervening task and before leaving for the cafeteria, participants were asked to perform a lexical decision task in an apparently unrelated experiment. Among the words presented in lexical decision task, the critical words were 'corridor', 'swing door', 'red' and 'fire hose'. As expected, participants, who had formed an implementation intention had shorter recognition times for the critical words and were more likely to collect the consumption coupon on their way to the cafeteria.

Furthermore, a mediation analysis showed that the impact of the type of planning task (i.e. implementation intention versus unrelated planning) on the likelihood of collecting the coupon became insignificant, when reaction time in the lexical decision task was statistically controlled for. This pattern is consistent with the assumption that the greater cognitive accessibility of the situational cues (i.e. swing door and red fire hose) mediated the impact of the implementation intention on behaviour. In other words, individuals who had performed an implementation intention were more successful in collecting the coupon, because they were more likely to be reminded by the situational cues to perform this action

Most research on implementation intentions has been conducted with approach goals, with individuals forming the intention to perform a specific action once a specific situation arose. In contrast to approach goals, where individuals at risk of failing to perform an intended action have to be reminded to get going, with avoidance goals people have to be reminded to suppress an unwanted response. Such unwanted responses can be the expression of prejudicial attitudes (e.g. Devine, 1989), or more relevant for consumer behaviour, indulging in some forbidden pleasure, such as eating high-calorie food while dieting, drinking too much or relapsing on the intention to quit smoking. There are several strategies individuals can use to form implementation intentions that help them to resist a specific temptation. In each case, they first have to identify situations in which the risk of yielding to the targeted temptation is particularly high, second think of a coping response that is likely to be effective in helping them to resist, and third cognitively rehearse linking the coping response to the situation. The effectiveness of this type of implementation intention will not only depend on whether they remember the coping strategy at the right moment, but also on whether this coping strategy is effective in helping them to resist the temptation. One possibility is to link the coping response to the tempting experience itself. For example, if we have a weakness for chocolate, we could recall the experience of temptation the last time just before we yielded and ate the chocolate. We could then form the implementation intention that whenever we experienced this type of craving, to think of our diet and of the many reasons why we wanted to lose weight. Alternatively, we could intervene earlier in the sequence by avoiding buying chocolate. We could form the implementation intention to think of our diet (or of how good we would look with a few pounds less) whenever we saw chocolate on a supermarket shelf and were tempted to put it into our shopping cart.

There are few empirical studies of the effectiveness of implementation intentions with avoidance goals. In one study, participants had to indicate their intention to halve their consumption of a favourite snack food (Achtziger, Gollwitzer & Sheeran, 2008). Half of these participants were then given the implementation intention that whenever they thought about this particular snack food, they should ignore that thought. All participants reduced their consumption of the chosen snack food, but individuals who had formed an implementation intention showed significantly greater reduction. In another study, participants formed the intention to snack on fewer unhealthy foods during the next two weeks (Sullivan & Rothman, 2008). Half of these participants were further instructed to form the implementation intention when and where to avoid eating a specific unhealthy snack (e.g. a bag of chips). Findings showed that individuals who had formed an implementation intention reported consuming significantly fewer calories and less fat over the two-week period of the study than individuals who had not formed such an implementation intention. Similarly, Adriaanse, de Ridder and de Wit (2009) demonstrated that implementation intentions, which specified motivational experiences (e.g. feeling bored, acting social), in which these participants tended to eat unhealthy snacks, and instructed them to replace the unhealthy with a healthy snack in these situations, resulted in a lower consumption of unhealthy and an increased consumption of healthy snacks.

With low effort actions such as phoning for an appointment or collecting a coupon, being reminded at a suitable moment to perform the action is probably sufficient to ensure that the action will be performed. If the action is well-learned and easy to perform, it might even be enacted automatically in response to the situational cue (Gollwitzer & Sheeran, 2006). With more difficult behaviours such as stopping smoking or reducing one's chocolate consumption, it would seem less plausible that merely being reminded of an intention would also ensure action. However, communication of an implementation intention to the experimenter might increase an individual's commitment to perform that behaviour in studies, where people had to record their implementation intentions during the experiment. Furthermore, forming such a specific intention should also increase the salience of a goal violation and thus of anticipated guilt feelings in the event that individuals fail to act on their intention (Stroebe, 2000). For example, if one forms the implementation intention to stop smoking at midnight on 31 December, any cigarette smoked on 1 January is in clear violation of this implementation intention. In contrast, if one violates the goal intention to stop smoking in the near future, one is unlikely to experience a clear goal violation effect, because it remains unclear at which point continuing to smoke violates this intention.

Implications for advertising

The research discussed so far has a number of important consequences for the planning of marketing campaigns, at least if one intends to use argument-based appeals. We learned from our review of dual process theories that one needs strong arguments to persuade people to change attitudes on issues that are important to them. However, these theories did not provide the criteria that would help us to design strong arguments, beyond the advice to have argument strength evaluated by members of the target population.

The research of Fishbein and Ajzen (1975; Ajzen, 2005) suggests several techniques, which allow us to design strong and effective argumentations. As a first step in developing an advertising campaign, marketers need to decide what precisely they want to influence with their advertisement or commercial, whether they want to improve brand awareness or would like to persuade people to buy a particular product. If their persuasive attempt is aimed at buying a particular product, they should use the techniques developed by Fishbein and Ajzen to assess whether the targeted behaviour is mainly determined by attitudes, subjective norms or perceived behavioural control (Ajzen, 2005; Fishbein & Ajzen, 1975). It is pointless to try to persuade people of the positive qualities of a product, if they are unlikely to buy it because their partners or other family members do not want them to buy it (subjective norms) or because they cannot afford it (perceived behavioural control). For example, in the area of food choice family preferences can have a strong influence (subjective norms) as can have the lack of skills in preparing specific dishes. Thus, despite the generally accepted health advantage, seafood is often not bought because of family dislike and because the persons responsible for cooking often do not know how to prepare seafood dishes (Scholderer & Trondsen, 2007). Perceived behavioural control can become important in decisions about buying expensive goods such as cars, furniture or even houses. In such cases control beliefs will often concern financing (concerns that can often be relieved through offering low interest loans for the specific purchase). Sometimes people also fear that they are unable to make the right choice due to lack of knowledge. For example, lack of knowledge about wine or computers might prevent people from buying these goods, even if they would like to do so.

Once one has decided whether to target behavioural outcome, normative or control beliefs (or a combination thereof), one needs to identify the specific beliefs which determine the targeted behaviour. These are relevant beliefs in which people, who own the targeted product or subscribe to the targeted service differ from those who do not intend to buy or subscribe. Such beliefs are likely to strongly influence the purchasing decision. For example, if people stay with a more expensive phone company rather than switching to a cheaper one, because they are worried that switching will involve a great deal of effort and also result in a disruption of their phone service, then persuading them that one can offer a better deal will not be effective. One will also have to convince them that the changeover would be easy and without risk of disruption. Focusing merely on the fact that one can offer a less expensive service would not persuade those people to change. And yet, at the time of writing this manuscript, most low-cost internet providers in the Netherlands base their advertising appeals nearly exclusively on their low prices.

The finding that individuals are more likely to act on their intentions if they have formed implementation intentions also has implications for advertising. If marketers would succeed not only to persuade potential customers to buy their product, but also to form an implementation intention, when and where to buy it, the likelihood that they would actually do so would be largely increased. Unfortunately it would be difficult to induce implementation intentions with an advertisement. One could imagine, though, that an advertisement, showing the Lindt chocolate chef making creamy pralines, would ask viewers to imagine for a second how wonderful this chocolate would taste and then follow this up with the instruction that 'if you want to enjoy the wonderful taste of Lindt pralines yourself, why not plan now that if you see Lindt pralines in your delicatessen when you are shopping next week, you will put them into your shopping cart.' (If one wanted to strengthen this manipulation, one should use a picture of the distinctive looking Lindt chocolate chef as a reminder cue next to the shelf on which the Lindt pralines are displayed.)

We could find only one study using implementation intentions in a consumer context. Kardes, Cronley and Posavac (2005) gave all participants in their study a sample of household cleaning liquid to take home. Whereas participants in the control condition were only asked their intention to use the product, participants in the implementation intention condition were asked to indicate the dates and times that they intended to use the product and the specific uses they were thinking of. A follow-up two weeks later showed that participants who had been induced to form the implementation intention were more likely to use the product and to use it in a greater variety of different situations. However, it is difficult to imagine that individuals who have been handed free samples of a product on the street or in a supermarket would be happy to answer questions about how they intended to use those samples. On the other hand, being provided with the opportunity to use a product first hand (e.g. through a free sample) might facilitate the formation of implementation intentions, because the consumer learns what the product does in which situation, something that potentially triggers the intention to acquire the product again, once the appropriate situational cues are encountered.

Beyond reasons and plans: the automatic instigation of behaviour

The theories discussed so far all assume that the impact of attitude on behaviour is mediated by intention. According to the theories of reasoned action and planned behaviour, attitudes, subjective norms and perceived behavioural control result in the formation of a behavioural intention. It is this intention which is assumed to be the most direct cause of behaviour. Although implementation intentions may result in a behavioural response being triggered automatically in the presence of the situational context specified by the implementation intention, individuals still have to form such an intention in order for the behaviour being performed.

In the last few decades, social and consumer psychologists have become increasingly interested in the automaticity of many higher mental processes (for a review, see Bargh 2007). **Automatic processes** are processes that occur without intention, effort or awareness and do not interfere with other concurrent cognitive processes. Thus, there is more and more research, which demonstrates that attitudes, norms and even goals can be primed by people's social or physical environment and influence behaviour without them being aware of being influenced. The second half of this chapter will review research on the automatic influence of attitudes, norms and goals (as well as the related concept of habit) on behaviour. The last part of this section will then discuss the implication of these findings for advertising.

Before reviewing this research, we would like to discuss the extent to which these findings are inconsistent with models of reasoned action and planned behaviour (for a discussion, see Ajzen & Fishbein, 2000, 2005). Although these theories assume that individuals are guided by relevant attitudes, subjective norms and control beliefs in forming behavioural intentions, the *activation* of behavioural, normative and control beliefs can be automatic and without conscious intent (Ajzen & Fishbein, 2000). Thus, priming or other processes that operate outside individual awareness can increase the cognitive accessibility of normative and control beliefs and thus influence the formation of behavioural intentions. However, since intentions involve some kind of planning, even if the planning is rudimentary, people are likely to be conscious of the process of intention formation. They are further likely to be aware of their intention, when instigating an action. Thus, findings that actions are automatically instigated are difficult to explain with theories of reasoned action and planned behaviour.

Automatic and deliberate influence of attitudes

As discussed earlier (chapter 4) implicit attitudes typically reflect people's automatic evaluative response to a stimulus object, whereas explicit attitudes reflect processes that can be cognitively controlled. Although implicit and explicit measures of attitudes often converge, there are certain conditions under which they diverge. One such domain is the area of prejudice, where some people react with prejudice on an implicit level, but try to consciously control such responses (chapter 4). Other domains are areas of self-regulation such as eating or drinking too much where individuals might be tempted to indulge but at the same time trying to control their temptation

In line with dual process models such as the MODE model of Fazio and colleagues (Fazio, 1990; Fazio & Olson, 2003) or the reflective–impulsive model of Strack and Deutsch (2004) one would expect implicit measures of attitudes to predict behaviour better than explicit measures when individuals are either unmotivated or unable to exert control. In contrast, explicit measures of attitudes should do better, when individuals are able and motivated to exert control over their behaviour.

Support for these assumptions comes from research on prejudice reported earlier, which demonstrated that implicit (but not explicit) measures predicted prejudicial behaviour that was outside the control of the individual. For example, Dovidio et al. (1997) found nonverbal behaviours displayed while interacting with a black or white interviewer to correlate with implicit but not explicit measures of prejudice. Thus, the implicit measure of prejudice predicted lower levels of visual contact with the black interviewer and higher rates of blinking, both not predicted by the measure of modern racism.

But prejudice is not the only domain where people's explicit and implicit attitudes diverge. For example, a dieter may feel attracted to chocolate or ice cream, but on further deliberation will reject these foods because of their high-calorie content. And yet when his motivational or cognitive resources are depleted, he might find himself buying and eating a large portion of ice cream. To test these predictions, Friese et al. (2006) assessed implicit and explicit attitudes towards chocolate and fruit and then allowed participants to choose five items from a large selection of different pieces of fruits and chocolate bars as compensation for their effort. Ability to control behaviour was impaired in half of the participants, by asking them to perform a cognitively demanding task (keeping in mind an eight-digit number). In support of prediction, the implicit attitude measure predicted choice better than the explicit measure under high cognitive load, whereas the reverse was true under low cognitive load. Along similar lines, alcohol consumption improved the capacity of an implicit attitude measure to predict candy consumption in an alleged market research study (Hofmann & Friese, 2009).

Another domain where implicit attitude measures have been shown to diverge from explicit measures is the choice between generic and branded products. In a study conducted in Germany, Friese, Waenke and Plessner (2006) made use of the fact that German consumers believe that generic products are manufactured by the same producers, who make the branded products, but are cheaper, because they are not advertised. And yet, probably as result of advertising, consumers often have a more positive attitudes to branded rather than generic products. Friese and colleagues (2006) therefore predicted that for consumers with divergent attitudes towards generic and branded products, explicit attitudes would predict product choice better when they had ample time to choose, whereas implicit attitudes would predict better when choices had to be made under time pressure. In support of these assumptions, 90 per cent of participants, whose explicit and implicit attitude diverged, made choices that were consistent with their explicit attitude under low time pressure. This pattern reversed under high time pressure. Now only 38 per cent of participants made choices that were consistent with their explicit attitude.

As one implication of these findings, it makes sense from the perspective of stimulating sales to display chocolates and other tempting goods at locations, where people have little time or cognitive resources to control their choice. The fact that supermarkets often display chocolate snacks next to the till might be motivated by similar reasoning. Not only will customers be exposed to these tempting items, but if the line is short and they have to transfer the choices from their shopping trolley to the conveyer belt that takes it to the cash-point, they may have no time for careful deliberation and thus yield to the temptation. Obviously from the perspective of protecting consumers against impulse buying, this is a devious and despicable strategy.

In contrast, if supermarkets want to sell their own brands rather than products from well-known brands, they should display them as far as possible from the exit, in areas where people are still leisurely shopping rather than being on the way to the exit. Furthermore, they should display their brands easily visible on the shelf directly below (or above) the competing product line with the prices of both sets of products shown clearly. Finally, they should make sure that the packaging of their own brands looks as similar as the law allows to that of the well-known brand. When consumers, who are not in a rush, see both similar-looking product lines displayed, with the supermarket's own brand considerably cheaper than the well-known brand, they might decide to risk buying own brand. However, whether they will choose the own brand again next time, will depend on whether the supermarket's own brand matches the quality of the well-known brand.

Another implication is that in cases where one could expect implicit product attitudes to diverge from explicit attitudes, both implicit and explicit attitude measures should be employed in predicting behaviour. Whereas explicit measures will predict behaviour better when people have the resources to control their behaviour, implicit measures will be better predictors when these resources are lacking. However, there is evidence to suggest that even in cases where a convergence between both types of measures can be expected, use of implicit measures can improve predictions based on explicit measures. For example, Maison, Greenwald and Bruin (2004) found implicit and explicit attitudes towards two yoghurt brands, two fast food restaurants and two soft drinks correlated. And yet, adding the implicit measure to the explicit measure significantly improved the prediction of behaviour, which suggests that behaviour is rarely totally controlled (or totally uncontrolled).

Automatic and deliberate influence of social norms

According to the theories of reasoned action and planned behaviour (Fishbein & Ajzen, 1975; Ajzen, 2005), the influence of subjective norms on behaviour should be mediated by intention. In contrast, Aarts and Dijksterhuis (2003) recently suggested that social norms might often guide behaviour automatically without individuals being aware of their influence. Norms are knowledge-based beliefs shaped by social influence and triggered by situational cues. They are if-then rules that state that in certain situations individuals should behave in certain ways, the behaviour being specified by the social norm. Thus, people should lower their voices when in a library or a church, and they should watch their table manners when eating in an elegant restaurant.

Many norms are tied to physical environments. For example, in contrast to football stadiums or railway stations, churches and libraries require one to be silent, and in contrast to fast food restaurants, elegant restaurants require one to be reasonably well-dressed. Aarts and Dijksterhuis (2003) argued that physical environments do not have such behavioural implications per se. People do not lower their voices when they drive past a library or a church. Thus, a pictures of a library should trigger the norm to speak quietly only if the picture was of behavioural relevance to the individual, for example because he or she was intending to visit the library. To test these assumptions student participants were asked to participate in an experiment that consisted of two parts. In the first part, they had to look at a set of pictures. Participants were either presented with pictures of a library or with pictures of a railway station. Half of the participants exposed to the library pictures were led to believe that they had to visit the library immediately afterwards, the other half did not expect to have to visit the library. In the second part of the study, participants responded to a lexical decision task with some of the words relevant to the norm of lowering one's voice (e.g. silent, whisper, quiet). In line with expectations, participants who had been exposed to library pictures *and* expected to visit the library immediately afterwards responded faster to these norm-relevant words than participants in the other two conditions. Thus, in people who had the immediate goal of visiting the library, the picture of the library triggered the relevant norm of speaking quietly.

These experimental manipulations were repeated in a second experiment, but their effect was assessed with a different dependent measure, namely a word pronunciation task. Participants had to pronounce a series of 10 words. No explanation was given for this task; voice intensity was measured while participants were pronouncing each of the words. Again, in line with predictions, participants who had been exposed to pictures of a library *and* instructed to visit the library immediately afterwards spoke less loudly when pronouncing these words than did participants, who did not expect to visit the library or were presented with pictures of a railway station. This study showed that triggering the norm had an impact on relevant behaviour.

In a last experiment, Aarts and Dijksterhuis (2003) studied the impact of a different norm, namely the norm to be well-behaved in restaurants. The study consisted of two parts, executed a month apart. In Part 1, participants had to perform an association task aimed at measuring how strongly behaving well was associated with the concept of exclusive restaurants in these participants. They were briefly shown a picture and immediately afterwards a verbal description of a behaviour. They had to indicate as fast as possible whether the verbal description referred to a behaviour that was appropriate for the environment shown in the picture. Association strength was inferred from the speed with which participants found well-mannered an appropriate behaviour in an elegant restaurant.

In the second part of the experiment conducted one month later, participants were first shown either a picture of a restaurant or of a railway station. They all expected that they had to visit the depicted environment immediately after the experiment. They were then seated at a table and had to eat a round biscuit that produced crumbs when one bit into it. The dependent variable consisted of the extent to which participants kept their table clean while they ate (assessed by external raters). These raters had to count the number of times participants removed crumbs from the table while eating. Consistent with expectations, participants in the restaurant-goal condition cleaned their table more often than participants in the railway-goal condition. Furthermore, the strength with which they had associated restaurants with good manners correlated significantly with their table cleaning behaviour in the restaurant-goal condition ($r = -.65$), but not in the railway-goal condition ($r - -10$). These findings demonstrated that for participants, who had the goal to visit the restaurant, priming them with pictures of a restaurant appeared to have triggered a behavioural norm, which subsequently influenced behaviour.

Although advertisements also frequently appeal to norms, these appeals are typically quite explicit. More subtle norm primes are used in shopping environments. For example, the aim of the endless Christmas music played in shops in the month before Christmas is not only to put people into a Christmas mood, but to remind them of their duty to buy presents for all their loved ones. Similarly, the aim of offering a glass of champagne (or more likely cremant or prosecco) to customers of shops that sell fine clothes is not only to impair their self-control through alcohol consumption but also to trigger the norm of reciprocity (chapter 7) according to which one should not accept the shop owner's booze without reciprocating by buying some of his wares.

Automatic and deliberate influence of goals

Recent research has challenged the assumption that goal pursuit necessarily reflects a conscious process with people being aware of a goal and of their intention to pursue this goal. There is increasing evidence that goal-directed behaviour can be triggered by environmental cues without an intention having been formed (Custers & Aarts, 2005; Moskowitz & Ignarri, in press). Theories of unconscious goal pursuit share with theories of conscious goal pursuit the basic assumption that goals are mentally represented as desired states relating to behaviour or outcomes (Custers & Aarts, 2005). Thus, **goals** are actions or outcomes towards which individuals hold positive attitudes. Furthermore, for a goal to motivate goal striving, there must also be a discrepancy between the actual state of the individual and the desired state (Custers & Aarts, 2005) and the goal must seem attainable to the individual (Kruglanski, Shah, Fishbach, Friedman, Chun & Sleeth-Keppler, 2002). Unconscious goals are therefore as much determined by attitudes, social norms and perceived behavioural control as are conscious intentions. The main difference is that theories of unconscious goal pursuit make the assumption that goals can be unconsciously activated and pursued, without the individual having formed a conscious intention. These theories assume that goals pre-exist in the actor's mind and form part of a knowledge structure that includes the goal itself, the context, in which the goal can be enacted (opportunity) and the actions that need to be performed to reach the goal (i.e. means).

Numerous studies have demonstrated that priming can activate goals without individuals being consciously aware of either the prime or the goal (for a review, see

Custers & Aarts, 2005). For example, Holland, Hendriks and Aarts (2005) exposed half of the participants in an experiment to the smell of an all-purpose cleaner without them being consciously aware of the presence of the scent. When participants were asked to list five home activities which they wanted to perform during the rest of the day, significantly more individuals who had been exposed to the smell of the cleaner included cleaning as their goal than individuals who had not been primed. This suggests that the smell of the cleaner increased the accessibility of the concept of cleaning, which was then used when participants were asked to retrieve plans and goals for home activities.

In this study goal priming was only shown to influence goal setting. However, there is also ample evidence that priming can influence goal enactment. For example, Bargh, Gollwitzer, Lee Chai, Barndollar and Trötschel (2001) unobtrusively exposed participants to words such as 'cooperative' and 'share' to prime the goal of cooperation. After that, participants took part in a resource dilemma task, in which they could either keep any profit for their own benefit or replenish the common pool. Participants who had been primed with the goal of cooperation were more likely to replenish the common source than were the (unprimed) control group participants. The same effects were observed with participants, who were given the explicit goal to cooperate. However, intentions to cooperate during the game (assessed afterwards) correlated with the extent of cooperative behaviour only for participants, who had been explicitly instructed, but not for those, who had formed the goal as a result of priming. Thus, people who were primed with words related to cooperation engaged in more cooperative behaviour without having formed a conscious intention to do so.

Goal priming has also been increasingly studied in the context of consumer research, where researchers have used brand images to prime goals. Brand images are the beliefs people hold about the attributes of a particular branded product. It is therefore possible to use brand images to prime specific goals. Support for this assumption comes from a study by Friedman and Elliot (2008), who used the brand image of the sports drink Gatorade as the prime. They established in a pre-test that their participants associated Gatorade with the trait of endurance. In their main experiment (Experiment 3), participants were first exposed to either a bottle of Gatorade or a bottle of Poland Spring water. In an apparently unrelated part of the experiment, they then had to undergo an effortful endurance task, which consisted of raising their dominant foot 12 inches (30.48 cm) above the ground and keeping it in this position as long as possible, while sitting on a chair with their back straight. While participants, who had been exposed to the bottle of water only managed to keep their leg in that position for 87 seconds, participants primed with Gatorade managed 187 seconds. Thus, having been primed with a brand of sports drink associated in people's mind with endurance, participants endured much longer on a physically demanding task than did participants, who had been primed with a different drink.

Brands are not only associated with characteristics that relate to the expected qualities of a product, they are often also associated with personality characteristics. This aspect of a brand image has been called 'brand personality' (e.g. Aaker, 1997). For example, the Apple computer firm has devoted a major proportion of their advertising budget to establish a brand personality that reflected nonconformity, innovation and creativity (e.g. with the 'Think different' campaign). In contrast, IBM is not particularly associated with creativity. Fitzsimons et al. (2008) made use of these differential associations by priming participants subliminally either with the Apple or the IBM logo. Creativity was then assessed with the unusual uses test of Guilford (Guilford, 1950). With this test, participants are asked to generate as many unusual uses for a common object as possible. In support of their hypothesis, participants primed with the Apple logo producing more creative uses than participants primed with the IBM logo.

A study by Fransen et al. (2008, Experiment 3) tested an even more indirect effect of exposure to a brand logo. These researchers hypothesized that certain types of brands could remind consumers of their mortality, and hence could activate the goal of terror management (see Greenberg, Pyszczynski, Solomon, Simon & Breus, 1994). Insurance brands were thought to induce this type of goal because of the close association between insurance and sickness, misfortune, misery and death. Terror management goals often manifest themselves as world view defense strategies to reaffirm one's important values and norms (Greenberg et al., 1986). In the realm of consumer behaviour typical of western societies, such salient norms involve materialism and consumerism (Arndt, Solomon, Kasser & Sheldon, 2004) and hence, terror management frequently translates into increased spending patterns, conspicuous consumption, a preference for luxury brands, and a preference for domestic products over foreign products (see Arndt et al., 2004; Rindfleisch and Burroughs, 2004; Maheswaran and Agrawal, 2004). After an earlier study had demonstrated that insurance primes significantly increased mortality thought, Fransen et al. (2008) primed participants subliminally with either the brand logo of a well-known insurance company or a control brand logo. In line with the notion of terror management, they found that participants subliminally primed with the insurance logo preferred brands of home-made products over brands of foreign products in the choice task.

That primes are not only useful in triggering goals, but also in channelling goal-directed behaviour in a specific direction has been demonstrated in studies by Chartrand, Huber, Shiv and Tanner (2008) and North, Hargreaves and McKendrick (1999), Chartrand et al. (2008) argued that the types of stores one passes on the way to the shop one is going to may well affect the type of choice people make at the point-of-purchase. Thus, if people walked past a number of shops selling cheap goods, they might be primed with the concept of thrift and therefore take the cheap alternative when making a buying decision later. To test these ideas, these researchers used the scrambled sentence test to induce either the concept of prestige or thrift and subsequently exposed participants to a product choice situation where they could choose between a prestige brand (Nike) or a US budget brand (Hanes). Not surprisingly, they found that those participants who were primed with prestige preferred Nike over Hanes.

That music in supermarkets can also be used to channel buying decisions has been demonstrated by North, Hargreaves and McKendrick (1999), who had customers in a supermarket exposed to either French or German music to influence the country of origin of the wines they bought. A selection of four French and four German wines was displayed on a shelf in the wine section of a supermarket. When French or German music was played on alternative days, the type of music influenced choice of wines, with more French wines being bought on days with French music and more German wines being bought on days with German music (Figure 6.2).

The problem with most of the consumer research on goal priming reported so far is that it is unclear whether the priming effects were driven by goal-based or

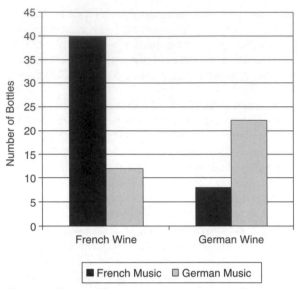

Figure 6.2 Influence of type of in-store music on country of origin of wines bought in a supermarket

Source: Adapted from North et al. (1999). The influence of in-store music on wine selection. *Journal of Applied Psychology, 84*, 271–276,Table 1, p. 274

cognition-based processes. For example, the prime in the Chartrand et al. study could have increased the cognitive accessibility of the concept 'thrifty' and this concept might have been associated with the budget brand Hanes rather than Nike. To ensure that goals rather than concepts are being primed, goal priming studies should incorporate a delay condition to assess whether the priming effect becomes weaker or stronger over time. Whereas memory effects fade over time, the motivational impact of unfulfilled goals increases over time.

Chartrand et al. (2008) therefore conducted a second study, in which they made use of the difference assumed to exist in the persistence of concept and goal primes over time. In this study the same goals (prestige versus thrift) were primed using the scrambled sentence task and a time delay was varied (three versus eight minutes) before participants could make product choices (in this study product choices again included a choice between the prestige brand Nike and the budget brand Hanes, but also between two brands of sound systems: Bose (prestige) and Toshiba (thrift), and between either a luxurious but expensive apartment or a simpler and cheaper one. Chartrand et al. (2008) found that the prime effects on product choice (higher preference for prestige related brands after prestige prime) increased rather than decreased over time and that reaching the goal diminished the effects of goal primes, but only when actual rather than hypothetical product choices were involved.

Even though they do not use subliminal techniques, marketers often make use of goal priming techniques in designing advertisements or commercials. In most of these advertisements pictures are used to prime a goal, whereas the text message is used to argue that the advertised product is the ideal means to reach the primed goal.

For example, travel tour operators will show pictures of beautiful beaches and of people enjoying these beaches to prime the goal of going on vacation. The text message will then point out that this travel operator offers travel packages that allow customers to go to beautiful vacation locations at reasonable prices.

That priming a goal before delivering a message increases the impact of relevant messages has been demonstrated by Strahan, Spencer and Zanna (2002, Experiment 2). Strahan and colleagues asked their participants not to eat or drink for 3 hours before coming to the laboratory. They then primed half the participants subliminally with thirst-related words (e.g. thirsty, dry), whereas the other half were primed with neutral words. Subsequently, participants were given a print advertisement describing a new drink, which was either called Super Quencher or Power Pro. Whereas Super Quencher was described as the best thirst quenching drink ever developed, Power Pro was described as an electrolyte-restoring sports drink. The argument that Super Quencher was extremely effective in quenching thirst was most persuasive for individuals who were not only thirsty, but for whom their thirst had been made cognitively accessible through priming. A measure of the persuasiveness of the two ads clearly indicated that thirst priming increased the persuasiveness of the Super Quencher but not of the Power Pro advertisement (Figure 6.3).

Goals, habits and behaviour

Many roads lead to Rome and the same is true for most goals. People usually have a choice from a multitude of means to reach a particular goal. To get a cup of coffee at our department, we can either make it ourselves, go down to the coffee automat in the canteen or go to the cafeteria in the library building, which offers a range of different coffees that would make Starbucks proud. While it is great to have such a choice, it also poses a challenge to our cognitive resources. Automatic behaviour would be

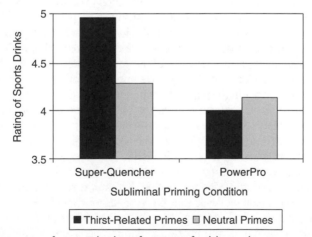

Figure 6.3 Rating of sports drink as function of subliminal priming condition

Source: Strahan et al. (2002). Subliminal priming and persuasion: Striking while the iron is hot. *Journal of Experimental Social Psychology*, 38, 368–383, Figure 2, p. 561

unlikely, if every time we would like to have a cup of coffee, we would ponder about the various means to reach this goal.

For goals to be implemented automatically, the selection of the relevant means to reach the goal needs to be routinized. In the research on goal implementation reported so far, the problem of means selection has been circumvented by presenting participants with *one* appropriate opportunity for goal directed behaviour. In everyday life, we often routinize the selection process by developing habits. **Habits** are 'learned sequences of acts that have become automatic responses to specific cues and are functional in obtaining certain goals or end states' (Verplanken & Aarts, 1999). Behaviour becomes habitual if it is performed frequently, regularly and under environmental conditions which are stable. Behaviour is unlikely to become habitual, if it is only performed once a year or under unstable environmental conditions. Thus, brushing one's teeth and having a shower in the morning are so habitual that we go through the whole routine without really thinking about it. Similarly, much of grocery shopping (e.g. choice of supermarket, choice of brands of washing powder, oil, margarine, toothpaste, etc.) is habitual and automatic. Buying Christmas presents, on the other hand, will need a great deal of deliberation.

In the case of well-learnt habitual behaviours such as driving, cycling, eating or dancing one speaks of goal-dependent automaticity, because starting out the behaviour involves an intention, but once the process has been triggered it runs off automatically (Bargh, 1994). We *decide* to drive to work, but once we sit in the car, we do not really have to think about starting the engine or engaging gears. By being enacted automatically and without need of deliberation, habitual behaviour has the great advantage of allowing us to use our (limited) cognitive resources for other purposes. Thus, while driving to work, we can plan our day in a leisurely way, rather than concentrating on performing the multitude of acts required when driving a car or on planning the route we have to take in order to reach our office.

The great disadvantage of the automaticity of habitual behaviour is that it is difficult to change, even if we have formed the intention to do so. This is also the reason why 'brand switching' for habitually acquired products is such a formidable challenge to marketers that no successful marketing strategies have yet been documented. In fact, even deviation from one's usual way home to pick up some shopping can prove a challenge. We might have promised to stop at the supermarket on our way home to pick up some supplies needed for dinner and yet we might find ourselves arriving at home, having totally forgotten about the planned deviation from our customary route. For this reason, behaviour that we perform regularly and under stable environmental conditions is probably better predicted by our past behaviour in these situations rather than by our intentions. In contrast, intentions will be a better predictor of behaviour that is performed infrequently and under conditions that vary a great deal.

These hypotheses were tested in a study of choice of travel mode by Verplanken, Aarts, van Knippenberg and Moonen (1998). The study was conducted in a small village and the target behaviour was the choice of car for travelling outside the village rather than alternative travel options. The authors measured habits as well as the determinants of behaviour of the model of planned behaviour. Habit strength was assessed through self-reported past behaviour (SPB) and with a newly developed response–frequency measure (RF)[16]. Behaviour was assessed through a diary in which individuals had to list their travel destinations and modes of travel for a three-week period. In line with predictions, habit and intention interacted to influence behaviour. As we can see from Figure 6.4, which presents the simple regression slopes of intention on behaviour for participants with weak, moderate and strong habits, this effect emerged for both measures of habit strength. Intention was a significant predictor of behaviour when habit was weak. However, when habit was very strong, the predictive power of intention decreased. In other words, for individuals who habitually went almost everywhere by car, behavioural intention became a poor predictor of their choice of travel mode.

Further support for these assumptions comes from a meta-analysis of studies that included measures of past behaviour in tests of theories of reasoned action and planned behaviour (Oulette & Wood, 1998). In line with predictions, intentions were a much better predictor than measures of past behaviour for actions that were only performed once or twice a year and in unstable contexts. In contrast, measures of past behaviour were better predictors than intentions of actions that were performed regularly and in stable contexts. These findings are indeed consistent with the assumption that habitual behaviour is automatic in the sense that it is triggered by situational cues rather than guided by conscious intentions.

If habits are a form of goal-directed automatic behaviour, they should be mentally represented as associations between goals and actions, which are instrumental for attaining these goals. Whenever a goal is activated, this should also activate the behaviour representations that present the appropriate means to attain the goal. Thus, if a student always uses her bicycle to travel to the university, activation of the goal to act (having to attend a lecture) should automatically trigger the habitual response (bicycle). This hypothesis was supported in a study with student participants, who varied in the extent to which they were habitual bicycle users (Aarts & Dijksterhuis,

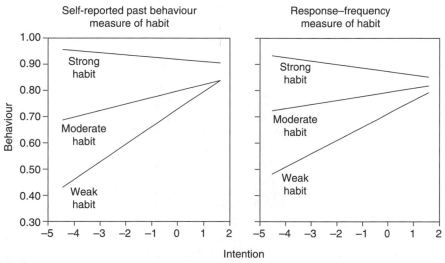

Figure 6.4 The relationship between intention and behaviour by habit strength

Source: Verplanken et al. (1998). Habit versus planned behaviour: A field experiment. *British Journal of Social Psychology, 37,* 11–128, Figure 1, p.119. Reproduced with permission from the *British Journal of Social Psychology,* © The British Psychological Society

2000). In a pre-test, the researchers established five locations in the university town, which could be reached by bicycle (e.g. shopping mall; university) and also the major reason, why students wanted to go to these locations (e.g. shopping; attending classes). Half the participants were then given sentences to read, which primed the five travel goals without mentioning locations (e.g. attending a lecture). The assumption was that reading these sentences would cognitively activate the five travel goals. Then, in an apparently unrelated task, all participants were presented with the five locations and a word presenting a travel mode and had to decide as quickly as possible whether the presented mode of transport was a reasonable way to get to that location. The dependent measure was the time taken to answer this question. In support of predictions, habitual bicycle users responded faster than non habitual bicycle users when bicycle was offered as a travel mode, but only if they had been primed with the relevant travel goals (Figure 6.5). Without goal priming, they did not respond faster to bicycle offered as a travel mode than did the non habitual bicycle users. This rules out the explanation that habitual bicycle users responded faster because they were more familiar with the concept of bicycle. The activation of a relevant travel goal was necessary to activate bicycling as a travel mode in habitual bicycle users.

If habits are cognitively represented as links between goals and actions that are instrumental for attaining these goals, then forming implementation intentions should operate through the same processes as the formation of habits. After all, in forming an implementation intention, individuals create a mental link between a situational cue

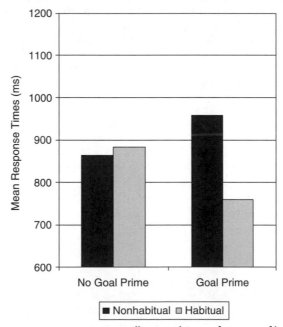

Figure 6.5 Mean response times (in milliseconds) as a function of habit strength and goal prime

Source: Aarts & Dijksterhuis, (2000). Habits as knowledge structures: Automaticity in goal-directed behavior. *Journal of Personality and Social Psychology, 78*, 53–63, Table 1, p. 56

and a specific action. Whereas with habits the association between the relevant situation and the behaviour is learnt through repeated performance of the behaviour, with implementation intentions the association is learnt through repeated mental simulation of performing that action in that specific situation. Support for this assumption comes from a study by Aarts and Dijksterhuis (2000), who used the travel goal paradigm described above. This time, they exposed all participants to the goal prime, but added an implementation intention condition as a factor, cross-cutting the extent to which individuals were (or were not) habitual bicycle users. Implementation intentions were formed by asking individuals to write down each of the travel goals and plan precisely, how to reach these goals. Again, the dependent measure was the time it would take individuals to recognize bicycle as a word in a lexical decision task. In support of predictions that the formation of implementation intentions would operate the same way as the formation of a habit, non habitual bicycle users recognized bicycle faster after they had formed an implementation intention than without such an intention (Figure 6.6). In fact non habitual bicycle users who had formed an implementation intention recognized the word bicycle as quickly as habitual bicycle users without implementation intention. Forming an implementation intention had no effect on habitual bicycle users.

So far we have mainly focused on cognitive processes that result in the automatic elicitation and/or execution of habitual behaviour sequences. However, if

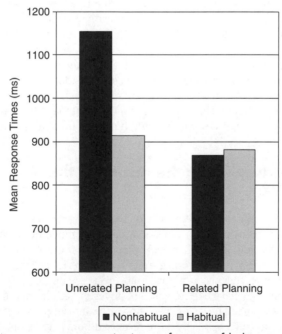

Figure 6.6 Mean response times (ms) as a function of habit strength and type of planning

Source: Aarts & Dijksterhuis (2000). Habits as knowledge structures: Automaticity in goal-directed behavior. *Journal of Personality and Social Psychology, 78,* 53–63, Table 2, p. 58

consumers continually frequent the same stores or buy the same brands, one can assume that they presumably do so because they are satisfied with those choices, or at least that they are more satisfied than they are with the alternatives available to them. Although this might have been true initially (i.e. at the time they first frequented the store or tried the product), it is quite possible that in the meantime better alternatives have become available. The problem is that once a particular choice has become habitual, people are no longer interested in searching for alternatives. In support of this assumption, Verplanken, Aarts and van Knippenberg (1997) demonstrated in a study of information search in deciding on a mode of travel that people who habitually used a particular travel mode (e.g. bicycle) acquired less information and gave evidence of less elaborate choice strategies in deciding how to travel to a new location than did people who did not habitually use a particular mode of travel.

Obviously, the fact that choices that are made on a habitual basis relieve one of the need to search for information about alternatives each time one has to choose, is one of the advantages of habit formation. For marketers, establishing habits is exceedingly desirable because they translate into brand-loyal consumers, who structurally buy the same brands. For this reason, marketers try to instill habits through what is known as 'frequency marketing', where repeat buying is rewarded with discounts and special benefits (e.g. frequent flyer programmes). However, there are other advantages as well. By habitually using a particular service, store, or product, people develop a particular skill in using this service, store or product. Once this skill has been acquired, switching would engender costs (i.e. extra effort and time) which lock consumers into making the same choice over and over again (Murray & Häubl, 2007). This phenomenon has been referred to as *cognitive lock-in* (Johnson, Bellman & Lohse, 2003). By shopping always at the same supermarket, customers save time and effort through knowing what is on offer and where to find it. Shopping in a different supermarket, where products have to be searched for, would cost considerably more time. Thus, the development of habits saves time and effort by reducing time for search and for using a particular facility or object. However, these gains are made at the risk of overlooking more advantageous alternatives, which might have become available in the meantime.

Implications for advertising: the return of the hidden persuaders

The finding that subliminal presentation of words or pictures can not only prime mental representations of words or objects in people's minds but also influence their behaviour raises the possibility that such procedures could be used for subliminal advertising. **Subliminal advertising** refers to advertising that uses messages (embedded in a film or television report) that are presented so briefly that viewers remain unaware that they have been exposed to advertising. This is probably a surprising suggestion, because subliminal advertising, after a brief period in the limelight in 1957, was declared as not feasible by more recent authors (e.g. Moore, 2000; Pratkanis & Aronson, 2002). Subliminal advertising was made notorious in 1957 through publicity surrounding James Vicary, a private market researcher, who claimed to have increased sales of Coca-Cola by 18.1 per cent and popcorn sales by 57.7 per cent in a movie theatre, by secretly and subliminally flashing the message 'Drink Coca-Cola' or

'Eat popcorn'. People became so upset by the idea that they could be manipulated without their awareness that subliminal advertising has subsequently been banned in Australia and Britain.

Nobody has ever been able to replicate the findings reported by James Vicary. The study has never been published and is now believed to have been a publicity hoax (Pratkanis & Aronson, 2001). The belief in the efficacy of subliminal messages was further decreased by the outcome of an assessment of the efficacy of self-help tapes that claim to use subliminal messages. Such tapes appear to be wildly popular among American consumers, who spend more than $50 million annually on audiotapes that contain subliminal messages to help them to improve their self-esteem, their memory and their study habits or to help them to lose weight and to stop smoking. (Pratkanis & Aronson, 2001).

To test the veracity of these claims, Greenwald, Spangenberg, Pratkanis and Eskenazi (1991) conducted a study in which they gave their participants tapes to listen to at home. Half received tapes that, according to the manufacturers, contained subliminal messages that should improve self-esteem ('I have high self-worth and high self-esteem') the other half received memory tapes ('My ability to remember and to recall is increasing daily'). Cross-cutting the (alleged) subliminal content of the tapes, half the respondents were led to believe that they listened to the memory tape, the other half that they listened to the self-esteem tape. Reassessment of their self-esteem and their memory on their return to the laboratory could detect no improvements. However, whereas the actual content of the tapes had no effect whatsoever, the *assumed* content resulted in a placebo effect. Participants believed that their memory (or their self-esteem) had improved, even though, objectively, there had been no improvements at all. Obviously, such beliefs guarantee satisfied customers and the continued sales of self-help tapes.

That these subliminal messages were ineffective is hardly surprising and does not necessarily rule out the possibility that subliminal advertising might work. First, these tapes used whole sentences and it is unlikely that sentences can be primed subliminally. Subliminal verbal primes have to consist of one or perhaps two (very short) words to be effective and not of whole sentences (Greenwald, 1992). Second, successful priming does nothing more than increase the accessibility of the primed concept and of thoughts related to that concept. Thus, even if it were possible to prime subliminally sentences such as 'My ability to remember is increasing daily' or 'I have high self-worth', they would be unlikely to improve our memory or our self-esteem.

Coca-Cola is a relatively short brand name and thus meets the first condition for a subliminal prime. Thus, if clever advertising technicians developed a technique that would enable them to successfully prime movie or TV audiences, this might increase the accessibility of Coca-Cola in the viewer's mind. But would this really result in higher sales? So far, only limited evidence on priming of brand choices is available (e.g. Cooper & Cooper, 2002; Hawkins, 1970; Dijksterhuis, Wegner & Aarts, 2005; Karremans, Stroebe & Claus, 2006; Strahan, Spencer & Zanna, 2002). Hawkins (1970) primed his participants either with 'Coke' or 'Drink Coke' for 2.7-millisecond intervals during the presentation of irrelevant supraliminal material. In a control condition, participants were subliminally exposed to nonsense syllables. Both Coke conditions resulted in higher thirst ratings, even though the differences between the 'Drink Coke' and the control group just failed to reach significance. In a rather similar study, Cooper and Cooper (2002) primed participants, who viewed a full episode of *The Simpsons* with 12 pictures of Coca-Cola cans *and* 12 presentations of the word 'thirsty', each frame being displayed for 33 milliseconds. (In the control condition blank frames were presented). Participants, who had to rate their state of thirst on a multi-item 'motivation states questionnaire' before and after the experiment showed a significant and positive effect of the experimental manipulation on thirst ratings. These studies indicate that subliminal exposure to the brand name of a (well-known) soft drink can increase self-ratings of thirst. However, since neither of these studies included a behavioural measure, it is unclear whether the increased thirst ratings really reflected greater thirst or simply an increased accessibility of the concept of thirst due to its association in memory with the word Coke.

A study of a subliminally primed drink or brand of beverage has been conducted by Dijksterhuis, Wegner and Aarts, 2001 (reported in Dijksterhuis, Aarts & Smith, 2005). Participants in this study were subliminally (15 ms) primed either with the word 'drink', the word 'cola' or four-letter random word strings. At the (apparent) end of the experiment, the experimenter mentioned that he was going to have a drink. He asked participants whether they wanted one and offered a choice between cola and mineral water. The dependent measure was the choice of drink and the amount drunk by participants, who wanted a drink. However, although participants in the two experimental conditions drank more than those in the control conditions, the cola prime did not result in a more frequent choice of cola.

Since the Coca-Cola company is unlikely to devote part of their advertising millions to a strategy, which is as likely to increase the consumption of mineral water as that of Coke, these findings are not supportive of subliminal advertising as a viable marketing strategy. However, Karremans et al. (2006) argued that these experiments disregarded a number of aspects that are important to get subliminal advertising to work. First, Coca-Cola is a highly accessible brand name. Priming might work better with a brand that is not as widely advertised as Coca-Cola and is therefore less congnitively accessible. Second, since priming does nothing more than increase the cognitive accessibility of the concept of Coca-Cola, effects will depend on the thoughts people associate with that brand and these thoughts might differ from the brand image that the Coca-Cola company conveys in advertisements. If participants find Coca-Cola too sweet a drink to quench thirst, priming will not change their opinion. On the other hand, if they associate it with great taste and great thirst quenching qualities, then priming might make them want to have a Coke, but only if they are thirsty at that particular moment. As Strahan, Spencer and Zanna (2002) pointed out, priming will influence behaviour only if the priming is goal relevant and people are motivated to pursue this goal. In the case of priming a brand of soft drink, this means that recipients have to be thirsty for the prime to be effective. The fact that priming slightly increased self-rated thirst in earlier studies (Hawkins, 1970; Cooper & Cooper, 2002) does not mean that they were sufficiently thirsty to go for a drink.

When Karremans, Stroebe and Claus (2006) tried to put this hypothesis to a test, they found in a pre-test that their Dutch students attributed the greatest thirst quenching qualities to Lipton Ice (an ice tea) and not to Coke. They therefore decided to use Lipton Ice in their studies. They conducted two experiments, in which half the participants were subliminally primed with Lipton Ice, the other half with a neutral control word containing the same letters. The primes were presented 25 times, but each time for only 23 milliseconds, so that participants were unaware of the priming procedure. Whereas in their first experiment, they used self-ratings of thirstiness to divide participants into thirsty and non-thirsty groups, they decided to manipulate thirstiness in the second study. Participants had to suck a salty sweet ('dropje'), supposedly to see whether they could identify with their tongue the letters that were impressed on one side of the sweet. (This sweet, which is popular in the Netherlands, is known to produce thirst.) Both experiments resulted in significant prime by thirstiness interactions on choice. When offered a choice between a brand of mineral water or Lipton Ice, participants who had been primed with Lipton Ice were significantly more likely to choose it over the mineral water, *but only if they were thirsty* (Figure 6.7). They also expressed greater intentions to choose Lipton Ice in a hypothetical situation (if they were now sitting on a terrace and ordering a drink). There was also a tendency for priming to work better for participants who did not drink Lipton Ice regularly than for those, who were habitual Lipton Ice drinkers.

Recently, Bermeitinger, Goelz, Johr, Neumann, Ecker and Doerr (2009) published a replication and extension of the Karremans et al. study (2006). This study made use of the fact that in Germany, dextrose pills are a popular means of concentration enhancement. Participants, who could be classified as tired or not tired according to self-ratings, were subliminally primed with one of two logos for (non-existent) dextrose pills, as well as the word 'concentration' while playing a computer game. Afterwards, they had to conduct a concentration task and were offered two bowls with dextrose pills, each bowl labelled with one of the two logos. In support of predictions, tired participants ate more of the primed than the non primed brand, whereas there was no difference in consumption between non tired participants.

Why did subliminally priming influence choice of soft drink in the study of

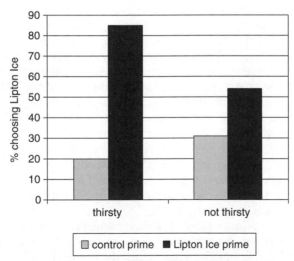

Figure 6.7 Percentage of participants choosing Lipton Ice as a function of thirst and prime

Source: Karremans et al. (2006). Beyond Vicary's fantasies: The impact of subliminal priming on brand choice. *Journal of Experimental Social Psychology, 42*, 792–798, Experiment 2

Karremans and colleague when Dijksterhuis and colleagues (2005) failed to find such an effect? We already mentioned several important reasons. Coca-Cola is a highly accessible brand and there might have been a ceiling effect. Furthermore, participants need to be thirsty and consider Coca-Cola thirst quenching. However, there is also a fourth reason and to explain this, we have to get a bit more technical. We already mentioned that priming is modality specific and that priming effects are considerably reduced or even absent when the target material is presented in auditory form or when participants study pictorial equivalents of words (Schacter, Chiu & Ochsner, 1993). Both Dijksterhuis et al. (2005) and Karremans et al. (2006) primed their participants with the name of the drink. But whereas Karremans and colleagues (2006) later measured consumer choice again with the name of the drink, Dijksterhuis and colleagues offered their participants a choice between two drinks referred to orally. In their study the experimenter said, 'I am going to have a drink. Do you want a drink as well? We have cola and mineral water' (Dijksterhuis et al., 2005, p. 95). Thus, whereas the prime was presented visually, the target was presented in auditory form. And as previous studies have shown, priming does not easily transfer across modalities (for a review see Schacter et al., 1993).[17]

Since readers might be interested in the reasons for this limitation of the generality of priming effects, we need to go into a bit of technical detail here and explain what memory theorists call *transfer appropriate processing* (Bransford, Franks, Morris & Stein, 1979). According to this view, a task like reading a word or a sentence requires a set of sensory-perceptual or conceptual operations and engaging in these operations has the same effect as practising a skill. It increases the efficiency with which this skill can be reenacted at a later time. Thus, remembering is less considered a process by which the individual accesses some residue of the studied information in memory than as a re-performance of an earlier act. The greater the similarity or overlap between the analytical processes engaged in during the learning and the retrieval phase, the better will be the performance on a memory task.

Most tests of implicit memory are data-driven. Because respondents are required to operate on perceptual information provided by the experimenter (e.g. fragment completion or perceptual identification), performance on these tests is more dependent on the match between the perceptual conditions during the study and the test phase (Richardson-Klavehn & Bjork, 1988; Roediger, 1990). In contrast, most explicit tests assess the encoded meaning of concepts, and are therefore sensitive to conceptual elaboration but insensitive to changes in the surface features of the information (e.g. type face, changes in modality) or in study-test manipulations (e.g. visual versus auditory). Thus, whereas explicit memory is mediated by processes that generalize across modalities and languages, implicit memory performance is mediated in part by processes that are modality and language specific (Richardson-Klavehn & Bjork, 1988; Roediger, 1990; Schacter et al., 1993).

What is the implication of all of this for subliminal advertising? Most importantly, we have to choose the subliminal prime to match the most likely consumer choice situation. If we want individuals to pick the primed brand from among other drinks, we should probably prime with the logo of the brand rather than the brand name. Second, the drink has to be considered thirst quenching and people have to be thirsty. But third, they also have to be in a situation, in which they are able to make that choice. A known limitation of subliminal priming is that effects wear off very quickly. Thus, even thirsty movie audiences would want the primed drink immediately after they had been primed and not three days afterwards. Thus, subliminally priming movie audiences just before the break might induce those who are thirsty to buy the primed drink during the break. However, it would not motivate them to stock up with it the next time they are at the supermarket.

Although we are continuously primed by our physical and social environment without being consciously aware of these effects, the possibility of becoming the target of subliminal advertising still raises ethical concerns. These concerns are somewhat alleviated by the fact that we now have a much better understanding of the processes underlying subliminal advertising than we did in 1957, when Vicary made his false claim. We now know that priming works by increasing the accessibility of cognitive concepts or of goals. Priming should not change attitudes. Since both the cognitive concepts and the goals must already be available in our minds to be made more accessible, this type of subliminal advertising would not guide us in directions we had no intention of moving.

More threatening is the possibility that instead of priming, one could use methods of subliminal evaluative conditioning. As we discussed in chapter 4, there is evidence that evaluative conditioning can affect attitudes towards brand-names. For example, one study on the long-term effects of conditioned attitudes towards a brand name associated positively evaluated images with a fictitious brand of mouthwash (Grossman & Till, 1998). Even three weeks after exposure, conditioning effects could still be observed. There is limited evidence for classical conditioning of attitudes to work when the evaluative stimuli are presented subliminally (e.g. Krosnick, Betz, Jussim & Lynn, 1992; but also see Pleyers et al, 2007). Thus, one could pair a brand name with evaluative stimuli (e.g. pictures of positive events), which are presented subliminally. It is this procedure, which must have been intended in a recent American election, when allegedly the concept of 'Democrats' was subliminally associated with 'rats'. Because this type of subliminal evaluative conditioning might result in attitude change without individuals being aware of the influence attempts, it would certainly be more ethically problematic than subliminal priming.

Summary and conclusions

- Once upon a time, social psychologists expected attitudes towards any attitude object to influence the whole range of individual behaviour that could be enacted towards that object and were upset by evidence, which disproved this assumption. We now know that the correct question to ask is not *whether* but *when* attitudes influence behaviour.

- The most important condition for measures of attitude to predict behaviour is that the two types of measures are compatible. Compatibility can be achieved by aggregating measures of behaviour to the level of generality of the attitude measure or by making the attitude measure so specific as to apply to the specific behaviour we want to predict.

- According to the theory of planned behaviour (which is an extension of the theory of reasoned action), a person's intention to perform a specific behaviour is the best predictor of that behaviour. People's intentions to engage in a specific behaviour are a function of their attitude towards that behaviour, their subjective norms (normative beliefs x motivation to comply) and their perceived behavioural control over performing that behaviour.

- The theories of reasoned action and planned behaviour assume that the influence of attitudes on behaviour is mediated by intentions. However, even though intentions are the best single predictor of behaviour, they predict less than 30 per cent of the variance in behaviour. This intention–behaviour gap can be reduced, if we motivate people to form implementation intentions. Implementation intentions differ from general intentions, because they specify the situation and time when the intended action should be performed.

- One reason why implementation intentions work is that by mentally simulating that if situation X arises one will enact behaviour Y, one partially or fully transfers the control over the instigation of the behaviour Y to environmental cues. Thus, once we have formed an implementation intention to do Y in situation X, situation X will trigger the behavioural response Y. With easy and well-learnt responses, this can lead to the automatic performance of that behaviour.

- The second part of the chapter discussed the influence of automatic processes on behaviour. There is increasing evidence that attitudes, social norms, habits and goals can be primed by one's social or physical environment and influence behaviour without individuals being aware of being influenced.

- Behaviour can be automatically and unconsciously influenced by our implicit attitudes, an effect that becomes apparent when implicit and explicit attitudes are discrepant. Under these conditions, explicit attitudes predict behaviour that is under the individual's control, whereas implicit attitudes are better predictors of behaviour when the individual lacks the resource (and motivation) to exert control.

- Norms can be triggered by environmental factors and influence behaviour without the individual being aware of this effect. For example, a picture of a library can induce individuals to lower their voices, but only if the norm is goal relevant (i.e. if they are planning to go to the library).

- There is increasing evidence that goals can be primed and that individuals often adopt goals without being aware of the environmental stimuli that acted as prime (e.g. the smell of cleaning liquid can make people aware that their house needs cleaning).

- Because there are usually different means available to reach a goal, the selection of means has to be routinized for goal directed behaviour to become automatic. One way to routinize the choice of means to reach a goal is the development of habits. Well-learnt habitual behaviours can be elicited by appropriate environmental cues and executed automatically. Habits work for the same reasons as implementation intentions, the difference being that the association between the situational cue and the behaviour sequence has been established through repeated performance of that behaviour rather than through mental simulation.

- The impact of subliminal priming on behaviour suggests the possibility of using such procedures in advertising. Subliminal advertising has been thought to be impossible for many decades, but recent research suggests that it might be feasible. For example, participants, who were subliminally primed with the name of a soft drink, were more likely to choose that soft drink over other drinks, but only if they were thirsty. Thus, when people have a particular goal, subliminally priming them with the means of reaching this goal, can influence their behaviour.

Chapter 7

Beyond persuasion: achieving consumer compliance without changing attitudes

Social influence and compliance without pressure	231
The principle of reciprocity	235
The principle of commitment/consistency	238
The principle of social validation	244
The principle of liking	248
The principle of authority	252
The principle of scarcity	256
The principle of confusion	258
Mindlessness revisited: the limited-resource account	261
Summary and conclusions	262

Have you ever wondered what made you buy that magical magnetized bracelet promising an end to your (non-existent) back problems, or why you ended up with four litres of processed cream cheese after your trip to the supermarket, despite your lactose intolerance? Then you're not alone! Although consumers typically do not intend to buy irrelevant, useless or unwanted products or services, they sometimes find themselves doing just that. In some situations, certain factors present at the point of purchase succeed in reducing consumer resistance and feeding the flame of desire ultimately leading to acts of purchasing, giving, spending or consuming that were typically not planned in advance. Consumers often end up complying with sales requests as a result of forces of social influence. It is these forces of social influence that we focus on in this chapter. As we will see, although one might not immediately think of compliance as a 'natural endpoint' of typical advertising, commercial messages do frequently play an important role in yielding to influence. Indeed, some advertising messages are designed to inform consumers, others are aimed at persuading them, but still others seek the overt behavioural response of compliance or acquiescence with a sales request. Therefore, a typical 'playing field' for the forces of social influence is *direct response* advertising.

Examples include the many mail-order catalogues consumers find in their mailbox. In addition, one might think of the often deceptive advertisements that promise consumers a great prize if only they dial a telephone number to buy a product. Principles of social influence can also be observed in tele-sales programmes where consumers can dial and directly purchase the advertised product, or in sales promotion actions where the advertiser promises a discount if the consumer complies with the sales request. Moreover, the forces of social influence can be seen at work in instances of in-store advertising and point-of-purchase product demonstrations where sales representatives show and hand out samples of a product hoping the consumer will agree to buy it after having seen, felt and tasted the product. Or think of advertising on the web, with increasing numbers of retail outlets depending solely on this channel for their sales. And then of course there are the numerous instances where consumers are approached and sometimes harassed by fundraisers, marketers and other compliance professionals either through telephone or in face-to-face interactions with the single goal of getting consumers to say 'yes' to their offer.

In the current chapter we review research on principles of social influence that are employed in each of these situations (see Cialdini & Trost, 1998). We will discuss the key mechanisms that are responsible for effective social influence, their manifestations in various commercial and non-profit contexts, and the conditions under which the impact of principles of social influence is enhanced or attenuated. We will review a large set of psychological studies that have examined why and when people 'give in' to a request posed to them by some influence agent. The bulk of this research deals with **compliance**, the overt behavioural acquiescence response when a specific request is posed. The request can be direct, as when an influence agent (say, a door-to-door salesman of encyclopaedias) addresses a consumer in a face-to-face context, or it can be more indirect, for instance when consumers see an ad for the encyclopaedia in a magazine which urges them to respond quickly in order to collect an attractive discount (Cialdini & Goldstein, 2004). As we will see, most of these principles of social influence aim at achieving compliance without changing consumers' attitudes towards a product.

Seminal work by Cialdini and colleagues (Cialdini, 1984, 2009, Cialdini & Trost, 1998; Cialdini & Goldstein, 2004) has identified a series of six principles of social influence: reciprocity, commitment and consistency, social validation, liking, authority, and scarcity. As a seventh principle, we will address a new addition to the study of social influence that has been labelled the 'confusion principle' (Kardes, 2002). We will conclude with an alternative theoretical account to explain the effectiveness of these principles on compliance behaviour based on fundamental premises of human self-regulation (Fennis, Janssen & Vohs, 2009; Janssen, Fennis, Pruyn & Vohs, 2008).

Social influence and compliance without pressure

There is a key difference between the influence principles discussed in this chapter and the persuasive impact of advertising as discussed in chapter 5. In contrast to conventional advertising to which consumers are typically exposed some time before the opportunity arises to buy the advertised product, the tactics used to foster com-pliance are frequently *proximate*, both temporally and spatially, in that they operate in the immediate action or choice environment of the consumer. The scripted sales request and the compliance response are typically in close proximity to each other rather than separated in time and/or space. In addition, the bulk of compliance gaining tactics are aimed at singular, overt actions in response to a well-defined behavioural request (e.g. to buy the product, donate to charity, sign a petition, or vote for a candidate). In terms of the DAGMAR model, or other hierarchy of effects models discussed in chapter 1, the principles of social influence typically function to foster purchase or purchase facilitation, but do not affect any of the other advertising object-ives, such as creating a category need, improving brand awareness or increasing brand knowledge. In addition, social influence principles affect singular behaviour and consequently are less effective in influencing behaviour patterns with a longer time frame, such as repeat buying, variety seeking or brand loyalty.

Automaticity has been proffered as the cornerstone of these compliance tech-niques (Cialdini, 2009; Kardes, 2002). Saying 'yes' to a sales request is frequently a mindless response: we do it without careful scrutiny of the merits of the request or the offer. Cialdini (2009) has used the metaphor of a **'click-whirr' response** to refer to this principle. Derived from ethological research, the click-whirr response entails a fixed action pattern, which unfolds more or less invariantly when suitable environmental stimuli are present in the influence context, similar to the involuntary squeaking of baby birds once they spot their mother approaching the nest. 'Click' refers to the stimulus that prompts the behavioural response, and 'whirr' to the actual unfolding of that response. In line with the notion of automaticity discussed previ-ously, click-whirr responses are fast, effortless, seemingly spontaneous, stable across situations, partly inherited, and frequently accompanied or triggered by emotions (see Adolphs, 2009). What is more, these fixed-action patterns are performed routinely and outside conscious awareness.

Although reference to the click-whirr response constitutes a persuasive meta-phor to illustrate automaticity to readers of a semi-popular book (Cialdini, 2009), it can hardly have been intended to serve as an animal model for the mechanisms that underlie the sales techniques discussed by Cialdini (2009). After all, these automatic fixed-action patterns in animals are based on inborn responses, whereas the reactions of clients to the sales tactics described below can hardly be assumed to rely on inborn processes. Furthermore, as we will argue below, it is doubtful whether our responses to compliance techniques are really automatic fixed-action patterns in the sense implied by the click-whirr metaphor. However, with this metaphor Cialdini (2009) succeeded in getting across the important point that these social influence techniques rely on processes that are subtle, indirect and outside the conscious awareness of the target consumers. According to Cialdini and others (e.g. Cialdini, 1993; Cialdini & Goldstein, 2004), the effectiveness of these techniques relies on what Langer (1992; Langer, Blank & Chanowitz, 1978) has called 'mindlessness'.

One consequence of mindlessness is that people re-enact **scripts** without paying attention to substantive information. Schank and Abelson (1977) defined scripts as 'a predetermined, stereotyped sequences of action that defines a well-known situation' (p. 41). Because we have detailed and 'scripted' knowledge about how to act in specific situations (e.g. when entering a restaurant), we do not really have to think about how to behave in such situations. We ask for a table, sit down, wait to be given a menu, order a meal, wait for it to be served, eat it, ask for the bill, pay and leave. However, as Moskowitz (2005) points out, for scripts to influence behaviour, people also need action rules that specify that certain actions need to be initiated when cues in the environment signal that a certain script and the 'scripted' action sequence are appropriate. For example, most people do not have one restaurant script, but several (e.g. fine restaurant versus McDonald's; US versus European restaurants). Furthermore, each part of the sequence of scripted actions in a restaurant has to be performed in response to specific cues. In elegant European (and all US) restaurants, you do not sit down at a table, but wait at the entrance until you are shown to your table, whereas in simple European restaurants you simply choose your own table and sit down. In US restaurants, you also do not give your order to the person filling your water glass, but wait for a proper waiter.

Langer et al. (1978) conducted a classic experiment to demonstrate that people often act mindlessly in such scripted situations. The unwitting participants in their experiment were people in a university library, who were just about to use the copy machine, when a confederate approached them with one of the following requests. In the 'no information' condition, the confederate simply asked, 'Excuse me, I have five copies, may I use the Xerox machine?' This is of course a simple request and, as Flynn and Lake (2008) have argued recently, denying requests for help violates social norms of being helpful to people in need. It is therefore not surprising that a substantial proportion of participants (60 per cent) agreed to let the confederate cut the waiting line.

People's willingness to help should be even be greater, if the person in need gives a justification for the urgency of his or her request. Langer et al. (1978) assessed this in a second condition, in which the confederate gave a reason for wanting to barge ahead. In this condition, she said, 'Excuse me, I have five pages, may I use the Xerox machine because I am in a rush?' Since the person was asking for a small favour and was giving a reasonably good justification for cutting ahead, the script in polite society for this kind of behaviour would require granting the request. And indeed, stating a reason increased the tendency to comply over the control condition: almost all participants (94 per cent) agreed.

What was most interesting in this experiment, however, was what happened in a third condition, the *placebic information* condition. In this condition the confederate stated, 'Excuse me, I have five pages, may I use the Xerox machine because I have to make copies?' The confederate gave a reason but it was a nonsensical one. If participants had made any effort to evaluate the request, this nonsensical reason should have been no more persuasive than giving no reason at all (perhaps even less so). However, if the people waiting at the copy machine were mindlessly following the script, any reason, even a totally ridiculous one, should be as good as giving a plausible reason. And indeed, supporting the mindlessness of the behaviour of the waiting students, a stunning 93 per cent, equivalent to the real reason, agreed to let the confederate go ahead.

According to the least-effort principle that underlies the motivational assumptions of dual process theories of information processing, people should only behave in this mindless manner if there is not sufficient reason to invest effort into mindful behaviour. Obviously, allowing another person to cut in front to make five copies will incur such a brief delay that it is not worth thinking much about the request. Matters would be different, however, if a big favour was being requested. To test this hypothesis, Langer et al. (1978) added a second set of conditions to their design, in which they used exactly the same reasons, but this time to be allowed to make 20 copies. As we can see, with the more substantial request, only the real reason increased compliance (Figure 7.1). With the placebic reason no more participants complied than when no reason at all had been given.

Scripts are only one of several knowledge structures, which help us to act efficiently in complex physical or social environments. Another type of knowledge structures, which people use to simplify complex decisions are cognitive **heuristics**

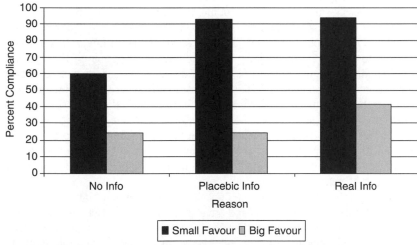

Figure 7.1 Compliance with request by importance and reason given

Source: Adapted from Langer et al. (1978). The mindlessness of ostensibly thoughtful action: The role of 'placebic' information in interpersonal interaction. *Journal of Personality and Social Psychology, 36*, 635–642

(simple decision rules discussed in chapters 3 and 6). In a state of 'mindlessness' consumers are not only prone to follow simple scripts they are also likely to employ simple heuristics that increase compliance rates. As we will see, in addition to (mis)using scripts, many of the compliance techniques to be discussed in this chapter also rely on consumers, who make 'mindless' low-effort decisions to use cognitive heuristics such as 'favours need to be returned' (reciprocity principle) or 'I agree with people I like' (liking principle).

At first glance these mindless strategies appear to be foolish, if not downright dangerous. However, researchers have underscored the adaptive functionality of such quick and dirty decision-making (e.g. Todd & Gigerenzer, 2007). In an age of ever-increasing information constantly fighting for our attention, it is efficient for people not to scrutinize every bit of information that impinges on the senses, and instead to resort to simple decision rules to save cognitive resources and aid in the day-to-day hassle of judgement and decision-making. Indeed, it is our 'default mode' to be as efficient as possible. Chen and Chaiken (1999) and others (e.g. Shiffrin & Schneider, 1977; Petty & Cacioppo, 1986) have pointed out that people tend to behave as 'cognitive misers' (Petty & Cacioppo, 1986), and 'economy-minded information processors' (Chaiken, 1980; Fiske & Taylor, 1984), guided by the rule of least effort. According to Chen and Chaiken (1999), the notion of least effort translates itself in what they term the **sufficiency principle** or the tendency to strike a balance between minimizing cognitive effort on the one hand and satisfying current motiv-ational concerns on the other. When there are no immediate motivational concerns to act otherwise, the sufficiency principle would predict that people tend to save their energy resources and fall back on simple decision heuristics as the prevalent mode of action.

Bargh (1984) and Moskowitz (2005) have argued that, although the mindless following of a script has some elements that are automatic, such as the triggering of a social-behavioural script by environmental stimuli (e.g. the request to use the copy machine in the case of Langer et al., 1978), it nevertheless requires conscious processing and conscious awareness at some stage. Thus, in line with the assump-tion that automatic and controlled processing form the endpoints of a continuum rather than dichotomous categories, the mindless behaviour discussed earlier is somewhere in the automatic half of this continuum. Whereas the features of the situation at the copy machine automatically activate the relevant script, the script then directs *conscious* search for further cues to verify that the script is adequate (Bargh, 1984; Moskowitz, 2005). When people are in a state of mindlessness, they simply fail to make an effort to think deeply and instead superficially scan the environment, often failing to detect important information (e.g. in the placebic informant condition).

Similarly, to use heuristics in their decision-making, individuals must perceive a relevant heuristic cue (e.g. a favour) and have an applicable heuristic at hand (favours need to be returned). When basing their decisions on heuristics rather than scanning the situation for all relevant information, people do not behave automatically in the sense of an automatic fixed-action pattern. They merely avoid having to think deeply, because potential decision outcomes are not sufficiently important to warrant the investment of a great deal of cognitive effort.

The principle of reciprocity

A powerful mechanism that people frequently resort to in influence settings is the motivation to return a favour, i.e. the **principle of reciprocity** (Gouldner, 1960). The norm that we should do to others as they do to us is widely shared across cultures. Reciprocity calls for positive responses to favourable treatment but negative responses to negative behavior. Gouldner (1960) argued that the norm of reciprocity is a social prescription that operates in most cultures.

The door-in-the-face technique

A technique that is assumed to hinge on this principle is the **door-in-the-face** (DITF) technique which is characterized by a sequence of rejection-then-moderation (see Cialdini et al., 1975; O'Keefe & Hale, 2001). In the DITF technique, a large request (which will probably be rejected) is followed by a more moderate target request. Although not uncontested, it is generally assumed the technique works because the influence agent, by sizing down the request, makes a clear concession. For the target, this should evoke the need to make a concession in return and thus to comply with the moderate request.

In a classic study, Cialdini et al. (1975) provided a first demonstration of the effectiveness of the DITF technique. They asked Arizona State University students to work as non-paid volunteers for the County Youth Counseling Program and act as a counsellor to a group of juvenile delinquents for two years. Not surprisingly, everyone rejected. Next, however, the request was made more moderate: they were asked to take a group of juveniles to the zoo for two hours. Under these conditions, half of the subjects complied with the request. In the target request-only control condition, where participants were only asked to take the juveniles to the zoo, only 17 per cent complied.

A follow-up study more directly tested the reciprocity account. In that study, participants were asked by either one or two influence agents to volunteer to assist low-income children for two years. After rejection, subjects were asked to take the group of children to the zoo for two hours. Compared to control conditions, the DITF condition again proved effective in bringing about compliance, but only when the same individual made both requests. When one person makes the large request and the second person the smaller request, the technique ceased to be effective. In the former scenario, the single requester clearly makes a concession, which evokes the norm of reciprocity, whereas in the two-requester scenario this norm is not made salient.

As part of a design where he also assessed the role of nonverbal behaviour, Fennis (2008a) took the DITF technique to an in-store advertising setting. In a supermarket in an urbanized area, consumers were approached by one of four confederates (two male, two female) acting as sales representatives. They tried to sell boxes of (Christmas) candy using either a DITF script or a control script. In addition, the sales representatives were trained to either exhibit nonverbal cues that indicate enthusiasm and professional confidence (e.g., showing sincere, authentic smiles, gazing at the customer, talking with a loud voice and using many hand gestures to underscore the sales pitch) or the reverse: embarrassment and lack of confidence (e.g. diverting one's gaze, talking with a soft voice and frequent body movements).

Similar to the procedure employed by Cialdini et al. (1975), the DITF technique involved preceding a moderate target request with a considerably larger initial request. In this condition the sales representative stated: 'Good afternoon sir/madam, Christmas is rapidly approaching, and so these boxes of Christmas candy are on special offer today! I may offer you six boxes of candy for €6'. The confederate then waited until the target responded (almost always by rejecting the offer) and continued' 'You think that six boxes is a bit too much? Ok, I understand. In that case I may also offer you one box for the price of €1!' In the target-request only condition, the consumer was only presented with the final sales request without preceding it by the more outrageous opening offer. The results showed that the DITF technique fared well in a commercial setting. 74 per cent of those exposed to the DITF strategy complied with the sales request, whereas 48 per cent of the participants in the target request-only condition did so. Interestingly, the nonverbal cues the sales representative exhibited boosted the effects of the technique: the impact of the DITF was highest when it lay embedded in a nonverbal context suggesting enthusiasm and confidence.

That's-not-all technique

The reciprocity principle not only underlies the effectiveness of the Door-In-The-Face technique but also plays a role in the related **That's-Not-All Technique** (TNA; Burger, 1986; Pollock, Smith & Knowles, 1998), where an initial request is followed by a second request that is made more desirable. Researchers have identified two basic forms of the TNA technique. In the reduced cost form, the opening bargain is improved by a decrease in the price of the offer, for instance when a new automobile is 'normally offered for the price of $20.000, but this week is on sale for $19.500.' In contrast, the added value form uses a fixed price, and instead adds desirable attributes or incentives to the initial offer to sweeten the deal, for instance when a prospective car buyer is seduced by an offer stating that the new automobile is 'listed for $19.500, but this week comes with a complementary CD player at no extra cost'. Both types of the TNA were originally tested by Burger (1986) in a campus cupcake sale. Passers-by on campus were either presented with a TNA offer or an equivalent control offer. The TNA either offered a cupcake for 75 cents with two chocolate chip cookies free of charge, or the cupcake with a discount of 25 cents to be sold for 75 cents, as opposed to the regular price of $1. For both types of TNA, 73 per cent of participants bought the cupcake offer, compared to 45 per cent in the control condition. Part of the explanation of the effectiveness of the technique (although again not entirely unequivocal, see Burger, 1986), is that consumers interpret the increased desirability of the offer as a favour, and in return are inclined to return the favour by complying with the sales request.

Importantly, in line with the notion of mindlessness set forth earlier, additional findings have underscored that the TNA technique works primarily when consumers are in a state of mindlessness, rather than mindfulness. That is, in a more recent exploration of the TNA technique, Pollock, Smith, Knowles and Bruce (1998) varied the price/volume of the offer to test this notion. In half the conditions, participants were confronted with a TNA technique for a low priced, small box of chocolates ($1), whereas for the other half the price and the volume of the box was substantial ($5). Presumably, having to pay a considerable amount of money would prompt more mindful information processing, which would undermine the effectiveness of the technique. In line with these notions, the technique indeed ceased to be effective when the price was raised.

An interesting additional feature of this study was that it also replicated the Langer et al. (1978) findings on the effectiveness of the types of reasons that are being given for buying the chocolate. In addition to varying the price, this study also varied the type of reason given for the offer. In the valid reason condition, the box of chocolates was offered with the argument, 'These Sweet Shop chocolates are fudge hand-dipped in chocolate with pecans. Also, Sweet Shop has been in business over 20 years'. In the placebic reason condition, in contrast, participants heard a trivial reason for buying the box of chocolates: 'This candy is made of chocolate and sold in this box'. Paralleling earlier results, the placebic reason produced as many purchases (68 per cent) as the real reason (68 per cent), but only when the small, cheap, box of chocolates was on sale. The placebic reason did not affect purchase rates when considerable expenditure was asked of consumers.

Beyond reciprocity

Recent research suggests that embedding a sales request in a cleverly scripted influence technique to increase the odds of compliance may not always be necessary. Flynn and Lake (2008) showed that in order for a target individual to comply with a request, all the requester has to do is simply ask for compliance. Since 60 per cent of the participants agreed with the small request made without any reason given in the study of Langer et al. (1978), this conclusion is hardly new. However, Flynn and Lake (2008) further demonstrated that influence agents systematically underestimate the intrinsic willingness of targets to say 'yes' to a request, regardless of its framing: they fail to appreciate sufficiently that for targets, the social costs of refusal frequently outweigh the instrumental costs of compliance. It is only when the request becomes extremely large (as in the initial request of the DITF technique) that the social costs no longer outweigh the instrumental costs of acquiescence and hence rejection is the result. These results may suggest that marketers sometimes waste resources on sales training programmes, in-store advertising and other persuasive communications where a simple request to buy might suffice.

Product samples as reciprocity traps. Notwithstanding the power of direct requests for compliance, the urge to return a concession or a favour with a countergesture of goodwill, is engrained in the consumer's repertoire. This fact has not been lost on marketers who have developed fairly straightforward marketing tools to trigger the reciprocity response, without having to risk outright rejection (as in the DITF technique). For example, a family of advertising techniques that makes use of the reciprocity principle centres around sales promotion. As stated in chapter 1, sales promotion advertising is a form of 'action communication' designed to generate a burst of extra sales by delivering a temporary incentive or deal. Hence, the TNA technique in either form can be considered sales promotion advertising, but there is a host of other sales promotion ad strategies in the marketer's toolbox, such as giving away coupons, cash refunds, contests, sweepstakes and lotteries, and of course free product samples and premiums that are offered to consumers.

As we shall see below, product samples serve a variety of psychological purposes making them powerful 'weapons of influence' (Cialdini, 2009), but one of the most important effects of free samples is to trigger a reciprocity response from the consumer. More often than not, free samples are offered at the point of purchase, e.g. in a supermarket where an in-store advertising stand gives away free samples of a new lemonade, shampoo or French cheese. According to Cialdini (2009) the reciprocity rule enforces uninvited debts. That is, although consumers have never asked for it, the fact that they have accepted the free offer induces a sense of indebtedness. What is more interesting from a marketing point of view is that the return favour need not necessarily be equivalent in value. As a result, people are inclined to return something of higher rather than lower value than what they have received. Hence, being offered a free sample of let us say $1 in monetary value may prompt a return favour of buying a regular-sized package of the advertised product often double the price!

The principle of commitment/consistency

People do not exhibit beliefs, attitudes, and preferences in a haphazard way. Rather, there is a strong tendency to show responses that are congruent and that show some coherence. People want to act in line with their previous behaviour and once they have committed themselves to a course of action, they tend to follow it through. The **commitment/consistency principle** captures this need to be consistent. This tendency to respond consistently comes both from external as well as internal forces. Not only do others expect us to say, feel and do things in a predictable way, and deviations from the consistency principle are sometimes seen as signs of mental illness (Dawes, 1994), there is also a strong internal drive to keep our mental world tidy and congruent (Cialdini, Trost & Newsom, 1995).

Advertisers are well aware that saying 'yes' once often leads to saying 'yes' again . . . and again. Recently, Dhar and colleagues (2007) have studied this phenomenon they dubbed the 'shopping momentum effect': the tendency to engage in repeated acts of purchasing after an initial and *unrelated* act of buying. Once consumers have passed a threshold, and have initially given in to the temptation to buy, the act of shopping becomes a self-perpetuating process, brought about by previous acts of compliance with sales offers, which then fuels subsequent acts of buying. The most prototypical example of the shopping momentum effect, that can truly turn into a shopping frenzy, occurs around Christmas, when shopping can frequently become a no holds barred, all or nothing affair. Indeed whenever consumers are seen to behave in a consistent manner, this must be the ultimate occasion!

Foot-in-the-door technique

The idea that an initial act of compliance spurs compliance with a second request lies at the root of the 'mother of all compliance techniques', the **Foot-In-The-Door**

(FITD) technique. The basic idea is that compliance with an initial, small request increases the likelihood of compliance with a second, much larger request, because the initial act of compliance triggers the principle of consistency. Telemarketers frequently use this tactic to sell their goods. They often start out by asking the consumer a series of small, ostensibly harmless questions. Once the consumer has agreed to answer the initial questions (which are frequently introduced as part of a market survey), the hook is set and the consumer is more likely to agree to the larger target request, which may involve buying a product the marketer is trying to sell.

Freedman and Fraser (1966) did a seminal series of studies on the FITD technique. In one study, they went door-to-door in a California neighbourhood and asked residents whether they would be willing to have a large and obtrusive sign reading 'drive carefully' placed in their front yard. Only a small minority directly agreed, but the overwhelming majority (83 per cent) initially said 'no'. This was the target request control condition in this experiment. A different picture emerged for the foot-in-the-door condition, though. In this condition, the large target request was preceded approximately two weeks earlier by a small, almost trivial, request, when homeowners were asked to post a small (three inches) sign reading 'be a safe driver'. Of these participants, a full 76 per cent later agreed to have their views obstructed with the large sign. Moreover, almost half of the participants still agreed with the target request, even when the small request was not about traffic safety but for a different issue (i.e. keeping California beautiful), or after complying with an initial request to sign a petition rather than to post a sign. Hence, compliance with the large second request was merely a function of compliance with the initial small request, regardless of the issue under consideration and regardless of the type of compliance that was requested.

It appears that for compliance with the second request to occur, consumers need to 'do' something first: it is not enough simply to agree with the initial request, the target also needs to sign the petition, actually place the small sign or engage in any other type of requested behaviour. This was ascertained in a second study by Freedman and Fraser (1966) in which they used the old telemarketing trick of preceding the target request with an initial request to answer a few questions. More specifically, in their FITD experiment, they approached households and before the larger target request was posed (in this study the request was to volunteer as a research participant in a large survey on household products), participants were asked whether they agreed to answer eight questions about the kinds of soaps they used. In addition, the authors varied the type of performance required with respect to the initial request: participants either proceeded to actually answer the initial questions or only agreed to do so. The results showed that compliance with the target request was higher when participants had actually performed the initial request (53 per cent) rather than simply agreeing to do so (33 per cent). The subtype of the FITD that Freedman and Fraser tested in this study where the target request is preceded by a series of semantically related questions has later been termed the Continuing Questions Procedure (CQP; Burger, 1999).

Fennis (2008a) used a similar technique to persuade homeowners to donate to charity. In the study on the role of nonverbal behaviour referred to earlier, three confederates (two male, one female) acted as fundraisers for an existing but relatively unknown charity named Sviatoslav, a foundation that aims to help children and adolescents (financially and otherwise) in former Soviet and East European states. The confederates again either displayed nonverbal cues associated with enthusiasm and self confidence or with embarrassment and lack of confidence. In addition, participants were either exposed to a CQP script in which the target request was preceded by a few (smaller) questions, or a control script in which only the request to donate money to the foundation was made. After a general introduction, the CQP script included three initial questions: 'May I elaborate on the mission of the Sviatoslav Foundation?' All participants agreed, as they did with the other two questions: 'Do you worry regularly about poverty in the world?' and 'What do you think about the idea that young people in Holland would help young people abroad who live in poverty?' After these initial questions, participants were asked to donate money to the charity. In the target-request only condition, only the request to donate was made. The results of this study showed that the type of technique affected compliance rates, such that exposure to a CQP resulted in higher amounts of money donated ($M = €1.69$) than exposure to a target request-only script ($M = €1.25$), see Figure 7.2. Although this difference doesn't appear too impressive (only a mean difference of 44 euro cents), we should keep in mind that using the CQP is still approximately 1.4 times more effective than a regular control script, which does make a difference in a mass-market and aggregated over many (sales) interactions. Similar to the previous DITF study, the present field experiment also revealed an interaction effect showing that the impact of the CQP was boosted by the nonverbal behaviour the fundraiser displayed: when the fundraiser displayed signs of confidence and enthusiasm, the impact of the CQP on monetary donations rose to an average of €2.19 compared to €1.25 when he did not (see Figure 7.2).

In line with Freedman and Fraser (1966), the present study did not simply require participants to agree with the initial request but also required them to actively

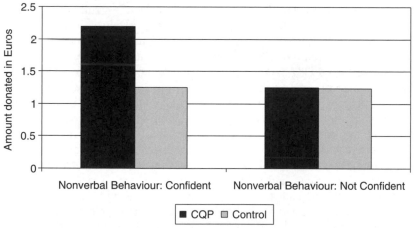

Figure 7.2 Compliance with request by influence technique (CQP) and nonverbal behavior

Source: Adapted from Fennis (2008a). Persuasion pleasure and selling stress: The role of nonverbal communication in consumer influence settings. *Advances in Consumer Research, 35,* 797–798

respond to the initial questions. Meta-analytic findings support the assumption that it is not the act of initial agreement per se that is the decisive factor in producing compliance, but rather how much *effort* is required to accomplish the initial request (Burger, 1999). This meta-analysis has also helped to clarify the underlying psychological processes that account for compliance in the FITD procedure. One important psychological principle that is related to the notion of consistency and commitment is self-perception (Bem, 1972). According to self-perception theory, people sometimes infer their attitudes from their overt behaviour, rather than vice versa. Hence, after performing the initial request, consumers infer from their behaviour that 'they must be the kind of person to comply with these kinds of requests'. This inference increases the likelihood of compliance with the target request.

The self-perception account assumes a few criteria that must be met. Involvement with the initial request should be high rather than low (albeit not so high as to provoke mindful scrutiny of the request), the initial request should be performed rather than only agreed to, and the initial request should be of considerable size (although not as substantial as the target request). Finally, although dissimilar requests still produce compliance with the target request, the self-perception account would hold that congruence of initial and target request will also contribute to compliance with the large request. A considerable number of studies has provided support for self-perception as a process underlying the effectiveness of the FITD technique.

Self-perception, more generally, refers to the self as the origin of consistency needs. That is, the consumer wishes to respond in such a fashion that his/her belief system remains consistent. This need for consistency can be a function of situational demands, but can also be thought of as an individual difference characteristic. That is, some people have a higher intrinsic need to behave consistently than others and this need is largely invariant across situations. Research by Cialdini et al. (1995) found that individuals scoring high on the Preference for Consistency scale were more likely to show compliance with an FITD-type of request than individuals low in this preference.

It is unclear whether FITD requires a state of mindlessness to operate. The explanation in terms of self-perception suggests that mindlessness underlies yielding to the FITD ploy. Rather than giving the decision to agree with the target request much thought, the self-perception process functions as a simple decision rule of the form, 'I did this, hence I must have liked it'. However, we have previously seen that agreement is only given mindlessly when the request that has been made is a small one. It seems to us that the request to put a large and ugly sign into one's forecourt is a rather large one that should have motivated people to give the decision serious thought. Nevertheless, as we shall see below, certain features endemic to the FITD script foster mindless rather than mindful responding to the target request.

Lowball technique

As the self-perception account and the work on the Preference for Consistency scale suggest, in the typical FITD procedure, the source of the pressure towards consistency in these experiments is primarily the need for self-consistency. However, consistency pressures can also arise from the need to be consistent in one's behaviour towards other people. As research by Burger and Petty (1981) has demonstrated, commitment toward a person making a request can often be a powerful force of social influence. Finally, commitment can be felt toward the deal or offer that is the object of the influence setting.

This latter type of commitment plays an important role in another powerful influence tactic, the **lowball technique**. The technique is used frequently by second-hand car salesmen and other low level sales personnel. The core of the lowball technique consists of soliciting commitment from customers with a particularly seductive offer and then changing the deal for the worse. Commitment sets in when the initial offer is presented.

To give an example, consider this scenario at a dealership: a customer walks in and is shown a particularly handsome car by a servile and all-too-friendly salesman. He says the car is on sale now, and is especially attractive because it is packed with fancy accessories that usually come at a higher price. The customer cannot believe his luck (in this example we picture a male customer, but women are probably equally susceptible to the technique) and before he knows it, he finds himself agreeing to the sales offer. The sales rep and the customer sit down and fill out a set of forms, and all the while the customer relishes his new acquisition, imagining himself behind the wheel, slowly cruising downtown to impress passers-by and showing the car to his envious neighbours. But then something happens. The sales representative is called away to his boss's office, and when he later returns he admits to having made a mistake. He might say that he forgot to mention that the price was without, rather than with all the extras, or he might say that his boss revoked the deal because the dealership would be losing money. Of course the car is still for sale, but with the extras, the customer would have to pay an additional $1400. What will happen now the deal is less attractive? More often than not, the customer will still agree and pay the extra money because he has already been hooked: while the sales representative was away, the customer has committed himself to his new acquisition, and has not reconsidered the deal when it changed. Of course, in all likelihood the sales agent was well aware of the commitment trap and there might even have been no interaction whatsoever between him and his boss. The whole show was staged in order for the commitment trap to do its work: he threw a lowball.

In line with the procedure outlined above, Fennis et al. (2009, Experiment 6) assessed the impact of the lowball procedure for a more charitable cause. They used a similar incentive scheme to ask for donations for an organization that provides toys, books, and financial resources to children in East European countries (the Mother Teresa Foundation, see www.moederteresa.com). In the lowball condition, participants were asked whether they would be willing to donate money to the charity organization. In return they were promised a small gift (i.e. a coffee mug). After obtaining an initial agreement by the participant, a confederate interrupted the fundraiser with the message that there were no more mugs available (see Burger and Cornelius, 2003, for a similar procedure). After the interruption, the lowball technique continued with the fundraiser asking, 'Would you still be willing to donate some money?' In the target-request only condition, only the request for a monetary donation to the Mother Teresa Foundation was made. In extension of the previous example, the lowball procedure was found to work for more noble causes as well: participants exposed to the lowball technique donated significantly more money than participants in the target request-only condition.

Cialdini and colleagues (Cialdini, Cacioppo, Basett & Miller, 1978) tested an alternative of the lowball procedure. Rather than removing an incentive as in the study above, these authors added an undesirable feature to an otherwise fairly neutral request. In this study, college students were approached on campus to volunteer as research participants in a study on 'thinking processes'. In the target request-only control condition, students were informed that the study was to be conducted at 7.00 am. This was not an attractive proposition and a mere 24 per cent agreed to participate at this unholy hour. In the lowball condition, however, students were approached with the same cover story but were initially only asked whether they would like to participate. Only after they initially agreed were they informed that the study would take place at 7.00 am and were then given the chance to change their mind. None of the agreeing participants (56 per cent) did, and in line with their previous commitment, 95 per cent actually showed up at 7.00 am as promised.

For the commitment principle to be most effective, commitment should be active, public, effortful and freely chosen (Cialdini, 2009). The meta-analysis on the FITD technique discussed earlier (Burger, 1999) demonstrates that these factors are important for the effectiveness of the technique. However, these factors are not characteristic for most situations in which target audiences are exposed to advertising and other types of commercial communications. Instead, the reception of advertising messages can usually be considered a passive, private and low-effort process. This raises the question of whether the commitment principle has any relevance for advertising and marketing?

Again, as discussed earlier, direct response advertising and product trials are marketing tools where commitment can have an important influence on consumer compliance. Direct response advertising and product trials frequently prompt more active and effortful responding. These marketing tools not only trigger a reciprocity response, but they do something else as well. Cialdini (2009) argues that active, public, effortful commitments 'grow their own legs' (p. 83). That is, after the compliance principle has brought the unsuspecting target to comply with a request as a function of the force of consistency (say, to buy an encyclopaedia after having answered a series of questions on the importance of general knowledge and education), there is no need to keep on reinforcing the behavioural change, because it is frequently accompanied by a cognitive change as well: the victim tends to generate cognitions supportive of the new behaviour. Because of the intrinsic need to be consistent within the system of beliefs he or she will generate assurances and other supportive arguments that buying the encyclopaedia was the right thing to do. In line with the notions outlined in chapter 5 on systematic or central route processing, these cognitions generally take the form of elaborations. Hence, the additional reasons and favourable arguments that the target consumer generates are frequently new and go beyond the arguments provided by the salesperson. As a result, persuasion in these instances becomes a case of self-persuasion (see Eagly & Chaiken, 1993). Such a process is also likely to have taken place in the lowball scenario with the car salesman described earlier. Thus, having greatly (albeit anticipatorily) enjoyed the possession of the new car, the consumer pays the extra price rather than relinquish his new possession.

The same principle may be at work when consumers find themselves accepting a free product sample. Rather than focusing on the act of *receiving* the sample (which sets in motion the reciprocity principle), the act of actually *using* the product similarly generates a rich set of newly formed associations and cognitions. The consumer feels, smells and tastes the product, finds out what it can do, how pleasing it is to the eye, whether it solves problems, makes life easier or just more enjoyable. In short, product samples generate new product knowledge on a first hand basis. Cognitions, based on direct experience are generally found to be a far more powerful predictor of future behaviour than second-hand sources of information (e.g. conventional advertising, see Kardes, 2002).

Hence, product trials through free sampling trigger a double edged marketing sword, with two powerful influence principles: reciprocity and commitment, and they do so efficiently and effectively. An additional marketing tool that can have similar effects are sales promotion actions such as prize contests and sweepstakes. Frequently, the consumer is offered a chance of winning a fabulous prize by completing a slogan of the following form: 'I like brand X because: . . .' Although the incentive to complete the sentence is an extrinsic one (i.e. the prize), completing the slogan also requires the generation of new and additional positive product arguments and hence fosters commitment through self-persuasion (see Eagly & Chaiken, 1993, for additional research on principles of self-persuasion).

The principle of social validation

The **social validation principle** involves turning an eye to others to assess the merits of some object, issue or offer. Advertising uses this principle in appealing to consensus information and highlighting the social dimension of consuming the product. For example, Volkswagen recently proudly advertised that it has sold over 700 million of its most successful model, the VW Golf. Similarly, McDonald's claims it has sold over one billion hamburgers. Sitcoms on television include canned laughter when jokes are presented to suggest an audience that clearly has fun watching the show (although most viewers do not like canned laughter; Cialdini, 2009). In each of these instances social validation is at work. It suggests that others (sometimes many others) like what is presented. This, in turn, should convince the target consumer that whatever is on offer can be trusted to be of value.

Social validation, or the principle of social proof as Cialdini (2009) labels it, is particularly effective under conditions of ambiguity and uncertainty, when consensus information is more readily accessible than more 'objective' forms of information. Products for which social proof as an influence tactic will be especially persuasive, are those with salient (inter)subjective or non-verifiable attributes. Scholars differentiate between 'experience' and 'credence' attributes in this regard (see Wright & Lynch, 1995). In contrast to 'search' attributes such as price and weight that can be known before buying the product, experience attributes are product attributes that can only be found out *after* product purchase, during consumption. The quality of bottles of wine, expensive dinners in restaurants, or vacations are examples of experience attributes. Credence attributes go even beyond that. These are attributes whose merits are difficult, if not impossible, to ascertain, even after consumption. An example is the professional advice of an interior architect or the quality of legal advice obtained from a lawyer. When experience or credence attributes are central to a product or service, we typically need to turn to others to assess the merits of the offer. It is in these cases that social proof will be most influential.

Reference groups

A straightforward tactic for advertisers to exploit the power of social validation is to include reference group appeals in their messages. Hyman (1942) coined the term **reference group**, defining it as 'a person or group of people that significantly influences an individual's behaviour'. Reference groups act as agents of social proof because they communicate standards, norms, beliefs and values that are shared by significant others and thus can act as a benchmark to determine what is right or wrong, what is good, what is valuable and how one should behave. Advertisers use this information when they show what 'your kind of people', your friends, your colleagues, your family members prefer. Frequently reference group appeals are incorporated in a 'testimonial' format where an 'average member' of one of these groups is questioned by an – often fictitious – interviewer and seen praising the merits of the advertised product. Alternatively, a 'slice of life' format is used where this same average consumer is portrayed buying or using the advertised product as part of his/her daily life.

Consumer theorists like Engel, Blackwell and Miniard (1990) have distinguished between primary and secondary groups, with the former being more influential than the latter because they are small and enable face-to-face interaction. The (extended) family is an example of a primary group as is a group of close friends. Secondary groups are a more remote sources of social proof where face-to-face interaction is still possible, but more sporadic, less comprehensive and with less impact. Examples of secondary groups include trade unions, community organizations and brand communities (e.g. the Rolls Royce owners' club). In addition, marketers frequently distinguish between membership groups, aspirational groups and negative reference groups. Membership groups are the groups one currently belongs to (e.g. family, a peer group or one's gender group). Aspirational groups are reference groups whose lifestyles, values, or norms one would like to adopt. Celebrities and sports heroes frequently figure as exemplars of this type of reference group in advertising.

The negative reference group is also a frequently used tool. Advertising cleverly portrays members of groups to which the target consumer would not like to belong. An uncaring mother, an unattractive partner or a commanding boss can fulfil this role in advertising. Such characters are frequently portrayed with an ineffective competing brand, providing a contrast effect which benefits the target brand, in an advertising format that Kardes (2005) has labelled the 'nerd alert'.

Individual differences and social proof

Nerd alerts and other types of reference group appeals can be surprisingly effective, especially for image-conscious consumers. These individuals tend to score high on self-monitoring (Snyder & DeBono, 1985), or the extent to which one is sensitive and responsive to normative social cues (see chapter 5). In addition, normative information on reference groups tends to be more effective for individuals with a collectivist rather than individualist orientation (Cialdini et al., 1999; Han & Shavitt, 1994). Individualists define themselves as independent from others and focus on personal goals, values and motives. Collectivists, in contrast, define themselves as interdependent, rather than independent. They tend to focus more on group membership, and group goals, values, norms and behaviour. Although this distinction reflects an individual difference characteristic rather than a cultural distinction, Western cultures (e.g. North America, Western Europe) are generally more individualistically oriented, and Eastern cultures (e.g. Japan, Korea, China) tend to be more collectivist in orientation.

Cialdini et al. (1999) examined the effectiveness of the commitment/consistency versus the social validation principle for consumers in the USA (an individualist society) and Poland (a collectivist culture). In addition, individual differences in individualism versus collectivism were also assessed with the Cultural Orientation Scale (COS; Bierbrauer, Meyer & Wolfradt, 1994). Both groups were asked to imagine being approached by a representative of the Coca-Cola company who asks them to participate in a 40-minute market survey about consumer preferences for a brand of soft drink. Participants were asked for their participation either after considering information on their own history of compliance with these kinds of requests or after considering information on their peers' history of compliance. More specifically, participants in the commitment/consistency condition were asked to rate their willingness to act as a volunteer for the market study while considering three instances in the past where they themselves either had always complied, had complied about half of the time, or had never complied with similar requests. Social validation was manipulated in this study by asking participants to rate their willingness to volunteer while either considering three instances where all their classmates had complied with similar requests, about half had complied, or none had complied.

The results of this study showed that both principles were effective in both countries. However, in line with predictions, evidence of what one had done in the past was relatively more impactful in the USA than in Poland, whereas evidence of what one's peers had done was relatively more impactful in Poland than in the United States. This pattern, which can be interpreted in terms of a relatively greater tendency towards collectivism in Poland and towards individualism in the United States, disappeared when individual difference scores were included in the analysis. Irrespective of nationality, commitment/consistency (i.e. information about their own compliance history) proved generally more influential for participants, who scored high on individualism, whereas social proof (i.e. information about the compliance history of their peers) was most influential for individuals who scored high trait collectivism.

Motivation and social validation

The principle of social proof states that we turn to others for assessing the merits of a message, an offer, a point of view or a behaviour. In short, we view something as correct to the extent that we see others believing it or doing it. As stated above, for social proof to have an impact, the situation must be characterized by uncertainty and ambivalence. The ambivalence or uncertainty due to the specific attributes of the product or service that is advertised can be further moderated by psychological make-up of the consumer. In chapter 5 we discussed three types of motivation which can affect the outcome of influence and persuasion attempts (Chen & Chaiken, 1999), namely defence motivation, impression motivation and accuracy motivation. Of these, strong accuracy and impression motivations are likely to increase the impact of social proof on beliefs, attitudes, and behaviour. When consumers have a strong need to hold accurate opinions, values and attitudes (an accuracy motive), and 'objective' sources of information are unavailable or inaccessible, socially validated information should have a large impact. Similarly, when consumers desire to hold attitudes and display behaviour that will satisfy salient social goals (i.e. strong impression motivation), social proof will also be very influential.

The role of impression motivation was assessed in a series of studies by White and Dahl (2006), who studied the impact of negative reference groups on consumer preferences. White and Dahl assumed that for their male participants the male gender group would be a positive, the female gender group a negative reference group. White and Dahl argued that when consumers have salient self-presentation concerns (i.e. when they have a strong impression motivation), information about the preferences of a negative reference group will produce a contrast effect (i.e. a shift *away* from these preferences). Male participants in this study were asked to imagine being at a business dinner. They were encouraged to select steak for their main course. The steak was either labelled in a neutral fashion (i.e. chef's cut) or in terms of the negative reference group (i.e. ladies' cut). Both cuts of steak were described as having the same weight. In line with predictions, males had more *negative* evaluations of, and showed a *decreased* tendency to choose the steak when it was associated with a female reference group. Moreover, consistent with the assumption that impression motives exert stronger influence on public rather than private behaviour, the negative reference group information was more effective in public than private consumption settings.

Other studies have also attested to the powerful role of reference group information in consumer decision-making (Bearden & Etzel, 1982). Membership groups and aspirational groups can exert considerable conformity pressures on individual consumers, and can elicit delinquent behaviours such as underage drinking and illegal drug use for consumers who would normally not consider these behaviours (Rose, Bearden & Teel, 1992).

Values and lifestyles

Since compliance professionals have understood the power of social proof in advertising and social proof is typically delivered by reference groups, marketers have attempted to segment groups of consumers based on commonalities in their attitudes, beliefs, values and lifestyles. The best known typology of this kind is the *Values and Life-Style* typology (VALS). In an extensive survey, the company that developed the VALS, SRI International, asked 2500 consumers to what extent they agreed with 43 statements about various values and lifestyles. The VALS claims to identify various groups of consumers along two axes, based on the availability of resources (e.g. income, intelligence, health, energy) and three types of orientation, namely principle, status and action orientation. According to the VALS, principle-oriented consumers tend to act on the basis of their own personal beliefs and values. These individuals should be relatively insensitive to group influence and hence, are comparable to low self-monitoring individuals with an individualistic orientation. Status-oriented consumers have a strong impression motivation, are higher in self-monitoring and are primarily concerned with the beliefs and values of others. These consumers are particularly susceptible to the principle of social proof. Action-oriented individuals are physically and socially active.

Based on their responses to the 43 statements, consumers are classified into one of eight segments. 'Actualizers' have the most resources and have achieved a balance between the three orientations. On the other end of the spectrum are the 'strugglers' who tend to be older, lack resources and are primarily focused on survival. In between are the other six segments. 'Fulfillers' and 'believers' tend to be principle-oriented with fulfillers having more resources at their disposal than believers. 'Achievers' and 'strivers' aim to impress others, but achievers are more successful in doing so, because they have more resources. Finally, 'experiencers' are impulsive, young, sensation-seekers with abundant resources, while 'makers' share the action orientation, but have to do with fewer resources, forcing them to focus their energy on attaining self-sufficiency

Although this taxonomy is widely used and might have a heuristic value for marketers, enabling them to match consumers to the type of advertising appeal to which they are most susceptible in order to sell them the kind of product or service they are most likely to be interested in, we should keep in mind that the instrument represents a commercial product. The research firm, SRI, does not publish data on the operationalizations of the items, the procedure, or the analysis of the data. This makes an assessment of the reliability and validity of the instrument difficult and scholars should be cautious in interpreting results from the VALS.

The principle of liking

The **liking principle** is probably the simplest and arguably the most effective of all influence principles at the disposal of the marketer. It simply states that we are more likely to comply with the requests of someone we like than someone we dislike or feel neutral towards. This may indeed seem simple, but it still presents a formidable challenge for any sales representative or advertiser. Imagine yourself in their shoes and try to think what it would take to be liked by a potential customer. After all, there are strong odds against you. First, you are probably unfamiliar with the other person and the other person is unfamiliar with you. Next, there is a clear asymmetry in the interaction: you want something of the other (i.e. compliance), and in all likelihood the other is well aware of your motive. And finally, the interaction is a singular one and you both know it: the chances are that you two will never see each other again. So what is there to like?

Nevertheless, research has accumulated evidence suggesting that becoming liked is not so hard after all, and is sometimes achieved by astonishingly small means, at the disposal of even the most unsympathetic sales representative (the fate of Ebenezer Scrooge being a case in point who, admittedly after a long investment period in which he had to endure a considerable amount of hardship, ultimately became liked by Tiny Tim and his entire family).

Determinants of liking in social influence situations

Several factors influence liking in social influence situations. As we mentioned earlier, one important factor is familiarity. Whereas lack of familiarity breeds dislike, there is ample evidence showing that familiarity breeds liking. In our discussion of the mere exposure effect (see chapter 4), we argued that simply being around someone is frequently sufficient for that person to like you. As the target of influence is repeatedly exposed to an influence agent, familiarity increases, and with it, a more positive attitude toward the agent develops. For example, Burger et al. (2001) showed that simply being exposed to a person even briefly and without engaging in a conversation was sufficient to increase compliance with that person's request.

The fundamental truth that friends are more powerful sources of influence than strangers, has not escaped the attention of the advertising and marketing world. Indeed, one of the most successful marketing formulae of all time, the Tupperware party, is based on this simple adage. Tupperware is the brand name for a home product line that includes preparation, storing and serving containers for the kitchen and the home. Tupperware parties are run by a consultant of the Tupperware company in the home of a host, who invites friends and neighbours to see the product line. The hostess (attendees of Tupperware parties are mostly women) is rewarded with free products based on the amount of sales that are made. The liking rule becomes a powerful instrument of social influence in this situation, because the request to buy Tupperware items does not come from a stranger, it comes from a friend. As a result, the warmth, attraction and kindness of friendship is transferred to the little plastic bags and boxes. This simple formula has resulted in purchase rates that are twice as high as those of conventional sales. The Tupperware party has become so successful that the company has decided to abandon retail sales entirely and concentrate fully on the in-home, entertaining, selling channel.

In a similar vein, other companies and charity organisations have resorted to a liking-based marketing technique that has come to be known as members-get-members campaigns. Recognizing that friends sell more than strangers, Vodafone, the telecommunications company, advertises with cheaper subscription rates 'for you and your friends'. The discount can be collected when customers bring in new customers, usually from their network of friends and relatives.

Another well-known application of the liking principle is a ruse frequently employed in telemarketing and door-to-door selling. Even when the unsuspecting consumer does not take the bait and refuses the offer, all is not lost from the agent's point of view. The sales representative frequently ends the conversation by stating something like, 'I understand our marvellous offer is not right for you at this time, but perhaps you know of some friends or colleagues who might be interested? Perhaps I could write down a few of their names and contact them with our offer?' For the customer who refused to buy anything, giving a few names may seem pretty harmless and a polite way to end the interaction. For the sales representative, it presents an opportunity to use the liking principle, as he/she might contact the next target and mention the 'friend who suggested I call on you' (Cialdini, 2009).

Physical attractiveness. One of the most effective ways to become liked is to be beautiful. This may indeed pose a challenge to the not-so-beautiful agent of influence, but even plastic surgery may be well worth the effort because the benefits do not end with being physically attractive. Research on the 'attractiveness halo' (Eagly, Ashmore, Makijani & Longo, 1991) suggests that, apart from being likeable, attractive people are also considered honest, kind, intelligent, persuasive and sociable. Hence, the attractiveness halo captures the tendency to overgeneralize from one feature (physical attractiveness) to other, unrelated, features.

An early demonstration of the 'attractiveness halo' can be found in a classic study by Dion, Berscheid and Walster (1972). These authors showed participants photographs of attractive and less attractive faces, ostensibly from students currently enrolled in another university, and asked to rate a number of dependent variables for each of the faces, including marital satisfaction, parental happiness, professional happiness and social happiness. In addition, job status was rated and a number of personality traits. As might be expected by now, more attractive faces were thought to represent happier, more successful people, with better lives, better marriages and higher status jobs.

The attractiveness halo has been used by advertisers and marketers for a long time and has proven its worth in selling products. If consumers tend to overgeneralize, then the halo should also rub off on a product that is associated with an attractive model, and recent research shows that it does (Strick, Holland & van Knippenberg, 2008). In this research, products (unknown brands of peppermints) were paired with faces that varied in attractiveness and gaze direction (to the participant or diverted away in other directions). In line with the halo effect, physical attractiveness affected product ratings, and did so particularly when the faces looked at the participant, rather than somewhere else.

Similarity. One of the best known factors contributing to liking is similarity. We tend to like people who are like us because, in general, we tend to like ourselves (Allport, 1961). That similarity in values and attitudes fosters liking has been known for many decades (Byrne, 1971; Newcomb, 1960). A more recent and more intriguing example of the similarity–liking relationship is the name–letter effect: the tendency to have a positive predisposition to the letters in one's own name, especially the first and last initials. Hence, we tend to like not only people who are similar to us, but also products that have something in common with us. Research has shown that people have a preference for products, street names, and even career choices that share the same letters as one's own name (see Brendl, Chattopadhyay, Pelham & Carvallo, 2005; Hodson & Olson, 2005; Jones, Pelham, Mirenberg & Hetts, 2002). Thus, Paul likes to become a professor and Lucy likes to become a lawyer.

Since the name–letter effect is also known to marketers, it is quite possible (and no coincidence) that the next time he picks up the phone, Bob Jones will be greeted by Bart Johnson, a telemarketer offering a great discount on an encyclopaedia. But the power of similarity does not stop there. Studies have shown that incidental similarities other than name letters can also be very effective in influence settings. Burger et al. (2004) showed that pretending to share someone's birthday, name or fingerprint increased compliance with requests.

Similarity is also enhanced when we use indirect associations, such as associating ourselves with a winning sports team, something that Cialdini (1976) has labelled 'basking in reflected glory'. Sharing the same items of clothing as the winning team in a sports match, or using items that bear the team's logo increases likeability. Of course, the team needs to win for the effect to occur. When it loses, there is nothing to bask in, so former fans are far less inclined to associate themselves with the team. This fact is reflected by the often dramatic drop in sales of promotional items such as mugs, baseball caps, shawls and team flags (Kardes, 2002).

Similarity-based liking is also induced in commercials using a 'testimonial' or 'slice of life' format as we have seen in our discussion of the social validation principle. In both formats, the message uses average-looking characters with beliefs, values and behaviours that are similar to those of the audience watching the commercial. Hence, message effectiveness of testimonial and slice of life commercials is partly a function of similarity-based liking.

Other research also suggests that you need not necessarily be beautiful or have something in common to be an effective influence agent. Even simple gestures, such as introducing yourself (Garrity & Degelman, 1990), a gentle touch (Segrin, 1993), asking about the well-being of the target of influence (Howard, 1990), remembering a client's name (Howard, Gengler & Jain, 1995) and mimicking someone's body language and verbal style (LaFrance, 1985; Tanner et al., 2008) may suffice to have the target like you.

Ingratiation. A blunt way of using the liking principle is through ingratiation. We tend to like those who flatter us, fuelled by our vanity (Gordon, 1996, Vonk, 2002). In a study assessing the effects of flattery on compliance, Hendrick et al. (1972) complimented targets of influence on their goodness and kindness and were rewarded with increased compliance with a request to complete a seven-page booklet (see Pratkanis, 2007). Similarly, Pratkanis and Abbott (2004) asked for volunteers for a 'stop junk mail' public communication campaign either after having flattered them about their clothing or after asking the time of day (control condition). This study too, reported elevated levels of compliance with the request, but was more equivocal about the mediating role of liking. Although flattery increased feelings of liking and affiliation, Pratkanis and Abbott (2004) found that the positive effects of flattery on compliance were observed regardless of whether the request to volunteer was made by the flatterer himself or by another person (immediately after the ingratiation took place). This finding suggests that flattery may also work through generalized positive mood that spills over to whoever asks for a favour or presents a sales offer. Nevertheless, the timing of flattery may make a difference. Campbell and Kirmani (2000) found that salesperson flattery right before a purchase was less effective, because it may elicit suspicion about the ulterior motives of the influence agent (i.e. pushing the sale). If the agent used ingratiation after the purchase, however, he/she was judged to be more sincere and an ulterior motive was less likely to be inferred, particularly when the consumer was cognitively busy.

Bringing good news. Finally, having some good news in store for a target of influence will almost invariably make him/her like you. Of course, flattery is a form of good news (about oneself), but other, unrelated types of good news also tend to rub off on the communicator, increasing the effectiveness of the liking principle. Unfortunately, the reverse tends to be true as well, as many a messenger bearing bad news has learned, sometimes the hard way as in ancient Persia where kings made carriers of bad news pay with their life. Less dramatic is the fate suffered by TV weather presenters reporting on bad weather, who seem to be frequently threatened and harassed for bringing the bad news (Cialdini, 2009).

The principle of authority

In 2009, a former investment banker, Bernard Madoff, was charged with fraud on a grand scale. Madoff was suspected of having engaged in high risk speculations with investment funds of countless individuals and corporations in unsecured pyramid constructions. In the process, his clients lost over $50 billion, making it the biggest swindle in banking history. An intriguing question is why even professional parties such as banks, financial institutions, hedge funds, and investment companies kept on trusting Madoff with their money despite the tell-tale signs that something was going wrong. The likely answer was given by one financial analyst who testified that the status and allure of Mr Madoff were beyond question. He was considered a man of authority and standing, someone of impeccable reputation who seemed to know his way around the world of high finance. As a result, even financial experts considered him a person you could trust with your money (Hofs, 2008). As it turned out, that trust was misplaced, and the $50 billion were lost without hope of recovering (part of) the damage.

Symbols of authority

Authority is the power to influence others into behaving in a certain manner either through coercion or with the aid of status and position related symbols. Typically, authority comes with social dominance, and dominance is conveyed through titles (e.g. CEO, PhD), specific items of clothing (i.c. a business suit, a white dentist's coat), or conspicuous products (e.g. jewellery or luxury cars) that impress others and communicate a high rank in the social pecking order. Since authority thrives on the display of symbols, marketers have been quick to capitalize on its influence. Brands are associated with competence and status. Products in advertising also use signs and symbols of power and authority to convey status, expertise and credibility. Toothpaste ads use white-dressed dentists (actually actors of course), perfume ads display smiling, beautiful, well-dressed, and obviously successful women and men (see Figure 7.3) and luxury brand car ads show admiring neighbours in awe over the new possession of a happy owner.

It is one thing to flirt with the symbols of authority, but it is entirely another to show that the advertised products and brands actually succeed in bringing about dominant and submissive behaviour. Can brands and products contribute to social hierarchies and induce such behaviours? Recent research by Fennis (2008b) suggests that they can. Moreover, this research sought to demonstrate that the branded items need not perform a leading role in an interaction between two individuals, but that incidental exposure to these brands suffices for hierarchisation behaviour (i.e. the establishment of a social hierarchy) to occur. This research focused on nonverbal

Figure 7.3 A perfume ad featuring a successful man, at least in a certain sphere of life

Source: Reproduced with permission of Hugo Boss. The permission of advertising visual photographer Terry Richardson and pack shot photographer (David Gill) and of the model (Nicholas Duvauchelle) is kindly acknowledged

indicators of hierarchisation behaviour. Over the years, a considerable body of literature has shown that hierarchisation in dyads involves the display of specific patterns
of nonverbal behaviour (see Buss, 1999). For instance, in series of studies, Tiedens
and Fragale (2003) reported that both nonverbal submissive and dominant behaviour
patterns (which they term 'power moves') were important contributors to hierarchisation. Nonverbal cues in their studies included expanding (dominant) and constricting
(submissive) postures. These authors have argued that hierarchisation is particularly
found in those settings where an a priori affiliation goal between both interaction
partners is absent, hence when two strangers meet without a preset agenda to like
each other, or become liked. Tiedens and Fragale (2003) demonstrated that a trained
confederate who displayed dominant nonverbal behaviour in such a setting could
nonconsciously induce submissive nonverbal behaviour on the part of the participant
and, conversely, evoke dominant nonverbal behaviour in the antagonist when exhibiting submissive behaviour him/herself, a pattern which Tiedens and Fragale (2003)
termed 'complementary' behaviour. In addition, although there was no affiliation goal
in these studies, their research showed that this complementary behaviour did have a
positive effect on the likeability of the confederate: participants rated the confederate
as more likeable in complementary conditions than in control conditions.

Extending these findings, Fennis (2008b) showed that the mere presence of
brands with specific salient attributes is sufficient to affect nonverbal hierarchisation
behaviour, without these brands playing any role of significance in the interaction. In
his first experiment, Fennis (2008b) had a male confederate exhibiting brands that
scored high on the brand personality dimension of competence (cf. Aaker, 1997), a
dimension closely linked to status and authority (established through a pre-test). The
pre-test revealed that Coca-Cola and Hugo Boss were considered 'competent brands' by
students. Therefore, in the experimental condition, the confederate engaged in a task
with the student interaction partner, while a can of Coca-Cola rested on the table to his
right and while he wore a sweater bearing the Hugo Boss logo. The brands played
no role whatsoever in the interaction and compared to control conditions, all other
elements of the interaction were held constant. Nevertheless, (male) participants in the
experimental conditions showed more frequent sequences of submissive nonverbal
behaviours in response to the high authority confederate such as looking at the confederate while listening to him, nodding affirmatively, and coyly smiling.

The effect, though, was not the same for every individual in the interaction, but
was moderated by individual differences in sociable dominance or the extent to which
individuals tend to take the initiative in social settings, to determine the group's
agenda, and the tendency to propose oneself as the (informal or formal) leader of
the group (Kalma, Visser & Peeters, 1993). The pattern of submissive nonverbal
behaviour in response to exposure to the competent brands was more pronounced for
individuals low in sociable dominance compared to individuals high in dominance.

In a second study using other brands and examining cross-sex dyads, Fennis
(2008b) found comparable results, but also observed that female participants were
more prone to exhibit these nonverbal cues of submissiveness in response to a male
confederate associated with high-status brands than male participants were in response to female confederates associated with these brands. This study further
revealed that female (but not male) participants rated their male interaction partners
as more likeable, when they were surrounded by high as opposed to low status

brands. These findings are consistent with the hypothesis suggested by evolutionary psychologists that women, in their interaction with men, are more prone to respond to status cues, than men in their interaction with women (cf. Buss, 1999).

Authority and obedience

Although this study shows that it does not take much for people to make use of the principle of authority (and that it pays to invest in high competence or high status brands if the aim is to secure a romantic partner or a business deal), the most striking demonstration of the powerful impact of the authority principle comes from what is arguably the best known and most (in)famous series of studies in social psychology.

These studies were conducted at Yale University by Stanley Milgram (1963) to assess the dynamics of obedience to authority. Participants in his studies were given the role of 'teacher' and met at the laboratory what appeared to be another participant who was assigned the role of 'learner' (in reality the learner was invariably a trained confederate). In a study presented as an investigation of the effects of punishment on learning, they were asked to perform a simple task involving memorized word pairs. The teacher would read out words to the learner and would punish errors (failure to supply the correct word in a word pair) by means of a large switchboard that enabled him to deliver electric shocks to the learner. The device contained 30 numbered switches from a low of 15 volts up to 450 volts. To indicate the strength of these shocks, labels were placed underneath each 'voltage' switch reading 'slight shock' via 'very strong shock' up to 'danger: severe shock'. The last two switches (435 and 450 volts) did not have a descriptive label, but merely a series of ominous Xes, leaving it to the imagination of the participant to figure out the damage it would do to the learner. Participants (teachers) were instructed to increase the strength of the shock each time the learner made an additional error. It should be noted that the learner did not receive real electric shocks. However, this was not known to the teacher, who genuinely believed that he delivered electric shocks with each turn of a switch. To strengthen the teacher in this belief, he was given the opportunity to try out the switchboard and received a very mild shock of 45 volts. As shock intensities increased, participants heard the learner scream louder and louder, eventually begging to be released from the apparatus. Any time the real participant hesitated to deliver a shock, the experimenter, an authority figure wearing a white lab coat, urged him to continue. The key question in this research was how far participants were willing to go in punishing the learner. The unsettling answer was that 65 per cent of all participants were willing to deliver the maximum shock of 450 volts which would have been lethal if it had really been delivered.

The most disconcerting aspect of this study, however, is the fact that Milgram and his co-workers did not need to use coercion to get people to deliver the deadly shocks. It was enough for them to urge the participants to continue with a graded series of 'prods', such as 'please continue', 'the experiment requires that you continue', 'it is absolutely essential that you continue', up to 'you have no other choice – you must go on'. Of course, participants *did* have another choice, i.e., they could refuse and leave the experiment. However, under the power of the authority principle, most of them chose not to opt for this course of action. Since 1963 this landmark series of studies has been replicated in Holland, Germany, Spain, Italy, Australia and Jordan, and results have been largely similar to the original findings (Meeus & Raaijmakers, 1986).

The principle of scarcity

The principle of **scarcity** involves the notion that consumers value goods that are scarce. If you think about it, the almost automatic response to scarcity is curious: what is valuable is sometimes scarce because it is made of rare materials (e.g. gold, diamonds). But the reverse is not necessarily true: what is scarce is not necessarily valuable. Nevertheless, people tend to value those things in life that are in short supply, difficult to obtain or rare, more than they value objects that are plentiful, or easy to obtain. It is no wonder then, that scarcity appeals are much used in advertising and marketing. Frequently, scarcity is the product of a deliberate marketing strategy. Luxury items, for example, derive a major part of their value from reduced availability. Jewellery brands such as Cartier, IWC or Rolex cannot be found in your average supermarket, but only at selected dealers. And even there, models are frequently sold out, or are sold as limited editions. Sometimes, scarcity is created unintentionally when products are banned (see for example the American ban on alcohol during prohibition or their ban on sales of Cuban cigars), something that marketers may capitalize on. Banned products also become more desirable (Mazis, Settle & Leslie, 1973). Moreover, time limits on availability and dwindling supplies may also be used to stir up scarcity perceptions (Brannon & Brock, 2001).

A demonstration of the influence of the scarcity principle comes from research by Worchel and colleagues (Worchel, Lee & Adewole, 1975). These researchers showed that presenting participants with few, as opposed to many, items exerted a powerful influence on desirability. In one study, participants were presented with a jar holding two or 10 chocolate chip cookies. When asked to give an overall evaluation, the cookies were rated more favourably when they were in limited rather than plentiful supply, although actual taste ratings were not affected. The effect was even more pronounced when availability changed while participants were watching, for example, when a second experimenter entered the lab and said he accidentally took the wrong jar of cookies and then switched the jar with ten for the one with two cookies. Changes in demand also affected product desirability, for example when the second experimenter said he needed more cookies, because his participants had almost finished theirs.

The scarcity principle is used frequently in what is known as the deadline technique in advertising (Cialdini, 2009) when promoting 'now or never' discounts, limited offers that suggest exclusiveness and special editions of various products (Inman, Anil & Raghubir, 1997). For example, the website www.onedayonly.nl hosts an online shop that has made scarcity into its unique selling proposition. It offers substantial discounts on products but only for one day: a clock is ticking the hours of the day away after which the original price of the product is reinstated. Scarcity is also frequently used by department stores or airlines which inform customers that some special offer will end on a given date or be only available for a limited time.

Sometimes the deadline is completely false: after the expiration date has passed, alert customers may notice that the product is still on the shelf, or the price discount is still valid. Nevertheless, the scarcity principle has probably already done its job and increased sales.

One well-known department store uses the scarcity principle to create a yearly shopping frenzy among young female consumers. Hennes and Mauritz (H&M) invites a well-known fashion designer to create a prêt-à-porter clothing collection at discount prices. In the past, such fashion gurus as Victor and Rolf, and Madonna have cooperated with the H&M corporation. The strategy evokes the scarcity principle along two lines: high fashion is rarely sold at discount prices and availability is limited (typically the fashion items are on sale for no more than a week per year). This is sufficient to create a mix of greed and desire turning even the most stolid customers into compulsive shoppers. At the advent of sales week, consumers gather before dawn at the shop entrance, sometimes even camping there to be certain of a good starting position, only to storm the place when it opens. At closing time, the H&M store typically looks like it has endured an air raid with the (few) remaining clothing items ripped apart and scattered across the shopping floor by frenzied customers who fought over them.

The scarcity principle serves an important heuristic function. As outlined by Cialdini and Sagarin (2005), because we think that objects that are of higher value are typically harder to obtain than less valuable objects, scarcity constitutes an important mental shortcut to infer the value or merit of something. Thus, scarcity should primarily affect consumer behaviour under conditions of mindlessness. However, there is some research suggesting that scarcity also prompts more systematic processing, and hence can increase consumer mindfulness. For example, Brannon and Brock (2001) have interpreted the association of scarcity and value in terms of their commodity theory (Brock, 1968). According to commodity theory, limiting the availability of an object, or limiting information (as in the case of censorship) should enhance the desirability of the object and the information not because scarcity acts as heuristic cue, but because increased scarcity instigates a tendency to form more extreme attitudes. This attitude polarization is assumed to be the result of enhanced thinking about the merits of the object due to scarcity. In line with dual process theories of persuasion (see chapter 5), scarcity thus motivates more extensive systematic, or central route processing, and Brannon and Brock (1998) found that such polarization under conditions of low availability was mediated by evaluative thinking and disappeared when this thinking was suppressed by a cognitive load manipulation.

To further test their commodity theory explanation, Brannon and Brock (2001) operationalized scarcity as limiting time for responding to a request and pitted their systematic processing account of scarcity information to the heuristic cue account. Following the dual process logic discussed in chapter 5, if scarcity would function as a heuristic cue, it would increase the favourability of attitudes toward a product or service regardless of the quality of any arguments supporting it. In contrast, if scarcity would prompt more extensive processing, then it would increase persuasion when arguments were strong and compelling, but decrease persuasion when arguments were weak and specious.

In one study Brannon and Brock (2001) instructed order takers of a local

Mexican food restaurant to sell customers an unusual food item, a cinnamon twist. In the high scarcity condition, the order taker offered the food item with the words, 'Would you like a cinnamon twist made with our special recipe today only?' In the low scarcity condition, the script read 'Would you like a cinnamon twist made with our usual recipe for this year?'. In addition a reason for ordering the food item was provided which varied in strength. In the strong argument condition, the order taker would say, 'The cinnamon twist goes great with Mexican food, you know'. The weak argument, in contrast, read, 'The cinnamon twist is not really Mexican food, you know'. The researchers found that the scarcity appeal indeed affected sales of the food item. Moreover, in line with their predictions, a scarcity appeal by argument quality interaction was observed, indicating that scarcity prompted increased sales of the cinnamon twist particularly when the reason for buying one was strong, rather than weak. Although this research cannot by itself discount the heuristic cue hypothesis of scarcity, or any of the other influence principles, it does suggest a complementary, more thoughtful process may also sometimes contribute to the impact of influence principles in advertising and marketing settings.

An alternative explanation of these findings could be derived from reactance theory (Brehm, 1966). As availability is reduced, we feel that we lose the freedom to choose. This reduction of our freedom prompts a strong motivation to restore freedom (Cialdini & Sagarin, 2005), a motivation, which has been called 'psychological reactance' by Brehm (1966). Gollwitzer (1990) has noted that the increase in volitional strength induced by reactance results in adopting a 'deliberative mind set' which involves a cognitive focus on issue-relevant information and the tendency to engage in careful scrutiny of the desirability of the object or issue under consideration.

The principle of confusion

In addition to the six principles of influence, recent research has examined a set of tools that marketers frequently use in advertising to confuse consumers into buying. Although at first glance one might argue that nothing good can come from distracting or disrupting consumers at the point of purchase, a series of studies suggest that it can. Research has shown that slightly confusing consumers can increase their tendency to comply with sales requests. These studies have examined the dynamics underlying an influence tactic, known as the **Disrupt-then-Reframe** (DTR) technique (Davis & Knowles, 1999; Fennis et al., 2004, 2006; Kardes et al., 2007). This technique is characterized by a small 'twist', or odd element, in a typical scripted request; the 'disruption', (for instance stating the price of an offer in pennies rather than dollars, i.e. 'they're 200 pennies . . . that's $2') is followed by a persuasive phrase that concludes the script, the 'reframe' (e.g. 'it's a really good deal'). Thus formulated, the original research on the technique found compliance rates to increase by more than 1.5 times compared to conventionally stated messages (Davis & Knowles, 1999). More specifically, Davis and Knowles (1999) had Christmas cards sold by two confederates who posed as representatives of a charity for disabled children (the profits actually went to this charity). After showing a set of Christmas cards to prospective buyers, these individuals were asked whether they wanted to know the price. Then, in some conditions, the disrupting phrase was inserted and after presenting this odd element, the confederate paused for two seconds before stating the reframe. The DTR condition would thus read' 'This package of cards sells for 300 pennies . . . That's $3. It's a bargain!' The original studies found purchasing rates to be more than 1.5 times and in several instances twice as high in DTR as opposed to control conditions.

The authors showed that both elements, the disruption and the reframe, were necessary to increase compliance. The DTR technique was tested against various control conditions, such as price only ('They're $3'), reframe then disrupt ('It's a bargain . . . They're 300 pennies. That's $3'), disruption-only ('They're 300 pennies . . . That's $3'), and reframe only ('They're $3. It's a bargain'). In all these instances, DTR conditions yielded significantly higher purchase rates than any of the control conditions.

Fennis et al. (2004) extended this research by testing the processes underlying the effectiveness of the DTR technique and its generalizability across various types of compliance behaviours and across differing types of persuasion settings. In line with the notion of consumer mindlessness, the DTR technique is assumed to gently confuse the target consumer without brutally 'awakening' him or her into a state of careful scrutiny of the sales script. Consistent with this reasoning, Fennis et al. (2004) argued that the disruption may function as a distracter, reducing the ability of the target individual to produce counterarguments in response to the sales script (cf. Harkins & Petty, 1981; Petty & Wegener, 1999; Petty, Wells & Brock, 1976). Thus, the disruption in the DTR reduces the extent of processing of the sales script. To be effective, the technique would thus require a persuasive reframe while participants are still distracted. This reframe would function as a simple decision heuristic to affect compliance with the sales request. This would explain why the DTR technique would outperform any of the control scripts listed above. Moreover, if the disruption reduces the recipient's ability to counterargue and consequently fosters mindless acceptance through heuristic processing of the reframe, than by the same token any *other* peripheral cue present in the influence situation would become more effective under DTR conditions than without. Thus, by distracting the target individual, the DTR technique would boost the impact of any additional persuasive elements that happened to be present.

These hypotheses were confirmed by the results of a total of five experiments (Fennis et al., 2004, 2006). In a first experiment, Fennis et al. (2004) employed a confederate to sell lottery tickets to passers-by in the centre of a large town on behalf of a company called 'Dayzers'. In the introduction, the confederate stated, 'I am with Dayzers. Are you familiar with Dayzers? Then you know it is an officially registered lottery that does not award millions of euros to just one winner, but gives many smaller prizes to millions of winners! You are now invited to join the lottery for eight weeks for the price of only four weeks!' Half of the participants were then exposed to the DTR technique whereas the other half received a control script. More specifically, in the DTR condition, the confederate proceeded by presenting the participant with a subtle disruption, followed by a reframe: 'Now is your chance to try your luck for 350 euro cents a week . . . that's €3.5. It's a bargain!' In the no-disruption condition the disruption was omitted, and the price was simply stated in euros: 'Now is your chance to try your luck for €3.5 a week. It's a bargain!' The results showed that the DTR was effective in selling lottery tickets: 43 per cent of participants exposed to the DTR bought the lottery ticket, whereas only 25 per cent of the individuals in the no-disruption condition did so. Moreover, to assess the thought disruption hypothesis, the confederate recorded the number of explicitly stated objections or critical comments and questions in response to the sales script and found that the DTR produced fewer counterarguments than the disruption-only control condition. It was further shown that this reduced counterargumentation mediated the effect of the technique on compliance. Hence, the findings support the notion that the DTR technique lowers the ability to critically process the sales message.

Recent research (Kardes et al., 2007) has demonstrated that the disruption serves a second function as well. Because the disruption confuses consumers, it may motivate the need for cognitive closure. The reframe, the persuasive conclusion to the script, may provide this closure and thereby increase compliance rates. In line with these notions, Kardes et al. (2007) demonstrated that the DTR effect is greater when individuals are high rather than low in the need for cognitive closure. Hence, the disruption in the DTR technique reduces the ability to counterargue the sales message and increases the motivation to attain a certain conclusion. The reframe thus acts as a peripheral cue providing this closure, resulting in increased compliance.

Fennis and colleagues (2004, 2006) provided further evidence for the notion that the DTR may boost the effectiveness of additional persuasive elements that are embedded in the influence context. For example, in one study, they crossed the DTR technique with the Continuing Questions Procedure (CQP) described earlier (Fennis et al., 2004, Study 2). As noted, in the CQP procedure, the target request is preceded by a series of initial questions that are semantically related to it. In this study a confederate approached students on campus with the request to sign a petition arguing for an increase in college tuition fees. Half of the participants were exposed to a DTR message, the other half to a disruption-only control script. Moreover, half of the participants were presented with the CQP and the other half was not. Consequently, the study employed a 2 (CQP: present versus absent) x 2 (influence technique: DTR versus no disruption) design. In the CQP condition, participants were asked a series of three simple questions before the target request of signing the petition was introduced. The confederate asked the target if he was allowed the opportunity to elucidate why it was necessary to ask for an increase in tuition fees. After the participant agreed, he or she was presented with two statements – both congruent with the final target question – and asked to indicate whether he or she agreed with each of the statements. The statements read: 'To improve the quality of academic education, more financial means need to be available', and 'High-quality scientific research is necessary to better understand and solve important societal issues and problems'. The script then continued to stress the importance of the increase in tuition fees to improve the quality of the scientific research and education and thus the need to argue for such an increase with the government. In the control condition, both the opening question and the two statements were omitted from the script. Then the scripted influence technique was presented. In the DTR condition, participants were informed that the pressure group argued for a €75 (approximately $75) increase in annual college tuition fees. In these conditions, participants were exposed to the subtle disruption, the two-second pause, and the reframe in the following way: 'College tuition fees need to be raised by 7,500 euro cents . . . that's €75. It's a really small investment!'.

In the no-disruption condition, the disruption was omitted. In this condition, the script simply stated, 'College tuition fees need to be raised by €75. It's a really small investment'. Signing the petition was the measure of behavioural compliance. The results showed that the DTR was again effective: the proportion of participants who complied with the request was significantly greater when they were exposed to a disruption (63 per cent) than when they were not (28 per cent). In addition, a greater proportion of participants agreed to sign the petition when they were exposed to multiple questions than when they were not (63 per cent versus 29 per cent) Of more interest was that this latter difference was significantly greater when participants had been exposed to the disrupt-then-reframe procedure (90 per cent versus 37 per cent) than when they had not (37 per cent versus 20 per cent). Hence, the effectiveness of the CQP was boosted by the DTR technique.

Mindlessness revisited: the limited-resource account

In the previous sections, we reviewed evidence of influence principles affecting consumer compliance primarily under conditions of automaticity or mindlessness. But where does this mindlessness in these and other social influence situations come from? In other words, what is it that makes people behave 'mindlessly' and fall back on engrained heuristics when presented with an influence technique? Although mindlessness has been proposed as a 'condition sine qua non' for the techniques to work, it is interesting to note that no study to date has directly addressed this key question.

Fennis, Janssen and Vohs (2009) argued that the origins of this mindlessness can be found in a characteristic that most influence techniques have in common: multiple decision moments, or sequential requests. That is, the target consumer has to respond to an initial request or series of requests before the actual target request is presented. For example, the foot-in-the door procedure starts with a small request, followed by a larger request. Similarly, door-in-the-face technique starts with a relatively large request, followed by a smaller request. Fennis et al. (2009) showed that these sequential request techniques essentially trigger *one* underlying psychological mechanism that accounts for their impact: that of **self-regulatory resource depletion** (Baumeister, Bratslavsky, Muraven & Tice, 1998; Muraven, Tice and Baumeister, 1998; Vohs & Heatherton, 2000; Vohs, Baumeister & Tice, 2008).

The basic premise of self-regulatory resource depletion (also termed ego-depletion) is that processes involving active self-regulation, such as exerting willpower, self-control, overcoming impulses, or resisting (unwanted) influence require resources that are finite: hence, the active self can become depleted. In line with these notions, Fennis et al. (2009) posited that actively responding to the initial stages of a sequential request technique also draws on this limited resource and hence results in a state of ego-depletion. This ego-depletion paves the way for subsequent compliance with the target request.

Fennis et al. (2009) developed and tested a *two-stage model* to account for the effectiveness of sequential request techniques. In the first stage, the initial request or series of requests is presented to the consumer. Yielding to the initial request(s) results in self-regulatory resource depletion. This state of low self-regulatory resources produces the mindlessness typically observed in studies on social influence. In the second stage, self-regulatory resource depletion fosters the use of heuristics that encourage yielding to the target request. Six studies provided empirical evidence for tenets of the two-stage model. Using various manipulations and measures of self-regulatory resource depletion and excluding alternative explanations, these studies showed that self-regulatory resource depletion was induced when participants yielded to the initial requests of a sequential request technique, and that a state of resource depletion increased the tendency to rely on simple heuristics for decision-making.

For example, in one study (Experiment 1), participants were exposed to either a CQP or a target request control condition. In the CQP condition participants were presented with an initial request, which asked them to answer a series of questions on their personal eating habits. This initial request was absent in the no-initial request condition. The target request in both conditions then asked participants whether they would volunteer to keep a food diary for two weeks, which involved describing what they consume, when, and how much. Self-regulatory resource depletion was measured by asking participants to generate as many arguments as they could opposing an issue that they favoured. Hence, participants were asked to actively override their primary evaluative response to the issue, an act known to require active self-regulation (see Wheeler, Briñol & Hermann, 2007). The number of arguments generated served as a measure of self-regulatory resource depletion. Results showed that the CQP induced higher compliance rates than the control condition. Of more interest was the observation that the initial questions in the CQP also induced self-regulatory resource depletion: participants in the CQP condition had a harder time overriding their existing attitude and thus generated fewer counterarguments than control participants. This finding was subsequently replicated using alternative measures of self-regulatory resource depletion and alternative influence settings.

In addition, another study demonstrated that self-regulatory resource depletion indeed mediated the effects of yielding to the initial requests of a foot-in-the-door technique on compliance with a charitable target request. Three other studies supported the notion that weak temporary and chronic self-control ability fostered compliance through reliance on compliance-promoting heuristics. In these studies, low self-control was found to increase susceptibility to the principles of reciprocity, commitment and consistency, and liking.

In sum, the two-stage model offers a more comprehensive account of the psychological processes underlying the various instances of influence governed by the basic heuristic principles identified in psychological research spanning more than five decades.

Summary and conclusions

- This chapter has reviewed principles of social influence designed to produce consumer compliance with (sales) requests. Several forms of advertising, most notably direct response advertising explicitly seek an overt behavioural response from consumers, and in the process employ one or more of the principles outlined in this chapter.
- Social psychological research has identified a series of six heuristic influence principles that compliance professionals such as advertisers and marketers can

employ to get consumers to say 'yes' to their offer. Heuristics are simple decision rules that consumers may use as a rule of thumb in a given influence setting. These heuristics are the principles of reciprocity, commitment/consistency, social validation, liking, authority and scarcity. In addition, recent research has identified the role of the confusion principle in consumer compliance and has stressed the role of consumer self-regulation in compliance settings.

- The first section discusses the role of consumer mindlessness. We also related mindlessness to automaticity and argued that the fact that most of the influence processes discussed in this chapter operate through processes which are subtle, implicit and frequently outside conscious awareness of the consumer does not necessarily mean that they are also automatic. Mindlessness drives the impact of the various influence heuristics on compliance. Heuristic decision-making is considered the default and frequently the most efficient way of behaving in many influence settings.

- The next section addresses the reciprocity principle or the motivation to return a favour. The door-in-the-face influence technique hinges on the reciprocity heuristic and is composed of a rejection-then-moderation sequence where the target consumer is first approached with a large offer or request, which is almost certain to be rejected, only to be followed by a more moderate target request. The target request is presented as a concession with the reciprocity rule provoking a counter concession on the part of the target consumer: compliance. The reciprocity principle also accounts for the impact of the that's-not-all technique, whereby an initial request is followed by a second request that is made more desirable. Sales promotion efforts such as handing out product samples also induce consumer reciprocity concerns, which partly account for their effectiveness

- Commitment/consistency is a heuristic principle that relies on the need to behave congruently across situations. The foot-in-the-door (FITD) technique, and a subtype, the continuing questions procedure (CQP), both use the consistency principle to produce compliance. In a FITD setting, the target request is preceded by a smaller initial request or series of requests. Scholars have pointed to a self-perception process to account for the effectiveness of the technique. Hence, from their compliance with the initial, small request, consumers infer that they must have a positive attitude towards compliance with such requests. This increases compliance with the bigger target request. The FITD and CQP procedures have been found to increase compliance across various compliance settings and types of requests. An additional technique that employs the commitment/consistency principle is the lowball technique where the deal or offer changes to a less attractive alternative after initial commitment.

- A third influence principle is the heuristic of social proof or social validation. It involves the tendency to look at other people to infer the 'correct' way of behaving in a given situation. The principle of social proof is mainly used in situations of ambiguity and uncertainly where other, more objective, sources of information are unavailable or inaccessible. Social validation is used frequently in advertising in messages using reference group appeals. Personality traits such as self-monitoring and individualism versus collectivism have been found

- to moderate the impact of reference group appeals and social proof in advertising and other influence settings.
- Another powerful influence heuristic is the liking principle. Consumers tend to comply with requests from sales representatives they like and research has identified several factors that affect liking. First, familiarity has been found to increase liking. Moreover, liking is induced by physical attractiveness. Similarity also facilitates liking as does ingratiation or brown-nosing. Finally, liking is stimulated by bringing good news. Liking-based ad formats include the testimonial and the slice of life.
- Authority is the power to influence others into believing, preferring or behaving in a certain manner either by coercion or with the aid of status and position related symbols. Authority is a function of status and hence is communicated through symbols such as clothing items and products. These symbols of authority are frequently portrayed in advertising. Research shows that symbols of authority actually succeed in bringing about hierarchisation behaviour. In addition, in the most famous research on authority, Milgram (1963) showed the ease with which naïve participants can be brought to inflict serious harm to others simply by obeying an authority figure.
- The heuristic principle of scarcity involves the tendency to infer value from limited availability rather than to infer availability from value. Scarcity is proposed as the basis of all economic thought. It manifests itself in product bans, dwindling supplies, limited availability, special editions or time restrictions. Research shows that scarcity increases product ratings due to enhanced desirability. Although scarcity may function as a heuristic, there is also research suggesting that it may prompt more extensive processing. Scarcity may be viewed as a loss of freedom to choose and hence triggers psychological reactance, or the tendency to actively restore what has been lost.
- In addition to these six heuristics, research has identified the confusion principle, or the notion that gently confusing a consumer can increase the tendency to comply with a sales request. This research has centred on the disrupt-then-reframe technique, which is characterized by a small 'twist', or odd element, in sales script, the 'disruption', followed by a persuasive phrase which concludes the script, the 'reframe'. Research has shown that the DTR technique results in higher compliance rates than conventional sales scripts. The technique works because the disruption distracts the consumer from counterarguing the message, and the reframe acts as a peripheral cue thus increasing persuasion. In addition, the disruption may increase the need for cognitive closure which the reframe subsequently provides.
- Finally, the limited-resource account provides an explanation for the mindlessness encountered in many influence settings, involving the notion of self-regulation failure brought about by resource depletion. The basic assumption is that actively responding to influence attempts requires self-regulation and consumes a limited resource available for such processes. The resulting state of self-regulatory resource depletion increases vulnerability to influence attempts through increased reliance on compliance promoting heuristics. This research has shown that sequential request techniques such as the FITD or DITF technique work in two stages. In the first stage, the initial request or series of

requests is presented to the consumer. Yielding to the initial request(s) results in self-regulatory resource depletion. This weakened state of low self-regulatory resources produces the mindlessness typically observed in studies on social influence. Once mindless, people are less able to defend themselves to unwanted influence attempts. Hence in the second stage, self-regulatory resource depletion fosters compliance but mainly when the influence setting harbours a powerful influence heuristic.

Notes

1   The Process Dissociation Procedure is a clever procedure to disentangle conscious from non conscious influences on responding. In the task, a word is flashed on a computer screen for a very brief duration (e.g. 50 milliseconds) followed by a mask. Participants are given a word-stem completion task that involves presenting them with the first three letters of the flashed word and asking them to complete the stem to form a word. Participants are instructed to *refrain* from using the words that have been flashed on the screen previously when completing the word stem. This puts conscious and unconscious influences in opposition. If the flashed word is consciously perceived, then there should be a *decreased* likelihood (compared to baseline) of completing the stem to form the flashed word, because participants were instructed not to use it. The influence of unconscious processes, however, are not within the participant's volitional control and so, if the word was unconsciously perceived then there should be an *increase* the likelihood (compared to baseline) that the stem is completed to form the flashed word. Additional provisions are sometimes made to account for partial correction of nonconscious influences by conscious interventions.
2   They used different traits and a different Donald story.
3   There is a distinction between memory-based *decisions* as defined by Hastie and Park (1986) and memory-based *brand choices* as they are typically understood by researchers in the marketing area (e.g. Lee, 2002). When we contrast memory-based with online decisions, the defining feature is the time interval between the exposure to the (product) information and the product evaluation. When we contrast memory-based with stimulus-based brand choices, on the other hand, the defining feature is the physical presence versus absence of a range

of products whilst we make our choice. Thus, both online and memory-based decisions can result in memory-based brand choices.

4   Attitudes that are reflected by self-reported evaluations are now referred to as **explicit attitudes** to distinguish them from 'implicit attitudes', which are measured indirectly through responses over which the individual has little or no control. This terminology has been imported from cognitive psychology. As you will remember, explicit memory is characterized by a person's conscious recollection of facts or events. In contrast, implicit memory effects are said to occur when previous experience facilitates our performance of subsequent tasks without us remembering the previous experience or being aware of its influence on our performance (chapter 3, this volume; Schacter et al., 1993).

5   Cards treated with a microfragrance coating that releases the fragrance when scratched. These cards can be inserted in magazines. Used for example in the advertising of perfume brands.

6   Although Bertolli sauce is imported from Italy, Bertolli is actually a brand of Unilever. The pasta sauce is an example of successful brand extension, because Bertolli was originally only a producer of olive oil.

7   By systematically attaching the adjective 'on occasion' to questions about pro-religious behaviour and 'frequently' to questions about anti-religious behaviour, these authors increased the frequency of reported pro- and decreased the frequency of reported anti-religious behaviour.

8   As we will discuss in chapter 6, Fishbein and Ajzen (1975) later integrated this expectancy-value conception of attitude as one of two predictors of behavioural intentions into their theory of reasoned action, which became the most prominent model for the prediction of behaviour in social psychology. According to this theory, the intention to perform a specific action is determined by an individual's attitude towards performing this action and by the individual's beliefs about how other people, who are important to her, expect her to act (subjective norms).

9   Since in those days researchers subsumed evaluation under the term 'affect', his theory became known as 'affective-cognitive consistency theory'. We will use the more appropriate term of 'evaluative-cognitive consistency'.

10   Maio and colleagues used a measure of structural ambivalence and did not assess experienced ambivalence. One would have expected these effects to be even stronger, if a measure of experienced ambivalence had been used.

11   Instead of instrumentality x value products, one could also use the more general belief x value products of the theory of Fishbein and Ajzen (1975; Σ $b_i e_i$).

12   Unfortunately, we have no direct information on the assumed processing differences, because Kang and Herr (2006) neither manipulated argument quality nor used a thought-listing measure to assess mode processing.

13   This last finding is actually unexpected and puzzling. While impression-motivated participants should use physical attractiveness as relevant information under high processing motivation, they should have used it as heuristic cue under low processing motivation.

14   From 1921 to the mid-1970s, Listerine was also marketed as prevention and remedy for colds and sore throats, but in 1976 the US Federal Trade Commission ruled that this claim was misleading and deceptive. Listerine had to include

a corrective statement in the next $10 million of Listerine advertisements. When the Warner-Lambert Company appealed against this decision, the United States Court of Appeals for the District of Columbia Circuit upheld this ruling in 1977 (LexisNexis Academic). This court experience did not prevent the company, which in the meantime had been taken over by Pfizer Inc., from claiming in its advertisements some years later that Listerine mouthwash was 'as effective as floss' in preventing plaque and gum disease. In 2005, a Manhattan Federal Judge ruled that these claims were false and could mislead consumers into thinking that using mouthwash could replace flossing (Lin, 2005). The final irony is that this court case against Pfizer was brought by a subsidiary of Johnson and Johnson, the nation's largest producer of dental floss, who bought the Listerine brand from Pfizer in 2006.

15   Although the authors explain these results in terms of evaluative conditioning, an alternative explanation could be based on balance theory (Heider, 1946). Balance theory is concerned with the consistency in the relations a person perceives between him/herself, other individuals and objects. According to Heider, the perception of such relations will tend towards a balanced state. A situation is balanced, if I likes the objects owned by a person one likes or dislikes the objects owned by a person one dislikes. A situation would be imbalanced, if a person one liked owned an object I disliked or if a person one disliked owned an object one liked. Thus, by disliking the brand worn by the disliked actor or liking the brand worn by the liked actor, participants created a balanced state in their perceptions.

16   To assess habit strength in the use of travel modes (e.g. car, bus, bicycle, and aeroplane) with the RF, research participants were presented with a number of locations for trips and had to indicate how they would travel to these locations. Habit strength for a given mode of travel was reflected by the proportion of times this mode had been chosen.

17   Although priming effects are mostly modality specific, there appear to be exceptions. A recent study by Berry, Banbury and Henry (1997) showed nearly perfect transfer of visual priming to auditory tests. Berry and colleagues further demonstrated that this asymmetry was due to the fact that participants subvocally rehearsed the visual stimuli. When rehearsal was suppressed through methods of articulatory suppression, transfer was impaired. It is questionable, however, whether these findings with supraliminal primes are also applicable to subliminal primes. It seems unlikely that participants can engage in subvocal rehearsal of prime words presented so briefly that they have been unable to read them.

References

Aaker, J.L. (1997). Dimensions of brand personality. *Journal of Marketing Research*, *34*, 347–356.

Aarts, H., & Dijksterhuis, A. (2000). Habits as knowledge structures: Automaticity in goal-directed behavior. *Journal of Personality and Social Psychology*, *78*, 53–63.

Aarts, H., & Dijskterhuis, A. (2003). The silence of the library: Environment, situational norm, and social behavior. *Journal of Personality and Social Psychology*, *84*, 18–28.

Aarts, H., Dijksterhuis, A., & Midden, K. (1998). To plan or not to plan? Goal achievement or interrupting the performance of mundane behaviors. *European Journal of Social Psychology*, *29*, 971–979.

Abelson, R. (1981). The psychological status of the script concept. *American Psychologist*, *36*, 715–729.

Abernethy, A.M., & Franke, G.R. (1996). The information content of advertising: A meta-analysis. *Journal of Advertising*, *25*, 1–17.

Achtziger, A., Gollwitzer, P.M. & Sheeran, P. (2008). Implementation intentions and shielding goal striving from unwanted thoughts and feelings. *Personality and Social Psychology Bulletin*, *34*, 381–393.

Adolphs, R. (2009). The social brain: Neural basis of social knowledge. *Annual Review of Psychology*, *60*, 693–716.

Adriaanse, M.A., de Ridder, D.T.D., & de Wit, J. (2009). Finding the critical cue: Implementation intentions to change one's diet work best when tailored to personally relevant reasons for unhealthy eating. *Personality and Social Psychology Bulletin*, *35*, 60–71.

Ajzen, I. (2005). *Attitudes, Personality and Behavior* (2nd edn) Maidenhead, UK: Open University Press.

Ajzen, I., & Fishbein, M. (1977). Attitude-behavior relations: A theoretical analysis and review of empirical research. *Psychological Bulletin*, *84*, 888–918.

Ajzen, I., & Fishbein, M. (2000). Attitudes and the attitude-behavior relation: Reasoned and automatic processes. In W. Stroebe & M. Hewstone (Eds.), *European Review of Social Psychology* (Vol. 11, pp. 1–33). Chichester: Wiley.

Ajzen, I., & Fishbein, M. (2005). The influence of attitudes on behavior. In D. Albarracin, B.T. Johnson, & M.P. Zanna (Eds.), *The Handbook of Attitudes* (pp. 173–222). Mahwah: Erlbaum.

Ajzen, I., & Timko, C. (1986). Correspondence between health attitudes and behavior. *Basic and Applied Social Psychology, 7,* 259–276.

Albarracin, D., Johnson, B.T., Fishbein, M. & Muellerleile, P.A. (2001). Theories of reasoned action and planned behavior as model of condom use: A meta-analysis. *Psychological Bulletin, 127,* 142–161.

Alden, S.L., Mukherjee, A., & Hoyer, W.D. (2000). The effects of incongruity, surprise, and positive moderators on perceived humor in television advertising. *Journal of Advertising, 29,* 1–15.

Allen, C.T., Schewe, C.D., & Wijk, G. (1980). More on self-perception theory's foot technique in the pre-call/mail survey setting. *Journal of Marketing Research, 17,* 498–502.

Allison, R.I., & Uhl, K.P. (1964). Influence of beer brand identification on taste perception. *Journal of Marketing Research, 1,* 36–39.

Allport, G.W. (1935). Attitudes. In C. Murchison (Ed.), *Handbook of Social Psychology* (pp. 798–884). Worchester, MA: Clark University Press.

Allport, G.W. (1961). *Patterns and Growth in Personality.* New York: Holt, Rinehart & Winston.

Alwin, D.F., Cohen, R.L., & Newcomb, T. (1991). *Political Attitudes over a Life-span: The Bennington Women After Fifty Years.* Madison: Madison University Press.

Andrews, J.C., & Shimp, T.A. (1990). Effects of involvement, argument strength, and source characteristics on central and peripheral processing of advertising. *Psychology and Marketing, 7* (3), 195–214.

Appleton-Knapp, S.L., Bjork, R.A., & Wickens, T.D. (2005). Examining the spacing effect in advertising: Encoding variability, retrieval processes, and their interaction. *Journal of Consumer Research, 32,* 266–276.

Areni, C.S., & Lutz, R.J. (1988). The role of argument quality in the elaboration likelihood model. *Advances in Consumer Research, 15,* 197–203.

Armitage, C.J., & Conner, M. (2000). Attitudinal ambivalence: A test of three key hypotheses. *Personality and Social Psychology Bulletin, 26,* 1421–1432.

Armitage, C.J., & Conner, M. (2001). Efficacy of the theory of planned behaviour. *British Journal of Social Psychology, 40,* 471–499.

Arndt, J., & Simon, J. (1983). Advertising and economies of scale: Critical comments on the evidence. *Journal of Industrial Economics, 32* (2), 229–241.

Arndt, J., Solomon, S., Kasser, T., & Sheldon, K.M. (2004). The urge to splurge revisited: further reflection on applying terror management theory to materialism and consumer behavior. *Journal of Consumer Psychology, 14,* 225–229.

Atkinson, R.C., & Shiffrin, R.M. (1968). Human memory: a proposed system and its control processes. In K.W. Spence & J.T. Spence (Eds.), *The Psychology of Learning and Motivation: Advances in Research and Theory* (pp. 89–195). New York: Academic Press.

Baddeley, A. (1966). Short-term memory for word sequences as a function of acoustic, semantic and formal similarity. *Quarterly Journal of Experimental Psychology, 18,* 362–365.

Baddeley, A. (1997). *Human Memory.* Brighton: Psychology Press.

Baddeley, A. (2000). The episodic buffer: a new component of working memory? *Trends in Cognitive Science, 11,* 417–423.

Baddeley, A. (2001). Is working memory still working? *European Psychologist, 7,* 85–97.

Baddeley, A. (2002). *Human Memory: Theory and Practice.* Hove, UK: Psychology Press.

Baddeley, A., & Hitch, G. (1974). Working memory. In G.A. Bower (Eds.), *Recent Advances in Learning and Motivation* (pp. 47–90), Vol 8. New York: Academic Press.

Baddeley, A., & Warrington, E.K. (1970). Amnesia and the distinction between long- and short-term memory. *Journal of Verbal Learning and Verbal Behavior, 9,* 176–189.

Baddeley, A.D., Thompson, N., & Buchanan, M. (1975). Word length and the structure of short-term memory. *Journal of Verbal Learning and Verbal Behavior, 14*, 575–589.

Baeyens, F., Crombez, G., Van den Bergh, O., & Eelen, P. (1988). Once in contact, always in contact: Evaluative conditioning is resistant to extinction. *Advances in Behaviour Research and Therapy, 10*, 179–199.

Bargh, J. A. (1984). Automatic and conscious processing of social information. In R.S. Wyer, Jr., & T.K. Srull (Eds.), *Handbook of Social Cognition* (Vol. 3, pp. 1–43). Hillsdale, NJ: Erlbaum.

Bargh, J.A. (1994). The four horsemen of automaticity: Awareness, intention, efficiency, and control in social cognition. In R.S. Wyer & T.K. Srull (Eds.), *Handbook of Social Cognition* (Vol. 1. Basic Processes; 2nd edn, pp. 1–40). Mahwah: Erlbaum.

Bargh, J.A. (2002). Losing consciousness: Automatic influences on consumer judgment, behavior, and motivation. *Journal of Consumer Research, 29 (September)*, 280–285.

Bargh, J. (2006). What have we been priming all these years? *European Journal of Social Psychology, 36*, 147–169.

Bargh, J.A. (Ed.). (2007). *Social Psychology and the Unconscious: The Automaticity of Higher Mental Processes*. New York: Psychology Press.

Bargh, J.A., Chaiken, S., Govender, R., & Pratto, F. (1992). The generality of the automatic attitude activation effect. *Journal of Personality and Social Psychology, 62*, 893–912.

Bargh, J.A., & Chartrand, T.L. (2000). The mind in the middle: A practical guide to priming and automaticity research. In H. Reis & C. Judd (Eds.), *Handbook of Research Methods in Social and Personality Psychology* (pp. 253–285). New York: Cambridge University Press.

Bargh, J.A.. Gollwitzer, P.M., Lee Chai, A., Barndollar, K. & Trötschel, R. (2001). The automated will: Non-conscious activation and pursuit of behavioural goals. *Journal of Personality and Social Psychology, 81*, 1014–1027.

Bargh, J., & Pietromonaco, P. (1982). Automatic information processing and social perception: The influence of trait information presented outside of conscious awareness on impression formation. *Journal of Personality and Social Psychology, 49*, 1129–1146.

Baron, R.M., & Kenny, D.A. (1986). The moderator-mediator variable distinction in social psychological research: Conceptual, strategic, and statistical considerations. *Journal of Personality and Social Psychology, 51* (6), 1173–1182.

Barone M.J., Miniard P.W., & Romeo J. (2000). The influence of positive mood on brand extension evaluations. *Journal of Consumer Research, 26*, 386–400.

Barry, T.E., & Howard, D.J. (1990). A review and critique of the hierarchy of effects in advertising. *International Journal of Advertising, 9*, 121–135.

Bassili, J.N. (1996). Meta-Judgmental versus operative indices of psychological properties: The case of measures of attitude strength. *Journal of Personality and Social Psychology, 71*, 637–653.

Bassili, J.N., & Fletcher, J.F. (1991). Response-time measurement in survey research: A method for CATI and a look at non-attitudes. *Public Opinion Quarterly, 55*, 331–346.

Basu, A.K., Basu, A., & Batra, R. (1995). Modeling the response pattern to direct marketing campaigns. *Journal of Marketing Research, 32*, 204–212.

Batra, R., & Ray, M. (1985). How advertising works at contact. In L.F. Alwitt & A.A. Mitchell (Eds.), *Psychological Processes and Advertising Effects* (pp. 13–44). Hillsdale, NJ: Erlbaum.

Baumeister, R.F., Bratslavsky, E., Muraven, M., & Tice, D.M. (1998). Ego depletion: Is the active self a limited resource? *Journal of Personality and Social Psychology, 74*, 1252–1265.

Beard, F.K. (2005). One hundred years of humor in American advertising. *Journal of Macromarketing, 25*, 54–65.

Bearden, W.O., & Etzel, M.J. (1982). Reference group influence on product and brand purchase decisions. *Journal of Consumer Research, 9*, 183–194.

Belch, G.E., & Belch, M.A. (2004). Advertising and promotion management: An integrated marketing communications perspective (6th edn). Boston: Irwin.

Bem, D.J. (1965). An experimental analysis of self-persuasion. *Journal of Experimental Social Psychology, 1*, 199–218.

Bem, D.J. (1972). Self-perception theory. In L. Berkowitz (Ed.), *Advances in Experimental Social Psychology* (Vol. 6, pp. 1–62). New York: Academic Press.

Berg, K.E. (1966). Ethnic attitudes and agreement with a Negro person. *Journal of Personality and Social Psychology, 4*, 215–220.

Bermeitinger, C., Goelz, R., Johr, N., Neumann, M., Ecker, U.K.H., & Doerr, R. (2009). The hidden persuaders break into the tired brain. *Journal of Experimental Social Psychology, 45*, 320-326.

Bernberg, R.E. (1952). Socio-psychological factors in industrial morale: I. The prediction of specific indicators. *Journal of Social Psychology, 36*, 73–82

Berry, D.C., Banbury, S., & Henry, L. (1997). Transfer across form and modality in implicit and explicit memory. *The Quarterly Journal of Experimental Psychology A: Human Experimental Psychology. 50*, 1–24.

Bessenoff, G.R., & Sherman, J.W. (2000). Automatic and controlled components of prejudice toward fat people: evaluation versus stereotype activation. *Social Cognition, 18,* 329–353.

Bierbrauer, G., Meyer, H., & Wolfradt, U. (1994). Measurement of normative and evaluative aspects in individualistic and collectivistic orientations: The Cultural Orientation Scale (COS). In U. Kim, H.Triandis, C. Kagitcibasi, S.–C. Choi, & G. Yoon (Eds.), *Individualism and collectivism: Theory, method, and applications* (pp. 189–194). Thousand Oaks, CA: Sage.

Bierley, C., McSweeney, F.K., & Vannieuwkerk, R. (1985). Classical conditioning of preferences for stimuli. *Journal of Consumer Research, 12*, 316–323.

Bishop, G.F. (1990). Issue involvement and response effects in public opinion surveys. *Public Opinion Quarterly, 54*, 209–218.

Biswas, D., Biswas, A., & Chatterjee, S. (2009). Making judgments in a two-sequence cue environment. The effects of differential cue strength, order sequence and distraction. *Journal of Consumer Psychology, 19*, 88–97.

Bizer, G.Y., & Krosnick, J.A. (2001). Exploring the structure of strength-related attitude features: The relation between attitude importance and attitude accessibility. *Journal of Personality and Social Psychology, 81*, 566–586.

Blair, M.H., & Rabuck, M.J. (1998). Advertising wearin and wearout: Ten years later – more empirical evidence and successful practice. *Journal of Advertising Research, 38* (5), 7–18.

Blankenship, A.B., & Whitely, P.L. (1941). Proactive inhibition in the recall of advertising material. *Journal of Social Psychology, 13*, 311–322.

Blanton, H., & Jaccard, J. (2006). Arbitrary metrics in psychology. *American Psychologist, 61* (1), 27–41.

Blanton, H., Jaccard, J., & Christie, C. (2007). Plausible assumptions, questionable assumptions, and post hoc rationalizations: Will the real IAT, please stand up? *Journal of Experimental Social Psychology, 43* (3), 399–409.

Bless, H., Bohner, G., Schwarz, N., & Strack, F. (1990) Mood and persuasion: a cognitive response analysis. *Personality and Social Psychology Bulletin, 16*, 331–345.

Bless, H., Fiedler, K., & Strack, F. (2004). *Social Cognition: How Individuals Construct Social Reality*. Hove: Psychology Press.

Bless, H., & Wänke, M. (2000). Can the same information be typical and atypical? How perceived typicality moderates assimilation and contrast in evaluative judgment. *Personality and Social Psychology Bulletin, 26*, 306–314.

Blüher, R., & Pahl, S. (2007). Der 'mere-exposure' Effekt und die Wahl von Produkten. [The mere-exposure effect and product choice]. *Zeitschrift für Sozialpsychologie, 38*, 209–215.

Bogardus, E.S. (1931). *Fundamentals of Social Psychology* (2nd edn). New York: Century.

Bray, D.W. (1950). The prediction of behavior from two attitude scales. *Journal of Abnormal and Social Psychology, 45,* 64–84.

Bohner, G., Moskowitz, G., & Chaiken, S. (1995). The interplay of heuristic and systematic processing of social information. In W. Stroebe & M. Hewstone (Eds.), *European Review of Social Psychology, 6,* 33–68.

Bolton, L.E., & Reed, A. II (2004). Sticky prior: The perseverance of identity effects on judgments. *Journal of Marketing Research, 41,* 397–411.

Bone, P.F., & Ellen, P.S. (1992). The generation and consequences of communication-evoked imagery. *Journal of Consumer Research, 19,* 93–104.

Boninger, D.S., Krosnick, J.A., Berent, M.K., & Fabrigar, L.R. (1995). The causes and consequences of attitude importance. In R.E. Petty & J.A. Krosnick (Eds.), *Attitude Strength: Antecedents and Consequences* (pp. 159–190). Mahwah, NJ: Erlbaum.

Bornstein, R.F. (1989). Exposure and affects: Overview and meta-analysis of research 1968–1987. *Psychological Bulletin, 106,* 265–289.

Bornstein, R.F., & D'Agostino, P.R. (1994). The attribution and discounting of perceptual fluency: Preliminary tests of a perceptual fluency/attribution model of the mere exposure effect. *Social Cognition, 12,* 113–148.

Bottomley, P.H., & Holden, S.J.S. (2001). Do we really know how consumers evaluate brand extensions? Empirical generalizations based on secondary analysis of eight studies. *Journal of Marketing Research, 38,* 494–500.

Bower, G.H. (2000). A brief history of memory research. In E. Tulving & F.I.M. Craik (Eds.), *Handbook of Memory Research* (pp. 3–32). New York: Oxford University Press.

Brannon, L.A., & Brock, T.C. (1998). *Scarcity claims elicit extreme responding to persuasive messages: Role of cognitive elaboration.* Unpublished manuscript.

Brannon, L.A., & Brock, T.C. (2001). Limiting time for responding enhances behavior corresponding to the merits of compliance: Refutations of heuristic-cue theory in service and consumer settings. *Journal of Consumer Psychology, 10,* 135–146.

Bransford, J.D., Franks, J.J., Morris, C.D., & Stein, B.S. (1979). Some general constrainst on learning an memory research. In L.S. Cermak & F.I.M Craik (Eds.), *Levels of Processing in Human Memory* (pp. 331–354). Hillsdale, NJ: Erlbaum.

Braun, K.A. (1999). Postexperience advertising effects on consumer memory. *Journal of Consumer Research, 25,* 319–334.

Braun-LaTour, K.A., & LaTour, M. (2005). Transforming consumer experience: When timing matters. *Journal of Advertising, 34,* 19–30.

Brehm, J.W. (1966). *A Theory of Psychological Reactance.* New York: Academic Press.

Brendl, M.C., Chattopadhyay, A., Pelham, B.W., & Carvallo, M. (2005). Name letter branding: Valence transfers when product specific needs are active. *Journal of Consumer Research, 32,* 405–415.

Briñol, P., & Petty, R.E. (2009) Source factors in persuasion: A self-validation approach. In W. Stroebe & M. Hewstone (Eds.), *European Review of Social Psychology, 20,* 49–96.

Briñol, P., Petty, R.E., & Tormala, Z.L. (2004). Self-validation of cognitive responses to advertisements. *Journal of Consumer Research, 30,* 559–573.

Britt, S., Adams, S.C., & Miller, A.S. (1972). How many advertising exposures per day? *Journal of Advertising Research, 12,* 3–9.

Broadbent, D.E. (1958). *Perception and Communication.* London: Pergamon Press.

Brock, T.C. (1968). Implications of commodity theory for value change. In A. Greenwald, T.C. Brock & T.M. Ostrom (Eds.), *Psychological Foundations of Attitudes* (pp. 243–276). New York: Academic.

Brown, S.P., & Stayman, D.M. (1992). Antecedents and consequences of attitude toward the ad: A meta-analysis. *Journal of Consumer Research, 19,* 34–51.

Brunel, F.F., Tietje, B.C., & Greenwald, A.G. (2004). Is the implicit association test a valid and valuable measure of implicit consumer social cognition? *Journal of Consumer Psychology, 14* (4), 385–404.

Bruner, J.S. (1957). On perceptual readiness. *Psychological Review, 64*, 123–152.

Burger, J.M. (1986). Increasing compliance by improving the deal: The That's-Not-All technique. *Journal of Personality and Social Psychology, 51*, 277–283.

Burger, J.M. (1999). The Foot-in-the-Door compliance procedure: A multiple process analysis and review. *Personality and Social Psychology Review, 3* (4), 303–325.

Burger, J.M., & Cornelius, T. (2003). Raising the price of agreement: Public commitment and the lowball compliance procedure. *Journal of Basic and Applied Social Psychology, 33*, 923–934.

Burger, J.M., Messian, N., Patel, S., del Prado, A., & Anderson, C. (2004). What a coincidence: The effects of incidental similarity on compliance. *Personality and Social Psychology Bulletin, 30*, 35–43.

Burger, J.M., & Petty, R.E. (1981). The lowball compliance technique: Task or person commitment? *Journal of Personality and Social Psychology, 40*, 492–500.

Burger, J.M., Soroka, S., Gonzago, K., Murphy, E., & Somervell, E. (2001). The effect of fleeting attraction on compliance to requests. *Personality and Social Psychology Bulletin, 27*, 1578–1586.

Burke, R.R., & Srull, T.K. (1988). Competitive interference and consumer memory for advertising. *Journal of Consumer Research, 15*, 55–68.

Burnkrant, R.E., & Unnava, H.R. (1995). Effects of self-referencing on persuasion. *Journal of Consumer Research, 22*, 17–26.

Buss, D.M. (1999). *Evolutionary Psychology: The New Science of the Mind*. Boston: Allyn and Bacon.

Byrne, D. (1971). *The attraction paradigm*. New York: Academic Press.

Cacioppo, J.T., Gardner, W.L., & Berntson, G.G. (1997). Beyond bipolar conceptualizations and measures. The case of attitudes and evaluative space. *Personality and Social Psychology Review, 1*, 3–25.

Cacioppo, J., & Petty, R. (1979). Effects of message repetition and position on cognitive response, recall and persuasion. *Journal of Personality and Social Psychology, 37*, 97–109.

Cacioppo, J., & Petty, R.E. (1982). The need for cognition. *Journal of Personality and Social Psychology, 42*, 116–131.

Cacioppo, J., & Petty, R. (1989). Effects of message repetition on argument processing, recall, and persuasion. *Basic and Applied Social Psychology, 10*, 3–12.

Cacioppo, J.T., Petty, R.E., Feinstein, J., & Jarvis, B. (1996). Individual differences in cognitive motivation: The life and times of people varying in need for cognition. *Psychological Bulletin, 119*, 197–253.

Campbell, D.T., & Stanley, J.C. (1963). *Experimental and quasi-experimental designs for research*. Boston, MA: Houghton, Mifflin and Company.

Campbell, M.C., & Goodstein, R.C. (2001). The moderating effect of perceived risk on consumers' evaluations of product incongruity: Preference for the norm. *Journal of Consumer Research, 28*, 439–449.

Campbell, M.C., & Kirmani., A. (2000). Consumers' use of persuasion knowledge: The effect of accessibility and cognitive capacity on perceptions of an influence agent. *Journal of Consumer Research, 27*, 69–83.

Carlston, D.E. (1980). The recall and use of traits and events in social inference process. *Journal of Experimental Social Psychology, 16*, 303–328.

Carpenter, G.S., & Nakamoto, K. (1989). Consumer preference formation and pioneering advantage. *Journal of Marketing Research, 26*, 285–298.

Carpenter, G.S., & Nakamoto, K. (1996). Impact of consumer preference formation on marketing objectives and second mover strategies. *Journal of Consumer Psychology, 5*, 325–358.

Castriott-Scanderbeg, A., Hagberg, G.E., Ceresa, A., Committeri, G., Galati, G., Patria, F. et al. (2005). The appreciation of wine by sommeliers: A functional magnetic resonance study of sensory integration. *NeuroImage, 25,* 570–578.

Celsi, R.L., & Olson, J.C. (1988). The role of involvement in attention and comprehension processes. *Journal of Consumer Research, 15,* 210–224.

Chaiken, S. (1980). Heuristic versus systematic information processing and the use of source versus message cues in persuasion. *Journal of Personality and Social Psychology, 39,* 752–766.

Chaiken, S., & Baldwin, M. (1981). Affective-cognitive consistency and the effect of salient behavioral information on the self-perception of attitudes. *Journal of Personality and Social Psychology, 41,* 1–12.

Chaiken, S., & Maheswaran, D. (1994). Heuristic processing can bias systematic processing: Effects of source credibility, argument ambiguity, and task importance on attitude judgment. *Journal of Personality and Social Psychology, 66,* 460–473.

Chaiken, S., Liberman, A., & Eagly, A.H. (1989). Heuristic and systematic processing within and beyond the persuasion context. In J.S. Uleman & J.A. Bargh (Eds.), *Unintended Thought* (pp. 212–252). New York: Guilford.

Chaiken, S., & Pomerantz, E.M. (1992). Structural consistency and temporal stability. Unpublished raw data.

Chaiken, S., Pomerantz, E.M., & Giner-Sorolla, R. (1995). Structural consistency and attitude stregth. In R.E. Petty & J.A. Krosnick (Eds.), *Attitude Strength: Antecedents and Consequences* (pp. 387–412). Mahwah, NJ: Erlbaum.

Chaiken, S. & Trope, Y. (Eds.). (1999). *Dual Process Theories in Social Psychology.* New York: Guilford.

Chartrand, T.L., Huber, J., Shiv, B., & Tanner, R.J. (2008). Nonconscious goals and consumer choice. *Journal of Consumer Research, 35,* 189–201.

Chen, S., & Chaiken, S. (1999). The heuristic-systematic model in its broader context. In S. Chaiken & Y. Trope (Eds.), *Dual Process Theories in Social Psychology* (pp. 73–97). New York: Guilford.

Chen, H.C., Reardon, R., Rea, C., & Moore, D.J. (1992). Forewarning of content and involvement: Consequences for persuasion and resistance to persuasion. *Journal of Experimental Social Psychology, 28,* 523–541.

Cialdini, R.B. (1976). Basking in reflected glory: Three (football) field studies. *Journal of Personality and Social Psychology, 34,* 366–375.

Cialdini, R.B. (1984). *Influence: The New Psychology of Modern Persuasion.* New York: Quill.

Cialdini, R.B. (1993). *Influence: Science and practice* (3rd edn). New York: HarperCollins.

Cialdini, R.B. (2009). *Influence: Science and Practice* (5th edn). Boston: Allyn and Bacon.

Cialdini, R.B., Cacioppo, J.T., Bassett, R., & Miller, J.A. (1978). Lowball procedure for producing compliance: Commitment then cost. *Journal of Personality and Social Psychology, 36,* 463–76.

Cialdini, R.B., & Goldstein, N.J. (2004). Social influence: Compliance and conformity. *Annual Review of Psychology, 55,* 591–621.

Cialdini, R.B., & Sagarin, B.J. (2005). Principles of interpersonal influence. In T.C. Brock & M.C. Green (Eds.), *Persuasion: Psychological Insights and Perspectives* (pp.143–171). Thousand Oaks, CA: Sage.

Cialdini, R.B., & Trost, M. (1998). Social influence: Social norms, conformity, and compliance. In D.T. Gilbert, S.T. Fiske, & G. Lindzey (Eds.), *The Handbook of Social Psychology,* (pp. 151–192).

Cialdini, R.B., Trost, M., & Newsom, J.T. (1995). Preference for consistency: The development of a valid measure and the discovery of surprising behavioral implications. *Journal of Personality and Social Psychology, 69,* 318–328.

Cialdini, R.B., Vincent, J.E., Lewis, S.K., Catalan, J., Wheeler, D., & Darby, B.L. (1975). Reciprocal concessions procedure for inducing compliance: The door-in-the-face technique. *Journal of Personality and Social Psychology, 31* (2), 206–215.

Cialdini, R.B., Wosinska, W., Barrett, D.W., Butner, J., & Gornik-Durose, M. (1999). Compliance with a request in two cultures: The differential influence of social proof and commitment/consistency on collectivists and individualists. *Personality and Social Psychology Bulletin, 25* (10), 1242–1253.

Clarkson, J. (2007). Volkswagen Phaeton: All the luxury you need but no Pizzazz. Times Online. Accessed February 2009. http://www.timesonline.co.uk/tol/driving/jeremy_clarkson/article2837650.ece

Claypool, H.M., Mackie, D.M., Garcia/Marques, T., McIntosh, A., & Udall, A. (2004). The effects of personal relevance and repetition on persuasive processing. *Social Cognition, 22,* 310–335.

Clore, G.L., Schwarz, N., & Conway, M. (1994). Cognitive causes and consequences of emotions. In R.S. Wyer, & T.K. Srull (Eds.), *Handbook of Social Cognition* (2nd edn, Vol. 1, pp. 323–417). Hillsdale, NJ: Lawrence Erlbaum.

Coates, S.L., Butler, L.T., & Berry, D.C. (2004) Implicit memory: A prime example for brand consideration and choice. *Applied Cognitive Psychology, 18,* 1195–1211.

Colley, R.H. (1961). *Defining Advertising Goals for Measured Advertising Results.* New York: Association of National Advertisers.

Collins, A.M., & Loftus, E.F. (1975). A spreading-activation theory of semantic processing. *Psychological Review, 82,* 407–428.

Conner, M. & Norman, P. (Eds.) (2005). *Predicting Health Behaviour* (2nd edn). Maidenhead: Open University Press.

Conrad, M.A., & Hull, A.J. (1964). Information, acoustic confusion and memory span. *British Journal of Psychology, 55,* 429–432.

Cooper, J., & Cooper, G. (2002). Subliminal motivation: A story revisited. *Journal of Applied Social Psychology, 32,* 2213–2227.

Corey, S.M. (1937). Professed attitudes and actual behavior. *Journal of Educational Psychology, 28,* 271–280.

Cornwell, T.B., Humphreys, M.S., Maguire, A.M., Weeks, C.S., & Tellegen, C.L. (2006). Sponsorship-linked marketing: the role of articulation in memory. *Journal of Consumer Research, 33,* 312–321.

Cowley, R., & Barron, C. (2008). When product placement goes wrong: The effects of program liking and placement prominence. *Journal of Advertising, 37,* 89–98.

Cowley, E., & Janus, E. (2004). Not necessarily better, but certainly different: A limit to the advertising misinformation effect on memory. *Journal of Consumer Research, 32,* 229–235.

Craik, F.I.M. (2002). Levels of processing: Past, present . . . and future? *Memory, 10,* 305–318.

Craik, F.I.M., & Lockhart, R.S. (1972). Levels of processing: a framework for memory research. *Journal of Verbal Learning and Verbal Behavior, 11,* 671–684.

Craik, F.I.M., & Tulving, E. (1975). Depth of processing and the retention of words in episodic memory. *Journal of Experimental Psychology: General, 104,* 268–294.

Cronley, M.L., Posavac, S.S., Meyer, T., Kardes, F.R., & Kellaris, J.J. (2005). A selective hypothesis testing perspective on price quality inference and inference-based choice. *Journal of Consumer Psychology, 15,* 159–169.

Crowley, A.E. & Hoyer, W.D. (1994). An integrative framework for understanding two-sided persuasion. *Journal of Consumer Research, 20,* 561–574.

Custers, R., & Aarts, H. (2005). Beyond priming effects: The role of positive affect and discrepancies in implicit processes of motivation and goal pursuit. In W. Stroebe & M. Hewstone

(Eds.), *European Review of Social Psychology* (Vol. 16, pp. 257–300). Hove: Psychology Press.

Das, E., de Wit, J., & Stroebe, W. (2003). Fear appeals motivate acceptance of action recommendations: Evidence for positive bias in the processing of persuasive messages. *Personality and Social Psychology Bulletin, 29,* 650–664.

Dasgupta, D., Greenwald, A.G., & Banaji, M.R. (2003). The first ontological challenge to the IAT: Attitude or mere familiarity? *Psychological Inquiry, 14,* 238–243.

Davis, B.P., & Knowles, E.S. (1999). A disrupt-then-reframe technique of social influence. *Journal of Personality and Social Psychology, 76* (2), 192–199.

Dawes, R.M. (1994). *House of Cards: Psychology and Psychotherapy Built on Myth.* New York: Free Press.

DeBono, K. (2006). Self-monitoring and consumer psychology. *Journal of Personality, 74,* 715–735.

DeBono, K.G., & Harnish, R.J. (1988). Source expertise, source attractiveness, and the processing of persuasive information: A functional approach. *Journal of Personality and Social Psychology, 55,* 541–546.

DeBono, K., Leavitt, A., & Backus, J. (2003). Product packaging and product evaluation: An individual difference approach. *Journal of Applied Social Psychology, 33,* 513–521.

DeBono, K.G., & Rubin, K. (1995). Country of origin and perceptions of product quality: An individual difference perspective. *Basic and Applied Social Psychology, 17,* 239–247.

De Houwer, J., Thomas, S., & Baeyens, F. (2001). Associative learning of likes and dislikes: A review of 25 years of research on human evaluative conditioning. *Psychological Bulletin, 127,* 853–869.

De Houwer, J., Hendrickx, H., & Baeyens, F. (1997). Evaluative learning with 'subliminally' presented stimuli. *Consciousness and Cognition, 6,* 87–107.

De Hoog, N., Stroebe, W., & DeWit, J. (2005) The impact of fear appeals on processing and accepting action recommendations. *Personality and Social Psychology Bulletin, 31,* 24–33.

De Hoog, N., Stroebe, W., & de Wit, J. (2007) The impact of vulnerability to and severity of a health risk on processing and acceptance of fear-arousing communications: A meta-analysis. *Review of General Psychology, 11,* 258–285.

De Hoog, N., Stroebe, W., & DeWit, J. (2008) The processing of fear-arousing communications: How biased processing leads to persuasion. *Social Influence, 3,* 84–113.

De Liver, Y., van der Pligt, J., & Wigboldus, D. (2006). Under pressure: Effects of integration goal and cognitive load on the experience of attitudinal conflict. *Journal of Experimental Social Psychology.*

DePelsmacker, P., Geuens, M., & van den Bergh, J. (2001). *Marketing Communications.* Harlow: Pearson.

Devine, P.G. (1989). Stereotypes and prejudice: Their automatic and controlled components. *Journal of Personality and Social Psychology, 56,* 680–690.

Dhar, R., Huber, J., & Khan, U. (2007). The shopping momentum effect. *Journal of Marketing Research, 44,* 370–378.

Dhar, S.K., & Hoch, S.J. (1996). Price discrimination using in-store merchandising. *Journal of Marketing, 60,* 17–30.

Dijksterhuis, A., Aarts, H., & Smith, P. (2005). The power of the subliminal: On subliminal persuasion and other potential applications. In R.R. Hassin, J.S. Uleman, & J.A. Bargh, *The New Unconscious* (pp. 77–106). New York: Oxford University Press.

Dijksterhuis, A., Wegner, D.M., & Aarts, H. (2001). Unpublished data set described in Dijksterhuis, Aarts, & Smith (2005).

Dion, K., Berscheid, E., & Walster, E. (1972). What is beautiful is good. *Journal of Personality and Social Psychology, 24,* 285–290.

Ditto, P.H., & Lopez, D.F. (1992). Motivated skepticism: Use of differential decision criteria for preferred and nonpreferred conclusions. *Journal of Personality and Social Psychology, 63,* 568–584.

Doll, J., & Ajzen, I. (1992). Accessibility and stability of predictors in the theory of planned behavior. *Journal of Personality and Social Psychology, 63,* 754–765.

Dovidio, J.F., Gaertner, S.L., & Saguy, T. (2007). Another view of 'we': Majority and minority group perspectives on a common ingroup identity. In W. Stroebe, & M. Hewstone (Eds.), *European Review of Social Psychology, 18,* 296–330.

Dovidio, J.F., Kawakami, K., & Beach, K.R. (2001). Implicit and explicit attitudes: Examination of the relationship. In R. Brown & S. Gaertner (Eds.), *Blackwell Handbook of Social Psychology* (pp. 175–197). Oxford, UK: Blackwell.

Dovidio, J.F., Kawakami, K., Johnson, C., Johnson, B., & Howards, A. (1997). The nature of prejudice: Automatic and controlled processes. *Journal of Experimental Social Psychology, 33,* 510–540.

Downey, K. (2002). Media Life, April 5. http://www.Medialifemagazine.com/news2002/apr01/5_fri/new2friday.html (accessed January 2007).

Dutka, S. (1995). *DAGMAR: Defining Advertising Goals for Measured Advertising Results.* Lincolnwood, IL: Business Books.

D'Ydewalle, G., van den Abele, P., van Rensberger, J., & Coucke, P. (1988). Incidental processing of advertisements while watching a soccer-games broadcast. In M. Gruneberg, P. Morris & R. Sykes (Eds.), *Practical Aspects of Memory: Current Research Issues* (pp. 478–483). New York: Wiley & Sons.

Eagly, A.H., Ashmore, R.D., Makhijani, M.G., & Longo, L.C. (1991). What is beautiful is good, but . . .: A meta-analytic review of research on the physical attractiveness stereotype. *Psychological Bulletin, 110,* 109–128.

Eagly, A.H., & Chaiken, S. (1984). Cognitive theories of persuasion, L. Berkowitz (Ed.). *Advances in Experimental Social Psychology* (pp. 268–361). Orlando FL: Academic Press.

Eagly, A.H., & Chaiken, S. (1993). *The Psychology of Attitudes.* Fort Worth: Harcourt Brace Jovanovich.

Eagly, A.H., & Chaiken, S. (2007). The advantage of an inclusive definition of attitude. *Social Cognition, 25,* 582–602.

Ebbinghaus, H. (1885/1964). *On Memory.* New York: Dover (originally published 1885; Leipzig: Duncker & Humblot)

Efron, R. (1970a). The relationship between duration of a stimulus and the duration of a perception. *Neuropsychologia, 8,* 37–55.

Efron, R. (1970b). The minimum duration of a perception. *Neuropsychologia, 8,* 57–63.

Engel, J.F., Blackwell, R.D., & Miniard, P.W. (1990). *Consumer Behavior* (6th edn). New York: Dryden

Engel, J., Kollat, D., & Blackwell, R. (1968). *Consumer Behavior.* New York: Holt, Rinehart & Winston.

Erber, M.W., Hodges, S.D., & Wilson, T.D. (1995). Attitude strength, attitude stability, and the effects of analyzing reasons. In R.E. Petty & J.A. Krosnick (Eds.), *Attitude Strength: Antecedents and Consequences* (pp. 433–454). Mawah, NJ: Erlbaum.

Erdem, T. (1998). An empirical analysis of umbrella branding. *Journal of Marketing Research, 35,* 339–351.

Escales, J.E., & Luce, M.F. (2004). Understanding the effects of process-focused versus outcome-focused thought in response to advertising. *Journal of Consumer Research, 31,* 274–285.

Etgar, M., & Goodwin, S.M. (1982). One-sided versus two-sided comparative message appeals for new brand introductions. *Journal of Consumer Research, 8,* 460–465.

Fabrigar, L.R., Krosnick, J.A., & MacDougall, B.L. (2005). Attitude measurement: Techniques for measuring the unobservable. In T.C. Brock & M.C. Green, (Eds.), *Persuasion: Psychological Insights and Perspectives* (pp. 17–41). Thousand Oaks, CA: Sage.

Fang, X., Singh, S., & Ahluwalia, R. (2007). An examination of different explanations for the mere exposure effect. *Journal of Consumer Research, 34*, 97–103.

Fazio, R.H. (1990). Multiple processes by which attitudes guide behavior: The MODE model as an integrative framework. *Advances in Experimental Psychology, 23*, 75–109.

Fazio, R.H. (1995). Attitudes as object-evaluation associations: Determinants, consequences, and correlates of attitudes. In R.E. Petty & J.A. Krosnick (Eds.), *Attitude Strength: Antecedents and Consequences* (pp. 247–282). Mahwah, NJ: Erlbaum.

Fazio, R.H. (2000). Accessible attitudes as tools for objects of appraisal: Their costs and benefits. In G.R. Maio, & J.M. Olson (Eds.), *Why we evaluate: Functions of attitudes* (pp. 1–36). Mahwah, NJ: Erlbaum.

Fazio, R.H., Chen, J-W., McDonel, E.C., & Sherman, S.J. (1982). Attitude accessibility, attitude-behavior consistency, and the strength of the object-evaluation association. *Journal of Experimental Social Psychology, 18*, 339–357.

Fazio, R.H., Jackson, J.R., Dunton, B.C., & Williams, C.J. (1995). Variability in automatic activation as an unobtrusive measure of racial attitudes: A bona fide pipeline? *Journal of Personality and Social Psychology, 69*, 1013–1027.

Fazio, R.H., & Olson, M.A. (2003). Implicit measures in social cognition research: Their meaning and use. *Annual Review of Psychology, 54*, 297–327.

Fazio, R.H., Powell, M.C., & Williams, C.J. (1989). The role of attitude accessibility in the attitude-to-behavior process. *Journal of Consumer Research, 16*, 280–288.

Fazio, R.H., Sanbonmatsu, D.M., Powell, M.C., & Kardes, F.R. (1986). On the automatic activation of attitudes. *Journal of Personality and Social Psychology, 50*, 229–238.

Fazio, R.H., & Williams, C.J. (1986). Attitude accessibility as moderator of the attitude-behavior relation: An investigation of the 1984 presidential election. *Journal of Personality and Social Psychology, 51*, 505–514.

Fazio, R.H., & Zanna, M.P. (1981). Direct experience and attitude-behavior-consistency. In L. Berkowitz (Ed.), *Advances in Experimental Social Psychology* (Vol. 14, pp. 161–202). Nw York: Academic Press.

Fennis, B.M. (2008a). Persuasion pleasure and selling stress: The role of non-verbal communication in consumer influence settings. *Advances in Consumer Research, 35*, 797–798.

Fennis, B.M. (2008b). Branded into submission: Brand attributes and hierarchization behavior in same-sex and mixed-sex dyads. *Journal of Applied Social Psychology, 38*, 1993–2009.

Fennis, B.M., & Bakker, A.B. (2001). 'Stay tuned – we will be back right after these messages': Need to evaluate moderates the transfer of irritation in advertising. *Journal of Advertising, 30* (3), 15–25.

Fennis, B.M., Das, E., & Fransen, M.L. (under review). Effectiveness of executional styles in advertising: The role of individual differences in vividness of visual imagery. *Journal of Business Research.*

Fennis, B.M., Das, E.H.H.J., & Pruyn, A.Th.H. (2004). 'If you cannot dazzle them with brilliance, baffle them with nonsense': Extending the impact of the Disrupt-Then-Reframe Technique of social influence. *Journal of Consumer Psychology, 14*, 280–290.

Fennis, B.M., Das, E.H.H.J., & Pruyn, A.Th.H. (2006). Interpersonal communication and compliance: The disrupt-then-reframe technique in dyadic influence settings. *Communication Research, 33*, 136–151.

Fennis, B.M., Janssen, L., & Vohs, K.D. (2009). Acts of benevolence: A limited-resource account of compliance with charitable requests. *Journal of Consumer Research, 35*, 904–924.

Fennis, B.M., & Pruyn, A.Th.H. (2007). You are what you wear: Brand personality influences on consumer impression formation. *Journal of Business Research, 60*, 634–639.

REFERENCES

Festinger, L., & Maccoby, N. (1964). On resistance to persuasive communications. *Journal of Abnormal and Social Psychology, 68*, 359–366.

Fichter, C., & Jonas, K. (2008). Image effects of newspapers: How brand images change consumers' product perception. *Journal of Psychology, 216*, 226–234.

Fishbein, M. (1963). An investigation of the relationship between beliefs about an object and the attitude toward that object. *Human Relations, 16*, 233–240.

Fishbein, M. & Ajzen, I. (1975). *Belief, Attitude, Intention, and Behavior: An Introduction to Theory and Research*. Reading, MA: Addison Wesley.

Fiske, S.T., & Taylor, S.E. (1984). *Social Cognition*. New York: Random House.

Fitzpatrick, K.R. (2005). The legal challenge of integrated marketing communication (IMC): Integrating commercial and political speech. *Journal of Advertising, 34* (4), 93–102.

Fitzsimons, G., Chartrand, T.L., & Fitzsimons, G.J. (2008). Automatic effects of brand exposure on motivated behaviour: How Apple makes you "think different". *Journal of Consumer Research, 35,* 21–35.

Fitzsimons, G.J., & Moore, S.G. (2008). Should we ask our children about sex, drugs and rock & roll? Potentially harmful effects of asking questions about risky behaviours. *Journal of Consumer Psychology, 18* (2), 82–95.

Fitzsimons, G.J., Nunes, J., & Williams, P. (2007). License to sin: The liberating role of reporting expectations. *Journal of Consumer Research, 34*, 22–31.

Flynn, F.J., & Lake, V. (2008). 'If you need help, just ask': Underestimating compliance with direct requests for help. *Journal of Personality and Social Psychology, 95* (1), 128–143.

Folkes, V.S., & Patrick, V.M. (2003). The positivity effect in perceptions of services: Seen one, seen them all? *Journal of Consumer Research, 30*, 125–137.

Fortin, D.R. & Dholakia, R.R. (2005). Interactivity and vividness effects on social presence and involvement with a web-based advertisement. *Journal of Business Research, 58* (3), 387–396.

Fox, S. (1984). *The mirror makers: A history of American advertising and its creator*. New York: Vintage Books.

Fransen, M.L., Fennis, B.M., Pruyn, A.Th.H., & Das, E. (2008). Rest in peace? Brand-induced mortality salience and consumer behavior. *Journal of Business Research, 61*, 1053–1061.

Freedman, J., & Fraser, S.C. (1966). Compliance without pressure: The Foot-in-the-Door technique. *Journal of Personality and Social Psychology, 4*, 195–202.

Frey, K.P. & Eagly, A.H. (1993). Vividness can undermine the persuasiveness of messages. *Journal of Personality and Social Psychology, 65* (1), 32–44.

Friedman, R., & Elliot, A.J. (2008). Exploring the influence of sports drink exposure on physical endurance. *Psychology of Sport and Exercise, 9*, 749–759.

Friedman, A., & Polson, M.C. (1981). Hemispheres as independent resource system: Limited-capacity processing and cerebral specialization. *Journal of Experimental Psychology: Human Perception and Performance, 7*, 1031–1058.

Friese, M., Hofmann, W., & Schmitt, M. (2008). When and why do implicit reaction time measures predict behaviour? Empirical evidence for the moderating role of opportunity, motivation, and process reliance. In W. Stroebe & M. Hewstone (Eds.), *European Review of Social Psychology* (Vol. 19, pp. 285–338) Hove: Psychology Press.

Friese, M., Wänke, M., & Plessner, H. (2006). Implicit consumer preferences and their influence on product choice. *Psychology & Marketing, 23*, 727–740.

Friestad, M., & Wright, P. (1994). The persuasion knowledge model: How people cope with persuasion attempts. *Journal of Consumer Research, 21*, 1–31.

Friestad, M., & Wright, P. (1995). Persuasion knowledge: Lay people's and researchers' beliefs about the psychology of advertising. *Journal of Consumer Research, 22*, 62–74.

Furse, D.H., Stewart, D.W., & Rados, D.L. (1981). Effects of foot-in-the-door, cash incentives, and follow-ups on survey response. *Journal of Marketing Research, 18*, 473–478.

Garbarino, E.C., & Edell, J.A. (1997). Cognitive effort, affect, and choice. *Journal of Consumer Research, 24,* 147–158.

Gardner, M.P., Mitchell, A.A., & Russo, J.E. (1985). Low involvement strategies for processing advertisements. *Journal of Advertising, 14* (2), 4–13.

Garrity, K., & Degelman, D. (1990). Effect of server introduction on restaurant tipping. *Journal of Applied Social Psychology, 20,* 168–172.

Gilbert, D.T. (1991). How mental systems believe. *American Psychologist, 46,* 107–119.

Gilbert, D.T., Krull, D.S., & Malone, P.S. (1990). Unbelieving the unbelievable: Some problems in the rejection of false information. *Journal of Personality and Social Psychology.*

Gilbert, D.T., Tafarodi, R.W., & Malone, P.S. (1993). You can't not believe everything you read. *Journal of Personality and Social Psychology, 65,* 221–233.

Glanzer, M., & Cunitz, A.R. (1966). Two storage mechanisms in free recall. *Journal of Verbal Learning and Verbal Behavior, 5,* 351–360.

Glasman, L.R., & Albarracin, D. (2006). Forming attitudes that predict future behavior: A meta-analysis of the attitude-behavior relation. *Psychological Bulletin, 132,* 778–822.

Goldberg, L.R. (1992). The development of markers for the big-five factor structure. *Psychological Assessment, 4,* 26–42.

Gollwitzer, P.M. (1990). Action phases and mind-sets. In E. T. Higgins & R.M. Sorrentino (Eds.), *Handbook of Motivation and Cognition: Vol. 2. Foundations of Social Behavior* (pp. 53– 92). New York: Guilford.

Gollwitzer, P.M., & Sheeran, P. (2006). Implementation intention and goal achievement: A meta-analysis of effects and processes. In M. Zanna (Ed.), *Advances of Experimental Social Psychology* (Vol. 38, pp. 69–120). San Diego: Academic Press.

Gordon, R.A. (1996). The impact of ingratiation on judgments and evaluations: A meta-analytic investigation. *Journal of Personality and Social Psychology, 71,* 54–70.

Gorn, G.J. (1982). The effects of music in advertising on choice behavior: A classical conditioning approach. *Journal of Marketing, 46,* 94–101.

Gouldner, A.W. (1960). The norm of reciprocity: A preliminary statement. *American Sociological Review, 25,* 161–178.

Grant, S.J., Malaviya, P., & Sternthal, B. (2004). Influence of negation on product evaluations. *Journal of Consumer Research, 31,* 583–591.

Greenberg, J., Pyszczynski, T., & Solomon, S. (1986). The causes and consequences of the need for self-esteem: A terror management theory. In R.F. Baumeister (Ed.), *Public self and private self* (pp. 189–212). New York: Springer.

Greenberg, J., Pyszczynski, T., Solomon, S., Simon, L., & Breus, M. (1994). Role of Consciousness and Accessibility of Death-Related Thoughts in Mortality Salience Effects. *Journal of Personality and Social Psychology, 67,* 627–637.

Greenwald, A.G. (1968). Cognitive learning, cognitive response to persuasion, and attitude change. In A.G. Greenwald, T.C. Brock, & T.M. Ostrom (Eds.), *Psychological Foundations of Attitudes* (pp. 147–170). San Diego, CA: Academic Press.

Greenwald, A.G. (1992). New look 3: Unconscious cognition reclaimed. *American Psychologist, 47,* 766–779.

Greenwald, A.G., Carnot, C.G., Beach, R., & Young, B. (1987). Increasing voting behaviour by asking people if they expect to vote. *Journal of Applied Psychology, 72,* 315–318.

Greenwald, A.G., & Leavitt, C. (1984). Audience involvement in advertising: Four levels. *Journal of Consumer Research, 11,* 581–592.

Greenwald, A.G., McGhee, D.E., & Schwartz, J.L.K. (1998). Measuring individual differences in implicit cognition: the implicit association test. *Journal of Personality and Social Psychology, 74,* 1464–1480.

Greenwald, A.G., Spangenberg, E.R., Pratkanis, A.R., & Eskenazi, J. (1991). Double-blind tests of subliminal self-help audiotapes. *Psychological Science, 28,* 191–194.

Grewal, D., Kavanoor, S., Fern, E.F., Costley, M., & Barnes, J.H. (1997). Comparative advertising: A meta-analysis of the empirical evidence. *Journal of Marketing, 61,* 1–15.

Grossman, R.P., & Till, B.D. (1998). The persistence of classically conditioned brand attitudes. *Journal of Advertising, 27,* 23–31.

Grunig, J.E., & Grunig, L.A. (1998). The relationship between public relations and marketing in excellent organizations: Evidence from the AIBC study. *Journal of Marketing Communications, 4,* 141–162.

Guilford, J.P. (1950). Creativity. *American Psychologist, 5,* 444–454.

Guilford, J.P., Merrifield, P.R., & Wilson, R.C. (1958). *Unusual uses test.* Orange, CA: Sheridan Psychological Services.

Gupta, P.B., & Lord, K.R. (1998). Product placement in movies: The effect of prominence and mode on recall. *Journal of Current Issues and Research in Advertising, 20,* 47–59.

Gurhan-Canli, Z., & Maheswaran, D. (1998). The effects of extensions on brand name dilution and enhacement. *Journal of Marketing Research, 35,* 464–473.

Haaland, G.A., & Vankatesan, M. (1968). Resistance to persuasive communication: an examination of the distraction hypotheses. *Journal of Personality and Social Psychology, 9,* 167–170.

Haddock, G. (2002). It's easy to like or dislike Tony Blair: Accessibility experiences and the favourability of attitude judgments. *British Journal of Psychology, 93,* 257–267.

Haddock, G., Rothman, A.J., Reber, R., & Schwarz, N. (1999). Forming judgments of attitude certainty, intensity, and importance: the role of subjective experience. *Personality and Social Psychology Bulletin, 25,* 771–782.

Han, S., & Shavitt, S. (1994). Persuasion and culture: Advertising appeals in individualistic and collectivistic societies. *Journal of Experimental Social Psychology, 30,* 326–350.

Hansen, R.A., & Robinson, L.M. (1980). Testing the effectiveness of alternative foot-in-the-door manipulations. *Journal of Marketing Research, 17,* 359–364.

Hanssens, D.M., Parsons, L.J., & Schultz, R.L. (1990). *Market Response Models: Econometric and Time Series Analysis.* Boston: Kluwer.

Harkins, S.G., & Petty, R.E. (1981). The multiple source effect in persuasion: The effects of distraction. *Personality and Social Psychology Bulletin, 7* (4), 627–635.

Harmon-Jones, E., & Allen, J.B. (2001). The role of affect in the mere exposure effect: Evidence from psychophysiological and individual differences approaches. *Personality and Social Psychology Bulletin, 27,* 889–898.

Harreveld, F. van, van der Pligt, J., de Vries, N.K., Wenneker, C., & Verhue, D. (2004). Ambivalence and information integration in attitudinal judgments. *British Journal of Social Psychology, 43,* 431–447.

Harris, R.J. (1977). Comprehension of pragmatic implications in advertising. *Journal of Applied Psychology, 62,* 603–608.

Hass, R.G., & Grady, K. (1975). Temporal delay, type of forewarning and resistance of influence. *Journal of Experimental Social Psychology, 11,* 459–469.

Hastie, R. (1983). Social inference. *Annual Review of Psychology, 34,* 511–542.

Hastie, R. (1984). Causes and effects of causal attribution. *Journal of Personality and Social Psychology, 46,* 44–56.

Hastie, R., & Park, B. (1986). The relationship between memory and judgment depends on whether the judgment task is memory-based or on-line. *Psychological Review, 93,* 258–268.

Haugtvedt, C.P., Herr, P.M., & Kardes, F.R. (Eds.) (2008). *Handbook of consumer psychology.* New York: Erlbaum.

Haugtvedt, C.P., & Kasmer, J.A. (2008). Attitude change and persuasion. In C. Haugtvedt, P.M. Herr, & F.R. Kardes (Eds.), *Handbook of Consumer Psychology* (pp. 419–435) New York: Taylor & Francis.

Haugtvedt, C.P., & Petty, R.E. (1992). Personality and persuasion: need for cognition moderates the persistence and resistance of attitude change. *Journal of Personality and Social Psychology, 63,* 308–319.

Haugtvedt, C.P., Schumann, D.W., Schneier, W.L., & Warren, W.L. (1994). Advertising repetition and variation strategies: Implications for understanding attitude strength. *Journal of Consumer Research, 21,* 176–189.

Haugtvedt, C.P., & Wegener, D.T. (1994). Message order effects in persuasion: An attitude strength perspective. *Journal of Consumer Research, 21,* 205–218.

Hauser, J.R., & Wernerfelt, B. (1990). An evaluation cost model of consideration sets. *Journal of Consumer Research, 16,* 393–408.

Hawkins, D. (1970). The effects of subliminal stimulation on drive level and brand preference. *Journal of Marketing Research, 7,* 322–326.

Hawkins, S.A., & Hoch, S.J. (1992). Low-involvement learning: Memory without evaluation. *Journal of Consumer Research, 19,* 212–225.

Heckler, S.E., & Childers, T.L. (1992). The role of expectancy and relevancy in memory for verbal and visual information: What is incongruency? *Journal of Consumer Research, 18,* 475–492.

Heider, F. (1946). Attitudes and cognitive organization. *Journal of Psychology, 21,* 107–112.

Hendrick, C., Borden, R., Giesen, M., Murray, E.J., & Seyfried, B.A. (1972). Effectiveness of ingratiation tactics in a cover letter on mail questionnaire response. *Psychonomic Science, 26,* 349–351.

Herr, P.M. (1989). Priming price: Prior knowledge and context effects. *Journal of Consumer Research, 16,* 67–75.

Herr, P.M., Kardes, F.R., & Kim, J. (1991). Effects of word-of-mouth and product-attribute information on persuasion: An accessibility-diagnosticity perspective. *Journal of Consumer Research, 17,* 454–462.

Higgins, T., Rholes, W.S., & Jones, C.R. (1977). Category accessibility and impression formation. *Journal of Experimental Social Psychology, 13,* 141–154.

Hildum, D.C., & Brown, R.W. (1965). Verbal reinforcement and interviewer bias. *Journal of Abnormal and Social Psychology, 53,* 108–111.

Himelstein, P., & Moore, J.C. (1963). Racial attitudes and the action of Negro- and white-background figures as factors in petition signing. *Journal of Social Psychology, 61,* 267–272.

Hintzman, D.L. (1976). Repetition and memory. In G. H. Bower (Ed.), *The psychology of learning and motivation* (pp. 47–91). New York: Academic Press.

Hoch, S.J., & Deighton, J. (1989). Managing what consumers learn from experience. *Journal of Marketing, 53,* 1–20.

Hoch, S.J., & Ha, Y.-W. (1986). Consumer learning: advertising and the ambiguity of product experience. *Journal of Consumer Research, 13,* 221–233.

Hodson, G., Maio, G.R., & Esses, V.M. (2001). The role of attitudinal ambivalence in susceptibility to consensus information. *Basic and Applied Social Psychology, 23,* 197–205.

Hodson, G., & Olson, J.M. (2005). Testing the generality of the name letter effect.: name initials and everyday attitudes. *Personality and Social Psychology Bulletin, 31,* 1099–1111.

Hofmann, W. & Friese, M. (2009). Impulses got the better of me: Alcohol moderates the influence of implicit attitudes toward food cues on eating behavior. *Journal of Abnormal Psychology, 117,* 420–427.

Hofs, Y. (2008). Kredietverleners letten teveel op reputaties. *Volkskrant, December 22,* p. 22.

Holland, R.W., Hendriks, M., & Aarts, H. (2005). Smells like clean spirit: Non-conscious effects of scent on cognition and behavior. *Psychological Science, 16,* 689–693.

Holland, R.W., Verplanken, B., & van Knippenberg, A. (2002). On the nature of attitude-behavior relations: The strong guide, the weak follow. *European Journal of Social Psychology, 32,* 869–876.

REFERENCES

Hong, S.-T., & Wyer, R.S. (1989) Effects of country-of-origin and product-attribute information on product evaluation: An information processing perspective. *Journal of Consumer Research, 16,* 175–187.

Hovland, C.I. (1951). Changes in attitude through communication. *Journal of Abnormal and Social Psychology, 46,* 424–437.

Hovland, C.I., Janis, I.L. & Kelly, H.H. (1953). *Communication and Persuasion.* New Haven, CT: Yale University Press.

Hovland, C.I., Lumsdaine, A.A., & Sheffield, F.D. (1949). *Experiments on Mass Communication.* Princeton, NJ: Princeton University Press.

Hovland, C.I., & Weiss, W (1951). The influence of source credibility on communication effectiveness. *Public Opinion Quarterly, 15,* 635–650.

Howard, D.J. (1990). The influence of verbal responses to common greetings on compliance behavior: The foot-in-the-mouth effect. *Journal of Applied Social Psychology, 20,* 1185–1196.

Howard, D.J., Gengler, C., & Jain, A. (1995). What's in a name? A complimentary means of persuasion. *Journal of Consumer Research, 22,* 200–211.

Howard, J.A., & Sheth, J.N. (1969). *The theory of buyer behaviour.* New York: Wiley.

Hyman, H.H. (1942). The psychology of status. *Archives of Psychology, 38.*

Inman, J.J., Anil, C.P., & Raghubir, P. (1997). Framing the deal: The role of restrictions in accentuating deal value. *Journal of Consumer Research, 24,* 68–79.

Insko, C.A. (1965). Verbal reinforcements of attitude. *Journal of Personality and Social Psychology, 2,* 621–623.

Jacoby, L.L. (1983). Remembering the data: analyzing interactive processes in reading. *Journal of Verbal Learning and Verbal Behavior, 22,* 485–508.

Jacoby, L.L. (1991). A process dissociation framework: Separating automatic from intentional uses of memory. *Journal of Memory and Language, 30,* 513–541.

Jacoby, J., Olson, J.C., & Haddock, R.A. (1971). Price, brand name, and product composition characteristics as determinants of perceived quality. *Journal of Applied Psychology, 55,* 570–579.

Jacoby, J., & Hoyer, W.D. (1982). Viewer miscomprehension of televised communication: Selected findings. *Journal of Marketing, 46,* 12–26.

Jalleh, G., Donovan, R.J., Giles-Corti, B., & Holman, C.D.J. (2002). Sponsorship: impact on brand awareness and brand attitudes. *SMQ, 8,* 35–45.

Janis, I.L., & Feshbach, S. (1953). Effects of fear-arousing communications. *Journal of Abnormal and Social Psychology, 48,* 78–92.

Janiszewski, C. (1988). Preconscious processing effects: The independence of attitude formation and conscious thought. *Journal of Consumer Research, 15,* 199–209.

Janiszewski, C. (1990). The influence of print advertisement organization on affect toward a brand name. *Journal of Consumer Research, 17,* 53–65.

Janiszewski, C. (1993). Preattentive mere exposure effects. *Journal of Consumer Research, 20,* 376–392.

Janiszewski, C., & Chandon, E. (2007). Transfer appropriate processing, response fluency, and the mere measurement effect. *Journal of Marketing Research, 44,* 309–323.

Janiszewski, C., Noel, H., & Sawyer, A.G. (2003). A meta-analysis of the spacing effect in verbal learning: Implications for research on advertising and consumer memory. *Journal of Consumer Research, 30,* 138–149.

Janssen, L., Fennis, B.M., Pruyn, A., & Vohs, K. (2008). The path of least resistance: Regulatory resource depletion and the effectiveness of social influence techniques. *Journal of Business Research, 61,* 1041–1045.

Jeannerod, M. (1994). The representing brain: Neural correlates of motor intention and imagery. *Behavioral and Brain Sciences, 17,* 187–245.

Johnson, B.T., & Eagly, A.H. (1989). The effects of involvement on persuasion: A meta-analysis. *Psychological Bulletin, 106*, 290–314.

Johnson, B.T., & Eagly, A.H. (1990). Involvement and persuasion: Types, traditions and the evidence. *Psychological Bulletin, 106*, 375–384.

Johnson, E.J., Bellman, S., & Lohse, G.L. (2003). Cognitive lock-in and the power law of practice. *Journal of Marketing, 67*, 62–75.

Jonas, K., Diehl, M., & Broemer, P. (1997). Effects of attitudinal ambivalence on information processing and attitude–intention consistency. *Journal of Experimental Social Psychology, 33*, 190–209.

Jonas, K., Broemer, P., & Diehl, M. (2000). Attitudinal ambivalence. In W. Stroebe & M. Hewstone (Eds.), *European Review of Social Psychology, 11*, 35–74.

Jonas, K., Broemer, P., & Diehl, M. (2000). Experienced ambivalence as a moderator of the consistency between attitudes and behaviors. *Zeitschrift für Sozialpsychologie, 31*, 153–165.

Jones, C.R., Fazio, R.H., & Olson, M.A. (2009). Implicit misattribution as a mechansm underlying evaluative conditioning. *Journal of Personality and Social Psychology, 96*, 933–948

Jones, J.T., Pelham, B.W., Mirenberg, M.C., & Hetts, J.J. (2002). Name letter preferences are not merely mere exposure: Implicit egotism as self regulation. *Journal of Experimental Social Psychology, 38*, 170–177.

Kahn, B.E., & Louie, T.A. (1990). Effects of retraction of price promotions on brand choice behaviour for variety-seeking and last-purchase-loyal consumers. *Journal of Marketing Research, 27*, 279–289.

Kahneman, D. (1973). *Attention and Effort*. Englewood Cliffs, NJ: Prentice Hall.

Kahneman, D., & Miller, D.T. (1986). Norm theory: Comparing reality to its alternatives. *Psychological Review, 93*, 136–153.

Kalma, A.P., Visser, L., & Peeters, A. (1993). Sociable and aggressive dominance: Personality differences in leadership style? *Leadership Quarterly, 4*, 45–64.

Kamins, M.A., & Assael, M. (1987). Two-sided versus one-sided appeals: A cognitive perspective on argumentation, source derogation, and the effect of disconfirming trial on belief change. *Journal of Marketing Research, 24*, 29–39.

Kamins, M.A., & Marks L.J. (1987). Advertising puffery: The impact of using two-sided claims on product attitude and purchase intention. *Journal of Advertising, 16* (4), 6–15.

Kang, Y.-S., & Herr, P.M. (2006). Beauty and the beholder: Toward an integrative model of communication source effects. *Journal of Consumer Research, 33*, 123–130.

Kaplan, K.J. (1972). On the ambivalence-indifference problem in attitude theory and measurement: A suggested modification of the semantic differential technique. *Psychological Bulletin, 77*, 361–372.

Kardes, F.R. (1986). Effects of initial product judgments on subsequent memory-based judgments. *Journal of Consumer Research, 13*, 1–11.

Kardes, F.R. (1993). Consumer inference: Determinants, consequences, and implications for advertising. In A.A. Mitchell (Ed.), *Advertising Exposure, Memory and Choice*. Hillsdale, NJ: Erlbaum.

Kardes, F.R. (1994). Consumer judgment and decision processes. In R.S. Wyer and T.K. Srull (Eds.) (2nd edn), *Handbook of Social Cognition: Volume 2: Applications* (pp. 399–467). Hillsdale, NJ: Erlbaum.

Kardes, F.R. (2002). *Consumer Behavior and Managerial Decision Making* (2nd edn). Upper Saddle River, NJ: Prentice Hall.

Kardes, F.R. (2005). The psychology of advertising. In T.C. Brock & M.C. Green (Eds.), *Persuasion: Psychological Insights and Perspectives* (2nd edn, pp. 281–305). Thousand Oaks: Sage.

Kardes, F.R., Cronley, M.L., & Posavac, S.S. (2005). Using implementation intentions to increase new product consumption: A field experiment. In F.R. Kardes, P.M. Herr, & J. Nantel

REFERENCES

(Eds.), *Applying Social Cognition to Consumer-focused Strategy* (pp. 219–233). Mahwah, NJ: Erlbaum.

Kardes, F.R., Fennis, B.M., Hirt, E.R., Tormala, Z.L., & Bullington, B. (2007). The role of the need for cognitive closure in the effectiveness of the disrupt-then-reframe influence technique. *Journal of Consumer Research, 34*, 377–385.

Kardes, F.R., & Gurumurthy, K. (1992). Order-of-entry effects on consumer memory and judgment: An information integration perspective. *Journal of Marketing Research, 29*, 343–357.

Kardes, F.R., Gurumurthy, K. Chandrashekaran, M., & Dornoff, R.J. (1993). Brand retrieval, consideration set composition, consumer choice, and the pioneering advantage. *Journal of Consumer Research, 20*, 62–75.

Kardes, F.R., Posavac, S.S., Cronley, M.L., & Herr, P.M. (2008). Consumer inference. In C. Haugtvedt, P.M. Herr, & F.R. Kardes (Eds.), *Handbook of Consumer Psychology* (pp. 165–191) New York: Taylor & Francis.

Karremans, J.C., Stroebe, W., & Claus, J. (2006). Beyond Vicary's fantasies: The impact of subliminal priming on brand choice. *Journal of Experimental Social Psychology, 42*, 792–798.

Karrh, J.A. (1998) Brand placement: A review. *Journal of Current Issues and Research in Advertising, 20*, 31–49.

Katz, D. (1960). The functional approach to the study of attitudes. *Public Opinion Quarterly, 24*, 163–204.

Keller, K.L. (1987). Memory factors in advertising: The effect of advertising retrieval cues on brand evaluations. *Journal of Consumer Research, 14*, 316–333.

Keller, K.L. (1991). Memory and evaluation effects in competitive advertising environments. *Journal of Consumer Research, 17*, 463–476.

Keller, K.L. (2009). Building strong brands in a modern marketing environment. *Journal of Marketing Communication, 15*, 139–155.

Kent, R.J., & Allen, C.T. (1993). Does competitive clutter in television advertising "interfere" with the recall and recognition of brand names and ad claims? *Marketing Letters, 4*, 175–184.

Kim, J., Allen, C.T., & Kardes, F.R. (1996). An investigation of the mediational mechanisms underlying attitudinal conditioning. *Journal of Marketing Research, 33*, 318–328.

Kirmani, A., & Shiv, B. (1998). Effects of source congruity on brand attitudes and beliefs: the moderating role of issue-relevant elaboration. *Journal of Consumer Psychology, 7*, 25–47.

Klein, C.T.F., & Webster, D.M. (2000). Individual differences in argument scrutiny as motivated by need for cognitive closure. *Basic and Applied Psychology, 22*, 119–129.

Klinger, E. (1975). Consequences of commitment to and disengagement from incentives. *Psychological Review, 82*, 1–25.

Klink, R.R., & Smith, D.C. (2001). Threats to the external validity of brand extension research. *Journal of Marketing Research, 38*, 326–426.

Knowles, E.S., & Linn, J.A. (2004). Approach-avoidance model of persuasion: Alpha and omega strategies for change. In E.S. Knowles & J.A. Linn (Eds.), *Resistance and Persuasion* (pp. 117–148). Mahwah, NJ: Erlbaum.

Kotler, P. (1997). *Marketing Management* (9th edn). Englewood Cliffs, NJ: Prentice Hall.

Kraus, S.J. (1995). Attitudes and the prediction of behavior: A meta-analysis of the empirical literature. *Personality and Social Psychology Bulletin, 21*, 58–75.

Krosnick, J.A., Betz, A.L., Jussim, L.J., & Lynn, A.R. (1992). Subliminal conditioning of attitudes. *Personality and Social Psychology Bulletin, 18*, 152–162.

Krosnick, J.A., & Petty, R.E. (1995). Attitude strength: An overview. In R.E. Petty & J.A. Krosnick (Eds.), *Attitude strength: Antecedents and consequences* (pp. 1–24). Mahwah, NJ: Erlbaum.

Krosnick, J.A., & Schuman, H. (1988). Attitude intensity, importance, and certainty and susceptibility to response effects. *Journal of Personality and Social Psychology, 54*, 940–952.

Kruglanski, A.W. (1989). *Lay epistemics and human knowledge: Cognitive and motivation bases*. New York: Plenum.

Kruglanski, A.W., & Freund, T. (1983). The freezing and unfreezing of lay inferences: Effects on impression primacy, ethnic stereotyping, and numerical anchoring. *Journal of Experimental Social Psychology, 19*, 448–468.

Kruglanski, A.W., Shah, J.Y., Fishbach, A., Friedman, R., Chun, W.Y., & Sleeth-Keppler, D. (2002). A theory of goal systems. *Advances in Experimental Social Psychology* (Vol 33, pp., 331–378). San Diego: Academic Press.

Kruglanski, A., & Stroebe, W. (2005). The influence of beliefs and goals on attitudes: Issues of structure, function, and dynamics. In D. Albarracin, B.T. Johnson, & M.P. Zanna (Eds.), *Handbook of Attitudes* (pp. 323–368). New York: Guilford Press.

Kruglanski, A. & Thompson, E.P. (1999). Persuasion by a single route: A view from the unimodel. *Psychological Inquiry, 10*, 83–109.

Kruglanski, A., Thompson, E.P., & Spiegel, S. (1999). Separate or equal? Bimodal notion of persuasion and a single process 'unimodel'. In S. Chaiken & Y. Trope (Eds.), *Dual Process Theories in Social Psychology* (293–313). New York: Guilford.

Kruglanski, A.W., & Webster, D.M. (1996). Motivated closing of the mind: 'Seizing' and 'freezing'. *Psychological Review, 103*, 263–283.

Krugman, H.E. (1965). The impact of television advertising: Learning without involvement. *Public Opinion Quarterly, 29*, 349–356.

Kumar, A., & Krishnan, S. (2004). Memory interference in advertising: A replication and extension. *Journal of Consumer Research, 30*, 602–611.

Kumkale, T.G., & Albarracin, D. (2004). The sleeper effect in persuasion: A meta-analytic review. *Psychological Bulletin, 130*, 143–172.

Kunda, Z. (1999). *Social Cognition: Making Sense of People*. Cambridge, MA: MIT Press.

Labroo, A.A., & Lee, A.Y. (2006). Between two brands: A goal fluency account of brand evaluation. *Journal of Marketing Research, 43* (3), 374–385.

LaFrance, M. (1985). Postural mirroring and intergroup relations. *Personality and Social Psychology Bulletin, 11*, 207–217.

Langer, E.J. (1992). Matters of mind: Mindfulness/mindlessness in perspective. *Consciousness and Cognition, 1*, 289–305.

Langer, E.J., Blank, A., & Chanowitz, B. (1978). The mindlessness of ostensibly thoughtful action: The role of 'placebic' information in interpersonal interaction. *Journal of Personality and Social Psychology, 36*, 635–642.

LaPiere, R.T. (1934). Attitudes vs. actions. *Social Forces, 13*, 230–237.

Lasswell, H.D. (1948). The structure and function of communication in society. In L. Bryson (Ed.), *The Communication of Ideas: Religion and Civilization series* (pp. 37–51). New York: Harper.

Lavidge, R.J., & Steiner, G.A. (1961). A model for predicting measurements of advertising effectiveness. *Journal of Marketing, 25*, 59–62.

Lavine, H., & Huff, J.W., Wagner, S.H., & Sweeney, D. (1998). The moderating influence of attitude strength on the susceptibility to context effects in attitude surveys. *Journal of Personality and Social Psychology, 75*, 359–373.

Law, S., & Braun, K.A. (2000). I'll have what she's having: Gauging the impact of product placements on viewers. *Psychology & Marketing, 17*, 1059–1075.

Lee, A.Y. (2002). Effects of implicit memory on memory-based versus stimulus-based brand choice. *Journal of Marketing Research, 39*, 440–453.

Lee, A.Y. (2004). The prevalence of meta-cognitive routes to judgments. *Journal of Consumer Psychology, 14* (4), 349–355.

Lee, A.Y., & Labroo, A.A. (2004). The effect of conceptual and perceptual fluency on brand evaluation *Journal of Marketing Research, 41*, 151–165.

REFERENCES

Leipkin, J.B. & Lipsky, M.S. (Eds.) (2003). *American Medical Association: Complete Medical Encycolpedia* ('Bad breath', p. 222–223).

Leventhal, H. (1970). Findings and theory in the study of fear communications. In L. Berkowitz (Ed.), *Advances in Experimental Social Psychology* (Vol. 5, pp 119–186). San Diego, CA: Academic Press.

Levin, I.P., & Gaeth, G.J. (1988). How consumers are affected by the framing of attribute information before and after consuming the product. *Journal of Consumer Research, 15*, 374–378.

LexisNexis Academic: Warner-Lambert Company, Petitioner, v. Federal Trade Commission, Respondent (No 76–1138). http://proxy.library.upenn.edu:8167/universe/printdoc (accessed July 2009).

Liberman, A., & Chaiken, S. (1992). Defensive processing of personal relevant health messages. *Personality and Social Psychology Bulletin, 18*, 669–679.

Lin, A. (2005). Listerine ads leave bad taste in judge's mouth. *New York Law Journal*, January 10. http://www.law.com/jsp/law/LawArticleFriendly.jsp?id=900005541818 (accessed July, 2009).

Loftus, E.F. (1980). *Memory*. Reading, MA: Addison Wesley.

Loken, B. (2006). Consumer psychology: Categorization, inferences, affect, and persuasion. *Annual Review of Psychology, 57*, 453–485.

Loken, B., Barsalou, B., & Joiner, L.W. (2008). Categorization theory and research in consumer psychology: Category representation and category-based inference. In C. Haugtvedt, P.M. Herr, & F.R. Kardes (Eds.), *Handbook of Consumer Psychology* (pp. 133–163). New York: Taylor & Francis.

Lucas, J., & Prensky, D. (1997). Evaluating the effectiveness of place-based media. In W.D. Wells (Ed.), *Measuring Advertising Effectiveness* (pp. 371–383). Hillsdale, NJ: Erlbaum.

Lumsdaine, A.A., & Janis, I.L. (1953). Resistance to 'counterpropaganda' produced by one-sided and two-sided 'propaganda' presentations. *Public Opinion Quarterly, 17*, 311–318.

MacKenzie, S.B., & Lutz, R.J. (1989). An empirical examination of the structural antecedents of attitude toward the ad in an advertising pretesting context. *Journal of Marketing, 53*, 48–65.

MacKenzie, S.B., Lutz, R.J. & Belch, G.E. (1986). The role of attitude toward the ad as a mediator of advertising effectiveness: A test of competing explanations. *Journal of Consumer Research, 23*, 130–143.

Mackie, D.M., & Ascuncion, A.G. (1990). On-line and memory-based modification of attitudes: determinants of message recall-attitude change correspondence. *Journal of Personality and Social Psychology, 57*, 27–40.

Madrigal, R. (2001). Social identity effects in a belief-attitude-intentions hierarchy: Implications for corporate sponsorship. *Psychology & Marketing, 18*, 145–165.

Maheswaran, D. (1994). Country of origin as a stereotype: Effects of consumer expertise and attribute strength on product evaluations. *Journal of Consumer Research, 21*, 354–365.

Maheswaran, D., & Agrawal, N. (2004). Motivational and cultural variations in mortality salience effects: Contemplations on terror management theory and consumer behaviour. *Journal of Consumer Psychology, 14*, 213–218.

Maio, G.R., Bell, D.W., & Esses, V.M. (1996). Ambivalence and persuasion: The processing of messages about immigrant groups. *Journal of Experimental Social Psychology, 32*, 513–536.

Maison, D., Greenwald, A.G., & Bruin, R.H. (2004). Predictive validity of the implicit association test in studies of brands, consumer attitudes, and behavior. *Journal of Consumer Psychology, 14*, 405–415.

Malaviya, P., Kisielius, J., & Sternthal, B. (1996). The effect of type of elaboration on advertising process and judgment. *Journal of Marketing Research, 33*, 410–421.

Malaviya, P., Meyers-Levy, J., & Sternthal, B. (1999). Ad repetition in a cluttered environment: The influence of type of processing. *Psychology & Marketing, 16,* 99–118.

Malof, M., & Lott, A.J. (1962). Ethnocentrism and the acceptance of Negro support in a group pressure situation. *Journal of Abnormal and Social Psychology, 65,* 254–258.

Mantonakis, A., Whittlesea, B.W.A., & Yoon, C. (2008). Consumer memory, fluency, and familiarity. In C. Haugtvedt, P.M. Herr, & F.R. Kardes (Eds.), *Handbook of Consumer Psychology* (pp. 77–102). New York: Taylor & Francis.

Marks, D.F. (1973). Visual imagery differences in the recall of pictures. *British Journal of Psychology, 64* (1), 17–24.

Markus, H. (1977). Self-schemata and processing information about the self. *Journal of Personality and Social Psychology, 35,* 63–78.

Marwell, G., Aiken, M., & Demerath, N.J. (1987). The persistence of political attitudes among 1960s civil rights activists. *Public Opinion Quarterly, 51,* 359–375.

Mazis, M.B., Settle, R.B., & Leslie, D.C. (1973). Elimination of phosphate detergents and psychological reactance. *Journal of Marketing Research, 10,* 390–395.

McConahay, J.B. (1986). Modern racism, ambivalence, and the modern racism scale. In S. Gaertner & J. Dovidio (Eds.), *Prejudice, discrimination and racism* (p. 91–126). Orlando, FL: Academic Press.

McDonald, C., & Scott, J. (2007). A brief history of advertising. In G.J. Tellis & T. Ambler (Eds.), *The Sage Handbook of Advertising* (pp. 17–35). Thousand Oaks, CA: Sage.

McGeoch, J.A., & McDonald, W.T. (1931). Meaningful relation and retroactive inhibition. *American Journal of Psychology, 43,* 579–588.

McGuire, W.J. (1968). Personality and susceptibility to social influence. In E.F. Borgatta & W.W. Lambert (Eds.), *Handbook of Personality Theory and Research* (pp. 1130–1187). Chicago: Rand McNally.

McGuire, W.J., (1969). The nature of attitudes and attitude change. In G. Lindzey & E. Aronson (Eds.), *Handbook of Social Psychology*, 2nd edn (Vol. 3, pp. 136–314). Reading, MA: Addison Wesley.

McGuire, W.J. (1985). Attitudes and attitude change. In G. Lindzey & E. Aronson (Eds.), *Handbook of Social Psychology*, 3rd edn (Vol. 2, pp. 233–346). New York: Random House.

McGuire, W.J. (1986). The myth of massive media impact: Savagings and salvagings. In: G. Comstock (Ed.), *Public Communication and Behavior* (Vol. 1, pp. 173–257). Florida: Academic Press.

McKinney, F. (1935). Retroactive inhibition in advertising. *Journal of Applied Psychology, 19,* 59–66.

Meenaghan, T. (2001). Sponsorship and advertising: A comparison of consumer perceptions. *Psychology & Marketing, 18,* 191–215.

Meeus, W.H.J., & Raaijmakers, Q.A.W. (1986). Administrative obedience: Carrying out orders to use psychological-administrative violence. *European Journal of Social Psychology, 16,* 311–324.

Melcher, J.M., & Schooler, J.W. (1996). The misremembrance of wines past: verbal and perceptual expertise differentially mediate verbal overshadowing of taste memory. *Journal of Memory and Language, 35,* 231–245.

Meyers-Levy, J., & Maheswaran, D. (1992). When timing matters: The influence of temporal distance on consumers' affective and persuasive responses. *Journal of Consumer Research, 19,* 424–433.

Meyers-Levy, J., & Peracchio, L.A. (1992). Getting an angle in advertising: The effect of camera angle on product evaluations. *Journal of Marketing Research, 29,* 454–461.

Milgram, S. (1963). Behavioral study of obedience. *Journal of Abnormal and Social Psychology, 67,* 371–378.

Millar, M.G., & Millar, K.U. (1996). The effects of direct and indirect experience of affective and cognitive responses and the attitude-behavior relation. *Journal of Experimental Social Psychology, 32*, 561–579.

Miller, G.A. (1956). The magical number seven, plus or minus two: Some limits on our capacity for processing information. *Psychological Review, 63*, 81–97.

Milner, B. (1966). Amnesia following operation on the temporal lobes. In C.W.M. Whitty & I.O. Zangwill (Eds.), *Amnesia* (pp. 109–133). London: Butterworths.

Miniard, P.W., Bhatla, S., & Rose, R.L. (1990). On the formation and relationship of ad and brand attitudes: An experimental and causal analysis. *Journal of Marketing Research, 27*, 290–303.

Mitchell, A.A., & Olson, J.C. (1981). Are product attribute beliefs the only mediator of advertising effects on brand attitude? *Journal of Consumer Research, 18*, 318–332.

Monroe, K.B., & Avila, R.A. (1986). Effectiveness of multiple request strategies: A synthesis of research results. *Journal of Marketing Research, 22*, 144–152.

Moore, T.E. (1982). Subliminal advertising: What you see is what you get. *Journal of Marketing, 46*, 38–47.

Moray, N. (1959). Attention in dichotic listening: Affective cues and the influence of instructions. *Quarterly Journal of Experimental Psychology, 11*, 56–60.

Morton, J. (1967). A singular lack of incidental learning. *Nature, 215*, 203–204.

Moskowitz, G.B. (2005). *Social Cognition*. New York: Guilford.

Muraven, M., Tice, D.M., & Baumeister, R.F. (1998). Self-control as a limited resource. Regulatory depletion patterns. *Journal of Personality and Social Psychology, 74*, 774–789.

Murray, K.B., & Häubl, G. (2007). Explaining cognitive lock-in: the role of skill-based habits of use in consumer choice. *Journal of Consumer Research, 34*, 77–88.

Muthukrishnan, A.V., & Chattopadhyay, A. (2007). Just give me another chance: The strategies for brands recovery from a bad first impression. *Journal of Marketing Research, 47*, 334–345.

Naik, P.A. & Raman, K. (2003). Understanding the impact of synergy in multimedia communications. *Journal of Marketing Research, 40*, 375–388.

Nedungadi, P. (1990). Recall and consumer consideration sets: Influencing choice without altering brand evaluations. *Journal of Consumer Research, 17*, 263–276.

Neisser, U. (1967). *Cognitive Psychology*, New York: Appleton Century Crofts.

Nenkov, G.Y., Inman, J.J., & Hulland, J. (2008). Considering the future: The conceptualization and measurement of elaboration on potential outcomes. *Journal of Consumer Research, 35*, 126–141.

Newby-Clark, I.R., McGregor, I., & Zanna, M.P. (2002). Thinking and caring about cognitive inconsistency: When and for whom does attitudinal ambivalence feel uncomfortable? *Journal of Personality and Social Psychology, 82*, 157–166.

Newcomb, T.M. (1960). Varieties in interpersonal attraction. In D. Cartwright & A. Zander (Eds.), *Group dynamics* (2nd edn). New York: Harper & Row.

Nickerson, R.S., & Adams, M.J. (1979). Long-term memory for a common object. *Cognitive Psychology, 11*, 287–307.

Nisbett, R.E., & Ross, L. (1980). *Human Inference: Strategies and Shortcomings of Social Judgment*. Englewood Cliffs, NJ: Prentice Hall.

Nordgren, L.F., van Harreveld, F., van der Pligt, J. (2006). Ambivalence, discomfort, and motivated information processing. *Journal of Experimental Social Psychology, 42*, 252–258.

Nordhielm, C.L. (2002). The influence of level of processing on advertising repetition effects. *Journal of Consumer Research, 29*, 371–382.

Norman, R. (1975). Affective-cognitive consistency, attitudes, conformity, and behavior. *Journal of Personality and Social Psychology, 32*, 83–91.

North, A.C., Hargreaves, D.J., McKendrick, J. (1999). The influence of in-store music on wine selection. *Journal of Applied Psychology, 84*, 271–276.

Nosek, B.A., Greenwald, A.G., & Banaji, M.R. (2007). The implicit association test at age 7: A methodological and conceptual review. In J.A. Bargh (Ed.), *Social Psychology and the Unconscious: The Automaticity of Higher Mental Processes* (pp. 265–292). New York: Psychology Press.

O'Keefe, D.J., & Hale, S.L. (2001). An odds-ratio-based meta-analysis of research on the door-in-the-face influence strategy. *Communication Reports, 14*, 31–38.

Oliver, R.L. (1980). A cognitive model of the antecedents and consequences of satisfaction decisions. *Journal of Marketing Research, 17*, 460–469.

Oliver, R.L. (1993). Cognitive, affective, and attribute bases of the satisfaction response. *Journal of Consumer Research, 20*, 418–430.

Oliver, R.L., & DeSarbo, W.S. (1988). Response determinants in satisfaction judgments. *Journal of Consumer Research, 14*, 495–507.

Olson, M.A., & Fazio, R.H. (2001). Implicit attitude formation through classical conditioning. *Psychological Science, 12*, 413–417.

Osterhouse, R.A., & Brock, T.C. (1970). Distraction increases yielding to propaganda by inhibiting counterarguing. *Journal of Personality and Social Psychology, 15*, 344–358.

Oulette, J., & Wood, E. (1998). Habit and intention in everyday life: The multiple processes by which past behavior predicts future behavior. *Psychological Bulletin, 124*, 54–74.

Oxoby, R.J., & Finnegan, H. (2007). Developing heuristic-based quality judgments: Blocking in consumer choice. *Psychology & Marketing, 24*, 295–313.

Page, M.M. (1969). Social psychology of a classical conditioning of attitude experiment. *Journal of Personality and Social Psychology, 11*, 177–186.

Park, C.W., & Young, S.M. (1986). Consumer response to television commercials: The impact of involvement and background music on brand attitude formation. *Journal of Marketing Research, 23*, 11–24.

Pechmann, C. (1992). Predicting when two-sided ads will be more effective than one-sided ads: The role of correlational and correspondent inferences. *Journal of Marketing Research, 29*, 441–453.

Peracchio, L.A., & Meyers-Levy, J. (1994). How ambiguous cropped objects in ad photos can affect product evaluations. *Journal of Consumer Research, 21*, 190–214.

Peracchio, L.A., & Tybout, A.M. (1996). The moderating role of prior knowledge in shame based product evaluation. *Journal of Consumer Research, 23*, 177–192.

Petty, R., Briñol, P., Tormala, Z.L., & Wegener, D.T. (2007). The role of metacognition in social judgment. In A. Kruglanski & T. Higgins (Eds.), *Social Psychology: Handbook of Basic Principles* (pp. 254–284). New York: Guilford.

Petty, R.E., & Cacioppo, J. (1980). Effects of issue involvement on attitudes in an advertising context.. In L. Percy & A. Woodside (Eds.), *Proceedings of the Division 23 Program* (pp. 75–79). Montreal, Canada: American Psychological Association

Petty, R.E., & Cacioppo, J.T. (1984). The effects of involvement on responses to argument quantity and quality: Central and peripheral routes to persuasion. *Journal of Personality and Social Psychology, 46* (1), 69–81.

Petty, R.E., & Cacioppo, J.T. (1986). *Communication and Persuasion: Central and Peripheral Routes to Attitude Change*. New York: Springer.

Petty, R.E., Cacioppo, J.T., & Goldman, R. (1981). Personal involvement as a determinant of argument-based persuasion. *Journal of Personality and Social Psychology, 41*, 847–855.

Petty, R.E., Cacioppo, J., & Schumann, D. (1983). Central and peripheral routes to advertising effectiveness: The moderating role of involvement. *Journal of Consumer Research, 10*, 135–146.

Petty, R.E., Fleming, M.A., Priester, J.R. & Feinstein, A.H. (2001). Individual versus group interest violation: Surprise as a determinant of argument scrutiny and persuasion. *Social Cognition, 19* (4), 418–442.

Petty, R.E., Ostrom, T.M., & Brock, T.C. (Eds.) (1981). *Cognitive Responses in Persuasion*. Hillsdale, NJ: Erlbaum.

Petty, R.E., & Wegener, D.T. (1998a). Matching versus mismatching attitude functions: Implications for scrutiny of persuasive messages. *Personality and Social Psychology Bulletin, 24*, 227–240.

Petty, R.E. & Wegner, D.T. (1998b). Attitude change: multiple roles for persuasion variables. In Gilbert, D.T., Fiske, S.T., & G. Lindzey (Eds.), *Handbook of Social Psychology*, 4th edn (Vol. 1, pp. 323–390). Boston, MA: McGraw-Hill.

Petty, R.E., & Wegener, D.T. (1999). The elaboration likelihood model: Current status and controversies. In S. Chaiken & Y. Trope (Eds.), *Dual-Process Theories in Social Psychology*. (pp. 37–72). New York, NY: Guilford Press.

Petty, R.E., Wells, G.L., & Brock, T.C. (1976). Distraction can enhance or reduce yielding to propaganda: thought disruption versus effort justification. *Journal of Personality and Social Psychology, 34*, 874–884.

Pfau, M., & Wan, H.H. (2006). Persuasion: An intrinsic function of public relations. In C.H. Botan & V. Hazleton (Eds.), *Public Relations Theory II* (pp. 101–136). Mahwah, NJ: Erlbaum.

Pham, M.T. (1998). Representativeness, relevance, and the use of feelings in decision making. *Journal of Consumer Research, 25*, 144–159.

Pham, M.T., & Johar, G.V. (2001). Market prominence biases in sponsor identification: Processes and consequentiality. *Psychology & Marketing, 18*, 123–143.

Pieters, R.G.M. & Bijmolt, T.H.A. (1997). Consumer memory for television advertising: A field study of duration, serial position, and competition effects. *Journal of Consumer Research, 23*, 362–372.

Pieters, R.G.M., & Van Raaij, F. (1992). *Reclamewerking*. Leiden: Stenfert Kroeze.

Pieters, R., & Wedel, M. (2007). Goal control of attention to advertising: The Yarbus implication. *Journal of Consumer Research, 34*, 224–233.

Plassmann, H., O'Doherty, J., Shiv, B., & Rangel, A. (2008). Marketing actions can modulate neural representations of experienced pleasantness. *Proceedings of the National Academy of Sciences, 105*, 105–1054.

Pleyers, G., Corneille, O., Luminet, O., & Yzerbyt, V. (2007). Aware and (Dis)Liking: Item-based analyses reveal that valence acquisition via evaluative conditioning emerges only when there is contingency awareness. *Journal of Experimental Psychology: Learning, Memory and Cognition, 33*, 130–144.

Plomp, R. (1964). Decay of auditory sensation. *Journal of the Acoustical Society of America, 36*, 277–288.

Poiesz, Th.B.C. (1989). *De transformatie van een karikatuur: Over de ontwikkeling van het consumentenbeeld in de psychologie van de reclame*. Inaugural Address, University of Tilburg.

Pollock, C.L., Smith, S.D., Knowles, E.S., & Bruce, H.J. (1998). Mindfulness limits compliance with the that's-not-all technique. *Personality and Social Psychology Bulletin, 24* (11), 1153–1157.

Posner, M.I., & Snyder, C.R.R. (1975). Attention and cognitive control. In R.L. Solso (Ed.), *Information Processing and Cognition* (pp. 55–85). Hillsdale, NJ: Erlbaum.

Postman, L., & Phillips, L.W. (1965). Short-term temporal changes in free recall. *Quarterly Journal of Experimental Psychology, 17*, 132–138.

Pratkanis, A.R. (2007). An invitation to social influence research. In A.R. Pratkanis (Ed.), *The Science of Social Influence: Advances and Future Progress*. New York: Psychology Press.

Pratkanis, A.R. (2007). Social influence analysis: An index of tactics. In A.R. Pratkanis (Ed.), *The Science of Social Influence: Advances and Future Progress*. New York: Psychology Press.

Pratkanis, A.R., & Abbott, C.J. (2004). Flattery and compliance with a direct request: Towards a theory of toady influence. Unpublished manuscript. University of California, Santa Cruz.

Pratkanis, A., & Aronson, E. (2002). *Age of Propaganda* (2nd edn). New York: Freeman.

Priester, J.R., Nayakankuppam, D., Fleming, M.A., & Godek, J. (2004). The A2SC2 model: The influence of attitudes and attitude strength on consideration and choice. *Journal of Consumer Research, 30*, 574–587.

Priester, J.R., & Petty, R.E. (2001). Extending the bases of subjective attitudinal ambivalence: Interpersonal and intrapersonal antecedents of evaluative tension. *Journal of Personality and Social Psychology, 80*, 29–34.

Randall, D.M. & Wolff, J.A. (1994). The time interval in the intention–behaviour relationship: meta-analysis. *British Journal of Social Psychology, 33*, 405–418.

Rao, A.R., & Monroe, K.B. (1989). The effect of price, brand name, and store name on buyers' perceptions of product quality: An integrative review. *Journal of Marketing Research, 26*, 351–357.

Ratneshwar, S., & Chaiken, S. (1991). Comprehension's role in persuasion: The case of its moderating effect on the persuasive impact of source cues. *Journal of Consumer Research, 18*, 52–62.

Reber, R., & Schwarz, N. (2001). The hot fringes of consciousness: Perceptual fluency and affect. *Consciousness and Emotion, 2*, 223–231.

Regan, D.T., & Fazio, R.H. (1977). On the consistency between attitudes and behavior: Look to the method of attitude formation. *Journal of Experimental Social Psychology, 13*, 38–45.

Reingen, P.H. (1978). On inducing compliance with requests. *Journal of Consumer Research, 5*, 96–102.

Reingen, P.H., & Kernan, J.B. (1977). Compliance with an interview request: A foot-in-the-door, self-perception interpretation. *Journal of Marketing Research, 14*, 365–369.

Rhodes, N., & Wood, W. (1992). Self-esteem and intelligence affect influenceability: the mediating role of message reception. *Psychological Bulletin, 111*, 156–171.

Richardson-Klavehn, A., & Bjork, R.A. (1988). Measures of memory. *Annual Review of Psychology, 39*, 475–543.

Rindfleisch, A., & Burroughs, J.E. (2004). Terrifying thoughts, terrible materialism? Contemplations on a terror management account of materialism and consumer behavior. *Journal of Consumer Psychology, 14*, 219–224.

Robinson, M.D. (1998). Running from William James' bear: A review of preattentive mechanisms and their contributions to emotional experience. *Cognition and Emotion, 12*, 667–696.

Roediger, H.R. (1990). Implicit memory: retentions without remembering. *American Psychologist, 45*, 1043–1056.

Rosch, E. (1973). Natural categories. *Cognitive Psychology, 4*, 329–350.

Rose, R.L., Bearden, W.O., & Teel, J.E. (1992). An attributional analysis of resistance to group pressure regarding illicit drug and alcohol consumption. *Journal of Consumer Research, 19*, 1–13.

Rosenberg, M.J. (1960) An analysis of affective–cognitive consistency. In C.I. Hovland & M.J. Rosenberg (Eds.), *Attitude Organization and Change* (pp. 15–64). New Haven, CT: Yale University Press.

Rossiter, J.R., Percy, L., & Donovan, J.R. (1991). A better advertising planning grid. *Journal of Advertising Research, 32* (5), 11–21.

Rothermund, K., & Wentura, D. (2004). Underlying processes in the implicit association test: Dissociating salience from associations. *Journal of Experimental Psychology: General, 133* (2), 139–165.

Rowsome, F. (1970). *They Laughed When I Sat Down: An Informal History of Advertising in Words and Pictures*. New York: McGraw-Hill.

Russell, C.A. (2002). Investigating the effectiveness of product placements in television shows: The role of modality and plot connection congruence on brand memory and attitude. *Journal of Consumer Research, 29*, 306–318.

Salancik, G.R., & Conway, M. (1975). Attitude inferences from salient and relevant cognitive content about behavior. *Journal of Personality and Social Psychology, 32*, 829–840.

Sawyer, A. (1981). Repetition, cognitive responses and persuasion. In R.E. Petty, T.M. Ostrom & T.C. Brock (Eds.), *Cognitive responses in persuasion* (pp. 237–262). Hillsdale, NJ: Erlbaum.

Schacter, D.L., Chiu, C.-Y. P., & Ochsner, K.N. (1993) Implicit memory: a selective review. *Annual Review of Psychology, 16*, 159–182.

Schank, R.C., & Abelson, R.P. (1977). *Scripts, plans, goals and understanding: An inquiry into human knowledge structures.* Oxford: Erlbaum.

Schemer, C., Mathes, J., Wirth, W., & Textor, S. (2008). Does 'passing the Courvoisier' always pay off? Positive and negative evaluative conditioning effects of brand placements in music videos. *Psychology & Marketing, 25*, 923–943.

Schlosser, A.E., & Shavitt, S. (2002). Anticipating discussion about a product: Rehearsing what to say can affect your judgments. *Journal of Consumer Research, 29*, 101–115.

Schneider, W., & Shiffrin, R.M. (1977). Controlled and automatic human information processing: I. Detection, search, and attention. *Psychological Review, 84*, 1–66.

Scholderer, J., & Trondsen, T. (2007). The dynamics of consumer behaviour: On habit, discontent, and other fish to fry. *Appetite, 51*, 576–591.

Schumann, D.W., Petty, R.E., & Clemons, D.S. (1991). Predicting the effectiveness of different strategies of advertising variation: A test of the repetition-variation hypothesis. *Journal of Consumer Research, 17*, 192–202.

Schwarz, N. (2004). Meta-cognitive experiences in consumer judgment and decision making. *Journal of Consumer Psychology, 14* (4), 332–348.

Schwarz, N. (2007). Attitude construction: evaluation in context. *Social Cognition, 25*, 638–656.

Schwarz, N., & Bless, H. (1992). Scandals and the public trust in politicians: Assimilation and contrast effects. *Personality and Social Psychology Bulletin, 18*, 574–579.

Schwarz, N., & Bohner, G. (2001). The construction of attitudes. In A. Tesser & N. Schwarz (Eds.), *Blackwell Handbook of Social Psychology: Intraindividual Processes* (pp. 436–457). Oxford, UK: Blackwell.

Schwarz, N., & Clore, G.L. (1983). Mood, misattribution and judgment of well-being: Informative and directive functions and affective states. *Journal of Personality and Social Psychology, 45*, 513–523.

Schwarz, N., & Strack, F. (1991). Context effects in attitude surveys: Applying cognitive theory to social research. In W. Stroebe & M. Hewstone (Eds.), *European Review of Social Psychology* (Vol. 2, pp. 31–50). Chichester, UK: Wiley.

Segrin, C. (1993). The effects of nonverbal behavior on outcomes of compliance gaining attempts. *Communication Studies, 44*, 169–187.

Sengupta, J., & Johar, G.V. (2002). Effects of inconsistent attribute information on the predictive value of product attitudes: Toward a resolution of opposing perspectives. *Journal of Consumer Research, 29*, 39–56.

Shallice, T., & Warrington, E.K. (1970). Independent functioning of verbal memory stores: a neuropsychological study. *Quarterly Journal of Experimental Psychology, 22*, 261–273.

Shapiro, S. (1999).When an ad's influence is beyond our conscious control: Perceptual and conceptual fluency effects caused by incidental ad exposure. *Journal of Consumer Research, 26*, 16–36.

Shapiro, S., & Krishnan, S.H. (2001). Memory-based measures for assessing advertising effects: A comparison of explicit and implicit memory effects. *Journal of Advertising, 30*, 11–13.

Shapiro, S., MacInnis, D.J., & Heckler, S.E. (1997). The effects of incidental ad exposure on the formation of consideration sets. *Journal of Consumer Research, 24*, 94–104.

Shavitt, S. (1990). The role of attitude objects in attitude functions. *Journal of Experimental Social Psychology, 26*, 124–148.

Shavitt, S, Swan, S., Lowrey, T.M., & Wänke, M. (1994). The interaction of endorser attractiveness and involvement in persuasion depends on the goals that guide message processing. *Journal of Consumer Psychology, 3*, 137–162.

Sheeran, P. (2002). Intention-behavior relations: A conceptual and empirical review. In W. Stroebe & M. Hewstone (Eds.), *European Review of Social Psychology* (Vol. 12, pp. 1–36). Chichester: Wiley.

Sheeran, P., & Orbell, S. (2000). Using implementation intentions to increase attendance for cervical cancer screening. *Health Psychology, 18*, 283–289.

Sheppard, B.H., Hartwick, J., & Warshaw, P.R. (1988). The theory of reasoned action: A meta-analysis of past research with recommendations for modification and future research. *Journal of Consumer Research, 15*, 325–342.

Sherman, D.A.K., Nelson, L.D., Steele, C.M. (2000). Do messages about health risks threaten the self? Increasing the acceptance of threatening health messages via self-affirmation. *Personality and Social Psychology Bulletin, 26*, 1046–1058.

Shiffrin, R.M., & Schneider, W. (1977). Controlled and automatic human information processing: II. Perceptual learning, automatic attending, and general theory. *Psychological Review, 84*, 127–190.

Shimp, T.A., Stuart, E.W., & Engle, R.W. (1991). A program of classical conditioning experiments testing variations in the conditioned stimulus and context. *Journal of Consumer Research, 18*, 1–12.

Shiv, B., Carmon, Z., & Ariely, D. (2005). Placebo effects of marketing actions: Consumers may get what they pay for. *Journal of Marketing Research, 42*, 383–393.

Simonin, B.L., & Ruth, J.A. (1998). Is a company known by the company it keeps? Assessing the spillover effects of brand alliances on consumer brand attitudes. *Journal of Marketing Research, 35*, 30–42.

Simonson, I., Carmon, Z., Dhar, R., Drolet, A., & Nowlis, S.M. (2001). Consumer research: In search of identity. *Annual Review of Psychology, 52*, 249–275.

Skurnik, I., Yoon, C., Park, D.C., & Schwarz, N. (2005). How warnings about false claims become reommendations. *Journal of Consumer Research, 31*, 713–724.

Smith, E.E. (1999). Mental representation and memory. In D. Gilbert, S. Fiske & G. Lindzey (Eds.). *Handbook of Social Psychology* (4th edn; Vol. 1, pp. 391–445). Boston: McGraw-Hill.

Smith, M.B., Bruner, J.S., & White, R.W. (1956). *Opinions and personality.* New York: Wiley.

Smith, R.E., & Hunt, S.D. (1978). Attributional processes and the effects in promotional situations. *Journal of Consumer Research, 5*, 149–158.

Smith, R.E., & Swinyard, W.R. (1982). Information response models: An integrated approach. *Journal of Marketing, 46*, 81–93.

Smith, T.M., Gopalakrishna, S., & Chatterjee, R. (2006). A three-stage model of integrated marketing communications at the marketing-sales interface. *Journal of Marketing Research, 43*, 564–579.

Snyder, M. (1974). Self-monitoring of expressive behavior. *Journal of Personality and Social Psychology, 30*, 526–537.

Snyder, M., & DeBono, K.G. (1985). Appeals to image and claims about quality: Understanding the psychology of advertising. *Journal of Personality and Social Psychology, 49*, 586–597.

Sperling, G. (1960). The information available in brief visual presentations. *Psychological Monographs: General and Applied, 74*, 1–29.

Squire, L.R., (1987). *Memory and Brain.* New York: Oxford University Press.

Squire, L.R., Knowlton, B., & Musen, G. (1993). *Annual Review of Psychology, 44*, 493–495.

Staats, A.W., & Staats, C.K. (1958). Attitudes established by classical conditioning. *Journal of Abnormal and Social Psychology, 57*, 37–40.

Stewart, D.W., & Furse, D.H. (1986). *Effective television advertising: A study of 1000 commercials.* Lexington, MA: Lexington Books.

Strahan, E.J., Spencer, S.J., & Zanna, M.P. (2002). Subliminal priming and persuasion: Striking while the iron is hot. *Journal of Experimental Social Psychology, 38,* 368–383.

Strack, F., & Deutsch, R. (2004). Reflective and impulsive determinants of social behavior. *Personality and Social Psychology Review, 8,* 220–247.

Strick, M., Holland, R., & an Knippenberg, A. (2008). Seductive eyes: Attractiveness and direct gaze increase desire for associated objects. *Cognition, 106,* 1487–1496.

Stroebe, W. (2000). *Social Psychology and Health* (2nd edn). Buckingham: Open University Press.

Stroebe, W., Hewstone, M. & Jonas, K. (2008). Introducing social psychology. In M. Hewstone, W.Stroebe & K. Jonas (Eds.), *Introduction to Social Psychology: A European Perspective* (pp. 3–19). Oxford: Blackwell

Stroebe, W. (2008). Strategies of attitude and behaviour change. In M. Hewstone, W. Stroebe & K. Jonas (Eds.), *Introduction to social psychology: A European perspective.* Oxford, UK: Blackwell.

Strong, E.K. (1925). *The Psychology of Selling.* New York: McGraw-Hill.

Stuart, E.W., Shimp, T.A. & Engle, R.W. (1987). Classical conditioning of consumer attitudes: Four experiments in an advertising context. *Journal of Consumer Research, 14,* 334–349.

Sullivan, G.L. & Macklin, C.M. (1988). Vividness and unvividness effects in print advertising: An experimental investigation. *Journal of Mental Imagery, 12* (3–4): 133–144.

Sullivan, H.W., & Rothman, A.J. (2008). When planning is needed: implementation intention and attainment of approach versus avoidance health goals. *Health Psychology, 27,* 438–444.

Sutherland, M., & Sylvester, A.K. (2000). *Advertising and the mind of the consumer: What works, what doesn't and why.* London: Kogan Page.

Swinyard, W.R. (1981). The interaction between comparative advertising and copy claim variation. *Journal of Marketing Research, 18,* 175–186.

Szibillo, G.J., & Heslin, R. (1973). Resistance to persuasion: Inoculation theory in a marketing context. *Journal of Marketing Research, 10,* 396–403.

Tanner, R.J., Ferraro, R., Chartrand, T.L., Bettman, J.R., & van Baaren, R.B. (2008). Of chameleons and consumption: The impact of mimicry on choice and preferences. *Journal of Consumer Research, 34,* 754–766.

Taylor, S.E. & Thompson, S.C. (1982). Stalking the elusive 'vividness' effect. *Psychological Review, 89* (2), 155–181.

Teigen, K.H., & Keren, G. (2003). Surprises: Low probabilities or high contrasts? *Cognition, 87* (2), 55–71.

Tellis, G.J. (2004). Effective advertising: Understanding when, how, and why advertising works. Thousand Oaks, CA: Sage.

Terry, W.S. (2005). Serial position effects in recall of television commercials. *Journal of General Psychology, 132,* 152–163.

Thomas, W.I., & Znaniecki, F. (1918). *The Polish Peasant in Europe and America* (Vol. 1). Boston, Badger.

Thompson, M.M., & Zanna, M.P., & Griffin, D.W. (1995). Let's not be indifferent about (attitudinal) ambivalence. In R.E. Petty & J.A. Krosnick (eds.) *Attitude Strength: Antecedents and Consequences* (pp. 361–386). Hillsdale, NJ: Erlbaum.

Tiedens, L.Z., & Fragale, A.R. (2003). Power moves: Complementarity in dominant and submissive nonverbal behavior. *Journal of Personality and Social Psychology, 84,* 558–568.

Till, B.D. & Priluck, R.L. (2000). Stimulus generalization in classical conditioning: An intitiaul investigation and extension. *Psychology & Marketing, 17,* 55–72.

Todd, P.M., & Gigerenzer, G. (2007). Environments that make us smart. *Current Directions in Psychological Science, 16,* 167–171.

Tormala, Z.L., & Petty, R.E. (2002). What doesn't kill me makes me stronger: The effects of resisting persuasion on attitude certainty. *Journal of Personality and Social Psychology*, *83*, 1298–1313.

Tourangeau, R., Rasinski, K.A., Bradburn, N., & D'Andrade, R. (1989). Belief accessibility and context effects in attitude measurement. *Journal of Experimental Social Psychology*, *25*, 401–421.

Tourangeau, R., & Rasinski, K.A. (1988). Cognitive processes underlying context effects in attitude measurement. *Psychological Bulletin*, *103*, 299–314.

Tuk, M.A., Verlegh, P.W.J., Smidts, A. & Wigboldus, D. (2009). Sales and sincerity: The role of relational framing in word-of-mouth marketing. *Journal of Consumer Psychology*, *19*, 38–47.

Tulving, E. (1983). *Elements of Episodic Memory*. Oxford: Oxford University Press.

Tversky, A., & Kahneman, D. (1974). Judgment under uncertainty: Heuristics and biases. *Science*, *185*, 1124–1131.

Tybout, A.M., Calder, B.J., & Sternthal, B. (1981). Using information processing theory to design marketing strategies. *Journal of Marketing Research*, *18*, 73–79.

Tybout, A.M., Sternthal, B., & Calder, B.J. (1983). Information availability as a determinant of multiple request effectiveness. *Journal of Marketing Research*, *20*, 280–290.

Underwood, B.J. (1957). Interference and forgetting. *Psychological Review*, *64*, 49–60.

Vakratsas, D., & Ambler, T. (1999). How advertising works: What do we really know? *Journal of Marketing*, *63*, 26–43.

Vanden Abeele, P., & MacLachlan, D. (1994). Process tracing of emotional responses to TV ads: Revisiting the warmth monitor. *Journal of Consumer Research*, *20* (4), 586–600.

Vaughn, R. (1980). How advertising works: A planning model. *Journal of Advertising Research*, *20* (5), 27–33.

Venkatraman, M.P., Marlino, D., Kardes, F.R., & Sklar, K.B. (1990). The interactive effects of message appeal and individual differences on information processing and persuasion. *Psychology & Marketing*, *7*, 85–96.

Verlegh, P.W.J., & Steenkamp, J.-B.E.M. (1999). A review and meta-analysis of country-of-origin research. *Journal of Economic Psychology*, *20*, 521–546.

Verplanken, B., & Aarts, H. (1999) Habit, attitude, planned behavior: is habit an empty construct or an interesting case of goal directed automaticity? In W. Stroebe & M. Hewstone (Eds.), *European Review of Social Psychology*, Vol. 10 (pp. 100–34). Chichester: Wiley.

Verplanken, B., Aarts, H., & van Knippenberg, A., (1997). Habit, information acquisition, and the process of making travel mode choices. *European Journal of Social Psychology*, *27*, 539–560.

Verplanken, B., Aarts, H., van Knippenberg, A., & Moonen, A. (1998). Habit versus planned behaviour: A field experiment. *British Journal of Social Psychology*, *37*, 111–128.

Veryzer, R.W., & Hutchinson, J.W. (1998). The influence of unity and prototypicality on aesthetic responses to new product designs. *Journal of Consumer Research*, *24*, 374–394.

Visser, P.S., Bizer, G.Y., & Krosnick, J.A. (2006). Exploring the latent structure of strength-related attitude attributes. *Advances of Experimental Social Psychology*, *38*, 1–68.

Visser, P.S., & Mirabile, R.R. (2004). Attitudes in the social context : The impact of social network composition on individual-level attitude strength. *Journal of Personality and Social Psychology*, *87*, 779–795.

Vohs, K.D., & Heatherton, T.F. (2000). Self-regulatory failure: A resource-depletion approach. *Psychological Science*, *11*, 249–254.

Vohs, K.D., Baumeister, R.F., & Tice, D.M. (2008). Self-regulation: Goals, consumption and choices. In C. Haugtvedt, P.M. Herr, & F.R. Kardes (Eds.), *Handbook of Consumer Psychology* (pp. 349–366). New York: Taylor & Francis.

Vonk, R. (2002). Self-serving interpretations of flattery: Why ingratiation works. *Journal of Personality and Social Psychology, 82,* 515–526.

Vroom, V.H. (1964). *Work and Motivation*. New York: Wiley.

Walster, E., & Festinger, L. (1962). The effectiveness of 'overheard' persuasive communications. *Journal of Abnormal and Social Psychology, 65*, 395–402.

Wänke, M. (2008). *Social Psychology of Consumer Behavior*. Hove: Psychology Press.

Wänke, M., Bless, H., & Biller, B. (1996). Subjective experience versus content of information in the construction of attitude judgments. *Personality and Social Psychology Bulletin, 22*, 1105–1113.

Wänke, M., Bless, H., & Igou, E.R. (2001). Next to a star: Paling, shining or both? Turning interexemplar contrast into interexemplar assimilation. *Personality and Social Psychology Bulletin, 27*, 14–29.

Wänke, M., Bohner, G., & Jurkowitsch, A. (1997). There are many reasons to drive a BMW. Does imagined ease of argument generation influence attitudes? *Journal of Consumer Research, 24*, 170–177.

Warlop, L., & Alba, J.W. (2004). Sincere flattery: Trade-dress imitation and consumer choice. *Journal of Consumer Psychology, 14*, 21–27.

Warrington, E.K., & Weiskrantz, L. (1970). Amnesic syndrome: consolidation or retrieval? *Nature, 228*, 629–630.

Webb, T.L., & Sheeran, P. (2007). How do implementation intentions promote goal attainment? A test of component processes. *Journal of Experimental Social Psychology, 43*, 295–302.

Webster, D.M., & Kruglanski, A.W. (1994). Individual differences in need for cognitive closure. *Journal of Personality and Social Psychology, 67*, 1049–1062.

Weilbacher, W.M. (2001). Point of view: Does advertising cause a 'hierarchy of effects'? *Journal of Advertising Research, 41* (6), 19–26.

Weiner, B. (1985). 'Spontaneous' causal thinking. *Psychological Bulletin, 97*, 74–84.

Wells, W., Moriarty, S., & Burnett, J. (2006). *Advertising: Principles and Practice* (7th edn). Upper Saddle River, NJ: Prentice Hall.

Wheeler, S.C., Briñol, P., & Hermann, A.D. (2007). Resistance to persuasion as self-regulation: Ego-depletion and its effects on attitude change processes. *Journal of Experimental Social Psychology, 43*, 150–156.

Wheeler, S.C., Petty, R.E., & Bizer, G.Y. (2005). Self-schema matching and attitude change: Situational and dispositional determinants of message elaboration. *Journal of Consumer Research, 31*, 787–797.

White, K., & Dahl, D.W. (2006). To be or not be? The influence of dissociative reference groups on consumer preferences. *Journal of Consumer Psychology, 16*, 404–414.

Wicker, A.W. (1969). Attitudes versus actions: The relationship of verbal and overt behavioral responses to attitude objects. *Journal of Social Issues, 25*, 41–78.

Wikipedia (2008a). Made in Germany. http://en.wikipedia.org/wiki/Made_in_Germany. (accessed August, 2008).

Wikipedia (2008b). Watch. http://en.wikipedia.org/wiki/Watch. (Accessed August, 2008).

Williams, P., Block, L.G., & Fitzsimons, G.J. (2006). Simply asking questions about health behaviours increases both healthy and unhealthy behaviours. *Social Influence, 1* (2), 117–127.

Williams, P., Fitzsimons, G.J., & Block, L.G. (2004). When consumers do not recognize 'benign' intention questions as persuasion attempts. *Journal of Consumer Research, 31*, 540–550.

Wilson, T.D., & Kraft, D. (1993). Why do I love thee: Effects of repeated introspections about a dating relationship on attitudes towards that relationship. *Personality and Social Psychology Bulletin, 19*, 409–418

Wilson, T.D., Kraft, D., & Dunn, D.S. (1989). The disruptive effects of explaining attitudes: The moderating effects of knowledge about the attitude object. *Journal of Experimental Social Psychology, 25*, 379–400.

Wilson, T.D., Lindsey, S., & Schooler, T.Y. (2000). A model of dual attitudes. *Psychological Review, 107*, 101–126.

Winkielman, P., Schwarz, N., Fazandeiro, T., & Reber, R. (2003). The hedonic marking of processing fluency: Implications for evaluative judgments. In J. Musch & K.C. Klauer (Eds.), *The Psychology of Evaluation* (pp. 189–218). Mahwah, NJ.: Erlbaum.

Witte, K., (1992). Putting the fear back into fear appeals: The extended parallel process model. *Communication Monographs, 59*, 329–349.

Witte, K., & Allen, M. (2000). A meta-analysis of fear appeals: Implications for effective public health campaigns. *Health Education and Behavior, 27*, 591–616.

Wood, W. (1982). Retrieval of attitude-relevant information from memory: Effects on susceptibility to persuasion and on intrinsic motivation. *Journal of Personality and Social Psychology, 42*, 798–810.

Wood, W., Kallgren, C.A., & Preisler, R.M. (1985). Access to attitude-relevant information in memory as determinant of persuasion: The role of message attributes. *Journal of Personality and Social Psychology, 21*, 73–85.

Wood, W., & Quinn, J.M (2003). Forewarned and forearmed? Two meta-analytic syntheses of forewarnings of influence appeals. *Psychological Bulletin, 129*, 119–138.

Worchel, S., Lee, J., & Adewole, A. (1975). Effects of supply and demand on ratings of object value. *Journal of Personality and Social Psychology, 32*, 906–914.

Wright, A.A., & Lynch, J. G. (1995). Communication effects of advertising versus direct experience when both search and experience attributes are present. *Journal of Consumer Research, 21*, 708–718.

Wright, P. (2002). Marketplace meta-cognition and social intelligence. *Journal of Consumer Research, 28*, 677–682.

Yang, M., & Roskos-Ewoldsen, D.R. (2007). The effectiveness of brand placements in the movies: Levels of placements, explicit and implicit memory, and brand-choice behavior. *Journal of Communication, 57*, 469–489.

Yeshin, T. (2006). *Advertising*. New York: Thomson.

Yeung, C.W.M., & Soman, D. (2007). The duration heuristic. *Journal of Consumer Research, 34*, 315–326.

Yoo, C.Y. (2008). Unconscious processing of Web advertising: Effects on implicit memory, attitude toward the brand, and consideration set. *Journal of Interactive Marketing, 22*, 2–18.

Zajonc, R.B. (1968). Attitudinal effects of mere exposure. *Journal of Personality and Social Psychology Monographs, 9* (2, pt 2), 1–27.

Zanna, M.P., & Rempel, J.K. (1988). Attitudes: A new look at an old concept. In D. Bar-Tal & A.W. Kruglanski (Eds.), *The Social Psychology of Knowledge* (pp. 315–334). Cambridge, UK: Cambridge University Press.

Zhang, S., & Sood, S. (2002). 'Deep' and 'surface' cues: Brand extension evaluations by children and adults. *Journal of Consumer Research, 29*, 129–141.

Zhao, X (1997). Clutter and serial order redefined and retested. *Journal of Advertising Research, 37*, 57–73.

Glossary

Accessibility   refers to the speed and ease with which information is retrieved from memory.

Advertising   refers to any form of paid communication by an identified sponsor aimed to inform and/or persuade target audiences about an organization, product, service or idea.

Advertising clutter   refers to the extent to which multiple messages compete for the **attention** of consumers.

Advertising wear-out   captures the phenomenon that advertising repetition ultimately hurts advertising effectiveness because every subsequent exposure enables the generation of ever more negative consumer responses, such as scepticism and irritation.

Affect-as-information hypothesis   refers to the use of the 'how do I feel about it' heuristic. Individuals use this heuristic to infer their attitude from their present mood state

Affect-based appeals   refer to the use of affect and emotion in advertising to appeal to consumers' feelings about a product in order to persuade.

Affective priming method   is an implicit measure of attitudes. Individuals are presented on each trial with a prime (the name or picture of an attitude object). Immediately afterwards they are presented with positive or negative adjectives (e.g. words such as 'useful', 'valuable' or 'disgusting') and are asked to decide as fast as possible whether the adjective is positive or negative. The time it takes people to make this judgement (i.e. response latency) constitutes the dependent measure.

Alpha strategies   in advertising are message tactics that generally increase the attractiveness of the offer and thus serve to influence a consumer's **approach motivation**.

Approach motivation. The tendency to move toward an object, advocated position, offer or idea.

Argument-based appeals use rational arguments to address consumers' beliefs about the attributes of a product in order to persuade.

Assimilation entails the notion that objects are classified as more similar to the parent category to the extent that the object and category are more congruent

Attention is the process by which information is held in conscious awareness and can be manipulated in **working memory**.

Attitude certainty refers to the confidence individuals have in the validity or correctness of their own attitude.

Attitude strength refers to the extent to which attitudes influence judgments and behaviour. Strong attitudes are characterized by four attributes: (1) high stability over time; (2) great impact on behaviour; (3) great influence on information processing; and (4) great resistance to persuasion.

Attitudes reflect the categorization of a stimulus object along an evaluative dimension.

Attitudinal ambivalence reflects a state in which an individual gives an attitude object equally strong positive or negative evaluation.

Automatic processes are processes that occur without intention, effort or awareness and do not interfere with other concurrent cognitive processes.

Avoidance motivation. The tendency to move away from an object, advocated position, offer or idea.

Beliefs refer to the opinions, knowledge or thoughts someone has about some attitude object. Beliefs are perceived links between the attitude object and various attributes. Beliefs often form the basis of evaluative judgments such as attitudes or preferences.

Brand is the label with which to identify an individual product and differentiate it from that of competitors.

Brand awareness refers to the ease with which exposure to a brand triggers the **brand image**.

Brand equity refers to the value added to a product by a brand name.

Brand image refers to the beliefs, feelings and evaluations associated with a brand name.

Categorization is the process by which incoming information is classified, that is, labelled as belonging to one or more categories based on a comparative assessment of features of the category and the incoming information.

Causal relationship refers to a relationship between two variables where change in one variable (the antecedent, or independent variable) *elicits* change in the other (the consequence, or dependent) variable. To infer causality, the antecedent must precede the consequence, changes in the antecedent must be associated with changes in the consequence and no other explanation for the change in consequence must be present than the change in antecedent.

Central executive allocates **attention** and coordinates the two subsystems of working memory of the memory system of Baddeley. It focuses the available attentional capacity and determines when the **phonological loop** and the **visuo-spatial sketchpad** are used and how they are used.

Classical conditioning refers to a process through which a neutral stimulus that is initially incapable of eliciting a particular response (the conditioned stimulus; CS) gradually acquires the ability to do so through repeated association with a stimulus that already evokes this response (unconditioned stimulus; US).

Click-whirr response.   Derived from ethological research, the click-whirr response entails a fixed action pattern, which unfolds more or less invariantly when suitable environmental stimuli are present in the influence context, similar to the involuntary squeaking of baby birds once they spot their mother approaching the nest. 'Click' refers to the stimulus that prompts the behavioural response, and 'whirr' refers to the actual unfolding of that response.

Cognitive response model   assumes that attitude change is mediated by the thoughts (cognitive responses) recipients generate while listening to persuasive arguments and that the magnitude and direction of attitude change will depend on the extent of message relevant thinking and the favourability of the thoughts generated in response to message arguments.

Commitment/consistency principle   captures the tendency to behave congruently across situations.

Compliance   is the overt behavioural acquiescence response that is sought in response to a specific request.

Comprehension   involves the process of forming inferences pertaining to the semantic meaning of a stimulus.

Consideration set   refers to the set of brands brought to mind in a particular choice situation

Consumer segment   is a group of consumers who share one or more feature(s) that differentiate them from other groups of consumers and that can be targeted by manufacturers and advertisers with products and advertisements to accommodate those features. Examples include age, education level, income, social class, interests, values and lifestyles.

Correlation   refers to an association between two variables where the change in one variable is systematically related to a change in the other.

Counterfactual thinking   is thinking about what might have been, or events that did not (yet) happen. This thinking on what might have been appears frequently in a 'what if' or 'if only' form.

Country-of-origin effect.   Consumers' use of knowledge about the country in which a product has been produced as a basis for evaluation and judgement of that product.

Dependent variable   is the variable that is expected to change as a function of changes in the independent variable. Observed changes in the dependent variable are seen as dependent on manipulated changes in the **independent variable**.

Direct mail   refers to a personalized form of advertising, where consumers are typically addressed individually by their names

Direct marketing   is a form of marketing communication where a firm communicates directly and individually with a potential customer, with the objective of generating a behavioural response from him/her, preferably in the form of a transaction.

Disrupt-then-Reframe technique (DTR).   An influence technique that is characterized by a small 'twist', or odd element, in a typical scripted request, the 'disruption', (for instance stating the prize of an offer in pennies rather than dollars, i.e. 'They're 200 pennies . . . that's $2'), followed by a persuasive phrase that concludes the script, the 'reframe' (e.g. 'It's a really good deal').

Distraction. While listening to a persuasive communication, individuals are distracted by having to perform an irrelevant activity or because of background noise. Distraction can either reduce or increase the impact depending on the strength of arguments contained in the message.

Door-In-The-Face (DITF). An influence technique which is characterized by a sequence of rejection-then-moderation. In the DITF technique, a large request (which will probably be rejected) is followed by a more moderate target request.

Dual Mediation Hypothesis of advertisements. According to this hypothesis, the attitude towards an advertisement influences brand attitudes through two pathways, namely indirectly, via brand cognitions and directly, via evaluative conditioning

Dual process theories of persuasion consider two modes of information processing, systematic and non-systematic (e.g. peripheral or heuristic processing). Modes differ in the extent to which individuals engage in message-relevant thought in order to decide on whether to accept message arguments. The mode used depends on processing ability and processing motivation. See **Elaboration Likelihood Model; Heuristic-Systematic Model**.

Durable goods refer to products that are not used up during consumption (like non-durable goods) but can be used more than once. Examples are refrigerators, cars or furniture.

Elaboration Likelihood Model of persuasion (ELM) is a **dual process theory of persuasion**. It assumes **persuasive communications** can induce attitude change through two different modes of processing (peripheral and central). Elaboration refers to the extent to which a recipient thinks about a message and scrutinizes message arguments. The probability that recipients think about a message (i.e. elaboration likelihood) is determined by processing motivation and ability.

Elaborative reasoning refers to the process by which a semantically represented stimulus is related to previously stored consumer knowledge that allows for simple or more complex inferences.

Encoding refers to the processes involved when an external stimulus is transformed into an internal representation that can be retained in the cognitive system. This requires that the external stimulus is related to prior knowledge in order to give it meaning.

Episodic buffer is a limited-capacity temporary storage system in the Baddeley model, capable of integrating information from a variety of sources, each involving a different set of codes.

Episodic memory refers to our recollection of a specific event that occurred at a particular place and time.

Evaluative-cognitive consistency refers to the consistency between people's attitudes towards an attitude object and the evaluative implications of their beliefs about the object.

Evaluative conditioning, see **classical conditioning**.

Event marketing refers to a marketing practice where a sports event or cultural event (such as a soccer match or a rock concert) is used as a 'vehicle' to get in touch with prospective customers, frequently through **sponsorship** of an existing event or the creation of an entirely new one, closely associated with the sponsoring brand.

Expectancy disconfirmation model.   Oliver (1980, 1993) developed this model to account for consumer (dis)satisfaction. According to the model, consumers form expectancies about product performance before buying a product. After they buy the product, consumers then compare the actual performance with the expected level of performance. To the extent that actual performance exceeds expectations, satisfaction is enhanced. To the extent that it falls short, satisfaction suffers.

Expectancy-value models.   According to these models attitudes can be predicted by multiplying the valuation of each attribute associated with the attitude object with the subjective probability with which it is perceived as linked to the object.

Explicit attitudes   are attitudes an individual is aware of and that are reflected by self-reported evaluations.

Explicit memory   is characterized by a person's conscious recollection of facts or events. Two subcategories of explicit memory are typically distinguished, namely **episodic** and **semantic memory**.

Factorial experiments   are experiments in which two or more independent variables (i.e. factors) are manipulated within the same design.

Fear-arousing communications   are messages which emphasize some health threat to persuade recipients to perform a recommended action described as reducing or eliminating the threat.

Figure-ground principle   holds that figural stimuli become focal whereas non-figural stimuli become nonfocal. Hence, the principle captures the process by which stimuli can grab attention and everything else fades into the background.

Foot-In-The-Door technique (FITD).   An influence technique where compliance with an initial, small request, increases the likelihood of compliance with a second, much larger request.

Free recall test   is a standard test of **explicit memory**. Respondents, who previously had to learn a list of words, are asked to recall as many of the recently presented words as possible.

Goals.   Desired states which are perceived as attainable and which are discrepant from the individual's present state.

Habits.   Learned sequences of acts that have become automatic responses to specific cues and are functional in obtaining certain goals or end states.

Hedonic fluency model   assumes that the increased ease of processing is experienced as pleasant and that this positive affect will be used as information in the evaluation of the stimulus.

Hemispheric lateralization   implies that our brain hemispheres have evolved specialized processing units for specific types of information. The right hemisphere is specialized in holistic, impressionistic processing. The left hemisphere specializes in bottom-up, data driven feature analysis. Therefore, picture processing involves relatively higher activation levels of the right hemisphere and textual processing involves relatively high levels of activation of the left hemisphere.

Heuristic processing. Use of simple **heuristics** (e.g. experts know; statistics do not lie) to evaluate the validity of arguments contained in a persuasive communication.

Heuristic-Systematic Model (HSM) is a **dual process theory of persuasion** that assumes that attitude change in response to a persuasive communication is mediated by two modes of information processing (heuristic and systematic), which can occur concurrently. **Heuristic processing** is the preferred mode when processing ability and/or motivation are low. With increasing processing ability and motivation, **systematic processing** becomes the preferred mode.

Heuristics are simple decision rules (rules of thumb), frequently of an 'if-then' type, that summarize more complex types of information and can function as a basis for judgement and decision-making.

Hierarchy-of-effects models refer to a class of advertising effects models that propose that the impact of advertising proceeds through a fixed learning sequence involving a cognitive stage, an affective stage, and a conative, or behavioural, stage.

Implementation intention. The intention to enact a certain behaviour in a specific situation and at a specific time.

Implicit Association Test (IAT). A procedure developed to measure implicit attitudes using the strength of an association between two concepts with positive and negative evaluations. It uses response latencies to infer implicit evaluations.

Implicit attitudes are evaluations, of which the individual is typically not aware and which influence reactions or actions over which the individual has no control.

Implicit memory effects occur when previous experiences facilitate our performance of subsequent tasks without us remembering the previous experience or being aware of its influence on our performance.

Independent variable refers to a variable which the experimenter manipulates or modifies in order to assess the effect on one or more **dependent variables**

Information Processing Model of persuasion. A **hierarchy-of-effects model** model developed by McGuire that assumed that there are different stages involved in the processing of persuasive communications and that attitude and behaviour change can only be achieved if individuals passed through the preceding stages (e.g. attention, comprehension, acceptance). The model further assumes that determinants of persuasion can have different impact at different stages.

Informational appeals use factual information on product attributes and availability to inform and persuade consumers.

Instrumental or utilitarian function of attitudes. The function attitudes serve in helping us to maximize our rewards and minimize penalties in interactions with our physical and social environment. They help us to approach those stimuli, which in the past have been associated with positive reinforcements and to avoid stimuli that have resulted in punishments.

Integrated Marketing Communications or IMC refers to the process of coordinating various elements in the promotional mix to create synergy between them and thus maximize the impact on consumer responses.

Interactive marketing   refers to marketing strategies involving two-way communication between firm and customers, frequently through the use of internet technology.

Involvement   refers to the extent of perceived personal relevance of a brand, product or product category.

Knowledge function of attitudes.   The function attitudes serve in helping us to organize and structure our environment to interpret and make sense of otherwise chaotic perceptions.

Lexical decision task.   A test that assesses the degree of cognitive accessibility of a concept. Participants are either presented with words or with non-word letter strings and are asked to decide as quickly as possible whether the presented item was a word or a non-word. There is evidence that lexical decisions about target words are made quicker the greater their cognitive accessibility.

Liking principle.   An influence principle that states that we are more likely to comply with the requests of someone we like than someone we dislike or feel neutral towards.

Long-term memory   is assumed to store nearly unlimited amounts of information for a nearly unlimited period of time.

Lowball technique.   An influence technique which consists of first soliciting commitment from customers with a particularly attractive offer and then changing the deal to a less attractive target request or offer.

Main effect   refers to the separate effects of each independent variable in a factorial experiment.

Matching activation hypothesis   assumes that when one hemisphere is activated by the information that accommodates the processing style of that particular hemisphere, the other hemisphere is encouraged to elaborate on secondary material. Thus, greater activation of one hemisphere (e.g. the left hemisphere) will be matched by an increase of processing resources in the opposing hemisphere.

Mediational analysis   attempts to identify the intermediary psychological processes that are responsible for the (i.e. mediate) the effect of the independent on the dependent variable.

Memory   is a system that not only allows us to record, store and retrieve the information that is acquired through our senses, but that also influences the way this information is perceived, encoded and stored.

Memory-based choice   refers to a choice made on the basis of information retrieved from memory rather than **stimulus-based choices** made from a range of products (e.g. in a supermarket).

Memory-based judgements   are judgements made on the basis of information retrieved from memory.

Mere exposure effect   increases the liking of an object as the result of being repeatedly exposed to it.

Meta-cognition   refers to 'thinking about thinking or feeling', or the phenomenon of reflecting on one's own inner states, and to infer something from that process.

Moderated or interaction effect   refers to a conditional effect where the effect of an independent on a dependent variable depends on the level of a third variable, the **moderator**.

Moderator is a variable that influences the strength and/or direction of the effect of independent on the dependent variable.

Multiple-role assumption. Assumption that the information contained in a persuasive communication can often serve multiple roles and, and depending on the extent of processing motivation, can serve as an argument as well as a source characteristic.

Need for cognition differentiates people according to the extent to which they enjoy thinking about the arguments contained in a message. Individuals high in need for cognition engage in more content-related thinking when exposed to a persuasive communication and are therefore more influenced by argument quality. Individuals low in need for cognition tend to be more influenced by heuristic cues.

Need for cognitive closure is an individual difference variable which refers to the desire of individuals for a definite answer on some topic, any answer as opposed to confusion and ambiguity. Individuals high in need for cognitive closure prefer the use of heuristics over elaborate message scrutiny.

Novelty refers to the perception of 'newness' of a stimulus, and is captured by the extent to which information is unfamiliar and the extent to which information about the products in advertising disconfirms existing consumer expectancies.

Object appraisal function combines the **utilitarian** and the **knowledge function** of attitudes.

Omega strategies can persuade and induce compliance because they reduce or minimize the tendency to move away from the position, and hence influence a consumer's **avoidance motivation**.

Online judgements are judgements made while being exposed to information.

Outcome-relevant involvement is the extent to which the acquisition and use of a product or brand is deemed to have significant personal consequences for the consumer

Perceived behavioural control refers to the individual's assessment of their ability to execute the intended behaviour. Perceived behavioural control can be assessed directly by asking respondents to indicate the extent to which performing a given behaviour is under their control. Alternatively, one can measure perceived behavioural control indirectly, by asking people to list the factors, which might prevent them from engaging in a specific behaviour as well as how likely this was going to happen.

Personal selling is a two-way, face-to-face form of communication between sales representative and consumer to inform and persuade prospective buyers with the aim of yielding a behavioural response from them, such as an initial or repeat purchase.

Persuasion refers to any change in beliefs and attitudes that results from exposure to a communication.

Phonological loop is a subsystem of Baddeley's multi-component working memory model. It is assumed to consist of two components, a phonological store that briefly holds sounds or speech-based information and an articulatory rehearsal system that uses subvocal 'inner speech'.

Pioneering advantage refers to the relative positive evaluation that first brands that enter a market or product category frequently enjoy in comparison to followers.

Preattentive analysis   refers to a general, non-goal directed, 'surveillance' of the environment.

Preferences   are relative evaluative judgments of one object in comparison to other objects.

Price-quality heuristic   refers to the expectancy that 'if expensive then good' and conversely, 'if inexpensive then bad'.

Priming   refers to the phenomenon that exposure to an object or a word in one context increases the accessibility of the mental representation of that object or word in a person's mind. Priming can be supraliminal or subliminal. In supraliminal priming the participant is exposed to the priming stimuli as part of a conscious task. In subliminal priming the prime is presented at very short exposure so that participants are not consciously aware of the prime.

Principle of compatibility: Measures of attitude will only be related to measures of behaviour, if both constructs are assessed at the same level of generality.

Principle of reciprocity.   The norm that we should do to others as they do to us, frequently in the form of returning an obtained favour.

Product life cycle   refers to an S-shaped curve which is related to the diffusion of a product across the marketplace from its initial introduction to its decline and ultimate demise. The product life cycle has an introduction stage, a growth stage, a maturity stage and a decline stage, each with its own managerial and advertising implications.

Product placement   (sometimes also called brand placement) refers to the paid inclusion of branded products or brand identifiers through audio and/or visual means, within mass media programming.

Product recall   refers to a type of advertising used when there is a problem with a product and consumers need to be informed that they are to return their product to the factory for repair or refunding.

Promotional mix   refers to the marketing communication modalities that make up the constituent parts for **integrated marketing communications** and include advertising, direct marketing, interactive marketing, sales promotion, public relations (PR) and personal selling.

Public relations   refers to a communication instrument that is used to promote favourable perceptions about an organization.

Random assignment   of participants to experimental and control conditions in such a way that each participant has an equal chance of being assigned to each condition. This procedure assures that participants did not differ significantly before the experimental manipulations and that any difference observed between participants afterwards is due to the experimental manipulation.

Recognition test   is a standard test of **explicit memory**. Memory of previously learned words is assessed by presenting participants with a list of words consisting of words that had been presented in the earlier list intermixed with words that had not been presented and asking them to identify those words that had been presented earlier.

Reference group.   A group of people that significantly influences an individual's behaviour, thoughts, evaluations or preferences.

Representativeness heuristic   which involves assessing the extent to which two stimuli belong to the same overall category based on the extent to which both share similarities.

Retrieval   refers to the processes that are involved when individuals retrieve information stored in **long-term memory** into **working memory**.

Sales promotion   refers to a type of marketing communication focused on generating a consumer behavioural response through the use of a temporary incentive which increases the attractiveness of the offer.

Sales-response models   refer to a class of models relating advertising inputs (such as expenditures) and outputs (such as market share or profitability) on the aggregate level.

Salience   refers to the extent to which a stimulus is noticeably different from its environment. Salience is context dependent, and varies over situations.

Scarcity principle.   The notion that people tend to value more what is scarce than what is in abundant supply.

Scripts   are predetermined, stereotyped sequences of action that define a well-known situation (e.g. restaurant script).

Self-monitoring scale.   An individual difference measure, which distinguishes people for whom image aspects of a product are particularly important from those, for whom these aspects are less important.

Self-perception theory.   According to this theory, people often do not know their attitudes and therefore infer their attitude from their own behaviour. They assume that their attitude is consistent with their own recent behaviour towards the attitude object.

Self-regulatory resource depletion.   The notion that repeatedly engaging in processes that involve deliberate, and active self-regulation, such as exerting will-power, self-control, overcoming impulses, or resisting (unwanted) influence, depletes the resources left for subsequent self-regulation.

Self-schema   refers to a cognitive generalization about the self that is comprised of a more or less comprehensive set of traits, values and beliefs that exerts a powerful influence on information processing

Self-validation   is a type of meta-cognition, reflecting the subjective confidence consumers have in their thoughts and evaluations in response to persuasive messages

Semantic memory   refers to the mental thesaurus, organized knowledge a person possesses about words and other verbal symbols, their meaning and referents, about relations among them, and about rules, formulae, and algorithm used to manipulate them.

Sensory memory   stores incoming sensory information for less than a second, before the information is either lost or transferred into the short-term memory.

Short-term memory   see **working memory**.

Sleeper effect.   The phenomon that the impact of a message attributed to a negative source increases over time, because after some delay, recipients of an otherwise influential message might recall the message but no longer remember the source.

Social validation principle.   This heuristic principle involves focusing on others to assess the merits of some object, issue or offer.

Source effects. The influence which attribution of a communication to a source has on the persuasive impact of that communication. According to **dual process theories of persuasion**, source effects are strongest when the issue addressed in the communication is of low personal relevance.

Sponsorship. A technique by which a commercial organization financially supports an entity (i.e. event, programme, team, person, cause) in order to associate the organization's name with this entity in the media and to use the entity for advertising purposes.

Statistical interaction refers to a pattern in a factorial experiment, where the impact of one factor on the dependent variable is moderated by the other factor.

Stimulus-based choices are choices made from a range of products (e.g. on the supermarket shelf).

Storage of information involves the retention of information in memory.

Subjective norms: People's expectations that others who are important to them expect them to behave in certain ways, weighted by their motivation to comply with these expectations.

Subliminal advertising refers to advertising that uses messages (embedded in a film or television report) that are presented so briefly that viewers remain unaware that they have been exposed to advertising

Sufficiency principle entails the notion of least effort that translates itself in the tendency to strike a balance between minimizing cognitive effort on the one hand and satisfying current motivational concerns on the other.

Stereotype refers to the beliefs about the attributes of members of an outgroup.

Systematic processing. Thorough and detailed evaluation of message arguments to arrive at a decision about the validity of the position advocated by a persuasive message.

That's-Not-All Technique. An influence technique where an initial request is followed by a second request that is made more desirable either by adding something attractive (e.g. an incentive) or reducing something less desirable (e.g. offering a price discount).

Theory of planned behaviour. The extension of the **theory of reasoned action**. In addition to the determinants of intention included in the theory of reasoned action (**attitudes** and **subjective norms**), perceived behavioural control is incorporated as the third predictor of intentions and behaviour.

Theory of reasoned action. A theory of the relationship between attitude and behaviour. Assumes that attitudes combine with subjective norms to determine behavioural intentions, which in turn influence behaviour.

Thought-listing technique enables one to assess the extent to which recipients of a message engage in message processing. Message recipients are asked to list all the thoughts that occurred to them while being exposed to a persuasive message. These thoughts are later categorized into those which are favourable of unfavourable to the position advocated by the message. Thoughts which do not fit either of these categories (e.g. neutral or irrelevant thoughts) are not considered.

Truth effect refers to people's tendency to initially uncritically accept information, even when certain elements are not fully comprehended.

Two-sided advertisements   differ from the usual one-sided ads in that they mention some negative features of a product in addition to emphasizing its positive attributes in order to increase credibility.

Unimodel   assumes that persuasion can be characterized as a singular process of drawing conclusions from available evidence, regardless of whether the evidence is argument- or context-based. The unimodel accepts the assumption of **dual process theories of persuasion** that the extent to which individuals engage in message processing is determined by processing motivation. The model rejects the assumption of a **necessary** relationship between ease of processing (or validity) and cue characteristic (i.e. whether information is a heuristic cue or an argument).

Unique Selling Proposition   is a summary statement used to meaningfully differentiate a **brand** from the competition.

Utilitarian function of attitudes.   See **instrumental function**.

Value-expressive function   refers to the function attitudes serve in reflecting values that are central to the self-concept of the individual or expression of which might help the individual to maintain relationships with important groups.

Visuo-spatial sketchpad   is a second subsystem of the working memory model of Baddeley. It is responsible for the brief storage and manipulation of visual material. It plays an important role in spatial orientation and the solution of visuo-spatial problems.

Vividness   refers to a variable with attention getting properties. Vividness is partly context-dependent and partly resides in the observer. Vivid stimuli are emotionally interesting, concrete and image provoking and proximate in a sensory temporal or spatial way. Whereas proximity may be an attribute of the stimulus and thus a situational variable, interest and ability for mental imagery are person variables.

Wants   refer to the translation of consumer needs to specific products and services that manufacturers can supply and that are able to satisfy the underlying needs.

Word fragment identification test   is a standard test to assess **implicit memory**. Participants are presented with a few letters of the word and are asked to name a word that fits.

Word-of-mouth marketing   refers to an unobtrusive, interpersonal form of advertising where an influence agent (usually a commited user of the product) tries to convince close relatives and friends to try the product as well.

Word stem completion test   is a standard test to assess **implicit memory**. Participants are presented with the first few letters of each word that had been presented earlier and are asked to present the first word that comes to mind to complete the stem.

Working memory   is that part of our memory that is currently activated. It is a unitary system where input from the different sensory memories is integrated with information from long-term memory to be briefly held in conscious awareness and manipulated. It has very limited storage capacity. Input of new information is only possible if old information is moved out.

Yale Reinforcement Approach.   An approach guided by the assumption that exposure to a persuasive communication which successfully induces the individual to accept a new opinion constitutes a learning experience in which a new verbal habit is acquired. Recipients of a persuasive message are assumed to silently rehearse the arguments contained in a message together with the recommended response and their own initial attitude. They will only accept the recommended attitudinal response if the incentives associated with this response are greater than those associated with their own original position.

Author index

Aaker, J.L. 61, 123, 254
Aarts, H. 203, 209–211, 212, 216, 217–219, 220, 221, 222, 224
Abbott, C.J. 251
Abelson, R. 89, 232
Abernethy, A.M 7
Achtziger, A. 204
Adams, M.J. 79
Adewole, A. 256
Adolphs, R. 231
Adriaanse, M.A. 205
Agrawal, N. 213
Ahluwalia, R. 127
Aiken, M. 119
Ajzen, I. 121, 134, 187, 197, 197–198, 199, 205, 207, 209, 268n8, 268n11
Alba, J.W. 69
Albarracin, D. 121, 122, 186, 202
Alden, S.L. 55
Allen, C.T. 26, 101, 102, 130
Allen, J.B. 128
Allen, M. 178
Allison, R.I. 123–124, 138
Allport, G.W. 112, 196, 197, 250
Alwin, D.F. 119
Ambler, T. 27, 30
Anderson, C. 250
Andrews, J.C. 35
Anil, C.P. 256
Appleton-Knapp, S.L. 103–104
Areni, C.S. 17

Ariely, D. 126
Armitage, C.J. 144, 145, 149, 202
Arndt, J. 27, 213
Aronson, E. 88, 220, 221
Ascuncion, A.G. 94, 158
Ashmore, R.D. 17, 250
Assael, M. 186
Atkinson, R.C. 74, 77, 79, 109
Avila, R.A. 26

Backus, J. 138, 139
Baddeley, A. 75, 77, 78–79, 80–82, 84, 85, 99, 109
Baeyens, F. 130
Bakker, A.B. 12
Baldwin, M. 132, 135, 147, 149
Banaji, M.R. 116
Banbury, S. 269n17
Bargh, J.A. 37, 42, 43, 85, 88, 141, 144, 207, 212, 216, 234
Barndollar, K. 212
Barnes, J.H. 68
Baron, R.M. 14
Barone, M.J. 56
Barrett, D.W. 246
Barron, C. 188, 189
Barry, T.E. 30
Barsalou, B. 56
Basset, R. 243
Bassili, J.N. 142, 144
Basu, A. 23

317

Basu, A.K. 23
Batra, R. 23, 35
Baumeister, R.F. 261
Beach, K.R. 117
Beach, R. 50
Beard, F.K. 4
Bearden, W.O. 247
Belch, G.E. 2, 17, 22, 23, 24, 135
Belch, M.A. 2, 17, 22, 23, 24
Bell, D.W. 145, 146, 147
Bellman, S. 220
Bem, D.J. 113, 132, 147, 150, 241
Berent, M.K. 142
Berg, K.E. 197
Bermeitinger, C. 223
Bernberg, R.E. 197
Berntson, G.G. 143
Berry, D.C. 99, 269n14, 269n17
Berscheid, E. 250
Bessenhoff, G.R. 117
Betz, A.L. 130, 225
Bhatla, S. 35
Bierbrauer, G. 246
Bierly, C. 128
Bijmolt, T.H.A. 104, 105
Biller, B. 69
Bishop, G.F. 147
Biswas, A. 19
Biswas, D. 19
Bizer, G.Y. 67–68, 141, 142, 143
Bjork, R.A. 83, 103–104, 224
Blackwell, R. 34, 245
Blair, M.H. 28
Blank, A. 232–233, 234, 237
Blankenship, A.B. 100
Blanton, H. 117
Bless, H. 42, 58, 59–60, 69, 163
Block, L.G. 50, 51
Blüher, R. 127
Bogardus, E.S. 196
Bohner, G. 69, 118, 119, 162, 163, 193
Bolton, L.E. 68
Bone, P.F. 53
Boninger, D.S. 142
Borden, R. 251
Bornstein, R.F. 127
Bottomley, P.H. 56
Bower, G.H. 83, 103
Bradburn, N. 145, 147
Brannon, L.A. 256, 257–258
Bransford, J.D. 224
Bratslavsky, E. 261
Braun, K.A. 107, 188, 189
Braun-LaTour, K.A. 107–108, 109

Bray, D.W. 197
Brehm, J.W. 185, 258
Brendl, M.C. 250
Breus, M. 213
Briñol, P. 69–70, 143, 262
Broadbent, D.E. 74
Brock, T.C. 14, 34, 158, 159–160, 165, 169, 256, 257–258, 259
Broemer, P. 143, 144, 146, 147, 149
Brown, R.W. 132
Brown, S.P. 136
Bruce, H.J. 236
Bruin, R.H. 209
Brunel, F.F. 116
Bruner, J.S. 89, 136, 137
Buchanan, M. 81
Bullington, B. 258, 260
Burger, J.M. 236, 239, 241, 242, 243, 249, 250
Burke, R.R. 100–101, 103
Burnett, J. 190
Burnkrant, R.E. 68
Burroughs, J.E. 213
Buss, D.M. 254, 255
Butler, L.T. 99
Butner, J. 246
Byrne, D. 250

Cacioppo, J.T. 10, 36, 43, 68, 140, 142, 143, 145, 154, 161, 162, 163, 165, 169–170, 172, 173–175, 176, 180, 234, 243
Calder, B.J. 9, 26
Campbell, M.C. 57, 185, 251
Carlston, D.E. 95
Carmon, Z. 34, 50, 126, 196
Carnot, C.G. 50
Carpenter, G.S. 57, 58
Carvallo, M. 250
Castriott-Scanderbeg, A. 82
Catalan, J. 235
Celsi, R.L. 35
Ceresa, A. 82
Chaiken, S. 10, 35, 36, 43, 63, 93, 112, 113, 118, 119, 132, 135, 140, 141, 142, 144, 145, 146, 147, 149, 154, 155, 158, 161, 162, 163, 167, 179, 183, 191, 193, 234, 243, 244, 247
Chandon, E. 50
Chanowitz, B. 232–233, 234, 237
Chartrand, T.L. 85, 88, 213, 214
Chatterjee, R. 22
Chatterjee, S. 19
Chattopadhyay, A. 62, 250
Chen, H.C. 185
Chen, J.-W. 121

Chen, S. 161, 234, 247
Childers, T.L. 55
Chiu, C.-Y.P. 43, 82, 87, 224, 268n4
Christie, C. 117
Chun, W.Y. 211
Cialdini, R.B. 26, 230–232, 235, 238, 241, 243, 244, 246, 250, 252, 256, 257, 258
Clarkson, J. 61
Claus, J. 221, 222–223, 224
Claypool, H.M. 170
Clemons, D.S. 55, 170, 181
Clore, G.L. 131, 163
Coates, S.L. 99
Cohen, R.L. 119
Colley, R.H. 32
Collins, A.M. 90
Committeri, G. 82
Conner, M. 144, 145, 149, 199, 202
Conrad, M.A. 78, 81
Conway, M. 131
Cooper, G. 221–222
Cooper, J. 221–222
Corey, S.M. 197
Corneille, O. 130, 225
Cornelius, T. 242
Cornwell, T.B. 191
Costley, M. 68
Coucke, P. 191
Cowley, E. 109
Cowley, R. 188, 189
Craik, F.I.M. 77, 79, 80, 85, 109
Crombez, G. 130
Cronley, M.L. 65, 125, 206
Crowley, A.E. 186–187
Cunitz, A.R. 77, 78
Custers, R. 211, 212

D'Agostino, P.R. 127
Dahl, D.W. 247
D'Andrade, R. 145, 147
Darby, B.L. 235
Das, E. 54, 178, 213, 258, 259, 260–261
Dasgupta, D. 116
Davis, B.P. 258–259
Dawes, R.M. 238
De Hoog, N. 49, 156, 178, 179
De Ridder, D.T.D. 205
De Vries, N.K. 144
De Wit, J. 49, 156, 178, 179, 204
DeBono, K.G. 17, 124, 137, 138, 139, 140, 167, 245
Degelman, D. 251
DeHouwer, J. 130
Deighton, J. 123

Del Prado, A. 250
Demerath, N.J. 119
DePelsmacker, P. 20–21, 22, 24, 25, 26, 28, 31
DeSarbo, W.S. 55
Deutsch, R. 208
Devine, P.J. 204
Dhar, R. 34
Dhar, S.K. 24, 50, 196, 238
Dholakia, R.R. 53
Diehl, M. 143, 144, 146, 147, 149
Dijksterhuis, A. 203, 209–211, 217–219, 220, 221, 222, 224
Dion, K. 250
Ditto, P.H. 179
Doerr, R. 223
Doll, J. 121
Donovan, J.R. 30, 31–32, 34
Donovan, R.J. 190
Dornoff, R.J. 57
Dovidio, J.F. 117, 123, 208
Downey, K. 100
Drolet, A. 34, 50, 196
Dunn, D.S. 119
Dunton, B.C. 115, 116, 117
Dutka, S. 32
D'Ydewalle, G. 191

Eagly, A.H. 10, 17, 35, 36, 42, 53, 68, 93, 112, 113, 118, 119, 140, 142, 145, 154, 155, 158, 161, 163, 191, 193, 243, 244, 250
Ebbinghaus, H. 83, 103
Ecker, U.K.H. 223
Edell, J.A. 68
Eelen, P. 130
Efron, R. 76
Ellen, P.S. 53
Elliot, A.J. 212
Engel, J.F. 34, 245
Engle, R.W. 128
Erber, M.W. 118, 119
Erdem, T. 60
Escales, J.E. 66
Eskenazi, J. 221
Esses, V.M. 145, 146, 147
Etgar, M. 186
Etzel, M.J. 247

Fabrigar, L.R. 117, 142
Fang, X. 127
Fazandeiro, T. 127, 128
Fazio, R.H. 115, 116, 117, 118, 119, 120–121, 130, 136, 137, 143, 149, 208
Feinstein, A.H. 55
Feinstein, J. 180

Fennis, B.M 12, 54, 61, 213, 231, 235–236, 239–240, 242, 252, 254–255, 258, 259, 260–262
Fern, E.F. 68
Feshbach, S. 155, 178
Festinger, L. 17, 158, 159
Fichte, C. 124, 138
Fiedler, K. 42
Finnegan, H. 126
Fishbach, A. 211
Fishbein, M. 130, 134, 187, 197, 197–198, 199, 202, 205, 207, 209, 268n8, 268n11
Fiske, S.T. 68, 234
Fitzpatrick, K.R. 25
Fitzsimons, G.J. 50, 51
Fleming, M.A. 55, 68
Fletcher, J.F. 142
Flynn, F.J. 232, 237
Folkes, V.S. 57
Fortin, D.R. 53
Fox, S. 4–5
Fragale, A.R. 254
Franke, G.R. 7
Franks, J.J. 224
Fransen, M.L. 54, 212, 213
Fraser, S.C. 239
Freedman, J. 239
Freund, T. 18
Frey, K.P. 53
Friedman, A. 46
Friedman, R. 211, 212
Friese, M. 208–209
Friestad, M. 69, 185
Furse, D.H. 26, 55

Gaertner, S.L. 117, 123
Gaeth, G.J. 106
Galati, G. 82
Garbarino, E.C. 68
Garcia-Marques, T. 170
Gardner, M.P. 35
Gardner, W.L. 143
Garrity, K. 251
Gengler, C. 251
Geuens, M. 20–21, 22, 24, 25, 26, 28, 31
Giesen, M. 251
Gigerenzer, G. 234
Gilbert, D.T. 63, 64–65
Giles-Corti, B. 190
Giner-Sorolla, R. 141, 146, 147
Glanzer, M. 77, 78
Glasman, L.R. 121, 122
Godek, J. 68
Goelz, R. 223

Goldberg, L.R. 61
Goldman, R. 173–174, 175
Goldstein, N.J. 26, 230, 231, 232
Gollwitzer, P.M. 203, 204, 205, 212, 258
Gonzago, K. 249
Goodstein, R.C. 57
Goodwin, S.M. 186
Gopalakrishna, S. 22
Gordon, R.A. 251
Gorn, G.J. 128
Gornik-Durose, M. 246
Gouldner, A.W. 235
Govender, R. 141, 144
Grady, K. 185
Grant, S.J. 9
Greenberg, J. 213
Greenwald, A.G. 14, 34, 42, 44, 50, 66, 116–117, 158, 165, 209, 221
Grewel, D. 68
Griffin, D.W. 143
Grossman, R.P. 128–129, 225
Grunig, J.E. 25
Grunig, L.A. 25
Giulford, J.P. 213
Gupta, P.B. 188, 189
Gurhan-Canli, Z. 60
Gurumurthy, K. 57, 58

Ha, Y.-W. 106–107, 108–109
Haaland, G.A. 159
Haddock, G. 143
Haddock, R.A. 138, 147, 148, 149
Hagberg, G.E. 82
Hale, S.L. 235
Han, S. 246
Hansen, R.A. 26
Hanssens, D.M. 27
Hargreaves, D.J. 213
Harkins, S.G. 259
Harmon-Jones, E. 128
Harnish, R.J. 17
Harreveld, F van 145
Harris, R.J. 66
Hartwick, J. 199, 202
Hass, R.G. 185
Hastie, R. 55, 65, 93–94, 267n3
Häubl, G. 220
Haugtvedt, C.P. 18, 42, 55, 181, 182
Hauser, J.R. 95
Hawkins, D. 221, 222
Hawkins, S.A., 65
Hayden, N. 104
Heatherton, T.F. 261
Heckler, S.E. 55, 96, 98

Heider, F. 144
Hendrickx, H. 130
Hendrik, C. 251
Hendriks, M. 212
Henry, L. 269n17
Hermann, A.D. 262
Herr, P.M. 42, 54, 65, 87–88, 176, 268n12
Heslin, R. 186
Hetts, J.J. 250
Hewstone, M. 154, 197
Higgins, T. 87, 88
Hildum, D.C. 132
Himelstein, P. 197
Hintzman, D.L. 103
Hirt, E.R. 258, 260
Hitch, G. 79, 80–82, 109
Hoch, S.J. 24, 65, 106–107, 108–109, 123
Hodges, S.D. 118, 119
Hodson, G. 145, 147, 250
Hofmann, W. 117, 208
Hofs, Y. 252
Holden, S.J.S. 56
Holland, R.W. 147, 148–149, 212, 250
Holman, C.D.J. 190
Hong, S.-T. 124, 167
Hopkins, C.C. 11
Hovland, C.I. 19, 154, 155, 156, 158, 186
Howard, D.J. 30, 251
Howard, J.A. 34
Howards, A. 208
Hoyer, W.D. 55, 63, 186–187
Huber, J. 213, 214, 238
Huff, J.W. 147
Hull, A.J. 78, 81
Hulland, J. 66
Humphreys, M.S. 191
Hunt, S.D. 186
Hutchinson, J.W. 57
Hyman, H.H. 245

Ignarri, C. 211
Igou, E.R. 59–60
Inman, J.J. 66, 256
Insko, C.A. 132

Jaccard, J. 117
Jackson, J.R. 115, 116, 117
Jacoby, J. 63, 138
Jacoby, L.L. 45, 85
Jain, A. 251
Jalleh, G. 190
Janis, I.L. 19, 154, 155, 156, 178
Janiszewski, C. 46, 47, 49, 50, 104
Janssen, L. 231, 242, 261–262

Janus, E. 109
Jarvis, B. 180
Johar, G.V. 66, 146, 191
Johnson, B. 208
Johnson, B.T. 42, 68, 202
Johnson, C. 208
Johnson, E.J. 220
Johr, N. 223
Joiner, L.W. 56
Jonas, K. 124, 138, 143, 144, 146, 147, 149, 154, 197
Jones, C.R. 87, 88, 130
Jones, J.T. 250
Jurkowitsch, A. 69
Jussim, L.J. 130, 225

Kahn, B.E. 24
Kahneman, D. 51, 55, 56
Kallgren, C.A., 142—143 167
Kalma, A.P. 254
Kamins, M.A. 55, 186
Kang, Y.-S. 176, 268n12
Kaplan, K.J. 144
Kardes, F.R. 5, 9, 12, 15, 20, 21, 26, 42, 50, 51, 53, 54, 57, 58, 63, 65, 66, 80, 94–95, 115, 125, 130, 206, 231, 244, 245, 251, 258, 260
Karremans, J.C. 221, 222–223, 224
Karrh, J.A. 187
Kasmer, J.A. 181
Kasser, T. 213
Katz, D. 136–137, 140
Kavanoor, S. 68
Kawakami, K. 117, 208
Kellaris, J.J. 125
Keller, K.L. 100, 102–103, 141
Kelly, H.H. 154, 155, 156
Kenny, D.A. 14
Kent, R.J. 101
Keren, G. 55
Kernan, J.B. 26
Khan, U. 238
Kim, J. 54, 130
Kirmani, A. 175, 177, 185, 251
Kisielius, J. 66
Klein, C.T.F. 180
Klinger, E. 51
Klink, R.R. 56
Knowles, E.S. 10, 19, 27, 32, 236, 258–259
Knowlton, B. 82
Kollat, D. 34
Kotler, P. 3, 10
Kraft, D. 119
Kraus, S.J. 198
Krishnan, S.H. 92, 101, 102

Krosnick, J.A. 117, 130, 140–141, 142, 143, 147, 225
Kruglanski, A.W. 18, 180, 183, 184, 211
Krugman, H.E. 35, 37
Krull, D.T. 63, 64–65
Kumar, A. 101, 102
Kumkale, T.G. 186
Kunda, Z. 90

Labroo, A.A. 44, 49, 50
LaFrance, M. 251
Lake, V. 232, 237
Langer, E.J. 36, 232–233, 234, 237
LaPiere, R.T. 114, 196–197
Lasswell, H.D. 155
LaTour, M. 107–108
Lavidge, R.J. 30, 95, 156
Lavine, H. 147
Law, S. 188, 189
Leavitt, A. 138, 139
Leavitt, C. 42, 44, 66
Lee, A.Y. 44, 49, 50, 69, 96–97, 98, 99, 267n3
Lee, J. 256
Lee Cahi, A. 212
Leipkin, J.B. 178
Leslie, D.C. 256
Leventhal, H. 178
Levin, I.P. 106
Lewis, S.K. 235
Liberman, A. 140, 142, 145, 161, 163, 179, 193
Lin, A. 269n14
Lindsey, S. 117, 118
Linn, J.A. 10, 19, 27, 32
Lipsky, M.S. 178
Lockhart, R.S. 79, 80, 85, 109
Loftus, E.F. 90, 108
Lohse, G.L. 220
Loken, B. 56, 59, 69
Longo, L.C. 17, 250
Lopez, D.F. 179
Lord, K.R. 188, 189
Lott, A.J. 197
Louie, T.A. 24
Lowrey, T.M. 176
Lucas, J. 30
Luce, M.F. 66
Luminet, O. 130, 225
Lumsdaine, A.A. 19
Luther, M. 3
Lutz, R.J. 17, 35, 135
Lynch, J.G. 107, 244
Lynn, A.R. 130, 225

Maccoby, N. 158, 159
MacDougall, B.L. 117
Macinnis, D.J. 96, 98
MacKenzie, S.B. 35, 135
Mackie, D.M. 94, 158, 170
MacLachlan, D. 12
Madrigal, R. 192
Maguire, A.M. 191
Maheswaran, D. 55, 60, 162, 167–168, 183, 193, 213
Maio, G.R. 145, 146, 147
Maison, D. 209
Makhijani, M.G. 17, 250
Malaviya, P. 9, 36, 66
Malof, M. 197
Malone, P.S. 63, 64–65
Mantonakis, A. 49
Marks, D.F. 54
Marks, L.J. 55
Markus, H. 67
Marlino, D. 21
Marwell, G. 119
Mathes, J. 189
Mazis, M.B. 256
McConahay, J.B. 116
McDonald, C. 2–3, 4
McDonald, W.T. 99
McDonel, E.C. 121
McGeoch, J.A. 99
McGhee, D.E. 117
McGregor, I. 144
McGuire, W.J. 37, 63, 93, 156–158
McIntosh, A. 170
McKendrick, J. 213
McKinney, F. 100
McSweeney, F.K. 128
Meenaghan, T. 190
Meeus, W.H.J. 256
Melcher, J.M. 82, 109
Messian, N. 250
Meyer, H. 246
Meyer, T. 125
Meyers-Levy, J. 36, 53, 55, 57, 67
Midden, K. 203
Middlestadt, S.E. 130
Milgram, S. 255, 264
Millar, K.U. 122
Millar, M.G. 122
Miller, A.S. 42
Miller, D.T. 55
Miller, G.A. 49, 77
Miller, J.A. 243
Milner, B. 79
Miniard, P.W. 35, 56, 245

Mirabile, R.R. 143
Mirenberg, M.C. 250
Mitchell, A.A. 35, 135
Monroe, K.B. 26, 125
Moonen, A. 216
Moore, D.J. 185
Moore, J.C. 197
Moore, S.G. 50, 212
Moray, N. 49
Moriarty, S. 190
Morris, C.D. 224
Morton, J. 79
Moskowitz, G.B. 42, 162, 163, 193, 211, 232, 234
Muellerleile, P.A. 202
Mukherjee, A. 55
Muraven, M. 261
Murphy, E. 249
Murray, E.J. 251
Murray, K.B. 220
Musen, G. 82
Muthukrishnan, A.V. 62

Naik, P.A. 22
Nakamoto, K. 57, 58
Nayakankuppam, D. 68
Nedungadi, P. 95, 96, 97–98, 99
Neisser, U. 75
Nelson, L.D. 179
Nenkov, G.Y. 66
Neumann, M. 223
Newby-Clark, I.R. 144
Newcomb, T. 119
Newcomb, T.M. 250
Newsom, J.T. 238, 241
Nickerson, R.S. 79
Nisbett, R.E. 53, 54
Nordgren, L.F. 145
Nordhielm, C.L. 28, 170, 172
Norman, P. 199
Norman, R. 135, 147, 149
North, A.C. 213
Nosek, B.A. 116
Nowlis, S.M. 34, 50, 196
Nunes, J. 50

Ochsner, K.N. 43, 82, 87, 224, 268n4
O'Dohery, J. 125–126
O'Keefe, D.J. 235
Oliver, R.L. 55
Olson, J.C. 35, 135, 138
Olson, J.M. 250
Olson, M.A. 117, 130, 208
Orbell, S. 203

Osterhouse, R.A. 14, 158
Ostrom, T.M. 34, 158
Oulette, J. 217
Oxoby, R.J. 126

Pahl, S. 127
Park, C.W. 35
Park, D.C. 65, 93–94, 267n3
Parsons, L.J. 27
Patel, S. 250
Patria, F. 82
Patrick, V.M. 57
Pechmann, C. 186, 187
Peeters, A. 254
Pelham, B.W. 250
Peracchio, L.A. 53, 56, 57, 67
Percy, L. 30, 31–32, 34
Petty, R.E. 10, 34, 36, 43, 55, 67–68, 69–70, 140–141, 142, 143, 144, 145, 154, 158, 159–160, 161, 162, 163, 165, 169–170, 172, 173–175, 176, 180, 181, 234, 241, 259
Pfau, M. 25
Pham, M.T. 131, 163, 191
Phillips, L.W. 78
Pieters, R. 54–55
Pieters, R.G.M. 11, 104, 105
Pietromonaco, P. 88
Plassman, H 125–126
Plessner, H. 208–209
Pleyers, G. 130, 225
Plomb, R. 76
Poiesz, Th.B.C. 10
Pollock, C.L. 236
Polson, M.C. 46
Pomerantz, E.M. 141, 146
Posavac, S.S. 65, 125, 206
Posner, M.I. 43
Postman, L. 78
Powell, M.C. 115, 141, 149
Pratkanis, A. 88, 220, 221, 251
Pratto, F. 141, 144
Preisler, R.M., 142—143 167
Prensky, D. 30
Priester, J.R. 55, 68, 144
Priluck, R.L. 128, 129
Pruyn, A.Th.H. 61, 213, 231, 258, 259, 260–261
Pyszczynski, T. 213

Quinn, J.M. 185

Raaijmakers, Q.A.W. 256
Rabuck, M.J. 28
Rados, D.L. 26

Raghubir, P. 256
Raman, K. 22
Randall, D.M. 202
Rangel, A. 125–126
Rao, A.R. 125
Rasinski, K.A. 118, 145, 147
Ratneshwar, S. 63
Ray, M. 35
Rea, C. 185
Reardon, R. 185
Reber, R. 43, 127, 128, 143
Reed, A. 68
Regan, D.T. 120, 121
Reingen, P.H. 26
Rempel, J.K. 112, 113, 119–120, 149
Rhodes, N. 157–158
Rholes, W.S. 87, 88
Richardson-Klavehn, A. 83, 224
Rindfleisch, A. 213
Robinson, L.M. 26
Robinson, M.D. 43, 48, 49
Roediger, H.R. 224
Romeo, J. 56
Rosch, E. 89
Rose, R.L. 35, 247
Rosenberg, M.J. 133–135, 137
Roskos-Ewoldsen, D.R. 188–189
Ross, L. 53, 54
Rossiter, J.R. 30, 31–32, 34
Rothermund, K. 117
Rothman, A.J. 143, 204
Rowsome, F. 4
Rubin, K. 124, 138, 139, 167
Russell, C.A. 187, 188, 189
Russo, J.E. 35
Ruth, J.A. 57

Sagarin, B.J. 257, 258
Saguy, T. 117, 123
Salancik, G.R. 132
Sanbonmatsu, D.M. 115
Sawyer, A.G. 103, 104
Schacter, D.L. 43, 82, 87, 224, 268n4
Schank, R.C. 232
Schemer, C. 189
Schewe, C.D. 26
Schlosser, A.E. 68
Schneider, W. 43, 234
Schneier, W.L. 55, 181, 182
Scholderer, J. 206
Schooler, J.W. 82, 109
Schooler, T.Y. 117, 118
Schultz, R.L. 27
Schuman, H. 147

Schumann, D.W. 55, 170, 174, 181, 182
Schwartz, J.L.K. 117
Schwarz, N. 43, 58, 65, 67, 69, 118, 119, 127, 128, 131, 143, 148, 163
Scott, J. 2–3, 4
Scott, W.D. 11
Segrin, C. 251
Sengupta, J. 66, 146
Settle, R.B. 256
Seyfried, B.A. 251
Shah, J.Y. 211
Shallice, T. 79
Shandrashekaran, M. 57
Shapiro, S. 44, 45, 49, 92, 96, 98
Shavitt, S. 68, 137, 138, 140, 176, 246
Sheeran, P. 203, 204, 205
Sheffield, F.D. 19
Sheldon, K.M. 213
Sheppard, B.H. 199, 202
Sherman, D.A.K. 179
Sherman, J.W. 117
Sherman, S.J. 121
Sheth, J.N. 34
Shiffrin, R.M. 43, 74, 77, 79, 109, 234
Shimp, T.A. 35, 128
Shiv, B. 125–126, 126, 175, 177, 213, 214
Simon, J. 27
Simon, L. 213
Simonin, B.L. 57
Simonson, I. 34, 50, 196
Singh, S. 127
Sklar, K.B. 21
Skurnik, I. 65
Sleeth-Keppler, D. 211
Smidts, A. 23
Smith, D.C. 56
Smith, E.E. 89
Smith, M.B. 136, 137
Smith, P. 222, 224
Smith, R.E. 35, 186
Smith, S.D. 236
Smith, T.M. 22
Snyder, C.R.R. 43
Snyder, M. 137, 138, 139, 245
Solomon, S. 213
Soman, D. 126
Somervell, E. 249
Sood, S. 57
Soroka, S. 249
Spangenberg, E.R. 221
Speigel, S. 183
Spencer, S.J. 215, 221, 222
Sperling, G. 75–76
Squire, L.R. 82

Srull, T.K. 100–101, 103
Staats, A.W. 128
Staats, C.K. 128
Stayman, D.M. 136
Steenkamp, J.-B.E.M. 124
Stein, B.S. 224
Steiner, G.A. 30, 95, 156
Sternthal, B. 9, 26, 36, 66
Stewart, D.W. 26, 55
Strack, F. 42, 118, 148, 163, 208
Strahan, E.J. 215, 221, 222
Strick, M. 250
Stroebe, W. 49, 154, 156, 159, 178, 179, 183,
    184, 197, 199, 205, 221, 222–223, 224
Strong, E.K. 29
Stuart, E.W. 128
Sullivan, H.W. 204
Sutherland, M. 63
Swan, S. 176
Sweeney, D. 147
Swinyard, W.R. 35, 186
Sylvester, A.K. 63
Szyibillo, G.J. 186

Tafarodi, R.W. 63, 64
Tanner, R.J. 214, 251
Taylor, S.E. 53, 68, 234
Teel, J.E. 247
Teigen, K.H. 55
Tellegen, C.L. 191
Tellis, G.J. 2, 10, 27
Terry, W.S. 104, 105–106
Textor, S. 189
Thomas, S. 130
Thomas, W.I. 196
Thompson, E.P. 183
Thompson, M.M 143
Thompson, N. 81
Thompson, S.C. 53
Tice, D.M. 261
Tiedens, L.Z. 254
Tietje, B.C. 116
Till, B.D. 128–129, 225
Timco, C. 198
Todd, P.M 234
Tormala, Z.L. 69–70, 143, 258, 260
Tourangeau, R. 118, 145, 147
Trondsen, T. 206
Trope, Y. 43
Trost, M. 230, 231, 238, 241
Trötschel, R. 212
Tuk, M.A. 23
Tulving, E. 80, 82, 83
Tversky, A. 56

Tybout, A.M. 9, 26, 56

Udall, A. 170
Uhl, K.P. 123–124, 138
Underwood, B.J. 99
Unnava, H.R. 68

Vakratsas, D. 27, 30
Van den Abele, P. 191
Van den Bergh, J. 20–21, 22, 24, 25, 26, 28, 31
Van den Bergh, O. 130
Van der Pligt, J. 145
Van Harreveld, F. 145
Van Knippenberg, A. 147, 148–149, 216, 250
Van Raaij, F. 11
Van Rensberger, J. 191
Vanden Abeele, P. 12
Vankatesan, M. 159
Vannieuwkerk, R. 128
Vaughn, R. 30
Venkatraman, M.P. 21
Verhue, D. 144
Verlegh, P.W.J. 23, 124
Verplanken, B. 147, 148–149, 216, 220
Veryzer, R.W. 57
Vincent, J.E. 235
Visser, L. 254
Visser, P.S. 141, 142, 143
Vohs, K.D. 231, 242, 261–262
Vonk, R. 251
Vroom, V.H. 197

Wagner, S.H. 147
Walster, E. 17, 250
Wan, H.H. 25
Wänke, M. 59–60, 69, 176, 208–209
Warlop, L. 69
Warren, W.L. 55, 181, 182
Warrington, E.K. 79, 83
Warshaw, P.R. 199, 202
Webb, T.L. 203
Webster. D.M. 180
Wedel, M. 54–55
Weeks, C.S. 191
Wegener, D.T. 18, 36, 140, 143, 161, 259
Wegner, D.M. 221, 222
Weilbacher, W.M. 29, 33
Weiner, B. 55
Weiskrantz, L. 83
Weiss, W. 186
Wells, G.L. 159–160, 165, 169, 259
Wells, W. 190
Wenneker, C. 144
Wentura, D. 117

Wernerfelt, B. 95
Wheeler, D. 235
Wheeler, S.C. 67–68, 262
White, K. 247
White, R.W. 136, 137
Whitely, P.L. 100
Whittlesea, B.W.A. 49
Wickens, T.D. 103–104
Wicker, A.W. 114, 197
Wigboldus, D. 23
Wijk, G. 26
Williams, C.J. 115, 116, 117, 118, 121, 141, 149
Williams, P. 50, 51
Wilson, D.T. 117, 118, 119
Winkielman, P. 127, 128
Wirth, W. 189
Witte, K. 178
Wolff, J.A. 202
Wolfradt, U. 246
Wood, E. 217
Wood, W. 142–143, 157–158, 167, 185

Worchel, S. 256
Wosinska, W. 246
Wright, A.A. 107, 244
Wright, P. 69, 185
Wyer, R.S. 124, 167

Yang, M. 188–189
Yeshin, T. 2, 29
Yeung, C.W.M. 126
Yoo, C.Y. 91, 92
Yoon, C. 49, 65
Young, B. 50
Young, S.M. 35
Yzerbyt, V. 130, 225

Zajonc, R.B. 126–127
Zanna, M.P. 112, 113, 119–120, 143, 144, 149, 215, 221, 222
Zhang, S. 57
Zhao, X. 104, 105
Znaniecki, F. 196

Subject index

Accessibility, cognitive 60, 85, 87, 95–99, 110, 121, 141–142, 144, 147–148, 204, 207, 212, 214, 221–222, 225, 301
Advertising
Defined 2
Clutter 48, 52, 65, 99–100, 101, 102–103, 110, 186, 191
Direct response 22, 23, 243, 262
Effectiveness 10–11, 19, 27, 30, 38, 49, 63, 64, 83, 90, 95, 110
Modelling approach to 27, 28, 40
Behavioural approach to 27, 28, 40
Functions of 5–10
Formats 251, 264
Testimonials 245, 251, 264
Slice of life 245, 251, 264
Main effects of 14, 92, 102, 104, 108, 139, 167, 307
Mediated effects of 14, 40, 85, 130, 135, 145, 155, 158, 160, 161, 172, 185, 193, 199–201, 204, 207, 209, 224, 226, 257, 260, 262, 303, 306
Moderated effects of 53, 109, 149, 157, 167, 179, 247, 254, 307
Media 3–4, 6, 11, 24, 25, 33, 37, 40, 49, 52, 65, 74, 122, 139, 142, 166, 188, 190, 191
Truth effect in 63–64, 65, 66, 71, 312
Origins of 2–5
Wear-out 28, 65, 301
Affect-as- information-hypothesis 126, 131, 150, 163, 301

Affect-based appeals 4, 17–22, 301
See also fear-arousing communications
See also emotional appeals
Argument-based appeals 4, 17–22, 301
See also informational appeals
Argument quality 17–19, 40, 67–68, 159, 160–184
Attention 6, 18, 19, 29–30, 38, 42, 43, 46, 48–49, 50, 51, 63, 65, 70–71, 77, 80, 81, 85, 91–92, 94, 96, 100, 102–104, 106, 109–110, 155–157, 176, 178, 186, 191, 232, 234, 302
Focal 38, 42, 43, 46, 49, 50, 51–61, 70, 71
Nonfocal 42, 43, 50
Attitude 10, 12–19, 26, 29, 31–39, 50–51, 54, 63, 67–69, 91–94, 98, 103, 110–202, 204–209, 211, 225–226, 229, 230, 238, 241, 247, 249–250, 257, 262–263, 268
Defining the concept 112–114, 119–120
Explicit 38–39, 114, 118,-119 149, 199, 208–209, 226, 268, 305
Implicit 39, 114–116, 118, 149, 192, 194, 208–209, 226, 268, 306
Measures of implicit 115–118
Relationship with behaviour 196–202
Attitude functions 136–140, 151
Ego-defensive 137
Instrumental or utilitarian 137, 306
Knowledge 137, 306
Social identity 137
Value-expressive 137, 312

Attitude Strength 140–146
    Ambivalence 141, 143–147, 151, 246, 268,
        302
    Certainty 143, 302
    Importance 142–143, 151
    Knowledge 142–143
Attitude structure 133–136
    Expectancy-value models 133–134, 305
Automatic processes 31, 38–40, 42, 69, 70,
        115, 116, 118, 205, 207–220, 226, 231,
        232, 234, 256, 302

Beliefs 6, 9–10, 12, 26, 35, 43, 60, 67, 68, 69,
        113–114, 120, 123, 130, 133–136, 141,
        146, 150, 151, 154, 155, 181, 185, 187,
        199, 206, 207, 210, 212, 221, 226, 238,
        243, 245, 247–248, 251, 268, 302
Brand
    Awareness 7, 12, 29, 32, 34, 37, 52, 95, 141,
        190, 205, 231, 302
    Equity 110, 123, 302
    Extensions 7, 56, 57, 60, 71, 268
    Familiarity 13, 49, 65, 71, 101, 102, 109,
        190, 249, 264
    Image 9, 44, 110, 112, 123–124, 212, 222,
        302
    Personality 61–62, 212, 254
    Switching 12, 24, 216

Categorization 12, 38, 56–62, 71, 120, 136,
        137, 149, 302
    Assimilation and 58, 71, 87, 301
    Contrast and 57, 58, 59, 61, 71, 88
    Pioneering advantage and 57–58, 71, 308
Causal relationships 12–15
Classical conditioning 128–129, 225, 302
Cognitive response model 34–35, 158–161,
        193, 303
    See also behavioural approach to
        advertising effectiveness
Comprehension 32, 38, 42, 43, 63–66, 77,
        155–157, 159, 160, 166, 303, 306
Consensus information 23, 66, 143, 145, 147,
        244
Consumer segments 4, 11, 22, 27, 303
    VALS typology of 247–248
Correlational relationships 12–15
Counterfactual thinking 55, 303
Country-of-origin-effect 106, 120, 123–124,
        138–139, 142, 167–168, 193, 213–214,
        303

Direct marketing 22, 23, 24, 40, 303, 309
    See also promotional mix

Distraction 2, 5, 10, 19, 55, 63–65, 92, 107,
        159–160, 162, 168–169, 258–259, 264,
        303
Dual-mediation hypothesis 135–136,
        150–151, 304
Dual process theories of persuasion 35, 39,
        63, 68, 94, 140, 142, 145, 160–162, 165,
        181, 193, 205, 233, 257, 304
    Elaboration Likelihood Model 36,
        161–165, 304
    Heuristic-Systematic Model 36, 161–165,
        306

Elaboration Likelihood Model 36, 161–165,
        304
Elaborative reasoning 38, 42, 66–70, 72,
        304
Emotional appeals 4–5, 21, 22
Evaluative-cognitive consistency 132, 135,
        141, 146–147, 151, 268, 304
Evaluative conditioning 113, 120, 126,
        128–130, 135–136, 150–151, 157, 161,
        191, 225, 269, 304
Expectancy-value models
    See attitude

FCB Grid 30–32, 40
Fear-arousing communication 20, 77–178,
        305
Frequency of exposure
    See mere exposure effects

Goals 42, 50, 54, 55, 66, 71, 94, 100, 134, 163,
        176, 199, 203–204, 207, 211–219,
        225–226, 246–247, 305

Habits 215–221, 226, 262, 305
Hedonic fluency 49, 50, 68, 69, 70, 128, 190,
        305
Heuristics 35, 36, 120, 123, 161, 163, 191,
        233–234, 261–264, 305
    Representativeness 56, 57, 71, 309
Heuristic cue 17, 123, 142–143, 161, 163, 165,
        167–168, 173–176, 180–181, 183–184,
        193, 234, 257–258, 298
Heuristic processing 120, 161–166, 178, 259,
        304, 305
Hierarchy-of-effects-models 28–34, 40, 231,
        306
    AIDA 29
    DAGMAR 32–33, 231

Implementation intentions 35, 202–207,
        218–219, 226, 306

Impression formation 61–62, 71, 93
Information processing 26, 31, 34–36, 38–40,
        43, 48, 51, 53, 56, 65–68, 71, 74, 141,
        178, 180, 192, 196, 233, 237, 302, 304,
        306, 310
    McGuire's model of 93, 156–158, 306
Informational appeals 4–8, 12
Integrated Marketing Communications
        22–27, 40, 306
Interactive marketing 23, 24, 306, 309
    See also promotional mix
Involvement 13, 14, 15, 19, 30–32, 35, 37, 40,
        42–43, 51, 56, 66, 173–175, 189, 190,
        192, 193, 241, 306, 308
    See also personal relevance

Lexical decision task 85, 203–204, 210, 219,
        307

Measures of implicit attitudes 115–118
    Implicit Association Test 116–118, 306
    Sequential priming Method 115, 310
Mediation analysis 14, 121, 135–136, 145,
        150, 151, 204, 304, 307
Memory 9, 74–110, 307
    Model of Atkinson and Shiffrin 74–75, 77,
        79, 109
    Declarative memory
        See implicit memory
    Encoding 63, 74, 79–80, 88, 103–104, 304
    Explicit memory 43, 82–83, 85–86, 91–92,
        96, 110, 188, 224, 268, 305, 309
    Implicit memory 43, 46, 70, 82–86, 90–92,
        96, 110, 188, 224, 268, 306, 312
    Levels of processing 79–80, 85, 100, 109
    Long-term memory 38, 74, 76–79, 80–83,
        88, 90, 109–110, 118, 307, 309, 312
    Short term memory 51, 74–79, 88, 90, 109,
        310
        See also working memory
    Storage 43, 74–78, 8–82, 109, 304, 311
    Working memory 42, 51, 64, 76–77, 80–82,
        109, 302, 308–309, 312
Mere exposure effect 98, 126–128, 150, 161,
        172, 249, 307
Message elaboration 42, 55, 68, 72, 93–95,
        158
    See elaboration likelihood model
Message repetition 28, 55, 65, 102–104, 110,
        169–172, 181–182, 301
    and cosmetic variation 55, 170–173
    and substantive variation 55, 170–173
Message sidedness 19, 168–167, 186–187
Message variables 15, 17–22

Meta-cognition 67, 68–70, 72, 307, 310
Moderation analysis 14
Multiple-role assumption 163, 307
    Individual differences in influenceability
        157

Need for closure,
    See processing motivation
Need for cognition,
    See processing motivation
Norm
    Subjective 199
    Social 39, 196, 199, 209–211, 226, 232
Novelty 51, 55, 70, 71, 308

Perceived behavioural control 196, 200–202,
        205–207, 211, 226, 308, 311
Perceptual fluency 49, 56, 98, 127, 172–173
    See also hedonic fluency
Personal selling 22, 26–27, 29, 40, 308–309
    See also promotional mix
Physical attractiveness 20, 36, 40, 161, 174,
        175, 176, 177, 250, 264, 268
    See also source attractiveness
Preattentive analysis 42, 43–51, 63, 70, 85
Preferences 6, 10, 12, 23, 24, 29, 51, 206, 238,
        246, 247, 308, 309
Price-quality heuristic 120, 125–126, 309
Principle of compatibility 197, 309
Priming 37, 50, 85–88, 96–99, 115–117, 207,
        211–215, 218, 222–227, 269, 309
Processing ability 151, 166–173
    and working knowledge 166–168
    and distraction 168–169
    and message repetition 169–173
Processing intensity 165–182
    and stability of change 181–182
Processing motivation 150, 173–182
    Accuracy 163, 247
    Defence 163, 247
    Fear as motivator 177–179
    Impression 163, 247
    Individual differences 180
    Need for closure 15, 180, 260, 308
    Need for cognition 15, 21–22, 53, 67–68,
        180–181, 308
    Personal relevance 13, 14, 173–174,
        178–179, 185, 193, 306, 311
Product placement 188–190, 309
Product life cycle 7–10, 309
Product samples 121, 206, 207, 230, 237–238,
        243–244, 263
Product trial 7, 12, 243–244
Promotional mix 14, 22, 28, 40, 306, 309

Psychological reactance 185, 258, 264
Public relations 9, 22, 25–26, 40, 309
   See also promotional mix

Resistance to advertising,
   Strategies of lowering 10, 184–192
Risk 20–21, 31, 32, 50, 52, 177–179, 206,
   252
Routes to persuasion
   Central 161 ff.
   Peripheral 161 ff.
   See also heuristic and systematic
      processing

Sales promotion 22, 24–25, 40, 42, 230, 237,
   238, 244, 263, 309, 310
   See also promotional mix
Sales response models 27–28
   See also modelling approach to
      advertising effectiveness
Salience 43, 51–53, 54, 55, 57, 71, 310
   Humour and 52, 71
Schema 85, 101
   Self 67–68, 72, 310
Self-monitoring 138, 139, 151, 245, 248,
   263
   Scale 138–139, 310
Self-perception theory 113, 132, 147, 150, 241,
   263, 310
Self-regulation 208, 261, 262, 263, 264, 310
Sleeper effect 65, 185–186, 310
Social influence 231–265
   Authority 252–256
      Status and 252, 254, 255, 264
      Obedience and 255–256
   Automaticity 231, 261, 263
      Click-whirr response in 231–232,
         302–303
      Mindlessness 36, 232–234, 236, 241, 257,
         259, 261–262, 263, 264
      Mindfulness 36, 233, 236, 237, 241, 257
      Using scripts in 36, 89, 232, 233, 234,
         310
   Commitment/consistency 238–244
      Foot-in-the-door technique 238–241,
         243, 263, 264, 305
      Continuing questions procedure
         239–240, 260, 262, 262, 263
      Lowball technique 241–243, 263, 307
   Compliance 26, 39, 229–265, 303
   Confusion 258–261
      Disrupt-then-reframe technique
         258–261, 264, 303
   Liking 248–252

Attractiveness and 250
   Similarity and 250–251
   Ingratiation and 251
   Bringing good news and 251–252
Limited resource account 261–262
   Self-regulatory resource depletion
      261–262, 264–265, 310
Reciprocity 235–238
   Door-in-the-face technique 235–236,
      237, 240, 264, 304
   That's-not-all technique 236–237
Social validation 244–248
   Reference groups 137, 142, 199, 245,
      246, 263, 264, 309
Scarcity 256–258
   Deadline technique 256–257
   Commodity theory 257–258
Source variables 15–17, 160 ff.
   See also heuristic processing
   Attractiveness 15–17, 250
   Credibility 15–17
Source effects 15–17, 122, 155, 311
Sponsorship 6, 23, 190–192, 311
Subliminal advertising 39, 88, 220–222,
   224–226, 311
Sufficiency principle 234, 311
Systematic processing 43, 161–162, 165–166,
   179, 181, 193, 257, 311

Theories of attitude change
   See theories of persuasion
Theories of persuasion 154–186
   Cognitive response model 34–35, 158–160,
      303
   Elaboration Likelihood Model 36,
      161–165, 304
   Information processing model 156–158,
      306
   Heuristic-Systematic Model 36, 161–165,
      306
   Unimodel of persuasion 182–184, 312
   Yale reinforcement approach 154–156,
      313
Theory of planned behaviour 199–200, 225,
   268, 311
Theory of reasoned action 199, 311
Two-sided advertisements 186–187
Thought-listing technique 14, 158, 160,
   165–167, 268, 311

Unconscious processes 10, 28, 37, 43, 48, 50,
   82, 196, 254, 267
   See also automaticity
   See also automatic processes

Unimodel of persuasion 182–184, 193, 312

Unique selling proposition 3, 256, 312

Vividness 43, 51, 53–55, 70, 71, 312

Word-of-mouth marketing 23, 54, 312
    See also promotional mix

Yale reinforcement approach 39, 154–156, 313